Brezhnev's Peace Program

Westview Replica Editions

The concept of Westview Replica Editions is a response to the continuing crisis in academic and informational publishing. Library budgets for books have been severely curtailed. Ever larger portions of general library budgets are being diverted from the purchase of books and used for data banks, computers, micromedia, and other methods of information retrieval. Interlibrary loan structures further reduce the edition sizes required to satisfy the needs of the scholarly community. Economic pressures (particularly inflation and high interest rates) on the university presses and the few private scholarly publishing companies have severely limited the capacity of the industry to properly serve the academic and research communities. As a result, many manuscripts dealing with important subjects, often representing the highest level of scholarship, are no longer economically viable publishing projects--or, if accepted for publication, are typically subject to lead times ranging from one to three years.

Westview Replica Editions are our practical solution to the problem. We accept a manuscript in camera-ready form, typed according to our specifications, and move it immediately into the production process. As always, the selection criteria include the importance of the subject, the work's contribution to scholarship, and its insight, originality of thought, and excellence of exposition. The responsiblity for editing and proofreading lies with the author or sponsoring institution. We prepare chapter headings and display pages, file for copyright, and obtain Library of Congress Cataloging in Publication Data. A detailed manual contains simple instructions for preparing the final typescript, and our editorial staff is always available to answer questions.

The end result is a book printed on acid-free paper and bound in sturdy library-quality soft covers. We manufacture these books ourselves using equipment that does not require a lengthy make-ready process and that allows us to publish first editions of 300 to 600 copies and to reprint even smaller quantities as needed. Thus, we can produce Replica Editions quickly and can keep even very specialized books in print as long as there is a demand for them.

About the Book and Author

Brezhnev's Peace Program:
A Study of Soviet Domestic Political Process and Power
Peter M. E. Volten

This analysis of the Soviet Union's foreign policymaking process
focuses on Brezhnev's Peace Program, a foreign policy plan undertaken
in the 1970s to normalize political-economic relations with the West
and to moderate military competition. Taking as his point of departure the issues and concerns expressed by the Soviet actors themselves, Dr. Volten defines the characteristics of Soviet decision making and the process of policy implementation, clarifies the distribution of power among leaders, and assesses the influence of domestic
circumstances and external events on the conduct of foreign policy.
He then deals specifically with the domestic factors affecting the
Soviet approach to arms control and defense policy. Many aspects of
Soviet military strategy and its development and implementation are
examined, with special attention given to civil-military relations.

Dr. Volten is a staff member of the Directorate of General Policy
Affairs, Ministry of Defense, The Hague, Netherlands. Previously, he
was visiting scholar at Stanford University's Kennan Institute for
Advanced Soviet Studies in Washington, D.C.

Brezhnev's Peace Program
A Study of Soviet Domestic Political Process and Power

Peter M. E. Volten

Westview Press / Boulder, Colorado

A Westview Replica Edition

Published in 1982 in the United States of America by
    Westview Press, Inc.
    5500 Central Avenue
    Boulder, Colorado 80301
    Frederick A. Praeger, President and Publisher

Library of Congress Catalog Card Number: 82-50688
ISBN 0-86531-910-3

Printed and bound in the United States of America

to KARIN

Contents

Tables

Acknowledgments

        This study is the product of collective endeavor in
more than one respect. Without the support of the
Foundation for the Promotion of East-West Contacts, and
of its Chairman, Rudolf Th. Jurrjens, in particular, the
research project would never have been started. The two
years I spent at Stanford University afforded me the
opportunity to do extensive research in the field of
Soviet studies. I am grateful to Stanford University
for its hospitality, and especially to the Hoover
Institution on War, Peace and Revolution, where I was
privileged to use its extensive library facilities and
received much kindness from the staff.
        I owe a debt of gratitude to the many persons with
whom I had useful and instructive discussions. It was
a special privilege that Alexander Dallin agreed to
cooperate in this project; his comments and advice were
a welcome--and sometimes badly needed--support and an
invariable source of inspiration. Among the many
"teachers" of Soviet studies I met, special thanks are
due to Paul Cocks, who helped me to understand the
Soviet System and political process. The Kennan
Institute for Advanced Russian Studies made it possible
for me on two occasions to spend valuable time in
Washington D.C. Its Executive Secretary, Frederick S.
Starr, kindly helped me to find my way to many scholarly
and political sources of information. I would like to
thank Gijs Kuypers for his invaluable comments in the
final stages of my research.
        In my work at the Ministry of Defense in The Hague,
many intricacies of military affairs have been clarified
with the help of General Gé C. Berkhof. His companion-
ship has been of strategic importance for this study.
I am also grateful to the Ministry of Defense and to
the Defense Staff for their generous practical assistance.
The final manuscript reflects the expert typing of
Willeke Loeffen and Edith de Visser and the time gener-
ously devoted to proof reading by my brother, Henk
Volten.

I owe a special debt of gratitude to my wife, Karin,
for her constant encouragement and support, and to my
children, who at a very early age learned the importance
of silence for scholarly research. Needless to say,
notwithstanding the collective effort involved, the
situation differs from that obtaining in the Soviet
Union in that I alone am responsible for the contents
of this book.

Peter Volten
The Hague

Introduction

> The superpowers often behave like
> two heavily armed blind men feel-
> ing their way around a room, each
> believing himself in mortal peril
> from the other whom he assumes to
> have perfect vision. Each side
> should know that frequently uncer-
> tainty, compromise, and incoher-
> ence are the essence of policy-
> making. Yet each tends to ascribe
> to the other side a consistency,
> foresight, and coherence that its
> own experience belies. Of course,
> over time even two armed blind men
> in a room can do enormous damage
> to each other, not to speak of the
> room.
>
> (Kissinger, Chapter XIII, "The
> Soviet Riddle," White House Years,
> p. 522)

The two concerns expressed in Kissinger's analogy
with the superpower relationship are the main subjects
of this study. Security and mutual understanding of each
other's political process and decision-making are central
parts of East-West relations, the former to a large
extent dependent on the latter. Averell Harriman's
mission to Moscow in 1976 to explain the presidential
elections and their impact on the dragging SALT-process
is just one example among many others of fear that the
other side misunderstands American willingness to
negotiate or misreads the administration's policy.
      The importance of our understanding of questions of

1

Peace and War is self-evident. Furthermore, when the
Soviet Union showed interest in improving East-West
relations and General Secretary Brezhnev launched the
so-called "Peace Program," a combined effort by scholars
in the field of Peace and War studies and Soviet studies
would have seemed not only a relevant, but also a likely
consequence. For even though the "Peace Program" would
soon entail a much broader sphere of interests in East-
West relations, it first of all advanced a number of
security proposals. In any case, when the Soviet Union
appears to be ready for serious military negotiations
for the first time in its existence, indeed, the change
may perhaps not be called "fundamental"--as some in the
West persistently point out--but important it is [1]. The
event is certainly important enough to delve into an
examination of the Soviet forces in favor of it, their
domestic strength and their possible impact on East-West
relations, above all on the control of the overloaded
weapons arsenals. Unlike other conflict, war is too
decisive to be acceptable in its consequences. The
strengthening of East-West security can be nothing but a
shared goal, if not an imperative need. In the final
analysis, avoidance of war prevails over any other East-
West conflict. One may recuperate from an economic
disaster and survive the suppression in a political system, but the loss in a military conflict is irreparable
and, if escalating into nuclear war, beyond calculation.
Whatever obstacles and irreconcilable ideas continue to
exist in East-West relations, the common overriding
concern with military security stands on its own because
of the terrifying dangers involved [2].
     However, there has hardly been a noticable rise of
a scholarly breed in which knowledge and expertise of
Soviet and defense matters are combined. With some
notable exceptions, most of which already had an established name and reputation in this regard, the academic
world and many institutions remained largely divided
along the same lines: defense and security specialists
on the one hand, students of the Soviet Union and the
domestic decision-making process on the other. This is
not to say that research in the two fields was or is
lacking. On the contrary, defense and arms control
studies are numerous and, as in the case of Sovietology,
many count for valuable and important contributions to
their field. Nonetheless, few have been the attempts--
besides those of Wolfe, Spielmann and Gallagher, Warner
and some others--to develop a more comprehensive approach
to Soviet politics and security [3].
     Paradoxically, as detente became more visible, pros-
pects of the development of an approach to the subject
as envisaged here seemed to become dimmer. The growing
controversy in the West about East-West security
increasingly tended to dominate the discussion and judgment about the Soviet Union. Security matters were

2

becoming the most important factor to determine where a
person stood politically and to some extent a criterion
for the way Soviet behavior should be approached academi-
cally. Politics and scholarly endeavor always interface,
but while the use of scholars and social studies is
natural in politics as a means to found and to sell
partisan views, social scientists should guard against
being drawn into the political struggle. If the services
of a long-standing and prominent expert on Soviet military policy and doctrine, Raymond Garthoff, are no longer
deemed necessary or useful for the American SALT delegation, it may be wise or regrettable but the decision is
fully a part of politics. However, when Soviet specialists are ready to "prove" the correctness of the CIA's
updated estimate of a doubled Soviet defense budget, they
not only compromise their own academic credibility, but
also risk transforming academic discussion into political
debate [4]. This is no plea to ascend the Ivory Tower;
rather to point out its relevant place amidst the complex
political structures which need careful observation,
preferably at some distance.
     The sensitivities of national security and the
emotions surrounding military power and arms have also
--notably in Western Europe--seen the opposite reaction:
a growing distance, perhaps separation between academia
and polity. While seeking support in society, peace
movements tended to turn away from what they saw as
policital machinations. In part, however they alienated
themselves from political reality in trying to separate
military power from international politics. Peace research or polemology, prompted by no doubt understandable
and very real concerns about peace, too, developed an
approach which was characterized by engagement rather
than inquiry. Political phenomena were observed and
described rather than analyzed by taking into account the
undeniably many complexities. The world was largely seen
in good and evil aspects: defense budgets were set
against (world) socio-economic development, civilian-
political against military-strategic considerations and
arms control against defense policy. Most evils were
found--explicitly or implicitly--in the West, particularly in the United States, not so much because the
Soviet Union was supposed to act differently or better,
but because serious efforts to examine the Soviet case
were lacking altogether [5].
     To be sure, a normative approach is not rejected [6].
On the contrary, the desired goal of international
security as defined in this study may be thought by some
to be too far from the real world. To many, greater
interdependence in the security issue area may even seem
a contradictio in terminis in an apparent Hobbesian East-
West environment. Such normative views on the
strengthening of East-West security, however, should not
be neglected by merely accepting reality as the only

3

standard for "objective" judgment. "There is a real danger of generating moral indifferences if 'objectivity' is pressed ruthlessly and without social and political responsibility." [7]
Unilaterally determined defense policy with which we have learned to live quite naturally, is not to be transformed into "a pattern of unilateral virtue." [8] For, if not controlled, this Hobbesian virtue may unintentionally lead to the dangerous situation--in East or West--of

> ...Hobbesian fear--that you yourself may vividly feel the terrible fear that you have of the other party, but you cannot enter into the other man's counter-fear, or even understand why he should be nervous. For you know that you yourself mean no harm, and that you want nothing from him save quarantees for your own safety; and it is never possible for you to realise or remember properly that since he cannot see the inside of your mind, he can never have the same assurance of your intentions that you have. [9]

International security is a complex subject on its own, but still more complicated by the Soviet riddle. Also today we are witness to such a contradictory development in the Soviet Union as the concurrent pursuit of "equal security" and equable military growth. Western views on these Soviet aims widely vary and sharply differ. The heated debate in the United States about the SALT-II agreements clearly demonstrated how difficult it is to analyze the two aspects simultaneously. Proponents and opponents alike tended to reduce the problem to a choice between one or the other feature of Soviet foreign policy. The former pointed to Soviet concessions in SALT-II and stress the necessity of arms control, while downgrading the significance of possible asymmetries between the military arsenals. The latter, on the other hand, emphasized the importance of military capabilities and demanded an increase in defense efforts in order to deter the Soviet Union from following possibly bad intentions. This view appears to guide the Reagan administration--in the eyes of many in Western Europe--to an astonishing degree. Regrettably, for foreign policy does not consist of either-or choices, but is rather the art "to strike a balance between the capabilities of the other parties and their intentions." [10] This study is an attempt to do that.
The analytical approach advanced in this study focusses on the concept of political leadership, defined as the ability to formulate and to implement policies. The paradigm of national leadership offers a number of advantages in comparison with other approaches. These will be outlined at greater length in Chapter I, but some

of the main aspects of the analytical approach can
briefly be enumerated as follows.

First, the approach is aimed at analyzing and
explaining the dynamic political process. Soviet foreign
policy is not designed by a unitary actor nor does it fit
the traditional, largely pre-designed approaches, whether
"cultural-Russian," "Bolshevik-ideological" or "totalitarian" in its paradigm. The Soviet and East-European
area specialists in the West have long tended to focus
primarily on unique features of the communist system,
which--certainly if the system is "viewed as a manifestation of a social sickness" [11] -- has impeded the use
of approaches developed in the social sciences. Neglect
of the dynamic interplay between the various and indeed
different actors in the Soviet political process and
Western emotional overtones are also likely to account
for "the troubling circumstance that one finds an empirically observable congruence between the political temper
of the times and the general thrust of dominant interpretations by specialists of the USSR." [12]

Second, the national political leadership is the
meeting point and pivotal element between domestic and
international processes. The leadership cannot serve two
masters or speak too long with two voices. Demands and
pressures from home and from abroad pass through it and
at some point must be reconciled. If the constitutional
rule does not provide a clear procedure and does not
assign the ultimate arbiter (e.g., parliament) the ruling
elite itself becomes the focus of decision-making.

Finally, since the political leadership deals with
problems in all issue areas and is made up of the various
"policy elites," [13] it is bound to set the general
political parameters of what is possible and what is not.
Continuity and change are determined within the leadership and specific proposals and demands are weighed
against the delicate balance of agreements reached among
its members. By focussing on consensus and disagreement
within the political leadership and on the domestic power
positions at stake, the analyst is confronted with the
dynamics of Soviet politics as portrayed by the Soviet
leaders themselves. It is not the analyst's theoretical
design or his selected issues, but the Soviet leadership's
concern about their nation and about the development of
the system that should be the point of departure. In
that way, fundamental issues can be distinguished from
less important ones [14]. Questions about the distribution
of power among actors may be answered. Characteristics
of decision-making and political style may be defined and
the process of implementation clarified.

When General Secretary Brezhnev emerged at the XXIV
Party Congress in 1971 as the first among equals in the
political leadership, he reached the analyst a helping
hand in several ways. First, the center of the political
leadership could be located. The policy proposals would

soon be identified with the name of Brezhnev and many
indicators would point to his personal efforts to pursue
the policies vigorously. Second, Brezhnev unfolded before his audience a comprehensive program linking domestic and foreign policy. Then and later on numerous
occasions, he pointed out the main issues of Soviet concern, while suggesting opportunities in the foreign
policy area to mitigate some of the system's difficulties.
Brezhnev stressed, in particular, the need for
changes in two areas if the Soviet Union was to become a
true developed socialist country and a proud world power.
These changes concerned as part of an overall, fundamental
upswing of Soviet political maturity, the economy and
East-West relations. Third, these proposed changes and
their likely consequence, if fully implemented, would
cause considerable unrest in the Party ranks and among
some policy elites. As will be argued, the political
struggle was at its most intense during the first half
of the 1970's. Tension within the Party increased as
detente succesfully proceeded. Foreign policy became the
outstanding issue in the period 1972-74. Therefore these
years are given the greatest attention.
After having examined the views and developments
within the Soviet political leadership at large and the
position of Brezhnev regarding the ability to implement
his proposed policies in particular, a closer look will
be given to the most important sub-system of the security
issue area, the military institution and its actors, the
military.
Soviet security policy involves three distinctive
but closely related processes on three levels of decision-
making: national, international and technical-strategic.
Of course, relations between the political leadership
and the military show many similarities with the domestic
process in general. This level of decision-making can be
referred to as the formulation and implementation of
defense policy.
Moving to the technical level of decision-making,
we are entering the realm of military strategy. "In
abstract terms, defence policy is the medium through
which force is organized, while strategy is the instrument with which it is organized." [15] Technical-strategic
decisions are by no means non-political. The Party
leadership is deeply involved and strategy forms an essential part of military power, which in turn is an
indispendable instrument in foreign policy. However the
military and for that matter their institution as a
whole--its tradition, esprit de corps, prestige, experience, proficiency, weapons, technological posture, and
so on--play a dominant role in the shaping and enforcement of strategy. Expertise and knowledge are, in this
respect, among the most important assets of the military
at the technical-strategic level of the decision-making
process.

At the international level, the conduct of policy
rests first and foremost in the hands of the political
leadership. Ultimately, it is the political leadership
that decides for or against particular wishes of the
policy elites. Unlike domestic politics, however, it
must also weigh these demands against those of the international actor. Given the antagonistic East-West relations and the sensitivities of national security, a bias
of the leadership in favor of those with whom it shares
power as well as interests is likely and fully understandable. In fact, in many instances the considerations
of the political leadership and the military will largely
coincide. Security is a concern shared by all actors and
images of the outside world are shared by many [16]. The
various views, still broadly distinguishable at national
and technical decision-making level, are largely fused
when it comes to East-West relations. An adverse international climate will be more helpful in advancing the
military interests and justifying defense programs than
friendly, normalized East-West relations and forms another important asset for the defense sector [17].
    The crucial point is thus not whether, but to what
extent the political leadership thinks or is willing to
act according to the military technical-strategic considerations. Political control over the military
institution, defense policy and arms control negotiations
is given by definition. In reality, however, some considerations are more important than others; some views
are more widely shared than others; and some policy
elites are more powerful than others. A distinction
between political and military views on security cannot
be made easily. The "military-powered" foreign policy
of the Soviet Union reflects the important role of the
military. But their views are just one factor. The
conduct of foreign policy is a complex process, in which
the political leadership must weigh many considerations
against one other, and in which it shares the military
viewpoint to a greater or lesser degree.
    In the light of the foregoing, the basic problem of
this study can now be stated as follows: How, to what
extent and by what considerations of Soviet actors have
domestic politics determined the implementation of the
Peace Program, in particular during the period 1971-1975
with regard to East-West security? The following main
questions, derived from this basic problem, wil next be
addressed: What conceptual framework fits the analyst's
task of unmasking the dynamic political process in the
Soviet Union with regard to the conduct of East-West
policy; How are the goals and the implementation of the
Peace Program perceived by Soviet actors in terms of
systemic needs and the distribution of power and
influence; What considerations of Soviet actors impose
restraints on the strengthening of international East-
West security; What is the impact of the "professional

7

soldier" on Soviet security policy?

The first two questions are the subject of Part I of this study concerning Soviet foreign policy in domestic perspective. In Chapter I, the conceptual framework concisely outlined above will be further developed and explained. A theoretical approach not only guides the analyst in his research, it is also a product of his work as it proceeds. A research project starts with a number of assumptions or choices. Some of these can be clarified and justified by the study itself. Still, it seems preferable to indicate these "compasses" at the outset. Others will remain cryptic because of the complexity of reality or the "incoherence of the system" [18] as well as because of our own limits as to comprehensiveness. The second part of Chapter I is devoted to the problem of security and to the question whether, and if so to what extent, military negotiations can contribute in theory to the strengthening of international security.

In Chapter II a "definition of the situation" at the time of the XXIV Party Congress is given. Against this background, the "Peace Program" and its goals as outlined by Brezhnev are analyzed and the new policy elements and main issues are indicated.

Chapters III and IV describe the process of implementation focussing on Brezhnev's position within the collective leadership. His ability to direct the policy is first seen in the light of the characteristics of collective decision-making, particularly with regard to the General Secretary's attempt to improve the Soviet economic organization and management. The following chapter extends these observations to the field of foreign policy. Accordingly, the central question addressed is whether or not Brezhnev strengthened his position by taking personal command of the conduct of foreign policy. The key issues of expansive trade and far-reaching normalization of relations with the West caused contention from the very outset and Brezhnev's determination to pursue them and to convince other leaders aroused further opposition. As tension mounted within the Party, the need to restore rest and unity within its ranks became all the more apparent. As will be argued, a solution to this pressing basic problem was found by 1975.

In Part II the emphasis will shift towards Soviet security policy, which encompasses both defense and arms control decision-making. Before turning to these two aspects in practice, the Soviet theory of questions of Peace and War will be described in historical perspective. Party-military relations, in particular the use of political-ideological views, to support military interests and their position, are analyzed in Chapter V. How the Soviet military have translated strategy into the current defense posture and what the impact of these architects of Soviet strategy is likely to be, are the subject of

investigation in Chapter VI. Thus, each chapter ad-
dresses one of the two main military concerns, which
Huntington has labeled "functional" and "societal" imperatives [19]. The former refers to the actual state of
the defense capability; the latter to the attitude and
support of the polity regarding the military institution.

Thus having characterized the civil-military relations, domestic politics will again be put in international perspective in Chapter VII, where political and
military views on East-West arms control will be
presented. It is here that Soviet strategic concepts and
security considerations meet with those of the West and
East-West asymmetries come to the fore. As in the West,
latent tension between military-strategic and political-
international considerations have also become manifest
in the Soviet Union. In this respect, attention is given
to the question whether the Soviet leadership is ready to
sacrifice the interests of a policy elite if the preservation or even intensification of the detente process in
general seems to require it.

In addition to indicating the confines of this
study which follow from the foregoing research outline,
two final remarks regarding its scope and length must be
made. First, Soviet foreign policy obviously involves
more than East-West relations. China, the Middle-East,
the Third World and the Islam countries have been factors
of growing significance in international relations. The
increased multi-polarity of world power is also a Soviet
concern--in the case of China, more or less supported by
United States, perhaps a nightmare [20]. Intensified
Soviet activities in Third World countries, particularly
during the second part of the 1970's highlighted by the
military invasion of Afghanistan, show the relative
importance of East-West relations and Soviet readiness to
compromise them. Little space in this study, however, is
given to the interplay of Soviet foreign policy and world
events outside the East-West framework.

Second, within this framework the text gives only
limited attention to Western views of defense policy,
strategy and arms control. This study would probably
double in length if, for example, American and NATO
strategy were described, the Alliance's planning and
policy programs and its decision were explained, and the
various arms control approaches and proposals were reviewed. An elaboration on the Western issues will be
undertaken only where an understanding of Western policies
is essential to the understanding of Soviet behavior. As
indicated, the main subject is not that part of political
science, of the behavior of states, which is called
international relations. Its focus is rather on one of
the issues which according to Hoffmann has been relatively left "in the dark," but "whose study is essential
to a determination of the dynamics of international
politics," domestic politics [21].

Part One:

Process, Power and Foreign Policy

1
Analyzing Soviet Foreign Policy and the Concept of Security

INTRODUCTION

In his review of 22 selected American studies of Soviet foreign policy, Welch calls for a greater "soundness of method,...defined essentially as providing clear-cut characterization well substantiated by the data." [1] His judgment of these studies by no means suggests that this scientific standard had been met by the end of the 1960's. He concludes that "with the notable exception of Triska there exists no thoughtful, dispassionate analysis of the subject in its temporal entirety." [2]

Welch stresses, in particular, two necessary improvements in the field of analysis. The first concerns the ending of the lively debate on methods, including such issues as the Soviet motivating force, the nature of the Soviet polity, and the validity of Kremlinology and comparative studies. According to him, these discussions "contribute little to resolution of the concrete problem of how to proceed in order to more firmly establish the nature of the specific subject under investigation." [3] Second, and most important, the conceptual framework should fit the data. Disquisitions on method in analyzing Soviet conduct in general and Soviet foreign policy should "center on the meeting point of general concept and datum, which is the crux of the whole matter." [4]

More than a decade has gone by since Welch's evaluation, but still the debate goes on and the fit between concept and datum remains the subject of contending approaches to Soviet foreign policy. This is not only justifiable; it cannot be otherwise. Unless the lively debate turns into scholarly dispute, or worse, envy, contending theories are instructive and useful for "raising an infant" of common concern, Sovietology [5].

In this chapter a few introductory remarks will be made about methodological and data constraints. Next, some major paradigms of Soviet politics will be described and their merits and shortcomings indicated. Proceeding

13

on the advances made in the field of Soviet studies some
general concepts of political theory which are equally
relevant for the Soviet case will be outlined. This
section will be concluded by listing the main elements
of an integrated approach to Soviet foreign policy. The
second section will look in greater detail at questions
of East-West relations, with reference to the concept of
security.

METHODOLOGICAL AND DATA CONSTRAINTS

     Despite Welch's rather pessimistic conclusion,
Soviet foreign policy analysis had--and has during the
past decade--made considerable progress in accumulating
knowledge as well as in applying social sciences theories.
The use of political theory has resulted in helpful explanations and in turn, the application of numerous
techniques and methods has clarified their relevance for
the political (Soviet) setting, thus helping "to facilitate their use by theorists." [6]
     Admittedly, scholarly appreciation of the multi-
faceted process of decision-making in the Soviet Union
has been rather slow, but few analysts today maintain the
notion of THE Soviet Union conducting foreign policy as a
unitary, rational actor. Although descriptions based on
rational state actors are of great help for first orientation, they are a far cry from explaining foreign policy
because of the total neglect of the question "how politics within a government influence decisions and actions
ostensibly directed outward." [7] Indeed, it is a safe
claim that the biggest bureaucracy, the "U.S.S.R. incorporated" [8] fits in more than one way the general conclusions of theories of large-scale organizations and
bureaucratic politics. The analyst should at least assume the presence of a number of "rational" actors. He
should assume a leadership oscillating between consensus
and conflict, working in a bureaucratic environment of
both footdragging and cooperation and of interwoven
dependencies between superiors and subordinates, as aptly
characterized by Rigby as "crypto-politics" and, more
recently, by Janos as "the politics of reciprocities
between leaders and their staffs and between administrative staff and the general population." [9]
     Explanations of Soviet politics have been only par-
tial, in most cases embracing merely some aspects of the
whole and thereby risking overemphasis on features inherent in that particular approach, while overlooking
others. The analyst "must be concerned with the total
behavior of a foreign state, not with some arbitrary
aspects of it." [10] Of course, since no framework will
ever extend "total behavior," imperfection is inevitable.
With regard to the use of social science models, Allison's
review and comments in his Essence of Decision are par-

ticularly worth mentioning. Using three different models
for his analysis of the Cuban missile crisis, he is concerned about the "differences in the ways the analysts
conceive of the problem, shape the puzzle, unpack the
summary questions and pick up pieces of the world in
search of an answer." [11]
He calls for an integrated approach in order to avoid
a twofold impact on the result of each model:

> While at one level three models produce different
> explanations of the same happening, at a second
> level the models produce different explanations of
> quite different occurrences. [12]

Thus the applicability of models is limited, but a
careful integration and combination of the partial
theories--or if one prefers, an eclectic approach--might
avoid the overemphasis inherent in different methods and
broaden the scope of analysis and comprehension of Soviet
politics and foreign policy. Moreover, this awareness
on the part of the analyst may further his contribution
to the development of a "rich" theory for understanding
and explanation "even though such a theory may not be
susceptible to rigorous verification." [13]
In addition to these theoretical shortcomings the
analyst of Soviet foreign policy faces great problems in
gathering evidence. More specifically, data constraints
considerably hamper the applicability of some approaches, since "successful manipulation of even the most
rigorous model must be based on a solid foundation of
prior established knowledge." [14] As Triska pointed out
with regard to the difficulty of linking the many pieces
of "micro-information" to the "political macro-level,"
"I see the problem less in terms of approach than in
terms of access and data." [15]
The evidence available for a study of Soviet foreign
policy consists of: (a) spoken and written words of
Soviet actors; (b) officially adopted policies; (c)
actual Soviet conduct of foreign relations; and (d) accu-
mulated knowledge in the West about the Soviet Union,
including quantitative data such as economic figures and
military capabilities. (a) and (b) differ mainly in
degree, but may indicate disagreement or conflict among
the actors. The "Peace Program" officially adopted at
the XXIV CPSU Congress in 1971 can be seen as the prevailing political line to which others are committed and
by which they are restricted in their own articulations [16]. Such an explicit program is however subject
to modification, especially during the stage of implementation. Besides, official programs such as the
"Peace Program" are often put in general terms and need
much elaboration and refinement. Also, after a policy
is adopted there is still room for contending views and
their expression.

With regard to the evaluation of Soviet data, two other observations would seem to be in order. The first concerns the critical assumption of how much credit one should give to Soviet sources and policy articulations of the leaders. The answer, bluntly put, is: quite a bit. Given its importance, considerable attention will be given troughout this study to the fact that Soviet leaders, too, communicate their views and that they need to clarify policy directions. Kremlinologists like Conquest and Tatu have proven the usefulness of an analysis of policy positions on the basis of communications, especially when tensions occur or changes are proposed [17]. In particular, Chapter II should be seen as an attempt to indicate how clearly and how much earlier the West could and even should have recognized the genuineness of the proposed policy changes in the Soviet Union [18].

This leads to a second observation concerning the perennial question--commonly surrounded by political confusion--of intentions and capabilities. It is regrettable that governments often pay little attention to policy analyses and--admittedly, on the much firmer ground of hard facts and figures--tend to adopt the popular, albeit questionable slogan that "intentions can change overnight." To be sure, Soviet military power is a hard fact, whereas intentions are enigmatic and uncertain, and are mostly not given the benefit of the doubt in the antagonistic East-West relations [19].

Yet, distinction must be made between capability analysis and policy analysis of Soviet power. Capability analyses allow the researcher to make conclusions about possibilities, the technical options to hand. The picture drawn from articulations of Soviet actors, however, enables the analyst to infer the more or less probable policies of the Soviet Union. There is no reason to give free rein to worsecase thinking and merely to plan according to the possible options of the adversary. Rational politics abide by more or less probable scenarios. Probability must therefore be based on the Soviet actor's perceptions and his views on facts and values, while taking into account the actual measurable possibilities of Soviet power [20]. Such balanced analyses of the available Soviet data can constitute a valuable contribution to Sovietology. Exaggerations and distortions of "hard evidence" and neglect of policy analysis, whether occuring in the political or the academic realm, can be redressed [21].

In sum, the analyst's framework for understanding and explaining Soviet foreign policy should correspond to the basic, though exacting, requirement that it fit the Soviet political setting and the available data, while at the same time making the maximum use of the integrated and combined theoretical knowledge. He should neither fill the evidence gap with conclusions derived from his model nor conceal theoretical deficiencies by inflated and abundant "evidence."22

WESTERN APPROACHES TO THE SOVIET POLITICAL SETTING

As in all political systems, the distribution of
power is of "critical importance" in Soviet politics.
Soviet studies, whether paradigmatically founded on totalitarian, Kremlinological or interest-group/pluralist
conceptions, largely describe and characterize the Soviet
system in terms of power relationships and "diffusion
of power." But, as argued above, characterization and
explanatory value vary with each approach. A brief review of the three approaches to this and other concepts
of "critical importance" may be useful here.

The totalitarian model. Odom, with this criterion
of Huntington in mind, seems to be on target when he
defends the totalitarian model precisely because it
"emphasizes what is truly important in Soviet politics;
a high degree of centralized power with policy initiative wholly reserved for the center." 23
There is indeed broad agreement in the West about
the location and centralization of power in the Soviet
Union. Odom is also right to warn advocates of the
"group approach," which "sins by encouraging one to notice the powerful center only dimly out of the corner of
one's eye." 24 But he seems to overreact regarding the
location of "initiative" in his rejecting rather than
"Dissenting View on the Group Approach." First, although
Party dominance is generally admitted, this "center of
power" is an elastic notion and involves many persons
and groups at various levels. Furthermore, however
centralized the level of an initiative may be, the totalitarian model does not explain the origin and nature
of that initiative. Except for this specific "critical"
characteristic, the political process remains obscure.
The totalitarian model is indeed on slippery ground when
facing Huntington's two other criteria: the comparative
and the dynamic strength. Has the totalitarian model
survived "comparative communism?" Brzezinski seems more
correct and more flexible than Odom when he reviews--in
more than one respect--his own contribution to Soviet
studies.

Many of the conventional concepts and tools of
research that were useful during the Stalinist era
no longer served to explain Soviet politics in the
post-Stalin era or the complex nature and functioning of fourteen different ruling Communist
parties, operating within a wide variety of geographical and cultural settings and in countries at
various stages of socio-economic development. It
was not surprising, therefore, that a new generation

17

of political scientists, recognizing the difference among Communist systems during the 1950's and early 1960's, turned to the new concepts and techniques being developed by their colleagues in other subfields of the discipline. [25]

Finally, the dynamics of politics--e.g., goal-orientation, choices of ways and means, and the complex processes involved--are somewhat clarified by the totalitarian model, but certainly not explained. The heavy emphasis on the uniqueness of the system and the attempts to derive change from general characteristics of totalitarian systems such as Brzezinski/Friedrich's classical six are too rigid for an understanding of the dynamic post-Stalin system [26].

Kremlinology. Centralized power is also fully recognized by Kremlinology, which approach has made important contributions, notably by calling attention to internal conflict. This notion has brought a dynamic element to the analysis of Soviet decision-making. Kremlinology stresses the personal power struggle and suggests that this struggle is of crucial importance, if not decisive for the outcome. However, it does not take into account the environment in which the struggle takes place or the influence of the various sub-systems in the Soviet Union. Instead, this approach assumes that the formulation and outcome of politics is wholly confined to a small oligarchy. Like in the case of the totalitarian model, generalization rests on too narrow a basis [27].

Another deficiency of Kremlinology is its neglect of possible agreement among the leaders. For sure, differences may be concealed, either deliberately as by the "collective leadership" that so abhorred the soloist, antagonizing practices witnessed in the time of Khrushchev, or because of fear to disrupt the existing power relations in the oligarchy. Also, the power struggle and the actual power relations between the leaders will certainly affect Soviet foreign policy. But they do not consitute the only determinant. The strong Kremlinological emphasis on internal conflict almost completely eclipses possible consensus among the leaders on various issues.

Nonetheless, Kremlinology points out some important phenomena. As stated earlier, there is little doubt about the primacy of the Communist Party in the Soviet political system, notwithstanding the increased opportunities of "interest groups."

We can be reasonably certain that the Kremlin will successfully resist changes that seem to threaten the leading role of the Party, control of the Party by seasoned professional functionaries, central planning of the economy, and Party-enforced cultural uniformity. [28]

18

With respect to inter-Party hierarchy there is also great unanimity in the literature. The Central Committee, but above all the Politburo, are the makers of "ultimate decisions." The nature of the political system thus strongly suggests--as the Kremlinologists do--concentration on the decision-making oligarchy, in which possible "groupings best attested in our empirical material on Soviet political conflict appear to be personal followings." 29

Interest group approach. The interest group approach extends Kremlinology in two ways. First, the approach takes into account the political environment and sub-systems and, second, it views the decision-making process as a struggle between several structured groups rather than persons. The central assumption is that a number of like-minded or professionally-organizationally united persons advance their common interests during the decision-making process 30. There is, however, little evidence that such personified aggregates (groups) act like persons or even that they have a coherent common interest. Studies of "interest groups" frequently reveal fragmentation within them and conflicts appear to divide the "interest groups." The analyst will inevitably have problems defining the boundaries of the group and determining the degree of involvement or influence of the various members with regard to a particular issue.

Furthermore, there is the disadvantage and danger of reification. A system is not a person possessing a will, nor can it itself influence policy. The "interest group" approach tends to view the communicated activities of persons in a rather rigid framework. The structure of the group rather than the interaction among its members seems to determine the influence on policy-making. Consequently, any explanation of the outcome of the decision-making process tends to stem too much from structured, if not pre-designed relationships.

The "interest group" approach has in common with Kremlinology that it takes too little account of the impact of "the autonomy of the political realm." 31 Studies of "interest groups" have proven to be instructive and useful for our insight in particular spheres of influence, e.g., the army, economy or agriculture. But they have failed to assess the relative impact of those groups on the political process. "Interest groups are treated as phenomena outside the top command in a formalistic, static system, almost as if they functioned in a vacuum." 32 Power and political process are however inseparable. Power is a prerequisite for the implementation of policies, while policies are used to obtain, maintain or enlarge power. Whereas "competition for power in the Soviet Union tends to magnify policy differences between the contestants," 33 the policy differences proper may on other occasions be the primary

19

reason for a power struggle taking place. The issues at stake, whether brought up deliberately or forced upon the political leadership, are often of critical importance in the political process. All three approaches fail to single out the significance of political issues. Again, neither centralized power, personal power nor other specific interests are the sole or predominant factors in the political process.

Finally, there is no reason to introduce typically Western concepts such as "interest groups" or pluralism as a means of showing that the Soviet Union is no mono- lith. Contrasting views are quite likely to occur; they are inevitable, as in Western democracies. But the Soviet policy does not grant these concepts the same "critical importance." LaPalombara is right in stating that it is of little help of

> ...placing qualifying adjectives before pluralism, (e.g., corporative pluralism, institutional plural- ism , quasi-pluralism, elite pluralism), restricting the idea of interest groups to those leaders who are inside the system more or less controlled by the Party, or coining expressions like "informal groups" of interest groupings. It may seriously impede our understanding of how Communist systems work. These tendencies, as Meyer points out, may even lead us backward in the sense of impeding our ever learning what these systems really are. [34]

In short, the advocates of an "interest group" approach stress sub-system dominance, accentuate the input of structured entities, view the Party as a broker of interests in trying to answer the question "Who governs?" In part, this approach may be explained as a reaction to persistent ideas inherited from the Stalin period; it may also be seen as a sign of Western pre-occupation with political change in general, and of wishful thinking with regard to the Soviet Union in particular.

THE POLITICAL ACTOR, THE PARTY AND THE SYSTEM

All characterization of the political process and order faces the perennial problem of the primacy of the "acting man" versus that of the "dominance of the system." The social sciences have experienced sharp controversies between adherents of these ostensibly exclusive views over the nature of the social order in which decisions are taken. This "fundamental difference" is clearly reflected in the various approaches developed. To sum- marize in the words of Silverman:

> One perspective--Structural-Functionalist, Trancen- dental, Holistic, or Systems--emphasized explana-

tions of behavior in terms of the interaction of
systems attempting to satisfy their need, and often
made use of an organic analogy to explain the nature
of the relationship between system-parts. The
other--namely, Action, Immanent or Atomistic--argued
that attention should first be paid to the orientations of the participants who might differentially
be attached to any aspect of social life and who
themselves create, sustain and change the rules of
the social game. [35]

Obviously, the more diffuse and more complex distribution of power since Stalin's personal dictatorship,
as clearly revealed by Soviet studies and their
methodological refinement, has complicated the assessment
of the character of the Soviet political leadership,
Party rule and political order [36]. The distinguishable
power sources of bases-see below--have not changed per
se, but some have become more, others less, important.
Most significantly, the category of "coercive" power--
possessed by an actor--has increasingly made room for
that of "consensual" power--recognized or agreed upon by
other actors [37]. The more this change is structured or
institutionalized--thus increasingly defining the political order--the more the functioning of the leadership is
prescribed and freedom of action is limited, or at least
controlled. It becomes difficult to distinguish between
the actor and his system; discussion about the primacy
of the one over the other becomes a matter of case by
case examination.
    Party rule is an unassailable fact and is in the
Soviet Union rather a problem of legitimacy than one of
legality. Socialist democracy and the actual role of
the Soviets in polity and society at large are a far cry
from what is envisaged ideologically and what is in the
longer run perhaps expected [38]. The Party is the source
of legitimacy as embodiment of the will of the whole
people. But the function of the Party is also, as everywhere, "to organize participation, to aggregate interest,
to serve as the link between social forces and the
government." [39] The legitimacy of the Party, therefore,
is not merely a theoretical but also a real concern for
the political leadership.
    This is not to say that communist ideals are lack-
ing popular adherence altogether. The Soviet system enjoys a fair degree of legitimacy, even according to victims of the unforgivable methods of that system such as
the exiled émigré, Zhores Medvedev, and the banned citizen, Sacharov [40]. But societal commitment to ideology
and socialist achievements are not matched by legitimacy
of the regime. As White concludes:

    The Soviet authorities appear to have had no compa-
    rable succes...in generating support for the insti-

21

tutions by which politics are determined and formulated, or in bringing about a popular commitment to Marxist-Leninist values which would be sufficient in itself to legitimate their rule. [41]

We have seen, Party dominance and intra-Party hierarchy are clearly defined. In practice, too, these general features are empirically observable. But beyond the general regulations of the Constitution and Party Statutes, clarity is quickly turned into obscurity as to the actual working of intra-Party rules. The question, briefly stated, becomes, "Who guards the Guards themselves?" This fundamental Soviet systemic problem complicates further the distinction between actor and system because the "guards" are--and have always been--reluctant, if nor unable, to institutionalize the roles of various Party actors on a legal basis and to accompany their privileges of power with legal demands of responsibility and accountability. The (limited) degree of political institutionalization within the polity is important for both leadership and society and directly affects the relations between these two entities.

First, in as far as political leadership is "a function of the political order" [42] in a narrow sense--that is, within the Party, the polity--limited institutionalization is likely to impede effective execution of the primary roles of "initiating, maintaining and protecting leadership" and the strengthening of "imitating, obeying and acclaiming" among the followership [43]. Since the communist Party lacks a built-in mechanism for political contestation--like free elections in the West--the establishment of authority as well as the creation of an unambiguous center of command is complicated and the use of leadership is hampered. Who is the ultimate arbiter: the General Secretary, an inner circle of the Politburo, the Politburo, with or without (parts of) the Central Committee? In short, how can the political leadership be characterized and how firmly are its characteristics-- nature, composition, number of persons, their level-- rooted in the Party institution and its internal order? These questions seem to be essential for an understanding of Soviet policy development, formation and implementation.

Second, the problems of intra-Party institutionalization also have a bearing on the role of the Party, viewed in a broad sense, as the embodiment of political leadership of the political order at large, society. Also at this level the leaders of the "directed society" face the problem of institutionalization. Political development towards the declared goal of communism implies increasing participation and institutionalization. This, however, seems a far from easy task for the political leadership in view of the troublesome intra-Party strength relations and the weak, unstable societal basis.

22

For, as Huntington concludes for all polities, the Soviet Union also faces the dual challenge and risk that "as political participation increases, the complexity, autonomy, adaptability, and coherence of the society's political institutions must also increase if political stability is to be maintained." 44

In sum, a description of the Soviet political leadership since Stalin's personal dictatorship must clarify the nature of power relations: that is, the degree of either coercive or consensual power of the leadership vis-à-vis policy elites. Furthermore, in spite of the gap between the polity and society, the political leadership cannot dismiss the problem of the regime's legitimacy and will have to take into account popular demands and rights expected on ideological and other grounds.

Third, within the polity the effectiveness of leadership is likely to be hampered if the organizational structure and governing rules are defined loosely and ambiguously, while sub-system autonomy grows and blurs all distinction between itself and "the autonomy of the political realm." Indeed, the latter is sought by authoritarian governments "not by default but by design." The crucial question is to what extent the Soviet political leadership actually succeeds in directing the polity as well as--by means of that polity--the society at large.

Since the very beginning of the Brezhnev-Kosygin regime in 1964, the principle of "collective leadership" has explicitly and emphatically been called the adopted and agreed style of leadership. Whether the principle has become characteristic and how well it has worked will be discussed in the following chapters. However, the foregoing theoretical considerations prompt a short digression at this point on a concept of increasing importance in more diffuse power relationships: that of political authority.

Political authority is defined by Friedrich as the "capacity for reasoned elaboration of communications," or, more specifically, of a policy. If the political leadership is able to explain its policies convincingly in terms of current opinions, values and beliefs, and perceived needs and interests of the society and polity, the followers' question "Why should I agree?" may be positively answered and political authority strengthened. Of course, there are other reasons for ascribing authority to leadership: power bases such as prestige or affection, charisma, previous successes, visible results, and so on. The point here, however, is that Friedrich's concept focusses our attention on the importance of convincing others in a basically consensual power relationship.

Political authority then has direct relevance to the three features of political leadership in relation to its environment, as summarized above. First, it is a source of power of the leadership; second, it is capable of creating and enhancing legitimacy of the leadership 45;

23

and third, political authority is a device to unite the
polity. It is an expression of agreement with the political acts of the leadership. To paraphrase Friedrich's
description of authority as "a bridge between power and
justice," which he defines as "the just political act,"
authority functions as a bridge between power and the
institutionalization and enforcement of ideological
images, values and beliefs in the Party [46]. Thus, authority appears to be useful for the political leader and
an important concept for an analysis of political leadership.

A final and sometimes neglected observation concerns
the concept of power in the context of the actors and the
Party on the one hand, and the system and organization
on the other. Besides the category "coercive power,"
which denotes an actor's possession and is primarily
characterized by the power bases physical means, wealth,
knowledge and skills, and the category "consensual power,"
which denotes an actor's dependence and is primarily
characterized by the power bases rights, affection,
ideological images and prestige [47], a third category can
be distinguished. This category may be called "structural
power" and denotes an actor's position in the system.

Structural power involves power bases of both other
categories. Structural power is however distinct from
the other categories by what may be called the "organizational power base." This power base is neither dependent
on other major actors nor is it defined by the actor's
possessions or personal characteristics. Instead, the
organization itself grants power to the actor's position [48]. An example is the different power base of
Podgorny vis-à-vis Brezhnev and Kosygin, the former leading the relatively weak state, the latter the strong
Party and Government organization, respectively. An
organization need not be bigger to be more powerful.
The power difference between the National Security Advisor
and the Director of ACDA in Washington is certainly not
related to the size of either organization, but to the
power that flows from the different places in the administration.

Another aspect of the organizational power base is
the possibility to direct or manipulate an organization
in order to achieve one's ends. One organization is
better, works faster or is more responsive than the other.
Improvement of the performance of apparently less efficient organizations may be possible, but only to some
extent and often at the expense of sacrifices in other
parts. The invisible power of bureaucracy--its resistance, sabotage, or simply proceeding on its own--is in
many ways beyond the control of policy makers, especially
during the stage of implementation. The experience with
systems management and PPBS in the U.S. is a case in
point. The motivations of the top leadership were

24

...the desire to regain control over a headstrong
bureaucracy, the need for better long-range policy
planning and evaluation to produce more rational
decisions, and the desire to make better use of
advanced technology and the administrative procedures that had been developed for the defense and
space sectors of the economy. [49]

However, opposition--also in the defense organization--
grew together with awareness of the consequences of
systems management, i.e., the devolution of power of the
sub-systems. In other cases the bureaucracies merely
paid lip-service but did not adopt the proposed structures and procedures. Elsewhere, the reforms died a natural death because of the weaknesses inherent in the systems approach [50]. No doubt there were more reasons for
the general disappointment about systems management.
Suffice to note here that organization is a power means
in the hands of leaders and that it matters where and in
what organization they act.
     For example, the organization along General Staff
lines of the Soviet military leadership quite probably
puts Marshal Ogarkov in a more powerful position vis-à-
vis the political leadership than his American counterpart, the Chief of the Joint Chiefs of Staff. The latter
has to compete in the defense organization with eight
other--partly mixed--civilian-military staffs [51]. Both
top military men stepped into their position and organizational power base as it was, but for the one the organization structure seems more conducive to manipulation
and exercise of power than for the other. Structural
power refers to the power that the dominant system,
however complex and incomprehensive that sometimes may
be, yields to the "acting man."

SOVIET STUDIES AND LINKAGE

     It is more than thirty years since George Kennan
called attention to "The Sources of Soviet Conduct," and
about fifteen years since Rosenau was among the most
ardent advocates of developing a rigorous "scientific
approach" to linkage politics [52]. The field of Soviet
studies has grown immensely since then, and not only in
the quantitative sense. But whereas Kennan devoted
considerable attention to internal factors, his--mostly
American--followers showed far more interest in Soviet
foreign policy as input in international relations. In
spite of the great advances made by political theory and
the rise of comparative politics, relatively little space
was given to the Soviet domestic factor as input in
international relations or to the notion that these two
variables meet at the "intermediate" level of foreign
policy [53]. Foreign policy in general was treated as a

distinctive issue area, a separate entity in the international world [54].

The studies reviewed by Welch are an example of "the neglect of issue areas in systematic inquiry." Unfortunately, Welch's suggestions for methodological improvement are no encouragement in this respect. By referring to Triska's framework proposed in 1958 and his positive judgment about Rosser's Introduction to Soviet Foreign Policy, Welch seems to propagate an approach which centers around Soviet ideology, the very concept that has proved to be insufficient for explanation and that has prompted so much emotional debate [55].

Indeed, that kind of debate should end. But the debate about a dynamic and comprehensive approach to the Soviet polity and its input in international politics should not. Progress in this respect has been rather slow. The first book-length study of domestic factors of Soviet foreign policy did not appear until 1975, and was according to its author, an effort to help remedy the deficiency of Western texts being "primarily historical or monographic" and lacking "an analytic perspective." [56] Of course there were Aspaturian, Brzezinski (and Huntington), and Dallin [57] in the 1960's who were later joined by others when the field of Soviet studies as a whole expanded and detente seemed to constitute an eye-opener for many scholars. Yet, "linkage politics" received only moderate attention.

The foundations for the analysis of Soviet "linkage politics" were laid in the 1960's , notably by those mentioned above: Brzezinski and Huntington by their pioneering work in the field of comparative politics, Political Power USA/USSR; and Aspaturian and Dallin by their comprehensive lists of variables, their penetrating analyses in historical perspective, and their stimulating analytic examples of the dynamics of Soviet politics [58].

Of course they raised more questions than they could possibly answer. Moreover, the time of appearance of their studies implied primary attention for the pre-Brezhnev/Kosygin period. Also, some of the conclusions reached deserve further scrutiny because of the central significance they assume in analyzing Soviet politics. Thus, for example, the basic problem of this study relates directly to the question of the primacy of domestic policy over foreign relations during a period when the issue of foreign policy seemed to gain the upper hand in Soviet politics. Or are such concepts as the "ideo-social interest" of the "security-productionist-ideological grouping" and the "consumptionist-agricultural-public services grouping" (Aspaturian) and the "left-right dichotomy" (Dallin) [59] still applicable for a "collective leadership" acting in a far more complex and more interdependent world? These and other questions remain central to our understanding of the Soviet Union.

It is regrettable in this respect that even today

the relevance of linkage politics and conflictual policy
positions is being questioned. For example, in his
otherwise thorough and fine contribution to Foreign
Policy Making in Communist Countries, Adomeit argues in
favor of developing--in fact, returning to--an approach
that "emphasizes coherence of policy and consensus about
basic principles of foreign policy rather than internal
conflict and suggests that distinctions between 'hawks'
and 'doves' in the Soviet leadership are blurred." [60]
There are probably few people working in government who
do not feel uneasiness when using the words "coherence of
policy." Even if Soviet circumstances are far better--
which is quite unlikely--consistency remains doubtful,
except of course for the worn-out and already well-
documented "basic principles of foreign policy." A return to approaches emphasizing "leadership consensus and
policy coherence" will provide no better clues to the
complex problems of the Soviet leaders and is--unlike
Dallin's criticized approach--a doubtful device for "the
analysis of the present era." [61]

MAIN ELEMENTS OF AN INTEGRATED ANALYTICAL APPROACH

     The foregoing observations do not by any means
exhaust the problem of analyzing Soviet foreign policy.
The concise review of some approaches, their strengths
and weaknesses, may nonetheless serve as an illustration
of where Soviet studies stand at the moment and as an
indication of the difficult choices the analyst must make
in the face of elusive, complex realities. It also
presents a first insight into the author's preferences
and assumptions regarding these realities and the
usefulness of various approaches devised to unravel them.

     The view of politics. The first and basic choice
concerns the view of politics as a struggle to achieve
ends, an attempt to bring about a desired future situation by the formulation and implementation of a policy.
A policy is a set of ends, ways and means, and moments
chosen by an actor [62]. These and other definitions and
concepts--such as power, influence, power bases--are
taken from the "Finalistic Approach" as developed at the
Department of Political Science of the Free University
of Amsterdam. Looking back to the foregoing discussion
of the primacy of the "acting man" or "the dominance of
a system," this view of politics tends to favor the
former. As Jurrjens quotes the core idea of Kuypers'
"Proto-theory": "science should consider "a human being"
as a producer of effects rather than a product of causes,
however much he may be bound to his given situation." [63]
     As Kuypers argues, the "Finalistic Approach" in no
way rejects other approaches of paradigms, e.g. politics
primarily viewed in terms of power, conflict, political

behavior, decision-making, allocation of values or of
system maintenance [64]. Rather, these are recognized and
integrated in the "Finalistic Approach." Furthermore,
with regard to Soviet actors themselves from Lenin to the
present, they actually interpret politics as a struggle
to achieve ends. Their orientation is embedded in
forecasting and futuristics, ideologically (victory of
socialism), cultural-socially (the new Soviet man) and
economically (planning).

Political process. A second central element of the
proposed integrated approach is the emphasis put on the
political process and its dynamics. This is done first
by focussing on the interplay of the goals and means of
various actors and, second, by taking the "acting man"
as the point of departure. In this way, Rosenau's
objections may be taken away when he asserts that despite
progress made in political studies,

> ...the dynamics of the processes which culminate in
> the external behavior of societies remain obscure.
> To identify factors is not to trace their influence.
> To uncover processes that affect external behavior
> is not to explain how and why they are operative
> under certain circumstances and not under others. [65]

Recently, Rosenau has again stressed the need to
focus on dynamic processes rather than static phenomena
like organizational structures of governments and
states [66]. However, his attempt to develop a new paradigm for coping with rapid changes in the world seems to
risk the same fate as his complex design of the matrix-
model for theory-building and comparison. This suffered
from its methodological rigor and complexity. Rosenau's
new paradigm of "aggregative processes," resulting in
"unintended, articulated and mobilized aggregations"
also seems to be a stimulating orientation, but again if
the "high level of abstraction" and the emphasis on
"processes rather than actors" (p. 135) are pushed too
hard, its applicability seems less promising. Problems
of reification and the pitfalls of defining the "collective interests" (p. 137) of the aggregetions will be
re-introduced. Admittedly, Rosenau's illustration of the
uses of the concept greatly reduces these fears; indeed,
he allows ample room in the analysis for where "action
is located, where it originates empirically and is
maintained, that is, in and by the individual." [67]
Another reason for avoiding concentration on static
phenomena like organizational and formal structures is our
limited knowledge about organizations in the Soviet Union.
To be sure, such notions as "the impact of the administrative structure," "maneuvers to affect information" or
"the limits on faithful implementation" inevitably probe
into the analyst's framework [68]. Likewise, knowledge

about Soviet Party and State organization remains useful and important. But placing great reliance on Standard Operating Procedures in influencing the organizational output, as exemplified by Allison's Model II, clearly does not fit the available Soviet data. Organization theory is often ambiguous and difficult to apply, particularly to the Soviet Union.

Given the paucity of information available to scholars about Soviet organizations involved in foreign and military policy decision-making, there is no reason to believe that explanations or predictions of Soviet behavior deduced from assumptions about "organizational behavior in general" will be intrinsically more reliable than or even add much to those derived from unitary rational actors assumptions that essentially "black-box" the policy process. [69]

The approach advocated here postulates the essence of an organization as "the view held by the dominant group in the organization of what the mission and capabilities should be." [70] This is just another way of saying that also at the sub-system level (ministries, High Command, Party etc.), attention is focussed on personal views held by actors. These actors will--or will try to--shape their institutions according to their views [71]. They are the participants in the multi-actor decision-making process. Questions like the following can then be asked: "What is the desired organizational output according to their views?" and "What are the constraints imposed on these actors in implementing these views?"

Finally, the concept of policy process has the advantage of incorporating the stage of implementation. As Dallin observes: "In general, the concern among Western scholars with decision-making may well have contributed to a neglect of the extent to which a policy can be subverted in the process of its implementation." [72] Implementation is in the present study viewed in a broad sense, including the process in which one or more actors seek support for a policy in order to make it the officially endorsed course to be pursued by the leadership as a whole.

Political leadership. Given the foregoing and earlier introductory remarks (pp. 4-5), only a few words need be devoted at this point to the concept of political leadership. Spielmann, who has developed and tested a similar approach regarding Soviet strategic decision-making, compares this concept with the rational actor and pluralist decision-making approach. He notes two basic points the national leadership approach helps to bring out:

29

First, contrary to the rational strategic actor
approach, a monopoly of decision-making power cannot
be automatically translated into decisions calculated
solely (or even predominantly) on strategic grounds.
Second, contrary to a pluralistic decision-making
approach, decisions that serve the interest of some
personalities or groups (other than the interests
that strict strategic calculation might serve) do
not automatically signify that power has been shared
in some significant way. [73]

How do these basic points relate to linkages between
domestic and foreign policy? As Dallin has pointed out
in this respect, there are two basic patterns of linkage:
congruence and reciprocity. If the political leadership
conducts domestic and foreign policies consistent with,
for example, a "leftist" orientation, this congruence
pattern may be called a "rational linkage." [74] Moreover,
if such a coherent policy of congruence is agreed upon
by policy elites and the sub-systems they represent, this
may be called a "political linkage." The latter situation
means that a general policy line is highly institutionalized and represents an eminently stable situation.
If, on the other hand, a "reciprocal" linkage pattern
prevails--e.g., a "rightist" foreign policy course
combined with "leftist" dominance at home--then foreign
policy may show instabilities or "zig-zagging," or at
least seem less rational to the other international actors.
For example, is it possible in the long run to combine
arms control efforts with rising defense expenditures?
For the purpose of the present study, an interesting
question raised by Dallin concerns domestic stability in
the case of a "reciprocal" linkage pattern, particularly
in a situation of a more diffuse power relationship
between political leadership and policy elites. For even
if the political leadership itself adheres to a "rational
linkage," the "political linkage" remains an uncertain
factor that needs further clarification regarding the
power means and actual influence of the policy elites.
The degree of conflict or consensus within the political
leadership and/or between this leadership and the polity
at large is of considerable importance for stability in
the Soviet Union and indirectly, in East-West relations.
A closer look at the patterns of linkage may add some
instructive insights into the Soviet political process.
For example, the verdict of Ulam's "pessimistic historian
of 1980" that the New Foreign Policy since the Party
Congress in "no more capable of being maintained for a
long time, no more compatible with the essence of the
Soviet system than was the New Economic Policy," [75]
suffers from both its generality and the equation of quite
different periods. The tenuous comparison between the
two "new" policies certainly needs clarification regarding
the different policy domains, their interrelationship and

relation to the Soviet system. Possibly true in itself, this pessimistic assessment does not tell us much about political change, however little that may be, nor does it explain how and why change did or did not take place. Political structure and culture--the Soviet system--of course have a strong impact on continuity and determine the--often rigid--parameters of the political feasibility of a policy. But they are not immutable. "Formal systems of belief are molded and repeatedly challenged or rein-forced by perceptions of events. And, in their turn, institutions and men and doctrines leave their own imprint on the course of events." [76]

   Political issues. The question of events influencing policies leads to the fourth central element of the analytical approach: issues and issue areas. There are many events in politics that do not become a political issue; other's are summoned for a governmental reaction by domestic actors and thus become an issue. Issues may also stem from own initiatives as part of policy; they may be exploited by the opposition. What makes a particular event or issue a politically significant issue is difficult to tell. However, the "nexus between issue and policy process" is of paramount importance "to specify the nature of the policy process (the identity of the major actors, the intensity of conflict)." [77] Membership of a coalition, the degree and level of participation, the interests involved, the consequences for power positions and budgets, and many other variables involved in the polity vary from issue to issue, but the nature of the issues in domestic and foreign policy is a significant factor in distinguishing and comprehending these variables [78].

   Core issues like national security can generate so strong a consensus--e.g., in war--that a nation acts as a unitary actor. In the other extreme situation, when "nothing happens" and "business is as usual," as Zimmerman points out, routine patterns may become predomimant, even to the extent that diplomatic behavior becomes predictable across the board [79]. For example, the MBFR negotiations are deadlocked, it may be argued, by a lack of political action and guidance; they have fallen victim to official-dom, to dug-in fixed positions. Reactions can be antici-pated and the negotiations increasingly become a routine issue.

   Issue areas can be distinguished according to the basic functions of a state. They are: [80]

   <u>Security</u>, concerning primarily military and intel-ligence operations. Although defense capabilities heavily depend on and will be affected by the state of the economy, including technology, defense itself, in theory and practice (doctrine and the actual build-up), lies primarily in the hands of a clearly

distinctive policy elite, the military;
Welfare, including the economy and its management.
Domestically, this involves the mode of production
and distribution of goods and services. Trade in
these goods and services represents the foreign
aspect of this issue area;
Diplomacy, which refers to all political relations
between actors. In foreign policy, diplomatic
actions are characterized by the means of communication (summits, negotiations, diplomatic notes) and
its results (agreements, treaties, international
law);
Culture, defined by ideas, values and beliefs in a
society.

Unlike Rosenau's definition [81] of an issue area,
reminiscent of attempts to formulate group interests,
an issue area is here viewed as the field of special
responsibilities and rights which assume pre-eminence at
the technical-professional level (cf. Introduction). Of
course, variables like organizational affiliation,
occupation, ideological images, responsiveness to authority and institutional environment are likely to account
for a certain "propensity of diverse actors to articulate
a similar approach to a given policy." [82] However, at
the non-technical, political level of decision-making,
other considerations may prevail. As Zimmerman suggests,
stimulating further investigation: "The ultimate conclusion may even be that differences in policy process
across issue areas within a given state...may be as
great as differences in foreign-policy process within a
particular arena of power for each." [83]

TENDENCY ANALYSIS

The foregoing attempt to discover an approach that
more fully integrates and combines existing frameworks
and that corresponds to what were termed "basic requirements" points to the method of analysis Griffiths has
labeled "tendency analysis."

One in which interaction among participants at different levels of the political structure generates
a conflict of dominant tendencies of articulations
through which alternate lines of policy are
identified, authoritatively decided and implemented
with regard to specific values. [84]

At the risk of calling too little attention to
Griffiths' thorough explanation of his method, the
following will be confined to two assumptions of particular importance. These concern the significance of
"intermediate actors" and of "system dominance" in

32

Griffiths' analysis. First, a tendency of articulation is regarded as a mass of common articulations which persist over time. However, these articulations are not limited to political actors. Griffith's approach also takes into account politically active actors who do not belong to the decision-making elite: intermediate actors. Such actors--for instance, Arbatov, Inozemtsev, Trofimenko, high ranking military or editorial writers--provide valuable information about the issues and problems under discussion. Their contributions obviously constitute a significant part of the available data on which tendencies of articulations can be based. Taking them together with the articulations and activities of the decision-makers, we may be able to construct a picture of the main issues in Soviet politics.

The relations of intermediate actors with the politicians are not altogether clear, but they may be seen as interpreters and "as an important and functional service elite." [85] No doubt political commentators must have the backing of the political leadership, or at least of a significant faction. When intermediate actors are recruited from the academic world, the relationship becomes more complicated. On the one hand, Soviet leadership since Stalin has shown great interest in the improvement of scholarly work, despite such appalling and almost inconceivable experiences as Lysenkoïsm [86]. One leading scholar of international relations, Arbatov, warns that imperialist propaganda uses "every manifestation of dogmatism, bigotry and die-hard adherence to obsolete formulas on the part of some champions of Marxism." [87] Arbatov calls for scholarship. The leadership is likely to agree that respectable scientists not only serve as a hedge against justified "bourgeois propaganda," but also serve Soviet development. On the other hand, the regime will not and cannot allow depoliticizing of the--social--sciences. Scholarly work, including that of intermediate actors, will continue to be handicapped by its explicit political function [88].

A central concept and assumption of Griffiths is "system dominance" implying that "despite the appearance of autonomy on the part of actors within the system, their activities are to be regarded as subordinate to the interaction of the whole." [89]
The extent to which this "autonomy of the political realm" cited earlier, or political leadership, exists is a basic problem, also in this study. Importantly, this orientation and starting point of analysis lead Griffiths--correctly and consistently--to emphasize the need to proceed the investigation from the general to the more specific issues [90]. Conflict and consensus may occur at the same time, but at several levels: core issues may be undisputed while budgetary fights are taking place. Following the stages from the general situation to specific cases may help to prevent conclusions about the

Soviet Union and its leaders based on only some characteristics of only some actors: for instance, the confu-
sion of military strategy with Soviet strategy could be
avoided [91].

To conclude, the approach sought in this chapter is
one that can promote the integrated use of social science
methods appropriate to the Soviet political setting and
data. Such a means of analysis is needed because most
Western studies focus on specific aspects, which does
not allow inferences about total Soviet foreign conduct.
The Griffiths approach seems to be promising with regard
to the requirement of maximum use of both the minimal
data and the partiality of methods.

The Soviet political setting and available data
suggest an application of a model that focusses on the
"acting man" rather than a model based on "system concepts." Griffiths' "tendency analysis" is actor oriented,
incorporates the "Finalistic Approach" in a multi-actor
process, and recognizes the "situational variable" at the
various levels of the political system.

The approach advocated opposes any attempt to
substitute theoretical constructions for that difficult
to fathom, but basic unit in human science: man. Analysis, by definition, requires an artificial division of
reality. The approach separates the analyst's and the
Soviet actor's common object, Soviet foreign policy.
Articulations of the latter are divided into many parts
(issues), which can be put together again in a meaningful
and enriched way after the investigation. The proposed
method does not divide the Soviet political leadership
at the outset into a number of particular men (blindly
dogmatic versus dissident or power maniacs, to mention
some extremes; or into military, apparatchiki, managers
and so on), since such a division is almost irreparable
or, if repaired, has been meaningless.

Analysis on an issue-to-issue basis facilitates our
comprehension of the complex subject matter without major
distortions. By reassembling the parts, the analyst can
examine the interdependence of issues according to "the
eye of the beholder or, better, the perception of the
decision maker" in seeking the ultimate linkage. Indeed,
"the idiosyncratic variable," "the cognitive map or
process," "the mind-set," the "operational code" or any
other concept used to refer to the individual attributes
of actors are the most difficult to ascertain, given the
data paucity [92]. But conflict of tendencies, interaction
between contending views and attention for the "loser"
as well as for the "winner" may contribute to our knowledge in this respect and the questions raised by
Aspaturian, Dallin, Rosenau, Zimmerman and others may
find an answer. Admittedly, neither this nor any other
approach can provide certainty. But certainty will never
be possible without

...openness in our approach. We must recognize that, even when we have consciously rejected the totalitarian model, it continues to color many of our assumptions about the rationale and dynamics of Soviet behavior. What is needed is a willingness--indeed a determination--to subject our assumptions to searching examination and to separate our distaste for the Soviet system from our descriptive analysis of it. [93]

FOREIGN POLICY AND SECURITY

The nature of foreign politics will differ in essence from that of internal politics as long as no legitimate global authority can enforce obedience to international "rules of the game." Unlike an economic system, for instance, where behavior can be explained by given rules and a fair degree of goal-orientation, national subsystems of the international system lack such guidance, rules and objectives in their highly unpatterned environment [94]. Even with regard to the ultimate goal of a national system--survival and maintenance of its sovereignty--the numerous views and possible orientations defy clear-cut definition of what the system should and should not do, or what is reasonably the "best" solution. Aron aptly summarizes the problem in his monumental study of international relations, Peace and War, as follows:

As long as each collectivity must think of its own safety at the same time as of that of the diplomatic system or of the human race, diplomatic-strategic behavior will never be rationally determined, even in theory. [95]

Given the severe limits of a theory of "undetermined behavior" [96] and the confines of this study outlined in the "Introduction," this section of the present chapter will describe the concept of security as defined in both national and international terms. The definition of security and the framework developed are intended to allow categorization of possible views or tendencies. Furthermore, a comparison of this framework with Soviet views and an assessment of their development in time will be possible [97].
The categories of the conceptual framework are primarily based on security considerations, but not exclusively in a military sense. Although the point of departure of this analysis is security in terms of military power rather than economic, ideological-cultural or diplomatic, the interplay between the military and political dimensions must be taken into account. For example, a definition of security must include a description of ways of enhancing stability other than military

negotiations. The inclusion of political aspects also allows us to define "detente," a concept embodying more than just military security and a phenomenon that in turn has a direct impact on the military issue area.

As already observed in the context of Soviet domestic politics, international military relations are for the political leadership just one issue area that must be weighed against other relations and interests. Whatever differences about "best" solutions in the field of security may exist, it cannot be claimed that security is more important to the one than to the other actor. Both political and military leaders are fully committed to the preservation of political sovereignty by military means. Security is a fundamental concern; yet views may differ on how to strengthen it. Furthermore, political and military leaders face the complex questions concerning arms control negotiations as an instrument to further international security. Clearly, it is in such negotiations that political and military dimensions merge and an integrated security policy of both defense planning and arms control is put to the test [98].

THE CONCEPT OF SECURITY

Security means two things in this study:

1. The preservation of territorial integrity and political sovereignty.
2. Reasonable confidence that threats to use force, pressures backed by force, or the actual employment of force cannot adversely affect these fundamental state interests. [99]

There is unlikely to be disagreement on the first point, which is the objective goal of every state. A reliable defense is a prerequisite for the protection of both fundamental state interests. Although foreign influence on political sovereignty cannot be completely excluded by military means, they should preclude all possibility of physical intrusion on the state's self-determination in domestic affairs. In the case of the Soviet Union, autonomy and self-reliance are relatively free from foreign influence, partly as a consequence of its outside contacts being kept deliberately limited, but largely because of its sheer size and huge natural resources [100]. Political sovereignty or freedom of action is evidently not attainable across the borders as easily and definitely as at home. Nor does it in most cases have the same priority, since many interests abroad, real as they may be, are not considered as "vital to national security." To the extent that a state has or assumes interests abroad, its global military power is quite likely to vary in direct proportion to the need

to protect those interests, provided the country possesses
the required capabilities 101. Military power projection may be perceived as essential, but it does not
relate per se to the guaranteed survival of the nation.
Power projection reflects a state's concern with the
"diplomatic system" and peace-time politics rather than
with its "own safety" as expressed in the first part
of the definition. At this point of the discussion, the
description of security policy primarily concerns the
national safety aspect rather than the "active" diplomatic use of military power; it involves "direct" rather
than "indirect strategy" and a protective rather than
offensive use of military power 102.

The second part of the definition introduces the
subjective aspect of security. Only the individual actor
himself has or has no "reasonable confidence" in a particular situation; he alone perceives a situation as
secure to a greater or lesser degree. The subjective
terms vary according to his "definition of the international situation" in relation to his perception of the
sufficiency of military means. At this point national
actors are likely to differ from one other, especially
in the matter of how they achieve greater security. Some
actors may aim first and foremost at an improvement of
the international situation by the strengthening of economic and diplomatic relations and a reduction in the
impact of military means. Others, on the other hand, may
stress unilateral measures in order to strengthen the
national military posture. Thus there are two ways
security can be understood, even though in reality an
actor's perception does not consist of just one. The two
situations (goals) that may be chosen will be called international security and national security. The absolute
form of both may be termed peace and self-guaranteed
peace respectively.

A CONTINUUM OF SECURITY SITUATIONS

Table I represents a continuum of possible security
situations and corresponding situations in the military
and diplomatic issue areas. The overall political situation and the international process are also characterized
according to the degree of unilateralism or multilateralism. Each of the security situations distinguished
above has its diplomatic and military way of being
achieved, maintained or strengthened. Both the military
and the diplomatic way contribute to the corresponding
security situation, but in a different way. Though the
two ways to achieve a security situation may reinforce
each other, one is not necessarily the result of the
other. Finally, the diplomatic and military way can be
an end as well as a means, depending on the situation at
a given moment. The following characteristics of the

37

TABLE I: INTERNATIONAL PROCESS AND POWER

ISSUE-AREA

SITUATION/GOAL

SECURITY	Peace	International Security	National Security	Self-Guaranteed Security	Self-Guaranteed Peace
POLITICAL	Integration	Interdependence	Dependence	Independence	Autarchy
MILITARY	Common Defense	Equivalence	At Least Parity	Superiority	Monopoly
DIPLOMATIC	Representation International Rule	Negotiation International Law	Power Politics National Influence	Offensive: Indirect Strategy Defensive: Autism	Hegemonism National Rule

NATURE

PROCESS	Power Devolution		Power Acquisition		Total Power
DESCRIPTION	World Government Police Force	Detente Arms Control	'Cold War' Intervention	Isolationism Potential Intervention	Pax Romana Occupation

Multi-(bi-)lateralism ←

→ Unilateralism

38

different situations can be distinguished.

First, international security is primarily based on multilateral (or bilateral) arrangements with the perceived adversary. National security, on the other hand, would be primarily based on unilateral action. "Unilateralism is essentially an attempt by a state...to preserve security values by its own efforts alone. The two principal forms on the unilateralist strategy are interventionism and isolationism." [103]

Peace and self-guaranteed peace would mean a complete multilateral or unilateral policy determination. Peace would involve an international authority in which all international actors were represented and which would govern all security arrangements. Self-guaranteed peace rules out any outside interference in internal security. Although peace appears to be an attainable goal in a cooperative relationship--for example the Common Market--this likelihood is extremely remote in a conflictive relationship such as that between East and West. The acquisition of (military) power may not be intended to serve defensive needs indefinitely, but may eventually be used for interventionist actions. The Cold War has shown that the acquisition of power serves one's own interventions while at the same time preventing interventionism on the part of the adversary.

Thus military power under isolationism may serve primarily defensive purposes, but the process of power acquisition does not reveal in what form unilateralist strategies will be followed in the future.

> Isolationism, the alternative unilateralist strategy, is an even less practical means for safeguarding security values in the modern world. Like interventionism, it usually implies neither reliance on commitments by other states nor willingness to give such commitments to other states. But interventionism explicitly implies some degree of participation in the affairs of the local, regional, or global system, whereas isolationism keeps transactions with other states to a minimum. [104]

Second, peace imposes very great constraints upon freedom of action, while self-guaranteed peace refutes any limitation on the use of any action. The former situation implies an almost complete coincidence as regards the policy and security goals; self-guaranteed peace exists exclusively in each other's perception of these goals. Peace implies to a very great extent irrelevance of the correlation of (military) means, since the actor's goals fundamentally coincide. The established, balanced relationship of means is to be maintained by multilateral arrangements. The situation of self-guaranteed peace, on the other hand, emphasizes the importance of means, since the goals of the others are not known, or are in any case uncertain. In the first situation the means are more or less rationally determined by agreement and are therefore probably balanced. In the opposite situation the means may only perhaps be balanced.

Both types of absolute security--peace and self-guaranteed peace--contain some inherent features endangering that particular kind of security. In a situation of peace, the actors may believe so strongly in a consensus of goals and values and may attach so much value to rational compromise that they neglect such phenomena as the continuing existence of their different goals, irrational behavior, changes in the relationship of means or the meaning of unanticipated events. The same can be said of self-guaranteed peace. Insecurity may arise through misperception of what was thought to be correct, poor knowledge which was believed to be sufficient or uncontrolled development of military power on one or both sides. Thus neither situation of absolute security in fact warrants such a claim. Each one contains inherent instabilities. For example, Fromm describes the unilateralist method as follows:

> In fact, the chase after absolute security is a boomerang: it creates more insecurity than it avoids. The goal of absolute security is damaging when it dominates foreign policies...In our obsession to consider all possibilities we end up by not considering the real probabilities. [105]

Third, when the two situations are compared, international security appears to have advantages over national security. The former concerns policies in terms of the probable maintenance or strengthening of security while the latter only involves its possible maintenance or strengthening. Negotiations are likely to enhance rationality in international policies since the negotiating parties probably correct each other. The assessment of military policies is likely to be more rational too, for communications between adversaries clarify these policies. Communication and information increase rationality and reduce the chance of wrong inferences. The situation of international security tends to constitute a balance of means so that one actor cannot adversely affect the state interests of the other by military power. Again, national security only offers a possibility for a basis of "reasonable confidence" in the actual security situation. Security situations can be defined in two ways:

> International (military) security is a situation in which the state actors coordinate defense policies towards each other and which is primarily based on agreement of security goals.

National (military) security is a situation in which the state actors individually formulate and conduct defense policies and which is primarily based on each other's means--perceived or real.

Analogous definitions could be given for economic, diplomatic and cultural issue areas and for overall (political) security. The political aspects of security in Table I include all different issue areas. This decreases the accuracy of description of the state of relations, since these may vary widely from issue to issue. For instance, the state of cultural relations may be autarchic, while economic negotiations flourish. However, the relationship between the diplomatic and military situations is central here and semantics follows the meaning closest to the described security situation. Suffice it to say that an actor pursuing military equality is probably in favor of military negotiations. His chances of achieving his goal are better than in the case of "power politics," where a kind of action-reaction sequence only might produce this equality.

POLITICAL AND MILITARY DETENTE

Detente can now be defined according to the security situations.

Political or military detente is the process by which political or military international security increases.

Obviously, detente is a complex phenomenon and difficult to define, especially since it has become an increasingly emotional and elusive concept in Western debates about its merits [106]. The definition given here acknowledges the complexity and sensitivity of detente and is an attempt to single out its most important characteristics. First, the complexity is indicated by the adjective "political" which includes all issue areas: from psychological warfare and human rights via acquisition of most-favored nation status to outright military reinforcements. The definition makes no difference between East and West as to the complexity of choices. How can one judge the pro's and cons if the Soviet Union is pictured so differently from the West, as for example in the following?

...there is a direct and inescapable connection between the Soviet desire for trade and the acquisition of Western technologies--on their own terms-- and the maintenance of an enormous military establishment which in itself tends to impel any Soviet leadership in the direction of thrusting, if not

41

downright aggressive, foreign policies. And the question whether there can be an evolution in these foreign policies comes in the end to turn heavily on the Western response, particularly in matters of trade. [107]

This deterministic "one way street" analysis of detente only underlines the complexity of Western decisions, while portraying Soviet choices as clear-cut and simple ones.

However manifold the aspects of detente may be, it is doubtful whether one should attach equal weight to all of them. It may not be very realistic--nor perhaps preferable--to monitor them all simultaneously. For instance, detente did not originate in the fundamental domestic contrasts between the two systems. It therefore seems to be beside the point if domestic, systemic change is advanced as the prime question at issue. Political sovereignty at home means the right of the nation-state to interpret, implement and protect what is "good" and desirable. To the extent that detente influences that right, nation-states may converge in the direction of the influencer. Convergence, however is distinct from integration because of the lack of voluntary change and adaptation [108]. Although detente cannot be entirely separated from the consequence of diminishing domestic sovereignty, detente policy was not and cannot be designed for this objective. Rather, detente stemmed from a situation in which "territorial integrity and political sovereignty" were endangered by the very defense of these characteristics of the nation-state. Therefore, the meaning of detente must primarily be viewed as "the relaxation of international tensions endangering security." [109]

Second, detente in the given definition is seen as a process. Detente is a dynamic, not a static, phenomenon. Detente is not a policy, but rather a goal to which a particular policy must lead. More security is a situation (goal) that might be realized by detente policy in one or more issue areas. Meanwhile no serious counter-actions should be undertaken in other areas. At least the international systemic rules and their understanding on both sides should be the same in all issue areas if the process is to be sustained. Policy implementation on both sides may differ in degree, but should not be in contradiction with each other. Asymmetries can--or rather must--be tolerated at the start, but they should not grow in the process of detente. Agreement on goals, e.g., the new situation, is essential. The "balance of interests" which Clemens has listed as a first condition for successful negotiations should not become more asymmetric or imbalanced during the process, at least with regard to issues on which understanding or agreement about objectives had been reached before [110].

Third, as detente proceeds, at some point changes might be expected to take place in both the national and international respect. In the political situation of interdependence, the concept of security undergoes an important modification since there is some common endeavor to define the preservation of territorial integrity on an international level. "International interdependence means that the life of societies as organized in sovereign states becomes more or less conditioned by the life of other societies. It means that the goal striving of societies, and their parts, is more or less interdependent..." 111

In the case of conflictive relations in which security issues are sensitive by definition, interdependence is bound to be an exceedingly delicate question. Moreover, if the Soviet leaders appear to live in a "garrison state"--as is sometimes argued 112 --then interdependence to whatever degree seems to be a vexed, if not intractable issue.

The notion of interdependence once more shows how much diplomatic and military-strategic factors are interlocked in domestic politics. Neither consideration can be neglected by the political leadership. However, it can also be argued that in the nuclear era--because of the changed nature of military force and diplomacy--military-strategic orientations must adopt the new realities of security. In this view, international security should abandon the traditional, military "truths" and schemes of classical war games. As Janowitz explains:

> The consequences of both (a) increased functional interdependence and "fundamental democratization" of residual power and (b) the fusion and moderation in the use of force and persuasion is a new level of complexity and fragility in international relations. It is not enough to assert that, because of nuclear weapons, there has been no major or total war between advanced industrial nations for more than a quarter of a century although levels of tensions and the scope of armed conflict have been persistent and unacceptably high. 113

Therefore more interdependent political relations at the international level must be accompanied by what Janowitz calls "stabilizing military systems." 114 This development would start with a review of the current domestic sociopolitical impact of the military institution and its technical-functional role on the assumption that the limits of military utility in the nuclear age have become narrower. These and other problems of political-military relations will be addressed later.

THE UTILITY OF MILITARY NEGOTIATIONS IN EAST-WEST RELATIONS

Can military negotiations, once agreed and proceeding, be an essential contribution to military and political detente? Or is their utility of an incidental nature? In order to answer these questions in theory, the characteristics of means distinguished by Kuypers [115], should be examined in the context of military negotiations.

Whether or not the negotiations as a means are essential for <u>military detente</u> depends on the simultaneous fulfilment of the conditions of necessity and sufficiency. Only then is there a causal relationship: military negotiations lead to military detente (ultimately to military peace). Communication and negotiation are by definition indispensable. As to the sufficiency of negotiations, the answer must be no. They are too complex; they cannot cover all types of armaments at the same time and require trust and confidence, enormous "good will" and so forth. Additional means are required.

However, one might say that such negotiations include a high probability of military detente. After all, communication is established, there are common interests, there are forces in favor of good results and so on. Hence there is no causality, though a probable relationship. There is no essential contribution to an increased international military security, but there is what could be called a substantial contribution.

With regard to the contribution of military negotations to <u>political detente</u>, the sufficiency condition is fulfilled even less. By definition, since political detente includes all issue areas, but also in reality because spill-over is highly questionable, e.g., successful military detente quite likely does not change ideological irreconcilability. Yet there is some probability that one party demands reconciliation in exchange for a desired favor or that interdependence in one issue area reaches a point having leverage elsewhere (issue-linkages). Hence there is certainly no essential contribution to political detente, but there is what might be called an aggregative contribution. This denotes a low probability of the contribution of means. This relationship is generally indicated by the contention "A tends to B." In this case, many other factors (means) are important but A is still necessary. When this means is not even necessary its contribution could be called incidental. In that case the contribution of the means merely depends upon the remaining four characteristics described by Kuypers, only possibly leading towards the achievement of the chosen goal.

Some of these characteristics of means may, in conclusion, be illustrated by a brief assessment of the two most important East-West military negotiations, the

Soviet-American Strategic Arms Limitation Talks (SALT), and the negotiations on Mutual and Balanced Force Reductions (MBFR) between NATO and the Warsaw Pact in Vienna. As regards the former, the SALT experience shows that with respect to its basic problem of unilateral deterrence versus mutual stability 116, the former has prevailed on both sides. The emphasis on unilateral defense policies seriously hindered the conclusion of a SALT-II agreement and presently hinders a serious START. Yet a fair conclusion also points out the contribution of SALT to mutual stability and arms control.

Although SALT-I confirmed the strategic situation and current military developments on both sides, the Moscow agreements also paved the way for greater mutual stability: first of all by the ABM Treaty, that guaranteed mutual vulnerability; second, by the Interim Agreement, seen as an effort to establish improved parity; third, by the fact that SALT-I was seen by the two parties as a first step. A first step in a long process of bargaining, learning, trusting, fighting and compromising, both at home and abroad.

SALT-II was not torpedoed by new technologies or by the complexities of existing weapons systems alone. To the same or perhaps an even greater extent SALT suffered from inexperience, novelty, unwillingness and, above all, from the "natural" problem of how to deal with the enemy in the fundamental question of a state's security. The political processes meant to solve strategic problems occasionally appeared to be too difficult to monitor. Internationally, action-reaction schemes for the arms race still provide some explanation: mistrust, misinformation, overreaction and the like are still keywords in American-Soviet relations. Domestically, views on security, the acceptability of war, the opponent's intentions, risks of the arms race, and so forth greatly vary.

Most important, however, was that despite all technical difficulties and political antagonism the SALT negotiators succeeded in formulating some goals of international security which in part enabled the two parties to find the difficult way to agree on limitations of the military means. Much time was lost before the admittedly limited contribution to international security of SALT-II was realized, but according to Bertram, the SALT-II agreement is nonetheless

> ...a success by the standards of arms control. It provides basic predictability for strategic planning, and it establishes a set of obligations against which the behavior of the other side can be measured. Without it the Soviet Union would not necessarily-- as some SALT supporters claim--continue forever the consistent increase in its strategic forces that has marked the past decade: but the resulting

unpredictability would leave worse case analysis
unchecked. SALT-II checks it. Further, without it
there would be no set of rules to which the other
side could be held accountable. SALT-II provides
it. Here--no more, but also no less-lies its
contribution to arms control. [117]

MBFR, on the other hand, has not yielded any tangible
results. Hence an assessment of whether MBFR can contribute to military and political detente is difficult to
make. With regards to the means, both quantitative and
qualitative reinforcements have taken place in Europe.
The wide range of troops and their weapons further
complicates the difficult technical questions. However,
MBFR, like SALT, has suffered not only from these technical problems. Political aspects of the negotiations
seem to be even more decisive here than in SALT. Whereas
SALT was given a framework in which some basic guidelines
were jointly agreed in order to put constrictions on
each other's military capabilities, the MBFR talks have
not even resulted in defining some general arms control
goals. Except for the doubtful assumption that reductions will increase European security, the parties have
not reached any common understanding about their objective, ways and means of achieving greater international
security. For example, where SALT clearly reveals the
objective of narrowing and offsetting disparities between
the respective strategic arsenals, MBFR is no more than
a discussion about numbers without knowing even which
arsenals should be included.
    To be sure, the military-technical and political
complexities of MBFR seem by far to exceed those of
SALT. The differences with SALT suggest a number of
reasons why the contribution of MBFR to international
security is even more limited: geographical and intra-
alliance disparities, and the unclear relationship between global, European and Central-European military
balances. All these factors seriously complicate the
formulation of a workable concept of international
security. However, without such a concept it seems
almost impossible to choose effective and efficient
means. In this situation, the contribution of MBFR seems
to be "possible rather than probable," and "incidental
rather than substantial." Arms control perspectives for
MBFR are no brighter in the political respect. "The
background to MBFR gives unusual encouragement to sceptics. The background invites the conclusion that nobody
wants MBFR for the purported purposes of gradual disarmament." [118]
    From the beginning, the history of MBFR points to
a poor concept of international security. The NATO
proposals were not primarily urged by this concern but
were much more inspired by intra-alliance, electoral and
economic motives. NATO's proposals did not reflect a

comprehensive approach to East-West security. In fact
they only refer to the maintenance of the existing
security at a lower level in one part of NATO's territory. MBFR's chances of success were already very much
reduced by the choices--still adhered to--of the limited
area of Central Europe and of some conventional armaments
of only one selected service, the ground forces.

A decade of East-West arms control has shown the
limits of the quantitative approach. SALT-I could
largely remain a counting exercise while some qualitative
differences between Soviet and American capabilities
could be offset. During SALT-II it became increasingly
apparent that technological and geographical factors
had to be taken into account, but only some qualitative
restrictions were incorporated in the agreements. MBFR
deals exclusively with numbers and it does not seem
possible to move towards qualitative considerations
without some basic agreement on facts and figures first.
That is to say, if the quantitative approach continues
to prevail in East-West arms control.

In an attempt to incorporate qualitative factors
Christoph Bertram has proposed as a point of departure
the "specific tasks to which military capabilities can
be put." 119 According to him, arms control negotiators
should first agree on military options neither party
wants the other to have. Only after defining these
fundamental concerns of both sides, could the parties
start negotiations on the technical aspects of the military options and the weapons systems involved. For
example, East and West could agree to ban a "first-strike"
capability or to regulate the deployment of forces capable
of a surprise attack. Bertram's method is no radical
departure from the present approach, for quantitative
limitations imply restrictions of options. But he
reverses--quite logically--the steps that are to be taken
first, arguing that "without an agreed aim, implementation talks will be useless." 120 The central questions
for the "arms controller" must become the same as for the
military planner: which option of the adversary is
intolerable and how can I redress this instability of
options? Arms control negotiations would thus correctly
be aimed at and reckon with the military-strategic
considerations on which security is so heavily based 121.
Then, and only then, can arms control be an integral part
of security policy. This is of course far from easy to
realize. "The greatest obstacles to the necessary reconstruction of our strategic order," writes Iklé, tempering
overoptimism, "may well be intellectual and institutional
rigidities." Indeed, apart from technical difficulties,
the fact that the "acting men" often turn logic and
common sense upside down is inhibitive to change of
whatever kind. The "primacy of goals", simple as that
may seem, finds difficulties in the political process.
Iklé illustrates this for the defense sector: "Means

outlive their ends among military organizations, for it
is to means that institutional loyalties and intellectual
craftsmanship are devoted." 122

In sum, the strengthening of security can be
described in terms of two basically different policies.
Each policy reflects the goals, ways and means simultaneously at work in East-West relations as well as in
individual countries. In reality, a clear-cut line between adherents to one or the other policy cannot be
drawn. The goal of international security is pursued,
contended and opposed by different actors; so is
unilateralism. In theory, the means of military negotiations are at the most a substantial contribution to
military detente and an aggregative contribution to political detente. In practice, the confrontation between
political and military orientations as well as the
manifold technical difficulties further complicate and
may even threaten tangible contributions to arms control.
There are no easy solutions in the complex East-West
security relations. Unilateral reductions, budget cuts,
a collective security system or the establishment of an
international authority seem to be illusory contributions,
or worse, a threat to security.

> A more constructive approach is to accept military
> power as a fact of life, and instead of seeking to
> abolish that which cannot be abolished, to try and
> manage it successfully so that wars become less
> rather than more frequent occurrences in interna-
> tional politics. This is the philosophy underlying
> recent arms control negotiations. For the disarmers
> it is a philosophy of despair; for the arms control-
> lers it is all there is. 123

2
Origins and Development of a New Foreign Policy: The "Peace Program"

INTRODUCTION

At the time of the XXIV Congress 1971 judgments varied widely as to whether the first term of the Brezhnev/Kosygin regime had brought seven fat or seven lean years to the Soviet Union. There were pessimists and optimists in both East and West, though far from equally divided. A number of apparent changes that oc-curred during this period gave particular cause for divergent views. Political observers and participants alike made up their own "definition of the situation" for the Soviet Union and accordingly produced a scala of assumed goals and tasks for the future. An extensive description of these manifold and multifaceted views does not seem either necessary or purposeful here. Instead, the international situation will be described briefly and some major issues and proposals identified; the former as seen primarily through the analyst's and Western eyes, the latter primarily according to Brezhnev. Aware of the incompleteness of a short and selective treatment, the description of the Soviet state of affairs given here will be confined to some major features and problems.

First, the state of East-West relations and Soviet foreign policy will be described. The chapter continues with an analysis of the "Peace Program" as presented by Brezhnev in his address to the XXIV Party Congress. The program's objectives, their attainability and genuineness are examined and an attempt is made to discover possible reasons for the proposed policy. Finally, attention will focus on the discussion following these policy plans during the months after the Party Congress, until November 1971 when the "Peace Program" was officially endorsed by the Central Committee.

The unquestionable successes of Soviet foreign
policy and the immense growth of the Soviet Union's
international prestige in the period subsequent to
the 23rd Congress of the CPSU were the best proof
of the correctness of the CPSU's policy founded on
a scientific analysis of the international situation
and on the great teaching of the Marxism-Leninism. [1]

Like all textbooks to a greater or lesser degree,
this one also pictures history in a partisan and self-
laudatory way. However, these writers and active participants in Soviet foreign policy have no hesitation
whatsoever about expressing the satisfactory results.
In fact, they merely dictate the view one should have of
Soviet foreign policy. However extreme and contrasting
it may be, the following evaluation of Soviet foreign
successes, prestige and use of Marxism-Leninism for
roughly the same period nevertheless seems more accurate:

The Soviet position in world affairs, instead of
being enhanced, diminished to that of a tired, worn-
out revolutionary power content with permanent status
as "Number 2" while the United States was left free
to flex its diplomatic and military muscles all over
the world and subtly to undermine the Soviet position
in Eastern Europe with seductive policies of "bridge
building" and "peaceful engagement..."

Furthermore, China had been progressively transformed
from an alienated ally into a hostile and threatening
neighbor while the world communist movement was
fractured and demoralized and the national-liberation
movement was deprived of its protective umbrella. [2]

Disregarding partisanship concerning the merits of
American foreign policy, the political competition between the superpowers had indeed not been an "unquestionable" success for the Soviet Union. But for other
relations as well, the kind of absolute judgment found
in Soviet writings seems to be born out of dogmatic
rigidity and prescription rather than recognition of
facts and knowledge of them.
The invasion in Czechoslovakia forms, quite contrary
to the foregoing Soviet conclusions, an example of the
unquestionable failure of foreign policy [3]: a socialist
ally could not be convinced or saved except through
military means; an act that no doubt hampered rather than
increased one's international prestige. Despite the
collective, "socialist" nature of the invasion, the world
was shown that the Soviet model might not be the best one
to adopt. Ota Sik's economic reforms were a far cry from
the Soviet example and political changes would have

dangerously interfered with the fundamental one-party system. Finally, the Czechoslovakian crisis may have pointed out quite clearly to leftist parties in Western Europe that a future socialist experiment should remain independent from Soviet authority over it. While order was successfully restored in Eastern Europe, at least for the time being, Soviet influence in Western Europe and its global prestige as the leading socialist power were damaged. Moreover, criticism from the communist world was bound to follow the invasion.

For instance, the Italian communist party openly condemned it, while Rumania, that had not joined the invasion forces, and Yugoslavia denounced this act of foreign interference. The sharpest attacks from a socialist country came from China, which accused the Soviet Union of hegemonial aspirations and traditional Russian imperialism. The Soviet Union

> ...has adopted the most despotic and vicious methods to keep countries under strict control and has stationed massive numbers of troops there, and it has openly dispatched hundreds of thousands of troops to trample Czechoslovakia underfoot and install a puppet regime at bayonet point.
> Like the old tsars denounced by Lenin, this gang of renegades bases its relations with its neighbors entirely on the feudal principle of privilege.

And about the so-called "Brezhnev doctrine," granting socialist countries the right to defend the socialist gains by military means if necessary:

> You have imposed your all-highest "supreme sovereignty" on the people of other countries, which means that the sovereignty of other countries is "limited," whereas your own power of dominating other countries is "unlimited." In other words, you have the right to order other countries about, whereas they have no right to oppose you... A "socialist community" indeed! It is nothing but a synonym for a colonial empire with you as the metropolitan state. [4]

That such a Chinese outburst came after their own experience with Soviet military power at the Sino-Soviet border in 1969 makes little difference. It merely underlines how greatly the two socialist giants are alienated from each other and, indeed, how little success the Brezhnev/Kosygin regime has had in normalizing the relations with China deteriorated under Khrushchev. Socialist unity with China had become even more distant; certainly not a success of Soviet foreign policy [5].

Although there was no immediate danger of a military encirclement of Russia's vulnerable frontiers, this traditional fear permeates diplomatic relations. Both the

West and China, each for its own reasons, oppose the
Soviet Union in world politics, although without forming
an alliance in any other sense. Yet the Soviet Union
faces them diplomatically as global powers and militarily
as strong neighbors and is inconveniently forced to
divide her attention in both cases. Particularly dramatic
is the need to allocate vast resources for the defense
of its far-flung borders. Keeping up militarily with the
West is no doubt an enormous strain on the Soviet economy,
but the build-up and maintenance of an equal strength in
the Far East may become unbearable. However, the 1969
border conflicts vividly pointed to such a possibility
when Soviet divisions were drastically increased and
nothing indicated that this trend could be reversed in
the following years.
    Either to preclude a Sino-American rapprochement or
to prevent unacceptable increases in defense expenditures,
the Soviet leadership was forced to come to better terms
with either adversary. Obviously, China was the least
feasible party to deal with at the end of the 1960's.

> Whatever Moscow's intentions, fears, and hopes con-
> cerning Peking, the Soviet position vis-à-vis China
> was bound to be weakened by a continuing high level
> of tension with the West. A decade had now passed
> since Khrushchev nourished his grand design: a general
> settlement with the United States that would enable
> the U.S.S.R. to keep China from becoming a nuclear,
> and hence a great, power. That was no longer
> practicable. The Kremlin's ambitions have of ne-
> cessity become more modest, and its apprehensions
> on account of China more vivid. To get any handle
> on the problem, Russia needed a more throughgoing
> detente with the United States. [6]

During most of the 1970's the Chinese were to remain
an annoying, if not threatening, factor in Soviet foreign
policy--militarily problematic and costly, ideologically
embarrassing and divisive, and diplomatically antagonistic
and undermining. When the Sino-American rapprochement
was developing into American assistance and economic
cooperation by the end of the decade, Chinese accusations
of Soviet betrayal of revolutionary zeal by siding with
the bourgeois enemy could be refuted by the same arguments [7]. What seemed to be more important than ideological intransigence, however, was the ever more manifest
confrontation between the two nation-states and the
trend towards closer ties between the United States and
China while at the same time Soviet-American relations
were deteriorating. A dark perspective from the Kremlin
and, moreover, one that was long feared. Indeed, despite
its China phobia, the collective leadership had not been
able to change the situation inherited from Khrushchev
and to improve its relations with China before the

United States did [8]. The state of Sino-Soviet relations of the 1960's also seems to support Aspaturian's conclusion:

> For five years the government of Leonid Brezhnev and Alexei Kosygin has postponed action on painful problems, has permitted events and situations to accumulate dangerously, and in general has allowed itself to be dominated by events rather than domesticating them. [9]

The present study considers the China factor as a constant fear of the Kremlin leaders. The "China Card" has become more visible during the past few years, but this potential threat has long been a reality in Soviet eyes. The tremendous military build-up along the Sino-Soviet border after the Ussuri incidents demonstrates the genuineness of Soviet fear. This fear cannot simply be dismissed as the "China Bogey" in Soviet propaganda [10]. Reportedly, the Warsaw Pact summit meeting in Budapest, 1969 was dominated by the recent hostilities and it was there "that Brezhnev's _Westpolitik_ was conceived."

> As one participant told the _Washington Post's_ Anatole Shub: "Brezhnev's face was red and he did not look well. He was nervous and impatient. His temper flared and he pounded on the table. He had only one thing on his mind--and that was China." [11]

Towards the West Soviet diplomacy showed much of the same powerlessness. Here too, Aspaturian's harsh judgment in 1969 seems more accurate than the mostly unrealistic and self-praising Soviet statements. Soviet references hardly went beyond ideological descriptions of dangerous, aggressive and hostile policies of the West, only vaguely expressing the wish to improve the situation. With regard to the traditional concern--security--the Soviet Union generally found the West suspicious and unresponsive to the holding of a European security conference, and totally uninterested in such issues as a world disarmament conference, abolition of NATO and the Warsaw Pact or the liquidation of foreign (American) bases. Basically, Soviet foreign policy was inert and purposeless, repeating without much fervour proposals that were mostly as old as the days of Khrushchev.

The most notable exception in the West was, of course, France, whose conception of independent European politics from the "Urals to the Atlantic" was highly praised. But again, it was De Gaulle's design, which was inspired by anything but Soviet foreign policy. The French example, limited as it was, might have had a greater impact on the West European outlook on the Soviet Union if the latter had not aborted such a possible trend in 1968. The invasion in Czechoslovakia damaged

De Gaulle's Eastern Policy, held up the beginning of SALT and abolished recently established trade relations, e.g., with Britain--to mention only a few direct consequences. Moreover, a strong tendency emerged in the West to demand some clear signs of Soviet goodwill before making any further moves on its own. A European security conference would not be held without the United States and Canada or before there was a reasonable chance of its success; a "satisfactory" settlement of the question of West Berlin was required before the conference could start; finally the NATO proposals of holding talks on mutual and balanced force reductions in Central Europe was soon to be added to the list of conditions made to the Kremlin and rein- forced after Czechoslovakia.

In sum, five years after Khrushchev's fall, Soviet foreign policy was not one step further in any direction; neither in terms of communist goals nor in respect of its state interests; neither towards strengthened security nor towards increased influence vis-à-vis its main oppo- nents. Soviet moves oscillated between a communist, an internationalist and a conventional state foreign policy in a way that resulted in sterility; an idle wait-and-see policy of safe opportunities while sitting tightly and brutally on former gains [12].

However, in the West important changes were about to happen. In two major powers a new leadership took office in 1969, in the United States and West Germany. These administrations were to take in hand a number of issues that in the previous years had merely been lingering possibilities for change in international relations. Nuclear wisdom had already brought three nuclear powers to take initiatives that resulted in the Non-Proliferation Treaty in 1968. More importantly, the two superpowers declared themselves ready to discuss "mutual limitations and subsequent reduction of strategic means of delivery of nuclear weapons, both offensive and defensive, in- cluding anti-ballistic missiles" as Gromyko described SALT [13]. And in the same year NATO expressed its willingness to negotiate mutual and balanced force reduc- tions in Europe with the Warsaw Pact countries, which in 1966 had already put forward the "Declaration on Strengthening of Peace and Security in Europe." [14] How- ever, all these signs of potential change remained vague and incidental until they were put into a framework of East-West relations that came to be known as detente. It was the assessment of the current situation by the new leadership and its fresh answers that greatly helped to provide that framework [15].

On the Soviet side, Brandt-Scheel's departure from formerly inflexible ideas, especially regarding intra- German relations, was soon noticed and swiftly reacted upon. Although the seriousness of the "more realistic statements" had still to be proven, prospects of removing the German obstacle to European security were seen as hopeful. "We have stood and continue to stand for an improvement in our relations with the FRG" [16]. The Soviet-German Treaty of Non-Aggression was signed on August 12, 1970 within one year after Brandt's election. The normalization of relations with Germany was certainly a great success of Soviet foreign policy. The Treaty opened new avenues of European security and beneficial contacts with this Western power "with its considerable economic and technical possibilities." [17] Without worrying unduly about East-German dissatisfaction or undoubtedly continuing intra-German quarrels, the Soviet Union had achieved the security priority in Europe.

As early as April 1970, Brezhnev spoke about the "prerequisite changes for the better in the European political climate" that would free the way to a European security conference. Soviet-German talks were hardly under way, but the fast pace desired together with apparent Soviet indifference to East-German uneasiness about events, to say the least, clearly showed Soviet eagerness to advance the conference. By the same token, Brezhnev was also willing to accede to the Western condition of a Berlin settlement in spite of the irreconcilable stand taken by East Germany. It was obvious that without a satisfactory agreement on West Berlin the Bundestag would not ratify the Soviet-German Treaty nor allow an expansion of economic relations with the Soviet Union. Indeed, it was only after the signing of the West Berlin agreement by the Big Four that political relations developed at a fast pace. Most notable in this respect was the private meeting between Brezhnev and Brandt in the Crimea in September, 1971, shortly after the Big Four agreement. Brandt's independent action was regarded with disfavor by his partners in NATO that had not been consulted. Probably in anticipation of frowning faces there, the communique of the meeting stated that the two leaders were acting "in a spirit of complete loyalty to their respective allies." [18]

With West Germany as a declared advocate in his basket, Brezhnev scored a winning point at home and abroad and brought the holding of the Conference on Security and Cooperation in Europe a step nearer. For that matter, both leaders had helped to free the way to multilateral negotiations that would not founder on les querelles allemandes. How their respective images of European security looked or differed, their common endeavor was a necessary condition for the removal of old-established insecurities.

In the case of the United States, the new administration faced a difficult situation made up of obvious problems and more latent issues yet to be spelled out [19]. Here, as in the case of Germany, national and international developments were imposed on the leadership. For the new administration, the diminution of clear-cut American dominance in general, and of military superior-

ity vis-à-vis the Soviet Union in particular, obliged the
United States to seek cooperation amidst the characteristic ongoing competition and conflict with the Soviet
Union. As one of the American architects of the new
relationship later explained:

> It can be said that in the broad sweep of history,
> Soviet Russia is only just beginning its truly
> "imperial" phase: its military forces have acquired
> intercontinental reach only fairly recently; its
> capacity to influence events in remote areas is of
> relatively recent standing; and it is only just
> acquiring the habit of defining its interests on
> a global rather than a solely continental basis.
> For us, therefore, the problem is that of building
> viable relationships with an emerging world power...

> Yet we also have been conscious of the fact that
> Soviet power has developed unevenly, that there were
> needs, shortcomings, and difficulties confronting
> Soviet decision makers and that there were in the
> international arena not only openings and oppor-
> tunities for Soviet gain but also substantial
> resistance to excessive Soviet influence. [20]

SALT was equally part of "an active policy conducted
over a broad front of issues, and based on hard realities." [21] SALT also represented an attempt to redefine
the power relationship with the Soviet Union. Containment
of Soviet power by military (superior) means alone was no
longer feasible. Additional measures such as military
negotiations, economic levers and diplomatic consultation
were necessary to place restraints upon Soviet influence.
Sonnenfeldt's remarks about Soviet weaknesses come to the
fore here. If a web of relationships were to be established, the United States might be able to use its
strength where the Soviets found "needs, shortcomings and
difficulties." This would apply not only to direct
relations, but also indirectly to Soviet behavior of
relevance in American foreign policy aimed at a stable
international system [22].
However, when President Nixon declared in June, 1970
that SALT could start within two months, the Soviet
official response was long in forthcoming. A number of
reasons can be given for this delay, although their relative weight remains unclear [23]. Was the Soviet Union too
preoccupied during this hot summer on the Sino-Soviet
border? Had the internal debate about SALT flared up
again? If so, which aspects were so controversial: military, the impact of the talks on international and/or
domestic policy, new doubts about Nixon's foreign policy
and "linkages"? Or did the Soviet Union just need more
time for preparations? Reaffirmations of Soviet readiness
by, for example, Kosygin and Gromyko on the one hand, and

the delay of official acceptance until the end of October
on the other, point to continuation of the internal
wavering and disagreement that had characterized Soviet
attitudes to SALT since Ambassador Thompson's first
soundings in 1967 [24]. On October 25 the world was to
learn that both sides had agreed to start talks in
Helsinki on November 17. It looked as though the faction
in favor of SALT had finally won the plea to commence
negotiations.

For some, argumentation in favor of SALT was dominated by concern about the subject matter itself: the
danger of further strategic developments. Gromyko's
speeches before the Supreme Soviet may be representative
in this respect. In 1968, announcing Soviet readiness to
negotiate for the first time, he pointedly and sharply
referred to the internal debate about disarmament:

> To the good-for-nothing theoreticians who try to
> tell us...that disarmament is an illusion, we reply:
> By taking such a stand you fall into step with the
> most dyed-in-the-wool imperialist reaction, weaken
> the front of struggle against it. [25]

One year later Gromyko made no mention of broader
Soviet-American relations such as those implied for
European development toward "detente" and "mutually advantageous relations." These common-places of only a few
years later were not yet applied to the United States.
Instead, security interests prevailed and SALT was rather
a "recognition of (the) great importance" of controlling
the weapons development, which meant becoming

> ...more and more independent of the people who create
> them. The thinking of statesmen and scientists must
> now be directed not toward determining the conditions
> in which new types of weapons can be used, an activ-
> ity that NATO military headquarters is very fond
> of, but toward disarmament since the arms race has
> long since become madness. [26]

To summarize, Soviet foreign performance, seen from
the international perspective on the eve of the XXIV
Party Congress, was neither as dim as Aspaturian concluded
in 1969 nor as bright as Soviet historians/politicians
wanted us to believe from the quotes at the beginning of
this section. Events since 1969 had considerably changed
the negative picture for the better.

First, the international situation was conducive to
new approaches in East-West relations. One might say
that more or less independent sequences of events during
the 1960's had created some necessary preconditions for
change in the political climate. For example, the Soviet
strategic build-up, aimed at a credible deterrence of an
American nuclear attack, led to rough parity, which was

an essential condition for strategic negotiations. Thus parity led to new opportunities to avoid nuclear war in addition to military deterrence. At the same time, both East and West were increasingly facing more complicated relations among themselves as well as with the non-aligned world [27]. The conjunction of international relations gradually taking place during the 1960's con-stituted a latent situation conducive to change.

Second, some Western leaders broke with old policies and assumptions. They made manifest what had so far gone unnoticed, whether intentionally or not. Each for their own purposes, the new leaderships in the United States and West Germany translated opportunities into political action.

Third, unlike in the West, the same leadership in the Soviet Union swiftly responded to the German events, though the reaction to President Johnson's SALT proposal was more hesitant. In 1968, the new president-elect, however, found the Soviets eager to negotiate. In both cases of positive reaction and assertive action, security considerations prevailed over mixed feelings--to put it mildly--about dealings with the two most "capitalist" and "aggressive" states. Apparently a changing environment influences Soviet doctrinal assumptions as well. "The men who make Soviet foreign policy are affected by events they perceive; their opportunities for influence, as well as their goals and expectations, are largely determined by their location in relation to events." [28]

Finally, this also sheds new light on our earlier conclusions concerning the "sterility" of Soviet foreign policy, since the leadership had less and less "allowed itself to be dominated by events rather than domesti-cating them." [29] Foreign policy towards the West was increasingly being conducted under the active guidance of Party leader Brezhnev. His detente policy, after its initial phase, was further elaborated in his report to the XXIV Congress, and particularly in the "Peace Pro-gram." This program of foreign policy, more firmly pursued under an apparently more dominant General Secre-tary among his equals, will be discussed next.

BREZHNEV AND THE XXIV CPSU CONGRESS: THE "PEACE PROGRAM"

After the first experience of Western readiness to negotiate a relaxation of tension in Europe and military security with the United States, the West soon became an issue of interest, action and change within the Soviet leadership that had so long been rather indifferent to broader East-West relations. At the XXIV Congress Brezhnev tried not only to consolidate but moreover to accelerate recent developments. Of course most of his statements had been heard before and only a few were really new. But Brezhnev's generally conciliatory and mild tone and his definite dissociation from previous articulations strongly suggest an assumption on his part that current foreign policy would assume a more permanent character. The Soviet Union proposed to conduct an active Western diplomacy aimed at relaxation rather than tension, trade rather than autarchy, and state-founded rather than communist-founded influence, provided of course no fundamental aspects of the latter categories were put seriously at risk. Brezhnev's ideas and proposals culminated in a concise form in the program of struggle for peace and international cooperation, soon to be called the "Peace Program." This program, praised as "comprehensive," "concrete," "realistic and offensive" etc. indicates an evolution in the opinions held about East-West relations. Obviously, its objectives, if meant to be striven after, would demand certain departures from the previous dogmatic, hostile and indifferent outlook on expanded ties with the Western world [30].

Brezhnev's report to the Congress differed considerably from official, as well as his own, previous formulations. His view on political reality in the West seemed more realistic. Compared with Brezhnev's speech to the XXIII Party Congress, reading the introduction and subheadings of the sections on foreign policy reveals a decrease in ideological terminology. Capitalism and imperialism were mentioned far less often; the struggle against imperialism had not grown "more intensive"; nor did Brezhnev say much about the "deepening of the capitalist crisis," as he had done so extensively and sharply in 1966; significantly, the sections dealing with the anti-imperialist struggle on the three revolutionary fronts were considerably reduced both in length and sharpness [31].

To be sure, support for the anti-imperialist forces continued with unabated force to dominate the internationalist part of the speech. Intra-communist communication was referred to in strong, ideological terms. First and foremost, the world communist system, viz., Comecon and the Warsaw Pact, was vital to the Soviet Union. The priority No 1 to control and preserve the socialist system lost nothing of its importance in the context of East-West relations. Neither its role in Soviet security nor its weight in the anti-imperialist struggle had been diminished in any sense. However, the Soviet Union had lost a great deal of its assumed role in the two other revolutionary movements: the class struggle in the West and the national liberation movement in the third world. Accordingly, a rather sober view of developments in these non-communist countries and the limited Soviet influence there pervaded Brezhnev's address. In the former area, the struggle for socialist unity had not yet been won, certainly not in the matter of solidarity with Moscow; indeed, the "main goal" of the international conferences in 1967 and 1969 had been "to bring about a turn toward cohesion of the Communist movement, toward the consolidation of its ideological basis. "The attractiveness of communism could not be said to have gained in the West.

Similarly, developments in the third world in the post-imperialist stage were not being shaped by Soviet influence. In fact, the leadership showed little interest in these areas. "Except where Soviet national interests were involved--little more than lip service was paid by the Soviet Union to its doctrinal commitment to support national liberation movements." [32]

In describing the evil, imperialism itself, Brezhnev was more cautious and less offensive than on earlier occasions. It was not treated as exclusively aggressive, but as potentially cooperative as well. This became clear when he dealt with Soviet foreign policy on the capitalist states, which were spared the lengthy tirade devoted to them in 1966. Brezhnev apparently took recent developments into account and did not want to impede the way to further developments. The changes in his judgments about the USA and FRG, usually designated as eminently dangerous and aggressive, were striking. Although he warned against the political forces in Germany opposed to the Ostpolitik, he no longer branded the political leaders "revanchists and militarists," "fascists and war criminals," striving to increase international tension in Europe; nor did he refer to their "predatory habits" during World War II, as he had done at the XXIII Congress and in more recent speeches. Instead he concluded that "new prospects in Europe are opening up as a result of the substantial change for the better in our relations with the FRG."

In the matter of Soviet-American relations, Brezhnev did not repeat the condition that the "USA cease its policies of aggression" in Vietnam before any improvement was possible. In spite of this ongoing war and doubts about other United States actions, he stated:

> We proceed from the premise that the improvement of relations between the USSR and the USA is possible. Our principled line with respect to the capitalist countries, including the USA, is consistently and fully to implement in practice the principles of peaceful coexistence, to develop mutually advantageous ties and--with those states that are ready to do so--to cooperate in the field of strengthening peace, making mutual relations with these states as stable as possible.

The General Secretary not only underscored the importance of peaceful coexistence with the United States--and the West in general--but also omitted all mention of the word "class" in this section on East-West relations. After Khrushchev the notion of peaceful coexistence had become only one slogan among many; if it was mentioned at all, it was immediately followed by rhetoric urging continuation of the class struggle as an inseparable and decisive tenet of peaceful coexistence. At the XXIV Congress, Brezhnev instead spoke about "normal and good relations" and "mutually advantageous ties" in the context of peaceful coexistence. Evidently the aspect of class struggle had not been given up by Brezhnev, but he pointedly ignored this fundamental feature in his recommendations concerning future East-West relations to the Congress--and possibly to the West. Furthermore, the other basic tenet of peaceful coexistence--the avoidance of war and the strengthening of peace--was underscored and extensively elaborated. Given the relatively stable situation, the Soviet Union intended to pursue "the <u>active</u> defense of peace and the strengthening of international security." The absence of war, up to then determined primarily by the military balance, was to be further ensured by negotiations and agreements, while the dangerous tensions stemming from that military balance had to be reduced and eliminated in cooperation with the Western powers, i.e. the adversary.

On the whole, Brezhnev's report on foreign policy concerning the West revealed the boosted importance of these relations, which in fact was to an appreciable extent at the expense of ideological themes and internationalist commitments. Even though the latter questions were vigorously and unmistakably upheld in one section, a shift in emphasis can be observed, namely from a Soviet revolutionary role in the inevitable victory of the proletariat towards an essential contribution of the indigenous vanguards themselves to "social and political changes" in the West. In general, Brezhnev's political approach to the West showed ideological and internationalist restraint, conventional state diplomacy and a reappraisal of the relative importance of the West in Soviet foreign policy. There was a tendency for the development of peaceful coexistence to prevail over socialist internationalism where these two fundamental principles were in conflict, except for the vital interests embodied in the world socialist <u>system</u>. Where communist rule did not prevail and control was not feasible, Brezhnev's approach diverged from previously dominant doctrines. To some extent he might have espoused the views Soviet foreign policy analysts adopted during the sixties, about which Zimmerman concluded:

> There has been a marked tendency for Soviet perspectives on international relations to converge with American analysis. For both, international relations was no longer a closed system with a solution at a single point. Instead, both entertained open-ended perspectives on the process of world politics...

61

Soviet commentary revealed the same preoccupation
with the political significance of technology,
especially weapons technology,..., and an analogous
attention to the constraints imposed on the behavior
of states by the atomic age. [33]

IS THE "PEACE PROGRAM" MEANT TO BE IMPLEMENTED?

Brezhnev's presentation of the "Peace Program" must
be seen in the context of his speech as a whole [34].
His title for this program of "struggle for peace and
international cooperation and for the freedom and independence of the peoples" might very well convey the
order of foreign priorities in Brezhnev's mind. First,
it is primarily concerned with security matters. Most
of the proposals consist of arms control measures aiming
at avoidance of war, military reductions and limitation
of damage, and the economic advantages stemming from
this. However, these facts alone do not make the program
a politically important statement. The Soviet Union had
repeatedly proposed disarmament measures that might have
increased security. But lack of credibility, real or
perceived, or the unlikelihood of the attainability of
the proposals always precluded success, often even first
attempts to implement them.

With regard to the attainability of the "Peace
Program" proposals two broad categories of goals can be
distinguished:

1. Those practically impossible or in any event
    extremely difficult to achieve during the next
    five years: a conference on disarmament of the
    five nuclear powers, liquidation of foreign
    bases, a world-wide conference on disarmament,
    annihilation of NATO and Warsaw Pact, reductions
    of military expenditures. This category also
    contains goals that might be achieved, but are
    far beyond Soviet influence and primarily depend
    on other actors, such as liquidation of "hotbeds"
    of war in Southeast Asia and the Middle East,
    and the improvement of Sino-Soviet relations.
2. Those conceivably achievable--at least par-
    tially--if actively supported and pursued by the
    Soviet Union: ratification of the treaty with
    the FRG, settlement of the West Berlin question,
    the holding of a European security conference,
    agreement on SALT, mutual force reductions in
    Central Europe, and measures against accidental
    war, bacteriological warfare, nuclear tests and
    proliferation of nuclear weapons and the like.

The first category may be described as idle hope
because of Soviet powerlessness in those matters, or as

62

sheer propaganda of the kind found in political programs.
But the second group involves realistic goals that are
attainable in the changed international environment as
described earlier. For example, SALT offers possibilities
of maintaining nuclear stability, and even of increasing
security. Presumably Brezhnev had noticed American
seriousness during the first rounds of the talks and was
clearly referring to the significance of their successful
continuation. With both sides interested, the expressed
goals become feasible. With regard to European security,
the "Peace Program" is still more explicit and Brezhnev
unmistakably stresses the significance of its goals for
security.
     But important as they are, particularly in a con-
ducive environment, Brezhnev's security proposals do not
in themselves make the "Peace Program" a serious document.
What makes this program substantially different from
previous "peace" proposals is that some credibility is
provided--at least by its author.
     First, Brezhnev significantly calls this program in
one breath one of "peace and international cooperation."
The main thrust of his report and the major difference
with the previous report on foreign policy concern the
consolidation and further normalization of East-West
relations. The last point--the sixth--of the "Peace
Program" accordingly puts all foregoing security matters
in a comprehensive, political perspective: "The Soviet
Union is prepared to deepen relations of mutually advantageous cooperation in all fields with states that seek
to do so."
     It is true that a comparable program of "most
important measures" at the XXIII Congress had included
similar proposals regarding European security. But not
the slightest indication was given of any political
extension beyond the largely old-established issues.
There was no question, as there was this time, of a
"fundamental shift toward detente and peace on this
continent."
     Second, if the security proposals were implemented
Soviet security would quite probably be strengthened.
The Soviet Union, according to Brezhnev, was seeking
"concrete results that would lessen the threat of war and
would prevent the peoples from getting used to the arms
race as an inevitable evil." Did Brezhnev also disagree
with the pessimists Gromyko so sharply rebuked? Later
Brezhnev was again to reject criticism about the feasibility of arms control, although he admitted that it was
a lengthy and complex process.

     Of course, the struggle for disarmament is a complex
     business. As in many other foreign policy issues,
     one meets stubborn resistance on this question from
     the imperialist forces. Nevertheless, we do not
     regard the proposals put forward by the XXIV Congress

as propaganda slogans, but as slogans for action
which reflect political objectives which, in our
time, are becoming ever more attainable. [35]

He also referred at the Congress to the positive
aspects of arms control saying that SALT "would make it
possible to avoid another round in the missile arms race
and to free substantial resources for constructive
purposes. "The Peace Program" undeniably included
chimeric goals whose realization was remote, to say the
least, but it revealed very real and realistic Soviet
security and economic interests as well.
Third and most important point is the Soviet assessment of the changed correlation of forces. Although
Brezhnev did not point this out so strongly in his speech,
the increased power of the Soviet Union would soon become
the first and foremost justification of detente. Few
articles and speeches fail to paraphrase Brezhnev's explanation of a few months later.

What, in fact, allows us to view the issue in this
way? Primarily the changed balance of power in the
world...both socio-political and military power.
Even a few years ago, the imperialists, and primarily
the American imperialists, hoped seriously, by using
the arms race, to reinforce their positions in the
world arena and to simultaneously weaken the economy
of the USSR and the other socialist countries, to
frustrate our plans for peaceful construction. The
failure of our enemies' calculations has now become
completely clear. Everyone can now see that socialism is sufficiently powerful to insure both a reliable defense and the development of its economy,
although, of course, without large defense
expenditures we and our economy would move ahead far
more quickly. (Emphasis added) [36]

Few observers in either East or West would disagree
with Brezhnev's appreciation of Soviet military power
and the burden it must impose on the economy. For example, the former Soviet citizen Zhores Medvedev writes
that detente "was induced by the feeling of military
equality, by the success of military science and technology." [37] But he adds a significant observation apparently aimed at Western critics of detente who fear an even
greater increase of military power as a result of "mutual
advantageous cooperation."

...it is wrong to think that detente will seriously
add to Soviet military power and the danger of
military aggression. In a highly centralized state,
military development is virtually independent of the
general standard of life or of international cooperation in other branches of science. Military tech-

nology is more often stimulated by bad relations
than by cooperation...

The influence of the USSR will grow in either case--
with detente or without it. With detente, the
influence is mutual and the situation is safer.
Without detente, the influence would still be felt,
but through military means. 38

In other words, military power will grow if the
Soviet leadership deems it necessary. It is precisely
this empirically confirmed fact that makes Brezhnev's
proposed departure from purely unilateral defense decision-making and preoccupation with national security so
important, if not opportune to the West. A former IISS
analyst of Soviet defense spending seems to be right on
target when he assumes--after having reviewed the various
methods used in the West--that "perhaps the weakest area
in Soviet defence expenditure analysis has not been the
estimation but the interpretation of results." And Cockle
concludes:

> Therefore, Western economic policies which affect
> the Soviet economy to some extent, and possibly
> could to a greater extent, are bound to have some
> bearing on the Soviet military-civil trade-off. The
> awareness of this higher defence burden should give
> the nature of its relationship to the Soviet economy
> and its policy far more importance to Western policy-
> makers. 39

Fourth, contrary to previous presentations of proposals, the "Peace Program" included concessions and answers
to Western demands. For the first time the Soviet Union
reacted to the mutual and balanced force reductions proposed by NATO in 1968. Interestingly, Brezhnev uses
practically the same language as Nixon a few weeks earlier.
Reportedly the State Department was later reminded to
this, when it seemed that the signal would pass unnoticed
in the United States. Besides the possible merits of MBFR
for foreign policy, Brezhnev's sudden readiness to hold
these talks should be seen too, as a concession in exchange for NATO's fiat for the long desired European
security conference (CSCE). Similarly, Soviet "motivation" for wishing to find a "satisfactory settlement"
for West Berlin had largely been a response to the demand
by NATO countries. Finally, eagerness for the CSCE had
also forced the Soviet Union to agree to the participation
of the United States and Canada in this conference. The
NATO position that European security could not be discussed without the United States was reluctantly accepted by the Warsaw Pact in 1970 40. The "Peace Program"
only implied acceptance of American participation. No
doubt Brezhnev was aware of this condition for any

negotiations on European security and presumably accepted
the failure of Soviet foreign policy to exclude the
United States from European affairs. Certainly MBFR, in
addition to the CSCE, would further nullify the traditional objective of separating the United States from
the question of West European security. Despite that
fact, this Western demand would be met [41].

Finally, the goals of the program whose implementation could start in a reasonably short time or was already
under way, all concerned long-term undertakings. Their
realization would require many years. The long-term
nature of the plans was due not only to the obviously
complicated military negotiations it entailed, but also
to Brezhnev's insistence on long-term trade contracts
and his frequent reference to the advantage of such deals
for economic planning at home.

To summarize, several factors point to the genuineness of the program's goals that were feasible. A fairly
broad political, long-term, flexible and business-like
approach aiming at stability and security prevailed over
a narrowly selective, expedient, dogmatic and uncompromising view backed up by nothing more than strength.

DOMESTIC FACTORS AND THE "PEACE PROGRAM"

In the foregoing section, the goals were analyzed in
international perspective; that must obviously be complemented by one or two fundamental considerations stemming
from the domestic situation. For possible international
gains from peace and cooperation could bring about a
number of benefits needed--or at least helpful--domes-
tically. The degree to which East-West normalization was
desired was likely to affect the sincerity underlying the
policy program.

First and foremost, Soviet economic prospects called
for "mutually advantageous cooperation" with the ever
further advancing West. Soviet economic performance,
especially in the scientific, technological and managerial
spheres, lagged behind the West. Of the two developed
industrialized systems, the capitalist states were not
only able to grow further, but also displayed a capacity
to manage more efficiently the complexities of modern
society. In this respect the Soviet Union stood to gain
rather than lose from Western experience. At the same
time, keeping up--at least--with the West was an absolute
political prerequisite in the competition between the two
social systems. In Brezhnev's words:

> The improvement of the system of foreign relations
> is an important reserve for increasing the economic
> efficiency of the national economy. Political fac-
> tors connected with the consolidation of the social-
> ist commonwealth and the strengthening of the econ-

omic basis of the peaceful coexistence of states, as well as factors stemming from the requirements of our national economy, make the expanded production of goods for export by all branches of industry an important matter. This will also help to increase imports of necessary commodities. There can be no doubt that the expansion of international exchanges will have a favorable effect on the improvement of the work of all our industry.

East-West ties were apparently of great economic and political importance and underline the policy of normalizing these relations. Nonetheless, Brezhnev's principal answer to the domestic economic problems was a highly ambitious increase in labor productivity, based on scientific and technological progress and greater efficiency in the Soviet economy itself. There was an urgent need for better organization and management, and for tighter control over the implementation of directives and central decisions. The political aspects of this question and Brezhnev's answers to it will be discussed later.

Besides plans to reorganize and restructure the economy, the policy designed for faster growth with more limited resources also included a reorientation of the allocation of means and social priorities. The domestic economic situation and the new Plan may indicate the degree to which Brezhnev's foreign policy was needed and hence serious. Prior to the Ninth Five Year Plan the growth of heavy industry had unquestionably prevailed over that of light industry, while the former's share in the total output was already overwhelming. Growth came from the productive sector and the consumer-oriented sector had to foot the bill. Similarly, the--non-productive--defense sector received generous and preferential treatment, enjoying priority over the consumer goods industry. The Ninth FYP departed from this tradition in Soviet economic policy by officially allocating a higher rate of consumer-oriented investments for the first time. The significance of this change must be seen in its official character and in the severe economic circumstances in which the decision was taken. The falling growth rate over the years could not have pointed to any consumer priority. Furthermore, even though a policy favorable to the consumer had been conducted by Brezhnev/ Kosygin during part of the Eighth FYP, this was never announced in a Plan, let alone with all the publicity attending this "main task" and "supreme goal" as in 1971 42. In view of this consumer priority, the much slower growth of economic inputs than in the previous Plan and the nevertheless ambitiously planned growth rate of the economy, one begins to wonder whether defense may not have been required to foot the bill this time, if the new policy was to be realized. This is not to say that

drastic changes were to be expected in the allocation of
funds. Drastic changes were unlikely to form part of the
Soviet process. Even the very small margin of investments
in consumer goods was likely to raise enough dust in the
political arena. It is more important and more sensible
to look for changes in trends, and not for dramatic
departures and break-throughs in Soviet institutional
arrangements.
     Nevertheless, in referring to heavy industry as the
foundation of further economic growth, the defense requirements and the people's well-being the latter seemed
in Brezhnev's view to have appreciably gained in relative
importance. He not only wished heavy industry "to expand
the production of consumer goods directly in their own
enterprises," but also defined "the ultimate goal of
heavy industry" as a substantial increase in the means of
production for consumer goods. He underscored this view
by quoting Lenin:

     In the final analysis the manufacture of the means
     of production is necessarily linked with the manu-
     facture of articles of consumption, since means of
     production are manufactured not for the sake of the
     means of production themselves, but only because
     more and more means of production are required by
     the branches of industry that manufacture articles
     of consumption.

To which he added:

     This, comrades, is the definitive instruction of our
     leader for our Party.

     The fact that the last sentence was omitted in Pravda
the next day indicates that Brezhnev leaned too much
towards consumer interests according to some. It also
showed the powerful position of the heavy-industry
lobbies 43.
     Brezhnev's attention to consumer priority could also
indicate the importance of political detente, or "good
relations" with the West. It is in precisely this sector
that the Soviet system is less equipped for rapid growth
because of the tremendous complexities surrounding the
planning and forecasting of consumer demand, the rising
expectations with respect to variety and quality, and the
inability of the system to cope with sudden needs and
unexpected shortages. Concerning the defense industry,
on the other hand, Brezhnev stated that its development
"will depend in large part on the international situation," even though he gave careful assurances that
national security would remain at the required level.
But on previous occasions Brezhnev had usually pointed to
the international situation as being responsible for the
substantial sums allocated to defense, and had frequently

guaranteed defense to be maintained "on the highest level." [44] At the XXIV Party Congress he dit not repeat this cliché. Instead, he referred to the adequacy of national defense, even implying the possibility of a shift of resources from military to "constructive purposes," as mentioned earlier. In other words, Brezhnev suggested that domestic economic priorities would benefit from detente, which would facilitate reallocation of the limited resources. If the Soviet consumer had indeed become a priority, then military detente could perhaps be the right means of promoting both the production of consumer goods and sustained economic growth.

The link between Soviet foreign policy and the possibility of freeing resources for "constructive purposes" was also made in a publication for internal propaganda, quoted by Sydney Ploss: "Experience has shown that only under conditions of a relaxation of tension is it possible to concentrate a maximum of resources for accomplishing the plans for the building of communism." [45]

Likewise, Soviet commentators stressed the "organic correlation" between the Five Year Plan and foreign policy, and urged the West to respond positively. Radio Moscow, for example, accused the mass media in some Western countries of having "ignored or pooh-poohed" Soviet proposals. The speaker wondered how the economic plan could ever be implemented without peace, adding: "It would be unwise to let the opportunity go by without attempting to exploit it to the best of one's ability.... As the saying goes, seize the moment." [46] The Soviet audience was likewise told that peace was a necessary condition. "This is why we may say with complete assurance that the new five-year plan of development of the national economy..., and the Soviet Peace Program mutually complement one another and, what is more, one is unthinkable without the other." Viktor Levin even assesses the direction of a causal relationship, possibly indicating his dislike of the current dominance of defense considerations in the economy and the impediment it formed for the implementation of the Peace Program.

> If the implementation of the Soviet Peace Program means an improvement of the external conditions of the building of communism in the U.S.S.R., then the fulfilment of the economic plans creates a reliable basis for carrying out an active peaceloving foreign policy. (Emphasis added) [47]

The "constructive purposes" Brezhnev actually had in mind were above all agriculture, to which huge sums had been allocated after a long debate during the previous years. This will be discussed in greater detail in Chapter V. Suffice it to say here that the military and heavy industry were indeed made subject to financial restraints in the new Five Year Plan.

Whether or not the "Peace Program" could bring about
military savings or prevent excessive increases in defense expenditures, a relaxation of (military) tensions
could contribute to domestic economic objectives. An
improved political climate--a clear aim of Brezhnev's--
could result in the expansion of trade even without
substantial military agreements. To be sure, Brezhnev's
pronouncements in favor of international military negotiations were certainly not matched by a similar clarity
with regard to national (domestic) measures aimed at
military reductions. No explicit recommendation for
a substantial relief on the defense burden was contained
in his outline of domestic policy. Yet his economic
priorities implied a shifting away from the absolute
defense preferences usual up to that time and such a
move, no matter what its scale, would be perfectly
consistent with the "Peace Program" goals.
    Finally, the feasibility of the "Peace Program"
depended to a considerable extent on the role and position assumed by Brezhnev personally and on his institutional power base. He had undoubtedly strengthened
his position since about 1969. It is not unlikely that
the Czechoslovakian events had plunged the collective
leadership into an internal crisis, which Brezhnev deftly
used to launch his initiatives from a strengthened
position [48]. This assertive move was most important,
for the Soviet political process was in dire straits.
Brezhnev appeared at the XXIV Congress with a positive
record of service in foreign policy and with the clear
intention of promoting a firm continuation of East-West
relations. That firmness was largely possible thanks to
his increased personal command over a number of issues.
    In fact he encroached upon the responsibilities
still entrusted to Kosygin. Prior to 1969 Soviet foreign
policy on the non-communist countries had been primarily
the domain of the Prime Minister. The rapprochement with
the FRG, however, emanated from Brezhnev's initiatives
and vigorous conduct. It is true that Kosygin was permitted to sign the Soviet-German Treaty in 1970, but this
may well be termed his last major act in East-West
relations. After the XXIV Congress Brezhnev was the
prominent authority in both the advocacy and conduct of
these relations [49]. Coincidentally--or not--he opened
a domestic offensive against Kosygin in 1969 [50]. In the
economic sphere the main themes that constantly recurred
were stressed with new vigor by Brezhnev: the role of the
scientific and technical revolution, the rapid introduction of findings and innovations in the production process, the need to increase labor productivity and
efficiency, managerial and organizational reforms, a
move from extensive to intensive economic growth, the
thrifty use of resources in view of future labor shortage
and capital construction, and so on [51]. Most unusual as
well as significant in view of its topicality, was for

70

instance the extensive attention paid by Brezhnev to the domestic problems facing the new (Ninth) FYP at a purely international gathering in 1969, the International Conference of Communist and Workers' Parties. But on other occasions, too, Brezhnev increasingly interfered in economic policies. Thus he sharply attacked the performance of ministries and, in more general terms, the economic reform of 1965 that had failed to respond effectively to the needs of the time. Likewise, the fact that Brezhnev delivered the "main speech" to the Council of Ministers in June 1970, and that he alone, and not Kosygin, signed the Directives of the Ninth Five Year Plan as the responsible Politburo member in both cases, illustrates once more his enhanced domestic position. The dominant role he played at the XXIV Congress merely underlined the trend of the preceding few years.

Whether Brezhnev's personal rise was accompanied by the institutional strengthening of his political leadership--i.e., the power to formulate and forcefully implement his policy--will be discussed throughout this study in the two contexts of domestic and foreign policy. It was precisely this fundamental issue in Soviet politics that was largely to determine the succes of the implementation of the "Peace Program."

To summarize, the new foreign policy pursued towards the West in the late 1960's culminated in the sweeping and offensive "Peace Program" that contained a number of realistic, though ambitious proposals. Whatever their attainability in terms of time and the necessary political will, Soviet sincerity was furthered both by favorable circumstances and political signals. Brezhnev's temperate tone and moderate ideological stand towards the West defied formerly expressed priorities; the more so as he showed an unprecedented readiness to yield to Western demands, deeming this necessary for the advancement of his foreign policy. The increased importance of East-West relations in Soviet policies was illustrated by topical, realistic concern about security and by strongly accentuated international cooperation.

However, the genuineness of Soviet foreign policy as represented by the "Peace Program" must primarily be explained in terms of the domestic situation and priorities. In particular, it should be assessed against the background of Brezhnev's (and company's) views on the dragging economy, the need to reform management and organization, and the problem of effectively "combining the achievements of the scientific-technical revolution with the advantages of the socialist system." 52 Though Brezhnev's ideas in these matters did not rule it out, a "new" defense policy did not seem to be accorded high priority on the list of domestic policies. There is no direct evidence that his interest in military negotiations included plans to redefine priorities or to reassess the political role of the defense-related

71

actors. Brezhnev had never risked his neck nor, presumably, did he intend to risk it this time vis-à-vis the sector of deep-rooted, traditional preference and power.

BREZHNEV'S FOREIGN POLICY ENDORSED

When the XXIV Party Congress ended it could not be said that the delegates were sent home with totally monolithic views on the issues, and especially not as regards foreign policy. Though they had heard and unanimously adopted the Party's policies, they had left the concrete answers to their leadership. Even though General Secretary Brezhnev appeared to be strongly in command in foreign policy, his recommendations were not always repeated by others and--more importantly--were given extremely little attention in the Congress Resolution. Although the Resolution approved "the proposals and conclusions contained in the Report of the CPSU Central Committee," [53] there was no specific reference to the "Peace Program" itself; nor did the Resolution contain any reflection of Brezhnev's extensive concern with arms control and disarmament problems--not even the propagandistic aspects. Instead, the Congress' document stressed--in the three traditionally separate sections-- the importance of the Soviet Union for anti-imperialist, revolutionary forces. By the same token, the fourth section dealing with relations with non-socialist states was dominated by familiar anti-imperialist themes which were counterbalanced by nothing more than a few remarks about positive changes in Europe and the promotion of the CSCE, and by the directive to expand ties with the capitalist countries, where this could be advantageous to both parties and world peace. The Resolution concludes:

> The Congress fully approves the basic directions, as
> formulated in the Report, of the struggle against
> the aggressive policy of imperialism and for peace,
> the security of the peoples and social progress. [54]

These basic directions do not contradict Brezhnev's words; at the same time, however, they fail to convey all his political projections, particularly those concerning East-West relations.

It was not until the November Plenum of the Central Committee in 1971 that this policy was cleared of the uncertainty surrounding it: only then was it possible to speak of a foreign policy course that had been publicly adopted by the Soviet leadership. For the first time in an official document the CPSU Central Committee clearly states that it

...unanimously approves and fully supports the work carried out by the Political Bureau of the Central Committee in carrying into life the foreign policy program put forward by the Congress...

The plenary meeting instructs the Political Bureau of the Central Committee to continue to abide consistently by the foreign policy program of the XXIV Congress... (Emphasis added) [55]

The Resolution pointed to the "further practical employment of the principles of peaceful coexistence and mutually beneficial cooperation of European states," called for a European security conference "with the participation of the United States and Canada," praised the diplomatic activities of and visits by Politburo members to so many countries, and noted "with satisfaction" the support of the fraternal parties for the Soviet international efforts. The Central Committee indeed seemed to endorse Brezhnev's "Peace Program," which was frequently referred to in the Resolution as "the foreign policy program." Whereas the Congress Resolution had not reflected--while not altogether ignoring--the presentation of Brezhnev's foreign policy, the November Plenum did. The Central Committee even assessed its first applications in a positive way.

This affirmative judgment seemed first and foremost to stem from the numerous activities Brezhnev had undertaken since the Congress in the domain of East-West relations. Apart from his successful efforts to win the support of the East European leaders for his policies [56], Brezhnev was pushing his plans very hard and persistently vis-à-vis the West. In May he unambiguously announced Soviet readiness to start the talks about military reductions in Europe (MBFR). In the same month the United States and the Soviet Union broke the dead-lock in SALT thanks largely to the revised Soviet position on American Forward Based Systems in Europe (FBS). Significantly, Brezhnev was by now the Politburo member in charge of these negotiations. "The first results" of these talks and of the "Peace Program," in one Soviet view [57], came in September when agreement was reached on improvement of the Hot Line and prevention of an accidental triggering-off of a nuclear war. Most important of all, only a few weeks later President Nixon confirmed his visit to Moscow, scheduled for May, 1972. In September the Big Four signed the agreement on West Berlin and the "private" Brezhnev-Brandt illustration of public Soviet-German togetherness in security matters was successfully concluded in the Crimea. Finally, in October Brezhnev once again was able to further his foreign policy ideas in France by means of the already exemplary Soviet-French relations, perceptibly framed in the "Principles of Cooperation" which he and President Pompidou signed.

Not surprisingly, the Soviet press frequently described the months following the XXIV Congress as "unprecedented Soviet diplomatic activity," "a great peace offensive of the Soviet Union" or "the Peace Program in action." This was certainly true of Brezhnev.

However, this period also reveals a lack of enthusiasm and hesitation concerning an active, cooperative policy towards the West. One even encounters outright advocacy of a more intransigent foreign policy, often accompanied by additions "as before," "since the Revolution," the "continuation of Lenin's course," "against the unabated aggressiveness of imperialism," and so on. Explanations of the meaning of the "Peace Program" were utterly conflicting, sometimes even in one and the same source. For example, the military daily, Red Star, wrote in an editorial, after referring to the "Soviet peace offensive" and the "exceptionally active diplomacy":

> Why not, we are really on the offensive, fighting
> for the peace and friendship of peoples. This great
> offensive began with October whose 54th anniversary
> the whole world will soon mark...
>
> This policy is based on the indestructible economic
> and military might of the land of the Soviets. [58]

But in another editorial in the same newspaper there was no downgrading of any change or possible initiatives in Soviet foreign policy nor any reference to the exclusiveness of Soviet economic and military power as peace-keeper. On the contrary, it was extremely positive about the "Peace Program that has found the way to the hearts of millions of people," that was already leading to a "turning point" in Europe's history, and that has been proposed "only seven months ago." [59]

Speeches and articles by Soviet leaders showed the same contradictions. Some did not mention the program at all and/or presented conflicting arguments [60]. Others ascribed it to the Congress report "made by Comrade L.I. Brezhnev," [61] in contrast to the standard phrase used after the November Plenum: "the Peace Program advanced by the XXIV Congress." Foreign policy as outlined by Brezhnev was apparently not yet regarded as being backed by a "unanimous" vote or as a policy that had to be presented as the "Leninist course".

Disagreement existed and continued to exist on more specific issues; for instance, to what extent security was to be determined in consultation with the adversary, the Soviet economy should be dependent on foreign trade or Soviet diplomacy should collaborate with capitalist states. The Resolution of the November Plenum leaves little doubt about the continuing friction between a certain dependency on the West and the self-reliance of the Soviet Union:

The plenary meeting stresses that the role of ideological struggle in the international scene increases more and more in the process of the party's further efforts to implement the foreign policy program of the XXIV Congress. The plenary meeting calls the attention of foreign policy, ideological and propaganda organs to the need of raising the level and effectiveness of their activities, vigorously upholding the interests of our country, the interests of socialism, of the entire communist movement in the struggle against imperialist propaganda and enemies of Marxism-Leninism...

The entire international activity of the Party rests on the steady growth of the Soviet Union's economic, political and defensive power. The successful fulfilment of the 9th Five Year Plan in all indicators is of primary importance for the further strengthening of the international position and prestige of the USSR, for the solution of the tasks facing our country in the international arena, for the achievement of new successes in the economic competition with capitalism. 62

Here those in favor of self-reliance rather than of any form of dependency speak up. This deep-rooted tendency toward national reliance will always remain present against the decision for some international reliance.

However predominant Brezhnev may have been in the foreign policy area at the Congress, his position in the political process as a whole probably underwent only a gradual change. In spite of his status of party leader and initiator in many fields, Brezhnev was part of a collective leadership with basically shared responsibilities. For all his plans, foreign and domestic alike, the essential point was whether he could transform his proposals into clear official decisions with more than merely nominal collective support. Though Brezhnev might make others change their tune, they were not yet dancing to his pipes.

3
Brezhnev: "The Embodiment of Collective Reason and Will?"

INTRODUCTION

Since 1964 Western analysts have been confronted with a remarkable phenomenon unknown in Soviet history since Lenin: the rule of a collective leadership. After the long period of personal dictatorship and power, with its accompanying fierce power struggles, a common question was: "How long will it last?" During the first years of their rule, however, Khrushchev's successors displayed a remarkable concern for the collective character of the regime and indeed appeared to seek stability as "the most salient characteristic of their style of government." [1] For example, when Brezhnev successfully consolidated his position as party leader in 1964-1966 at the expense of some of his colleagues, his responsibilities did not increase. The effect of the demotion of some competitors, notably Podgorny and Shelepin, and of the promotion of Brezhnev clients was limited, causing little change in the power distribution. Even then, according to Dornberg, the General Secretary's enhanced position was nevertheless criticized in Pravda.

> The collegial spirit asserts itself when respect for authority does not go beyond reasonable limits and when secretaries of party committees have the tact, caution and self-critical spirit which are necessary for the collective exchange of opinions...
>
> The secretary of a party committee is not a na-chalnik--its chief--he is not invested with the right to give orders. He is merely the senior man in the collective leadership. True, a greater responsibility rests upon him, but his rights are on a par with those of the other members of the committee. [2]

The division of work and authority was still maintained after the reshuffle of friends and foes.

Politburo members continued to perform their particular
duties, emphatically presented to the outside world as
collective decisions taken in full agreement. Nonetheless, this state of affairs, so un characteristic of
the Soviet polity, was followed with scepticism and
disbelief in the West. For example, Schapiro concludes
his comprehensive study of the Communist Party of the
Soviet Union in 1970 as follows:

> Perhaps the single most important question in Soviet
> politics in the next few years will be the survival
> of collective rule, or the re-emergency of a single
> supreme leader who has been a characteristic feature
> throughout Soviet history.[3]

Indeed, the years following the XXIV Party Congress
were marked by Brezhnev's emphatically pursued influence
on foreign policy and some key areas of domestic policy.
The emergent _primus inter pares_ had clearly assumed a
dominant position while striving to increase the momentum
his policy plans had gained after the Party Congress.
Abroad and at home, his articulations became the major
indication of the official policy direction. The Party
and the government acknowledged in their greetings to
Brezhnev on his 70th birthday that it had been he who put
forward the "Peace Program." [4] His contribution to "the
formulation and implementation of Soviet foreign policy"
became a standard reference for the spoken and written
word. This personification of Soviet foreign policy was
further underlined by direct contacts with foreign
leaders, highlighted by the superpower summits in 1972,
1973 and 1974. Furthermore, since the end of 1973 and
beginning of 1974 Brezhnev was almost routinely said to
"head" the Politburo and the Central Committee. With a
few exceptions, Politburo members referred to Brezhnev
as the leader _(rukovoditel)_ whose strategic insights and
plans were followed by Party and Government. An
increasingly thriving personality cult appeared from
decorations, publications of his speeches, his promotion
to Marshal of the Soviet Union and Chairman of the Defense
Council, and his nomination as Soviet President. All
these marks of honor and public recognition were reminiscent of the era of Brezhnev's predecessors: the rule of
a supreme leader, prompted by the cult of his personality [5].

The central question of this chapter, bearing on
both domestic and foreign policy, is whether Brezhnev
could and/or wanted to become a single leader who, like
Stalin, could bring "support at last for almost any
policy as long as it promised a way out of the present
standstill." [6] Had Brezhnev increased his power and
authority as policy-maker or was he an interest-broker
and, as Suslov characterizes his leadership, the "embodiment of collective reason and will of the CPSU?" [7]

The following attempt to characterize the political
leadership will embrace some political issues pertinent
to the perceived systemic needs for development and
include an examination of the working power relationship
within the polity. First, how serious was the
"standstill," if any, in Soviet politics and what was
Brezhnev's response? Second, what was Brezhnev's position in the Party, in particular in the Central Committee
and the Politburo?

DETERIORATION OF POLITICAL LEADERSHIP

The apparently successful attempt in the 1960's to
prevent the emergence of a dominant leader and to install
genuine consensus decision-making, reinforced by mutual
control, evidently bore the serious risk of immobilism.
If full agreement among the leaders was becoming an
actual goal or prerequisite, then the consequence of
meaningless compromises, hesitant leadership, sham decisions or no decision at all was looming and, if prolonged,
likely to become a real danger in a one-Party system.

Some problems do, indeed, go away if left, but
others, such as those concerned with economic
planning and administration, are more basic or
pervasive, and the ill-effects of irresolute decision-making are cumulative, so that the acuteness
and potential devisiveness of these problems tend
to grow with time. [8]

Immobilism, earlier observed with regard to foreign
policy, threatened to render the domestic scene dangerously undirected by 1969. The lack of authoritative
leadership most probably had a negative influence on both
higher and lower levels. It seriously jeopardized the
implementation of decisions, even decisions that were
adequate and unanimous. For instance, the chances of
economic reform were diminished not only by the compro-
mised design and limited application at the top level,
but also by the slow or even negative response at the
enterprise level during its implementation [9]. By the
same token, the dissatisfaction frequently ventilated by
Brezhnev and others with the way ministries were carrying
out the Plan and central decisions illustrates the
considerable and persistent freedom of parts of the sub-
system. Although the leadership did not ride rough-shod
over (party) officials or virtually oppose bureaucratic
interests as had Khrushchev, it experienced to the same
extent the tremendous impact of the giant Soviet bureaucracy.
This regime may not have displayed Khrushchev's
administrative faults, but the basic problems seemed to
counteract the ability to control the organizational

process even more vehemently. One such problem was the complexity of modern society, as Brezhnev fully admitted: "The higher the level that society reaches, the more complicated and larger in scale the tasks that it sets for itself become." 10

Obviously the stage of "developed socialism" would bring with it a great number of new and major problems for the centralized government. The scale and complexity to which Brezhnev referred left their imprints, among other things, on the decision-making process. Incrementalism, bureaucratic competition and bargaining, pluralistic-professional pressures, indispensable knowledge and expertise, all took their toll of the autonomy and authority of the dominant--centralized--system. Sub-systems had not only increased their operational freedom over the years, but also enhanced their decision-making autonomy within their own sub-system and asseverated their input in the dominant central system. The top leadership was increasingly confronted with loss of direction because of the dwindling of effective and legitimate guidance. As Tatu concluded in 1969:

> The most strictly Marxist analysis leads to the conclusion that the country's forces of production (the living forces of the nation and the needs of development) have come into conflict with the yields of production (the political and economic super-structure) and that the USSR thus presents a typical case of pre-revolutionary situation. 11

Once again, Brezhnev was the most vigorous of the leaders in defying the challenges. Significantly, soon after the failure of the Communist Party in Czechoslovakia he told an international communist conference in 1969:

> The scale and complexity of the tasks of communist construction increase the importance of a conscious, organizing vanguard in the life of society. Such a vanguard is the Communist Party, which bases all its activity on Marxism-Leninism, has close ties with the broadest masses of working people and imparts an organized and planned character to all work involved in the construction of communism. In exercising its leadership role, the Party does everything necessary so that the masses of working people can actively influence the formation and implementation of state policy and can have a real opportunity to display their initiative and their inventiveness. The Party is waging a resolute struggle against bureaucratic tendencies, against which the administrative apparatus is not completely immune even under socialism. The heightening of the Party's leadership role intensifies its responsibility for everything that is done in the country and for the present and future

of the Soviet State. This means that the Party itself must develop, raise the fighting efficiency of its ranks and strengthen its ideological and organizational unity. [12]

At the December Plenum of the Central Committee he reiterated his points: the Party must regain its (lost) initiative and dynamic guiding role in these modern times which required "new methods and new decisions." [13] And later, at the XXIV Party Congress, Brezhnev stressed the importance of new economic management and organization by the _Party_ aimed at its single, clear command over a vast range of interests and issues. New methods must be found to "strengthen and modernize the role of the Communist Party as the ruling mechanism of government." [14] In short, Brezhnev wished to re-establish the role of the Party as the dominant institution, decisive and zealous in furthering its cause and policy.

Brezhnev's overriding concern was the development of the political system; the red thread running through the "new methods and new decisions" was the way the Party could and should be used in this respect. The most important aspect for our further analysis is the way various actors received and acted upon the specific proposals. The consequences, perceived or real, of the development envisaged, particularly where current power positions were affected, are the focus of the following examination. No attempt will be made to examine the economic aspects proper or the likely usefulness of the proposed changes. Before turning to the functioning of the political leadership, however, a few major features of the comprehensive domestic socio-economic policy should be mentioned [15].

First, Brezhnev's economic plans reflect to a considerable extent the views normally ascribed to Kosygin. On the left-right continuum, he seems to have moved somewhat towards advocacy of economics and evolutionary development. As shown before, Brezhnev had sided with Kosygin on the issue of the revival of consumer interest and encouragement of a more self-sustaining economic mechanism by greater independence and economic incentives. In the words of a "liberal" economist: "A sound economy is one that operationally reacts to desirable social shifts and reflects their rhythm.... In this situation guidance of the economy must correspond to the dynamism of development and give collectives greater independence." [16]

Furthermore, economic growth was primarily to be maintained by the introduction of technology and by an increase of labor productivity. The reserves for extensive growth were exhausted, particularly the labor force, and the solution had to be found in intensive growth. Brezhnev thus recognized and strongly emphasized the significance of the "Scientific-Technical Revolution." [17]

Third, the degree of planning and administrative centralization was also questioned by Brezhnev. The difficulties of central planning have been extensively commented upon both in Eastern and Western publications. So it does not seem at all unreasonable to ask, as Grossman does, "Is the Plan a Plan?" In addition to his own well-founded doubts, Grossman cites a Gosplan top official who had written:

As we know, the preparation of a five-year plan... requires about three years. As a result, such plans are generally prepared at the same time as the annual plans, which complicates the work of planning bodies, especially the central ones, which are preoccupied with annual plans for 7-8 months a year and can work on the longer term ones only in the remaining parts of the year. This frequently has led to the termination of five-year plans. Sometimes (the planners) limited themselves to the preparation of Control Figures, which were never communicated down to the executants, which reduced their significance (deistvennost). 18

There was an almost endless stream of complaints about the many shortcomings in the planning system. Norms were not defined, information and data were insufficient, sometimes mere "calculated guesses," and they often arrived too late at the ministries and Gosplan. Planning was fragmented between the branches and sectors, even with regard to the parts of a single end product 19. To be sure, planning had to be improved, but must not become an immutable law:

However the centralized plan is improved, it must not be turned into a fetish, into an absolute, and regarded as a plan that must be carried out in every detail. Certain deviations from the original plan are dictated by new situations. 20

In this view, automated systems and the use of computers can be of considerable assistance, but cannot in themselves make the system function. Therefore Brezhnev talked in terms of "planned guidance," geared particularly to long-term forecasting of both quantitative and qualitative changes. In this respect he repeatedly stressed the need for a more flexible 10-15 year plan 21.

Fourth, part of the solution to these problems was sought by Brezhnev in a new variant of "economic reform": the establishment of huge production and science and production associations. These "cartels" were to enjoy a fair degree of autonomy and were intended to integrate the research, planning and production processes at their own level, while being able to function at higher levels as major furnishers of information and planning data.

The system certainly aimed at a greater degree of decentralization [22]. The center was to deal through fewer and shorter lines with these economic units. This would allow the center to improve communication and cooperation with the lower levels and to make explicit the cognitive features of planning [23].

> The key task of the times is to develop not only modern technical hardware, but also an effective and distinctive software that is appropriate to Soviet conditions as well as capable of accelerating technological change and managing the innovation process. Indeed, that is the essence of Brezhnev's call, articulated at the 1971 CPSU Congress and reiterated at the 1976 Congress... [24]

Brezhnev also reminded the latter Congress that this was the "agreed policy and correct line," "the decisive element is its organization" [25].

This agreed policy was in no way a departure from centralized leadership in the economy. Decentralization through the associations was intended to relieve the central planning agencies from micro-level problems to increase their overall insight and to enhance planning and control [26]. Indeed, planning had to be improved, not abolished. Nor were the planning agencies to disappear. They were however to give up some of their autonomy in favor of the managers of the associations and of Party officials. Shcherbitsky, First Secretary of the Ukrainian Central Committee and, like other regional and republican secretaries, an advocate of management reform, explained:

> Naturally, solving these tasks requires an intensification of political leadership of the country's economic life and necessitates a rise in the party's role as the directing and organizing force of our society...
>
> The most important avenue for improving the organizational forms of management is the formation of large-scale associations, which makes it possible under the conditions of the scientific and technical revolution to organically combine centralized leadership with the independence of current economic activity granted to enterprises by the economic reform...
>
> Management under socialism is not an uncoordinated set of diverse ways and means of organizing managerial activities but a systematically organized process led by the party with a clearly expressed economic and socio-political aim--the building of a communist society. [27]

Planning and control were the subject of Party
concern and had to be brought closer to it. To be sure,
Ministers and Heads of State Committees were Party members. But these men and their bureaucracies were fairly
independent and possessed the knowledge and information
which could only be observed by the central party organs
from the outside and not from the inside. Under the new
system the Party Committee and primary Party organizations were expected to guide and check from within by
actually taking part in economic activities. The State
organs were to become executives, not policy-makers.
Their performance in concert with the enterprises had to
be controlled on the spot and in time; not from a
distance and after plan fulfilment [28].
     It was at this point that the "agreed policy"
entered the realm of power and faced the difficult test
of putting theory into practice. The problem of power
distribution between the Party Committee, the manager
executive or Minister, and the primary Party organization
was an old and unsolved one; indeed, there was doubt
whether it was in fact solvable at all. As Jerry Hough
convincingly demonstrated a decade ago for the local
level, the complex web of overlapping responsibilities
and the vague, often arbitrarily described power positions of the various participants defy an answer to the
question of who, in fact, was in charge of the economy [29].
The situation at the central level was no different.

> Despite the conflict that must exist between the
> officials of the Central Committee and governmental
> hierarchies, it just as surely would be incorrect
> to see this relationship in purely adversary terms.
> The very logic of the situation in which the Central
> Committee officials find themselves often pushes
> them into representing the interests of those they
> are supervising. [30]

Soviet writings to date still reflect the intractable
problem of implementing administrative theory, This is
a Herculean task anyway, but even more so in Soviet
theory because of the many contradictions and inherent
conceptual tensions. For example, Varlamov, loyal to the
official theory that democratic centralism was the principle of economic management, summed up a number of
concepts that were difficult to "link" or "unite."

> The indivisible link between centralism and democ-
> racy is manifested in the control sphere through
> the unities of discipline and initiative, of the
> collegial and one-man management principles, and of
> administrative and executive activity, This link
> is also expressed in the combination of adminis-
> trative and economic methods of control, of the
> state and social forms of control, and of represen-

tative _and_ direct leadership. (Emphasis added) 31

In a lengthy but far from conclusive explanation of
Socialist Management: The Leninist Concept, the same
expert exposed the many existing and possible frictions
between the party-political (partiyny) style and
economic and managerial leadership. Not surprisingly,
he noted that "there was not a single Party Congress in
Lenin's lifetime that dit not discuss matters relating
to the interaction of Party and government bodies." 32
This has not changed.

The actively pursued restructuring of economic
leadership advanced extremely slowly in the 1970's,
particularly at the ministerial level. Party committees
did exist in the ministries and had the right to exercise
control, as stated in the Resolution on Party Statutes
adopted by the XXIV Congress. However, a _Pravda_ editorial in 1974 admitted that in spite of this right--"which
has considerably expanded the opportunities for the
communists' influence on improving the style of management
actively and on the consolidation of state discipline 33"
--the Party committees were unable to redress the shortcomings and inertia of the bureaucracy. During the XXV
Party Congress, the republican and regional secretaries
left no doubt about the attitude of the Ministers and
their apparatus. For example, Romanov cynically advised
them to change not only "their 'nameplates,' but also the
very principles of relations between enterprises and
organizations." 34

Thus at the central level in Moscow the distribution
of power with regard to the organization of economic
management remained basically the same. The government
agencies were still deeply involved in running the
economy, including the increasingly important part of the
associations. Brezhnev and his associates had only
marginally succeeded in increasing Party influence at the
expense of that of the government. The Party Committee
penetrated, but did not conquer the ministries.

Obviously the institutionalization of Party rule in
economic management and social development was not a
minor undertaking. At all levels in the hierarchy,
specialists fiercely resisted the intrusion of Party
officials, as they had done rather successfully in the
early years of the Brezhnev-Kosygin leadership 35. At
that time power positions as well as competence had been
at issue. In the 1970's complaints about Party officials
recurred, but in a somewhat different vein.

It was not so much competence, but a better partition
and delimitation of work and responsibilities that was
stressed notably, and repeatedly, by Podgorny 36. The
specialist was to remain the expert. His expertise and
skills were not to be dismissed or replaced but, on the
contrary, had to be used and included in the decision-
making by the Party secretaries and committees. Ideally,

the expert was conceived as functioning in a "participatory model" in which policy-making proper was the domain of the Party [37]. What was required of the expert was advice, not decisions; the power of knowledge and skills was recognized, even applauded; expert influence, however, was denied.

On the other hand, of course, the Party official had to be as knowledgeable and well-equipped as possible. In this respect the Party showed sensitivity to earlier reproaches and embarked on a large-scale program of training and retraining of the cadres [38]. Again, this educational effort was not aimed at replacing the expert--although this side-effect seemed inevitable to some extent [39]--but at providing the cadres with the necessary tools for leadership and effective control. Comprehension of the technical problems as well as the ability to integrate them in a comprehensive policy was the Party's goal [40]. It seems, however, that implementation here was developing at a snail's pace as well. Kapitonov, Central Committee secretary in charge of the cadres, recapitulated the dragging problem in 1978. What was still needed was

...a fundamental re-orientation of the thinking of officials, a new approach to the evaluation of the results of business activity. It is no secret that we still frequently judge the performance of enterprises basically in terms of sold output, overlooking indicators of labor productivity, production cost, quality of output, and the adoption of new technology. It is clear that such an approach is now obsolete and is at odds with the Party's policy regarding the enhancement of production efficiency.[41]

Brezhnev's plans also point to awareness within the leadership of the need to stress the responsibility of Party members towards the population. Party authority could only be restored by showing real concern for the Soviet citizen, which would give badly needed legitimacy to the superimposed caretaker. Mobilization of the masses, in factories or in the Soviets [42], was impossible without some sort of respect and good example. The improvement of socialist democracy and public participation would remain utopian ideals if the Party failed to provide the kind of leadership that Brezhnev had in mind [43]. The concerns of the Soviet leaders like other leaders in Eastern Europe, "involve not only power and efficiency but the character of political authority and social relations." [44]

Whether and to what extent the political leadership, at this point personified by Brezhnev, was concerned about systemic societal development is hard to tell, but there are signs that warrant an affirmative answer. However, the envisaged political and social development towards greater participation and responsibility of the population and social forces was made dependent on the strengthening of policy guidance and control by the Party. It was this absolute condition of Brezhnev that--at least--postponed that development. Unless leadership within the Party was improved, the leadership of the Party in the system was unlikely to allow greater socio-political participation.

The foregoing leads to the following conclusions. First, the implementation of the major points of Brezhnev's domestic policy was characterized by grad-ualism, by a movement "away from change" to "adaptation" and "from major changes" to "marginal improvement." [45] Furthermore, the major problem of putting theory into practice was extremely time-consuming. True, Brezhnev had a right to pride himself on the enhanced role of the Party in economic management during the 1970's. When he introduced the Draft Constitution in 1977, he must have had some satisfaction in announcing the registration of the "important principle of the socialist economy as the combination of planned centralized management with the economic independence and initiative of enterprises and associations." [46] Technical competence in the cadres had also probably been improved and the number of asso-ciations as the most important economic unit had grown considerably. Moreover, he could conclude that the Party's "actual place in Soviet society and the Soviet state" was more clearly reflected than in the 1936 Constitution. Finally, the combination of the function of General Secretary with that of Chairman of the Presidium of the Supreme Soviet made it plain that Party rule was to be visible in "all key questions of state life." The Party leader as head of the Soviets--"the political foundation of the state of all the people [47]"--was a significant expression of the absolute condition of Party control. Successful political development, however, required more. A prerequisite for success in promoting closeness between regime and citizens was, for example, "that the repre-sentatives of the regime should have not only power but authority in the community." [48] Whether Party members actually behaved in this manner, genuinely leading and daring to go beyond formal plans and resolutions, showing concern and initiative, is very much open to doubt; it seems in any case to have been the exception rather than the rule [49]. Was Brezhnev not trying to reconcile the irreconcilable by attempting to strengthen Party and popular rule simultaneously? It seems that Brezhnev's rationalization of Party control was "caught in a crossfire between politics and techniques, a tool to be molded by political will and political hands." [50]

Second, policy development--or the outline of pol-itical strategy--was presumably to a large extent coor-dinated with Kosygin. Concerning the content of the proposed plans, Brezhnev sought the partnership of the Premier in more than one respect. However, policy formulation--or official adoption--by a greater part of the leadership is something else again. Brezhnev had certainly not become a "supreme leader" who could impose his will on others. In the process of policy formulation in the polity, Brezhnev was not endowed with coercive power. He had to persuade a majority to back his proposals and try to establish "a more confident, institutionalized party, with a policy of its own and with its own distinctive, corporate existence." 51   It was this alternative to "supreme leadership" that became decisive for the actual formulation and implementation of Brezhnev's comprehensive policy.   How he operated in the Party and tried to make his ideas part of those of the Central Committee and Politburo, and his position in these bodies, will be examined next.

POLITICAL LEADERSHIP AND THE CENTRAL COMMITTEE

     Gradualism as exemplified by the creeping implementation of management reform can be attributed to more than one cause.   Factors such as an immense bureaucracy, the difficulties inherent in reorganization, especially when comprehensive changes are involved, and educational and learning processes are universal features all taking their share of the time needed for reform.   It is impossible to say how much more time these factors would take under a weak, divided leadership than under a strong, united leadership.   But there is no doubt of the fact that one leadership manages better and achieves more than the other.   The foregoing suggests that Brezhnev, the major spokesman of policy changes, had only limited influence and that collective leadership prevailed in the 1970's.   As will be shown, however, the Party lived through some tense years during which it was far from clear which "majority" represented the Party collective.
     As a general observation, it is in no way surprising that the survivors of Stalin's reign of terror and Khrushchev's rule of rapidly changing coalitions should have had a common interest in a continuing, well-established collective rule.   Politicians in the Central Committee and Politburo had long experience in the game of power politics and survival and knew only too well what the consequences of revived one-man rule could be. The experience of fear and uncertainty under Stalin and memories of the erosion of political authority in Khrushchev's terms were likely to unite these men against too much personal power.   The public admission of the harm done to the Party cause by Stalin, and the minimum attention paid to Khrushchev's death and his absence from the list of deceased Party members in 1971, are indicative enough of the aversion to the personal rule of these former leaders 52.   Likewise, ten years after the October Plenum at which Khrushchev was ousted, Kommunist reminded

its readers that this event had "reaffirmed in full the "Leninist principle of collectivity as the highest principle of party leadership." It ensured "the elimination of the vestiges of and prevention of relapses into the voluntarist, subjective approach to the solution of political and economic problems." 53

The Kommunist editorial did not stop at this conclusion. It also dwelt on the current political and economic problems, and, as will be argued, at a very timely moment. A few weeks before a historical meeting of the Central Committee, the theoretical journal again reiterated the main points of the new economic policy, which was based on "long experimentation" and on Central Committee studies of the "positive experience of management under the new conditions of enterprises, associations, industrial sectors and also the experience of party committees on the leadership of industry." It left no doubt about the correctness and "scientific substantiation" of what was basically Brezhnev's economic policy 54.

Of special interest in the present discussion is Kommunist's assertion that it was the Central Committee which determined the political line and directed the development of the Party. It was certainly not only the General Secretary, however praised, nor the Politburo that was "totally responsible to the Party." It was the Central Committee that

> ...guards the Party's principles from Congress to Congress and is the interpreter of those principles... The Central Committee includes the most experienced and politically mature members of the Party... Plenums discuss the most important national economic problems and fundamental questions of the Soviet State's domestic and foreign policy. And the fact that the Party's best forces are represented in the Central Committee is a guarantee that the decisions adopted will be thoroughly studied and well thought out. 55 (Emphasis added)

The actual power of the Central Committee is often doubted in the West, and for good reasons. How can such a large body that meets two--sometimes three--times a year for only one or two days really influence policy-making 56? Yet there is evidence that the Central Committee and its secretariat played a greater role during the Brezhnev era. First, stability and job tenure had become the dominant principle in the Central Committee. The percentages of re-elected members at the XXIV and XXV Party Congresses were 76.5 and 83.4 respectively, and the distribution of institutional representation remained about the same 57. Tenure of Central Committee membership under Brezhnev was dependent on job tenure in Party and State organizations rather than on either the caprice of a supreme leader or a power struggle at the top.

A fierce power competition between the top leaders attempting to promote their own protégés and to demote those of others, as well as a similar struggle within the Central Committee, would probably result in a much higher turnover of membership. The low turnover suggests a "business-like" rather than a "person-bound" approach to individual membership and a tendency, if no more, to preserve security for the individual and collegial rule for the whole.

> Brezhnev has not imposed himself on the Soviet leadership in the Stalin and Khrushchev manner; rather, he has worked with the existing material, allowing himself--perhaps by force of necessity--to be the representative and the reflection of the existing bureaucratic hierarchy rather than the architect of a new political machine designed in his own image. [58]

Some of the newcomers in the expanded Central Committee--from 195 to 241 in 1971 and to 287 full members in 1976--may have been Brezhnev clients, but their number is unknown. There is no evidence that their impact--or indeed that of any other client grouping--affected the previously existing division of opinion and coalitions. The relationship between Brezhnev and this assembly of representatives of institutions and regions seems to have been one of distinct and considerable dependency on the part of the former, whereas on the individual level "Central Committee member and General Secretary are mutually vulnerable and mutually dependent." [59] The lack of a clear majority for the General Secretary reflected the institutionalization of collective rule and made the Central Committee a strong force for continuity. Had the General Secretary--or any senior contestant--sought domination, this alliance for stability and continuity would have had a definite interest in checking his power and could ultimately have been the force to remove him.

Second, stability among these "watch-dogs" of collective rule was also significant in that it put the Central Committee in a better position to participate in the discussion of fundamental issues and to act as arbiter in Politburo disputes. For example, besides the Plenums devoted to the obviously important plans and budget-- usually held in December--the plenary sessions' agenda contained the issue of foreign policy precisely at times when this was a fundamental and highly disputed issue [60]. As we have already seen, the Central Committee approved "the international activity of the Politburo" in November 1971. This tribute to the collective instead of to Brezhnev's personal efforts was followed by a session in May 1972 when the Politburo was "instructed" to proceed on the current course. In April 1973 the Plenum discussed only foreign policy. The agenda does not mention foreign policy in 1974, but it was discussed--unusually--at the meeting in December (for reasons that will be examined in the next chapter). After the April 1975 Plenum, where the foreign policy issue was "settled," as will be argued, five years were to go by before foreign policy was announced again as the sole discussion topic. Afghanistan was quite probably subject of discussion at the June 1980 Plenum.

Another indication of a more profound involvement than appears from the frequency of Central Committee meetings is the increasingly emphasized significance of the policy agreed by this body in resolutions, and perhaps also the number of resolutions and decrees. Resolutions pertaining to disputed issues are carefully formulated in compromising language which shows that discussion has actually taken place. A Pravda editorial contends that since the XXIV Party Congress much has been done "to improve the organization of plenums and to increase their effectiveness."

> As a rule, plenum speeches are distinguished by their businesslike approach, and the decisions they adopt by purposefulness. Committee members are enlisted in the practical implementation of measures that are mapped out and are better informed about the progress being made translating them into reality. 61 (Emphasis added)

Pravda does not say whether these improvements and the active involvement of committee members also apply to the Central Committee. The work of this Committee is certainly carried on between the Plenums, but it is not clear whether and to what extent Committee and Secretariat members, working in central organs and agencies in Moscow, formulate and prepare plenary decisions. Who are the thousands of men in the apparatus of the Central Committee Secretariat, and how are the Secretariat and its apparatus related to the ministries? One can only speculate. Pravda understandably states that "a decision adopted by a party committee plenum should be regarded as the most important document determining the substance of the entire party organization's activity for the coming period." 62 There will certainly be a need for one single point of reference, and the effort to ascribe this function or right to the (Central) Committee plenary sessions is significant and apparently not without success.

The area in which the Party apparatus has probably advanced most is foreign policy. The number of institutions and ministries in this field is much more limited than in, say, economic policy. The clear command over foreign policy taken by Brezhnev and the Politburo had already been announced by Gromyko in his speech to the XXIV Party Congress 63. The extent to which this strengthened Party leadership would also mean greater involvement of the central apparatus below the top was not made clear. However, according to the first deputy head of the International Department of the Central Committee, Zagladin, not only the Politburo but also the Secretariat of the Central Committee examines foreign policy in detail "at practically every meeting." He repeats Brezhnev's revelation during the XXV Party Congress, that the Politburo and Secretariat had met 215 and 205 times respectively between that and the previous Congress [64]. Taking into account holidays and vacations, this means a frequency of about once a week. Moreover, Zagladin asserts that foreign policy implementation by the "diplomatic apparatus" takes place under the "direct guidance" of the Central Committee. Thus neither Brezhnev nor the Politburo would seem to have a free hand in the field of foreign policy. They are closely super-vised and to a certain extent directed by the Central Committee and its apparatus.

The situation is probably quite different in domestic politics, in which a great many actors at various levels are involved. The overlapping positions in the State and Party hierarchies noted above make it impossible to determine which individuals or groups in the Central Committee are actually involved in day-to-day policy-making [65]. Moreover, as Hough and Fainsod conclude with regard to the overlapping positions of high officials:

This fact alone makes it virtually impossible to conceive of the Central Committee Secretariat and apparatus pre-empting the policy-making role--or the policy-initiating role, even in a narrow sense--and of the government simply being limited to the execution of policy. [66]

Brezhnev was undoubtedly well aware of the reactions his considerable changes in Soviet politics would stir up, the more so when it became clear that he was talking seriously. Moreover, this experienced and shrewd politician knew perfectly well where opposition would be fiercest and most difficult to overcome and to win for his policy: in the Central Committee and its apparatus. This "Parliament" of the Party and custodian of the political system had officially endorsed the new economic and foreign policy course,but in a grudging and grumbling manner. Various groups represented in the Central Committee indeed had reason to resist changes in domestic or foreign policy, or even in both. An outright confron-tation with the conservative majority of the Central Committee would have amounted to political suicide. Brezhnev is obliged to respect the power of the Central Committee as a whole. He can select only a particular section of its members as his target, while at the same time trying to enlist the support of other members. He acts as servant to the Party (Central Committee), but can

use his authority as Party leader vis-à-vis particular
groupings which do not follow his and the Party's
instructions.

Brezhnev undoubtedly regrets the slow pace of
decision-making in the Central Committee, but he can only
respect this "established" rule. This does not prevent
him, however, from naming those whom he finds responsible
for the dragging pace of implementation.

> The Central Committee is against hasty, ill-con-
> sidered reorganization of the managerial structure
> and of established methods of economic management.
> As the saying goes, we must measure the cloth not
> seven but eight or even ten times before we cut it.
> But once we have done the measuring, once we realize
> that the framework of the existing management
> mechanism has become too cramped for the continuously
> developing national economy, it must be drastically
> improved. This is the direct duty of the Council
> of Ministers, the State Planning Committee and the
> central economic agencies. [67]

Harsh attacks on these state organs had been
launched by Brezhnev and regional secretaries not only
before the Congresses, but also on numerous other
occasions and in particular during the December Plenums
of the Central Committee. As stated earlier, the Party
committees in the ministries are not well-placed for
gaining influence as "primarily the necessary system of
control over the executing of adopted decisions is
lacking." [68] The "decisive" element of organizing and
restructuring economic leadership continues to be hampered
by fragmented planning and out-dated management of
ministries and ministers whose positions seems to be
almost untouchable. A Pravda editorial in January 1980,
for example, does not significantly differ in its complaints and appeals from the 1974 editorial just
quoted [69]. It was perhaps Brezhnev's long-felt irritation
about this fact that prompted him to attack a number of
the "comrade" ministers personally for the first time in
an almost Khrushchevian way. At the Central Committee
November Plenum in 1979 he actually threatened the
"specific persons" who were to blame, stating that they
"must be found and punished." This threat may not have
been an entirely hollow one [70], especially as far as the
lower levels are concerned. For example, a few years
before Brezhnev wrote that in 1976 "nearly 10,000
administrators were removed from their posts" because of
non-fulfilment of their socio-economic duties and
responsibilities, and 347,000 cummunists had not received
a "new-style party card" (Kapitonov) after the exchange
which was ordered by the XXIV Congress [71].

Nor have Brezhnev's attacks been confined to state
actors; he does not eschew threats to Party members

either. For example, at the XXIV Party Congress he addressed in clear language those who might not be willing to change "their approach to consumer goods." This approach had been understandable in the earlier and more difficult days of the Soviet Union, and consequently

> ...could not but have its effect on the attitude to consumer goods, to their quality and variety. But what was explicable and natural in the past when other tasks were in the foreground is inacceptable, comrades, in present conditions. And if some comrades do not take this into account, the Party has the right to see in such attitudes either a lack of understanding of the essence of its policy...or the desire to justify their inactivity.

At the XXV Party Congress he complained about the lax manner in which Party organizations used their rights of control and verification. Although he reassured his audience that no alarming situation had developed in the Party, he deemed it necessary to warn: "Steadfast adherence to a Leninist style in work is a prerequisite for the successful activity of all Party, Soviet, and economic organizations and for the realization of all our plans." 72

In short, the high demands Brezhnev made on Party work must have been alarming, for the "Leninist style" he envisaged was to be taken seriously. Indeed, he was determined to condition the powerful and privileged position of Party members. Power is "inseparably linked with great personal responsibility for the entrusted section, for the fulfilment of Party decisions." 73 Here, at the Central Committee December Plenum in 1973, he vigorously strove for a majority to back his economic policy, but he left no doubt of the fact that the (re-) establishment of Party rule was unthinkable without real evidence of responsibility and correct behavior on the part of its members.

Throughout the 1970's Brezhnev was seriously determined to implement the "agreed" economic policy, and he was apparently ready for a confrontation with Party members of all ranks, high and low. His determination, the large-scale efforts to improve the cadres' technical and economic expertise and knowledge, the purge of about 347,000 members during the exchange of Party cards, and his attempts to impose personal responsibility and accountability were more than enough, however, to cause uneasiness among the central, regional and local "czars," who feared that some day they might actually have to change their attitude. The state and regional representatives in the Central Committee probably reflected this concern and were either afraid or simply unwilling to accept a responsible power position. Yanov describes this faction as "Little Stalins," 74 whose powerful position is largely based on chaos and lack of organization of the economy, and which consequently makes managers and directors dependent on them. They have nothing to lose but their privileges. For many, therefore, the prospect of change from ideological commitment without engagement to ideological obligations of genuine social progress, linked with responsibility, was probably highly undesirable, if not alarming.

To conclude, power relations in the Central Committee--or for that matter in the Party at large--are complex. On the one hand, the top leadership headed by Brezhnev and the regional and local representatives may adhere to the official policy and form a coalition vis-à-vis the central economic agencies. If that is so, Brezhnev's power base will be founded primarily on the former group of representatives, and the successful restructuring of economic leadership in favor of the Party is likely to enhance the authority of both. It would provide an essential asset for the realization of social development and political maturity in the Soviet Union.

On the other hand, the regional representatives may avoid the risks of delegated power and responsibility and join the presumed opposition of the state representatives. It is of course unknown how many in the two major power blocs in the Central Committee actually oppose the reform of economic management and leadership. But the slow implementation, the continuing discussion and complaints about the reluctant compliance with the "agreed policy," indicate at least that Brezhnev and his supporters have been unable to convince the Central Committee and to strengthen Party rule on a basis of unity and consensual power. At any rate, the authority of Brezhnev as the economic leader has remained ambiguous and continues to be contested. The Party leader addressed himself to some real and urgent problems, but the Central Committee as a whole followed the agreed line only if hard pressed. It is quite likely that only a minority of the Committee has taken the same direction as its leader and actively pursued it.

If the Party had been a monolith and had acted as a united vanguard and guide, as envisaged by its leader, the "Ideal Type" of political and economic development could have been achieved in some measure. But the Party was not a monolith, and the distribution of power among its members did not allow the formation of a majority. Worse, Brezhnev and his supporters, in vigorously pursuing their goals, threatened its unity--or the agreement to disagree. In 1973 and 1974, particularly when the new policies were being vehemently pushed, the situation in the Party was becoming very tense. Domestic and foreign policy issues divided the Party into several groups of varying and complex composition. The need to restore unity was pressing, and soon assumed priority over the solution of the issues at stake.

In a lengthy article about freedom of discussion and criticism, Petrenko lauds these two rights as strong weapons against "personality cults" and "subjectivism." The October 1964 Plenum and "the XXIV Party Congress demonstrated with new vigor the vivifying rule of the Party's wide discussion of current economic and socio-political problems." Petrenko warns, however, that at some point along the line, when a majority had reached a decision, discussion should stop: "The Party is no debating society."

> The principle of subordination to the majority is not only just from the viewpoint of a reflection of the general fundamental interests and goals of the Party, but is also extremely necessary to preserve the Party as a whole. A refusal by a minority to act in unity with the majority would be a serious obstacle to the Party's resolution of tasks before it. It would paralyse its work and inevitably would lead to a split in the Party. [75]

Petrenko also urges some ministries not to stand in the way of implementation, and calls for patience to await results first before criticizing. After quoting Lenin, who refuted "any criticism undermining or hindering the unity of an action decided by the Party," he adds:

> There is no need to prove that the Party would inevitably fall to pieces ideologically and organizationally if Party discipline did not exist in its life along with discussion and criticism. [76]

About this time it became usual for Politburo members to call Brezhnev "head" of this body and unanimously to praise his great "personal" contribution to foreign policy. Some--found, not surprisingly, among the Party and Central Committee secretaries--even referred to his economic leadership [77]. Others, like Podgorny, explicitly stressed the "synthesized collective wisdom of the Party and the people" with regard to the "new" national economy, while reassuring their audience that "no radical reorganization of the existing system of management is involved (Emphasis added)." [78] Not unity, but sharp differences, characterized the situation during this period. This became the overriding concern. The Central Committee urged Brezhnev to slow down his "crusade" for the new policies in order to restore unity. The Central Committee indeed adhered to collectivity before anything else. How the top leaders in the Politburo acted in this situation and how Brezhnev's position as political leader developed there, will be examined next.

POLITICAL LEADERSHIP AND THE POLITBURO

However important the Central Committee may be, its power in the Party is not absolute. Day-to-day politics and decision-making belong to its Secretariat and, above all, to the Politburo. Even though the precise distribution of power among these top Party sections cannot be given, the Politburo is the center of power of the polity, from which policy initiatives and guidance flow into the Party and state system for formalization and implementation. It is clear that the stronger the unity within the apex of centralized leadership and the more precise the directives given, the greater the chance that the system will respond in conformity with the guidance from the top. Ambiguity and divisiveness are harmful for effective leadership. All Politburo members therefore have an interest in unanimity or at least in consent among the greatest possible majority.

One way to secure control is to enlist enough protégés and supporters in the Politburo. Counting these protégés is a popular albeit questionable method of measuring Brezhnev's standing among the senior leaders [79]. Therefore, a short digression on the composition of the Politburo would seem to be useful. As stated before, Brezhnev successfully consolidated his position during the 1960's and we may speak of the accession to power of the so-called "Dnepr Mafia." Politburo members Kirilenko, Shcherbitsky and Grechko, and Ministers Shchelokov, Smirnov, Novikov, and Tikhonov--to name some who found their way to the top--had all worked with Brezhnev in Dnepropetrovsk during and after World War II. During the 1970's some very close followers--Chernerko in 1979 and Kunaev in 1971; both clients since the 1950's--as well as presumed supporters--e.g., Romanov in 1976, Andropov in 1973 and candidate member Gorbachev in 1979--strengthened Brezhnev's position in the Politburo. Finally, outspoken opponents in one or more areas, such as Shelest and Voronov, and assumed potential rivals could either be removed (Shelepin) or transferred to a less promising position (Solomentsev). The conclusion that his power base, defined here as the number of favorably disposed leaders in the Politburo, has been strengthened would thus seem to be warranted.

However, the changes were not decisive in the sense that they have made Brezhnev a supreme leader. First, unlike Stalin and Khrushchev, the present Party leader has not had a chance to appoint merely his protégés in order to gain a clear majority, either in the Politburo or in the Central Committee. Even the Secretariat of the Central Committee, pre-eminently the domain of the General Secretary, has always contained a number of secretaries whose careers have been independent of Brezhnev. Some of them, moreover, have not always appeared to favor Brezhnev's policies, but this has not affected their own

power position--e.g., Suslov, Kirilenko and Ponomarev.
These "independent" colleagues have remained in
office and continued their own particular responsibilities. Except for a few obvious followers, loyalty to
Brezhnev cannot be ascertained on the basis of the
simple fact of having worked with him in the past. While
a personal relationship may have grown over the years, it
seems unlikely that sympathy or support for Brezhnev's
policies would automatically follow. Too many other
factors determine a personal power base, and few of these
educated manipulators of power are inclined to put their
political fate completely into the hands of one of the
senior leaders of a body dedicated to collective decision-
making.
     Secondly, the few personnel changes that have taken
place seem to have occurred in a well-considered and
balanced way. For example, the most dramatic change in
the Politburo occurred in 1973, when the foreign policy
sector of the State organization was included. But
neither the three men concerned (Andropov, Gromyko,
Grechko) nor the institutions they represented (KGB,
Foreign and Defense Ministry, respectively) can be said
to have suscribed to the "Peace Program" in exactly the
same way. Proponents of the program may have seen this
move as an attempt to encapsulate the suspicious and more
sceptical elements in government. The latter, in turn,
may have viewed access to the top level as an asset in
tempering or even countering the course towards detente
80. Policy differences between the newly-elected men
will be examined later. Suffice it to note at this point
that the addition of foreign policy representatives of
the government to the Politburo reflected support for
collective rather than personal rule.
     By this move, moreover, a nearly perfect balance
between representatives of the Government and the
Secretariat was achieved. As Table II shows, the dominance of the Secretariat was instituted after the Anti-
Party Coup of Khrushchev in 1957, but this was changed
into a more equal distribution after 1964. However,
Party representation was increased by the addition of
Republic and Gorkom First Secretaries. At the XXIV Party
Congress, Grishin, Kunaev and Shcherbitsky became full
members 81; they were joined by Romanov in 1976. From
that moment on one can speak of a neatly balanced
Politburo with five (or four) voting members for the
Secretariat and the Government, and four for the regional representatives. The enhanced status of the Republican
Party Committee is also reflected in the elevation of
other Republican First Secretaries as candidate members
of the Politburo: Masherov in 1966 and Aliev in 1976 82
(see Table III). The representation of the most important
regional and local Party organizations should not be seen
as a way of outvoting the government representatives in
the Politburo. Rather, their growing importance is a

YEAR	GOVERNMENT	STATE	SECRETARIAT	OTHER	TOTAL
1957	7	1	2	1	11
1958	3	1	7	4	15
1964	3	1	6	2	12
1965	3	1	4	4	12
1971 (XXIV)	4	1	4	6	15
1973	6	1	4	5	16
1976 (XXV)	5	1	5	5	16
	Kosygin	Podgorny	Brezhnev	Pelshe	
	Mazurov		Suslov	Grishin	
	Andropov		Kirilenko	Kunaev	
	Gromyko		Kulakov	Romanov	
	Grechko		Ustinov	Shcherbitsky	
1981 (XXVI)	4	0	5	5	14
	Tikhonov ***	(Brezhnev)*	Brezhnev	Pelshe	
	Ustinov **		Suslov	Grishin	
	Andropov		Kirilenko	Kunaev	
	Gromyko		Chernenko ****	Romanov	
			Gorbachev ****	Shcherbitsky	

TABLE II. DISTRIBUTION OF FULL MEMBERS OF THE POLITBURO, 1957 - 1981

* Podgorny was succeeded by Breznev in 1977.

** It is not clear whether Ustinov has retained as Secretary any of his responsibilities for the military, the defense industry and the police. Ustinov was appointed Minister of Defense in 1976. His successor in the Secretariat, Ryabov, was relieved of his duties early in 1979 and the post has since remained vacant.

*** Tikhonov replaced Mazurov in 1979, who lost his membership in 1978. Kosygin retired in October, 1980 and the position of Prime Minister passed to Tikhonov. The first deputy Prime Minister, Arkhipov, may be expected to become a full member in the future.

**** Kulakov died in July, 1976. It soon became apparent that Chernenko was designated by Brezhnev to replace Kulakov as his successor. Chernenk o became Central Committee Secretary in 1976, candidate member of the Politburo in 1977, and full member in 1979. Gorbachev became Secretary of Agriculture. Suslov died in January, 1982.

98

further indication of the tendency towards decentralization and Party rule within territorial boundaries. One
economist, Milner, who does not conceal his objections
to central management by the ministries and strongly
advocates territorial associations that are able to
develop, coordinate and implement "the comprehensive
program from start to finish," goes even further and
points to the role of the Soviets.

> Enhancing the role and expanding the authority of
> local agencies in ensuring the comprehensive
> accomplishment of territorial production tasks,
> especially the timely creation of the necessary
> infrastructure, is becoming a question of paramount
> importance. This calls for a further increase in
> the influence of the local Soviets and their planning
> agencies on the formation and implementation of all
> production programs within a given territory. [83]

The realization of such a program is inconceivable
under the leadership of the ministries in Moscow.
Therefore the inclusion in the Politburo of a firm bloc
of eight supporters of Brezhnev's reform of economic
management must be seen as a real asset to him. In
foreign policy decision-making these Secretaries probably
do not carry much weight, except of course for the four
votes. But in domestic politics they are extremely
important because they have the best opportunities to
actually start and implement the Party's policy in their
region. In fact, such "entrepreneurs" can circumvent the
seemingly endless decision-making process and political
discussion.
    For example, in 1973 there were 80 associations and
major industrial enterprises and combines producing more
than 60 per cent of all industrial output in the
Leningrad Obkom [84]. This means that the "improvement of
the economic reform" was actually underway before the
Central Committee and the Council of Ministers had
adopted the Resolution "On Certain Measures for the
Further Improvement of Management in Industry," the main
reference in this field since then. In other words,
Leningrad figured as "a kind of laboratory of advanced
experience of Party work." [85] These experiments were,
according to Leningrad's Party boss, Romanov, inspired by
Brezhnev personally [86]. They are being expanded steadily
and quickly and the Leningrad experience is expected to
become a nation-wide practice in the early 1980's. Thus
agreement with both Brezhnev's economic policy and the
structural power of the regional Party leaders is of
paramount importance for Brezhnev's political leadership.
    Alliances in the Politburo are, however, complex and
diffuse, as is illustrated in Table IV. Only when tension
in the Party grows, as happened in 1974, does the Politburo seem--or is forced--to close its ranks and to show

MEMBERS	YEAR OF BIRTH	YEAR OF ELECTION	POSITION (since)
BREZHNEV	1906	1957	General Secretary (64) Chairman of the Presidium of the Supreme Soviet (77)
ANDROPOV	1914	1973	Chairman of the KGB (67)
GORBACHEV	1931	1980	Secretary CC; Supervision of Agriculture and Food Industry (78)
GRISHIN	1914	1971	First Secretary of the Moscow Gorkom (67)
GROMYKO	1909	1973	Minister of Foreign Affairs (57)
KIRILENKO	1904	1962	Secretary CC, General supervision of the Economy and Party Organization (66)
KOSYGIN*	1904	1948 and 1952	Chairman of the Council of Ministers (64)
KUNAEV	1912	1971	First Secretary of the Kazakhstan CC (64)
PELSHE	1899	1966	Chairman of the Party Control Committee (66)
ROMANOV	1923	1976	First Secretary of the Leningrad Gorkom (70)
SHCHERBITSKY	1918	1971	First Secretary of the Ukrainian CC (72)
SUSLOV **	1902	1952 and 1955	Secretary CC; General supervision of Ideological Affairs and Foreign Policy (early 1950)
TIKHONOV*	1905	1979	First Deputy Chairman of the Council of Ministers (76)
USTINOV	1908	1976	Minister of Defense (76) Possibly acting Secretary CC, supervising the military, defense industry and the police (65)
CHERNENKO	1911	1979	Secretary CC; General supervision of the Secretariat and Bureaucracy

CENTRAL COMMITTEE SECRETARIAT 1981

CANDIDATE MEMBERS	YEAR OF BIRTH	YEAR OF ELECTION	POSITION (since)
ALIEV	1923	1976	First Secretary of the Azerbaidzhan CC (69)
DEMICHEV	1918	1964	Minister of Culture (75)
KISELEV	1917	1980	First Secretary of the Belorussian CC (80)
KUZNETSOV	1901	1977	First Deputy Chairman of the Supreme Soviet (77)
PONOMAREV	1905	1972	Secretary CC; Head of the International Department, Relations with non-Communist countries (55)
RASHIDOV	1917	1961	First Secretary of the Uzbekistan CC (59)
SHEVARDNADZE	1929	1978	First Secretary of the Georgian CC (75)
SOLOMENTSEV	1913	1971	Chairman of the RSFSR Council of Ministers (71)

* Kosygin retired in October, 1980. He died in December, 1980. His position was taken by Tikhonov.

** Suslov died in January, 1982.

SECRETARIES (non-members of Politburo)	YEAR OF BIRTH	YEAR OF ELECTION	SUPERVISION
DOLGIKH	1924	1971	(Heavy) Industry
KAPITONOV	1915	1965	Lower Party Apparatus
RUSAKOV	1909	1977	Relations with Ruling Communist Parties
ZIMYANIN	1914	1976	Ideology and Mass Media

TABLE IV: LIKELY VIEWS ON PRIORITIES

	I	II	III
BREZHNEV	[+ +]	+	+
ANDROPOV	−	+ +	+ +
GRECHKO *	−	− −	[− −]
GRISHIN	+ +	+ +	+
GROMYKO	−	+	−
KIRILENKO	−	− −	[− −]
KOSYGIN*	− −	+ +	[+ +]
KUNAEV	[+ +]	+	−
MAZUROV*	−	−	[+ +]
PELSHE	+	+	+
PODGORNY*	−	[+ +]	+ +
POLYANSKY*	−	−	[+ +]
ROMANOV	[+ +]	+ +	−
SUSLOV *	−	−	−
TIKHONOV*	−	+ +	− −
USTINOV	+ +	−	−
CHERNENKO*	+ +	+	+
SHCHERBITSKY	[+ +]	+ +	+

+ +   positive
+   moderately positive
−   unsympathetic
− −   negative
[   ]   dominant issue for the leader

SOURCES: Speeches 1970 - 1976

* Tikhonov and Chernenko became full members in 1979 and 1978; Polyansky, Podgorny and Mazurov lost their membership in 1976, 1977 and 1978, respectively, Grechko died in 1976; Kosygin died in 1980; Suslov died in 1982.

The issues described in the text are schematically presented according to the likely views on the preferred direction of development in the given situation. Even though the 'definitions of the situation' will differ among the leaders, the situation at the turn of the decade is seen here as generally being in favor of (1) the central government and planning agencies; (2) centralization; and (3) heavy industry. Thus the marks (-) and (--) represent the preservation of the status quo to a greater of lesser degree. Proposed changes of the 'new' policy are shown as the alternatives: (1) and increasing role of the Party organization in economic management and control; (2) greater decentralization, either on a territorial or sectorial basis; (3) an upswing of the material well-being of the Soviet citizen. The leaders are grouped in one figure for each issue. The positions are determined by the number of times, the preferences are discussed and the alternatives are rejected (or ignored) and by the consistency and intensity of the discussions. Variations are likely to occur within the 'grouping area', but such refinements are not made. (For example, Tikhonov's score in the (+ +) area of Issue II is probably higher on the horizontal axis - and thus closer to Kirilenko's views on centralization - than is Kosygin's.) Nor are changes of views in the course of the period taken into account. (For example, Ustinov is found to be more decidedly in favor of Brezhnev's economic policy before he became Minister of Defense. Ustinov is both an economist and a representative of military interests, and it is extremely difficult to decide whether he accords priority to economic of military considerations). In some cases the leader's position was (partly) determined by inference, for example by taking the degree of support for Brezhnev's economic policy. This is certainly the case with Chernenko's views, which is why his position regarding Issues II and III is in parenthesis. Given its speculative character, TABLE IV should be considered to be no more than an illustration of the positions of persons and groupings as seen by the present author. It is his interpretation of the selected speeches.

OF SOME DOMESTIC ISSUES

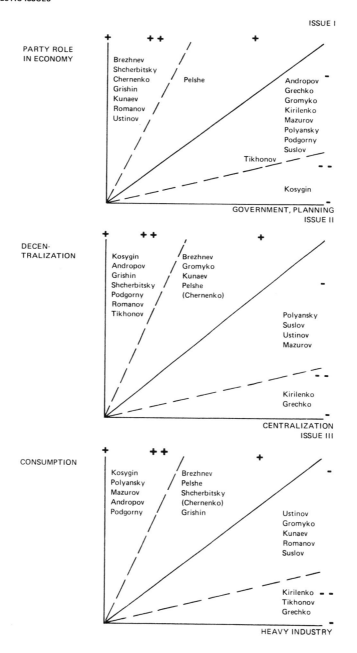

ISSUE I

PARTY ROLE
IN ECONOMY

Brezhnev
Shcherbitsky
Chernenko   Pelshe
Grishin
Kunaev
Romanov
Ustinov

Andropov
Grechko
Gromyko
Kirilenko
Mazurov
Polyansky
Podgorny
Suslov

Tikhonov

Kosygin

GOVERNMENT, PLANNING
ISSUE II

DECEN-
TRALIZATION

Kosygin   Brezhnev
Andropov   Gromyko
Grishin   Kunaev
Shcherbitsky   Pelshe
Podgorny   (Chernenko)
Romanov
Tikhonov

Polyansky
Suslov
Ustinov
Mazurov

Kirilenko
Grechko

CENTRALIZATION
ISSUE III

CONSUMPTION

Kosygin   Brezhnev
Polyansky   Pelshe
Mazurov   Shcherbitsky
Andropov   (Chernenko)
Podgorny   Grishin

Ustinov
Gromyko
Kunaev
Romanov
Suslov

Kirilenko
Tikhonov
Grechko

HEAVY INDUSTRY

103

unity. Obviously this must happen around a symbol and the only possible person is the Party leader. Even Kosygin, who was the first to doubt Brezhnev's honoring of collective leadership, says these days that

> ...the successes of Soviet domestic and foreign policy...are to a considerable extent dependent on that atmosphere of ideological unity, comradely trust, high exactingness and party principles which has become apparant in the past 10 years in our Party, its Central Committee, and the Politburo, led by Comrade Brezhnev, General Secretary of the CPSU Central Committee. [87]

In reality, Kosygin and others were in considerable disagreement with the course pursued in foreign policy and also in domestic policy. Indeed, the alleged majority favoring Brezhnev's plans found itself in a difficult position. For example, Kosygin, who favors the enhancement of economic rationality in the Soviet system, greater decentralization, and intensive growth by the introduction of modern management methods and new technology, cannot disguise the fact that he is a representative of the central planning and economic institutions. He is not the person to tell Baibakov and his central planners not to effect further improvements to the plan, its indices or forecasting capability, or to discourage the envisaged role of the nation-wide automation of planning information. Although Kosygin admits its shortcomings, he calls the plan "an immutable law"; although he agrees with criticism of the ministries, he certainly supports their place in economic management [88]. He largely shares--and is probably the major inspirator of--Brezhnev's economic views but, like Podgorny, he is not at all convinced that the Party apparatus is the best means for its realization.

On the other hand, Kirilenko, senior Central Committee Secretary for the supervision of the ecomony and diehard _apparatchik,_ appears to be a steadfast upholder of the existing political and economic order, resisting all change. He is the personification of the bold conservatism that by the time of the December Plenum of the Central Committee in 1974 had regained much of the ground lost to modernist tendencies. Kirilenko is often seen in the West as a close associate of Brezhnev with almost identical views [89]. True, both have a conservative record, both have close ties with heavy industry and the military, both are determined to build communism à la russe, that is by domination . But their views, even if fundamentally very close, also conflict. Whereas Brezhnev shows concern about political and social development and is ready to try new, perhaps even idealist ways to improve the endangered system, Kirilenko clings to worn-out methods and dispassionate phraseology [90].

Appeals to socialist competition, shock labor, collective
counterplans and labor discipline are means "that stood
the test of the time" for the one, but are insufficient,
or even useless if lacking in persuasion, for the
other [91].

The tendency exemplified by Kirilenko is powerful
and--in alliance with opponents of too much Party
intrusion--forced Brezhnev's retreat at the Central Committee Plenary session in December 1974. Peace and unity
in the Party ranks were largely restored by the
reformulation of a number of issues. Reports about the
Plenum and articles and speeches in the following months
reveal a return to the familiar socialist appeals, and
to the traditional priorities, notably heavy industry and
the need to strengthen national defense [92]. Brezhnev's
foreign policy goals were seriously affected by this
Plenum, as will be shown later. Podgorny was basically
right in saying to Brezhnev on his 70th birthday in 1976:

> Leonid Ilyich, your contribution to strengthening
> the unity and monolithic solidarity of the Party
> and the people is invaluable. You deserve principal
> credit for firmly establishing the Leninist style,
> principles and norms in Party and state work,
> collective leadership and collegiality in the res-
> olution of all questions. [93]

After 1974 Brezhnev's ambitious "policy package"
outlined at the XXIV Party Congress was reduced to fewer
issues, while the implementation of those remaining was
impeded by opposition or lack of enthusiasm. The success
of management reform and the constitutional re-affirm-
ation of Party rule were overshadowed by their creeping
effect in practice and by setbacks with other issues.
Admittedly, the desire for economic rationality and for
more and better consumer goods is not dead [94]. But such
intentions cannot be realized by piecemeal reform.
Indeed, "the system has an inner logic which resists
partial change." [95] By even further curtailing the
partial changes envisaged by Brezhnev, his opponents only
reinforced this systemic bias.

To conclude, the diffuse distribution of power and
the complex composite of resistance made up of the
system's "inner logic," anonymous social and political
forces, and outright opposition, appear to be key factors
impeding Brezhnev's political leadership in Soviet
decision-making and implementation. They also explain
the "fundamental inconsistency" between Brezhnev's
modernizing strategy and his implementation tactics, as
aptly formulated by Paul Cocks with reference to the
management of science in Soviet socio-economic development.

While his strategy emphasizes the need for a total
system's outlook and approach to the problem of
Soviet Russia's development, Brezhnev's tactics
recognize the need for a piecemeal, experimental,
and incremental form of implementation that is political "muddling through." [96]

A factor of major importance seems to be the political failure to establish "a more confident, institutionalized Party, with a policy of its own and with its
own distinctive, corporate existence." Brezhnev's
authority was too narrow a basis to raise the Party above
the various sub-systems. Instead, the Party remained one
of the sub-systems, leaving the existing autonomous
realms intact. Gromyko indicated the problem, when he
described the debate of the 1973 December plenary session
as a "Party matter, a political matter." [97] The issues
at stake were vitally important because they raised the
question of power relations between various institutions,
and also between the Party top--the Politburo and partly
the Secretariat--and the lower echelons. In particular,
the Central Committee had included itself in the guiding
collective leadership and, as a consequence, Brezhnev's
"daring new plans of communist construction" [98] were
neutralized. Brezhnev's leadership could henceforth be
glorified and recognized "universally." The "ability
to listen to the opinions of comrades" [99] and to remain
a "simple leader gifted with the Leninist style" hailed
by his colleagues is undoubtedly closer to reality than
some Western conclusions about the direct relationship
between his personal glorification and power. Brezhnev
tried, but the preservation of collective leadership
paralyzed his personal, political leadership and his
policies. Full recognition of his authority in the
second half of the 1970's became possible because he had
proved to be first and foremost the "embodiment of the
collective reason and will of the CPSU."

4
Brezhnev's Conduct
of Foreign Policy:
Asset or Liability?

INTRODUCTION

Brezhnev's much disputed economic leadership, his
vulnerable power base in the Politburo and even more so
in the Central Committee, and the slow institutionalization of Party rule as envisaged by him, could only
marginally strengthen his personal authority. In general,
reorganization and reform are a far from grateful undertaking and gradualism never completely silences opposition to measures likely to threaten power positions [1].
In the Soviet Union, the strait-jacket of collectivity
complicates political leadership even further. The
limits of power are largely set by a consensual power
relationship and political authority. In domestic
politics Brezhnev had shown his determination to adhere
to the principle of progressing towards communism. His
authority was to a large extent based on this perception
of his "just political act" (Friedrich) and of the
substance of the policy pursued.
It is not surprising that Brezhnev chose an additional and well-known way to underscore his authority
and statesmanship: the conduct of foreign policy. Unlike
the domestic politics scene, leadership in this area is
not so much hindered by a large number of actors and by
their possible footdragging. Brezhnev could become a
visible leader and channel his efforts to match those of
Gromyko, in this respect a loyal ally. Indeed, both by
the expedient use of the available opportunities and
by purposeful action Brezhnev soon mastered the field of
East-West relations [2].
Nonetheless, just as in domestic politics, changes
in foreign policy entail questions of both collegial rule
and policy substance. In this chapter, we shall first
see that foreign policy became the major issue of discord,
and shall discuss the aspects of Brezhnev's policy which
were so disquieting. Next, it will be argued that
Brezhnev was increasingly forced into a defensive position. After a glance at the role of ideology in Soviet

foreign policy, the chapter will be concluded with an
examination of the theoretical-ideological "solution"
to the problem of discord in the Soviet polity.

FOREIGN POLICY AS "THE MAIN PROBLEM OF DOMESTIC POLICY"

     Soviet foreign policy has generally been the indi-
vidual and separate task of a limited number of leaders,
among whom the General Secretary has often assumed command. During the "first term" of the Brezhnev-Kosygin
regime the Politburo was preoccupied with domestic affairs. At the XXIV Party Congress, however, Gromyko
welcomed and encouraged the greater and especially the
more continuous attention "this leading organ" apparently
intended to devote to his field of responsibility [3].
     The "Peace Program, the concentrated expression of
our country's foreign policy course [4]" indeed soon brought
this field to the forefront of attention. As mentioned
earlier, two Central Committee Plenums discussed the
international activity of the Politburo, and an outspoken
opponent of detente, Shelest, was demoted at the meeting
held in April, 1972. Furthermore, the inclusion of the
foreign policy troika of the government in the Politburo--
Andropov, Gromyko and Grechko--established a firm link
between decision-making and implementation [5]. The
organizational structure was to Brezhnev's liking: policy
formulation by the Party's leadership provided with
expertise and technical information while at the same time
ensuring the commitment of the heads of the policy elites.
The executive was brought closer to the political leadership. Finally, as in the case of Brezhnev's domestic
initiatives, foreign policy formulation was purposeful,
programmatic and comprehensive. "The fundamental special
feature of the Peace Program is that it has brought to
the forefront of world politics an interrelated complex
of tasks and aims oriented toward the fundamental
restructuring of the whole system of present day international relations." [6]
     By 1973, the international climate had appreciably
changed. The swift successes and early results of Soviet
diplomacy had contributed to a strengthening of international security and, of equal importance, had molded the
political will of a majority of the Politburo to pursue
this course. In 1973 Brezhnev urged that detente be made
"irreversible," and made a forceful attempt at the Central
Committee Plenum in April to consolidate and extend the
current trend. Not without success. The Resolution
praised Brezhnev's "great personal contribution," adding
that "the propositions and conclusions of Leonid
Brezhnev's report should be taken as a guide." [7] Support
for his personal achievements was also underscored by the
award of the International Lenin Prize for Peace to the
Party Leader shortly after the meeting.

Brezhnev had "brought home" foreign policy, especially at this April Plenum, which was called "a historic landmark in the struggle for peace." [8] The references to Brezhnev's rather than the Central Committee's instructions on the one hand, and the ostentatious public appearance of unity and agreement on the other, were however the first indications of a growing controversy within the polity. Reportedly, Brezhnev even told the Plenum that "foreign policy is now the main problem of domestic policy." [9]

The problem, more specifically, was the Central Committee, which was assuming a far more assertive role than in the past when its "plenums invariably approved the Politburo's foreign policy activity." [10] In the 1970's it was said that the "most important condition" for a correct and successful conduct of foreign policy was the guidance of the Party, "its Central Committee, which is concerned with key foreign policy problems on a daily basis." [11]

Though the April Plenum approved Brezhnev's report, it was neither unanimously nor "ardently," as the weekly publication of the Ministry of Foreign Affairs, Novoye Vremya, wished its readers to believe. The weekly's emphasis on the role of the Politburo was unusual and thus significant. "It is precisely the Politburo which is the ideological and organizing center whose consistent work is of decisive significance for the practical implementation of this program." [12]

While Brezhnev was apparently supported by the Politburo, or at least by a majority, a large part of the Central Committee still did not seem to be convinced. Its members had difficulty in adjusting to the new international developments. Two articles published in Kommunist shortly after the Plenum pointed to the differences between the top and sub-top levels. The first, by Gantman, ascribed the lack of support and understanding to the speed of developments. "In their minds our contemporaries find it difficult to get used to the fact that the pace and scale of the current improvements in world politics belong to a time period spanning a mere two years." His assessment of the actual situation, though too optimistic, was indicative of the psychological change he envisaged and deemed necessary. "The implementation of the Peace Program has led to a new deployment of all currently active political forces with respect to their attitude toward international activity." [13]

It was precisely this attitude of the Central Committee members that had not changed. Nowhere in Gantman's article was there any reference to the rigidity of Western thinking or to the other bourgeois shortcomings commonly used in the Soviet press to explain international difficulties. Instead, he pointed to the Party members who were not in a position to fully grasp foreign

policy. This "mass of lower grades (cadres) who are
prisoners of the dogmas and the primitive views of the
world [14]" was also the target of the second article in
Kommunist. The editorial's wording was somewhat different
from Tatu's language, but left no doubt about whose
"opinion" was to be changed.

> At the foot of a high mountain you cannot always see
> the summit. In the rapid stream of often contra-
> dictory events of various magnitudes it is sometimes
> hard for a man to discern the significance of each
> of them. But there cannot be two opinions about the
> times in which we are now living. These are times
> of an important shift in international relations,
> a shift from dangerous tension and "cold war"
> towards relaxation and peace. [15]

In order to mobilize support and to provide more
information for the Party at large, Soviet foreign policy
was widely discussed at all levels during the summer and
fall of 1973. Politburo members went round the country,
delivering speeches that were largely devoted to foreign
policy [16].
Of course the level of these discussions and their
effect are unknown; just the same, they should not be
over-estimated. To give just one example, a lecturer
from the Latvian Central Committee--an intellectual
"at the foot of the high mountain"--made the following
comment on the April plenary session:

> It is well-known that the CPSU Central Committee
> April 1973 Plenum drew attention to the need to
> further raise the level of party organizations'
> ideological work and to display constant vigilance
> and readiness to repulse any intrigues of the
> aggressive, reactionary circles of imperialism
> and any hostile ideological sabotage. [17]

These appeals may have been heard, but they were
certainly not the main thrust of the discussion. The
Plenum Resolution did not devote one word to "party
organizations," nor was anything in the nature of an
ideological appeal apparent in any later official or
high-level comment. This regional Party member was
nevertheless correct in that the matters discussed in
April were soon to be subject to ideological struggle.
He also anticipated the crack-down of the KGB on dissi-
dents and intellectuals that summer which was the price
to be paid for a more liberal foreign policy [18]. Finally,
the orthodox version of the plenary discussion also
indicated that high-level opposition to Brezhnev's plans
had grown strong enough to permit this kind of comment
by regional Party members.

DETENTE AND "MUTUALLY ADVANTAGEOUS COOPERATION"

What, then, were the disturbing "propositions and conclusions" made by Brezhnev in the Central Committee? The answer should not primarily be sought in the security issue area. SALT-I was not likely to be considered detrimental to Soviet security, having in fact been received positively, and MBFR had not yet begun.

The ideas that must have been so shocking had to do with the future content and further deepening of detente. The far-reaching measures of economic cooperation with the West, in particular, must have caused feelings of disquiet among Brezhnev's audience [19].

It is true that Brezhnev had indicated earlier what the catch phrase "mutually advantageous cooperation" was to mean. In March and December 1972, he had declared his willingness to establish contact between the EEC and the COMECON, thus implicitly recognizing the Common Market for the first time [20]. During the first Moscow summit it was Brezhnev more than anyone else who had insisted on the development of Soviet-American trade [21], and before the end of the year he was able to produce to the Central Committee a signed economic agreement. The Party must have known that what Brezhnev meant by trade was extensive and large-scale trade. Once detente was under way his message was also received in the West, not without amazement. Visiting the FRG shortly after the April Plenum, Brezhnev astonished his hosts by his extremely high expectations of Soviet-German trade. On T.V. he dismissed the traditional image of the Soviet Union. "Our plans are by no means plans designed for autarky. We are not steering a course aimed at the isolation of our country from the outside world. On the contrary..."[22]

In the months following the April Plenum, it became increasingly clear from articles and speeches that the meaning of detente was to be normalization in the strictest sense of the word, based on a "network of common interests" and on the use of economic "springboards," "levers" and "bridgeheads." [23] The "breakthrough" in relations with the major capitalist states was intended to go beyond the security aspects "leading to a shift of the center of gravity of struggle to non-military spheres," [24] in particular to economic relations.

> Peace is not only a matter of security. It is the most important precondition for solving the major problems of contemporary civilization. [25]

As always, the new course was explained and justified by references to Lenin, who had stressed the importance of the link between domestic and economic development and pointed to the compelling force in the West, greater than hostility, to embark on the path of economic relations with the Soviet Union [26]. Lenin's theory of peaceful cooperation between the systems advanced fifty-one years before was to be revived. The time had come to "revisit Genoa." 27

However, Brezhnev's extension of detente and his liberal interpretation of peaceful coexistence stirred up opposition in more than one respect. First, his expectations of East-West economic relations were far too optimistic, perhaps even unrealistic. For even assuming political readiness on both sides to develop large-scale trade and joint ventures, there were many obstacles which could not be overcome without drastic reform based on economic rationality. Western economists did not deny the potential benefits of the Soviet use of foreign "reserves" in order to increase efficiency. But the real effect was largely dependent on how imported technology and management methods were assimilated in the Soviet system 28. Furthermore, the volume of imported goods was severely limited by the lack of hard currency and by the economic restrictions imposed on borrowing. Moreover, the lack of experience in marketing and the slow production responsiveness to demand, together with the general sluggishness of Soviet businessmen, all added up to a real impediment to economic relations 29.

The feasibility of significantly expanding trade was doubted not only by Western economists, but by their counterparts in the Soviet Union as well. An even more serious impediment, however, was the unfertile political soil. Soviet views on the desirability of vastly expanded East-West trade were not overly enthusiastic. From the viewpoint of a central planner, for example, a large flow of goods between East and West would complicate the plan considerably and, worse, threaten it with disruption through short-term deals, sudden changes in the political mood ("freezes" and "boycotts") and uncertainties as to whether the Soviet Union herself could meet delivery deadlines and quality standards. When Kosygin was asked about his "desire to expand trade," he first mentioned the condition of long-term, planned trade and added: "This means that, having studied the market...we can outline a whole series of measures for the development of certain industrial sectors and include them in a plan insuring the export of these goods." 30

As argued above, Kosygin found himself in an extremely difficult position as head of the government economic leadership. He had to reconcile many different and competing views: those of the Gosplan, of reformers, of consumer advocates and of proponents of a technological influx from the West. Personally, he is quite likely to have favored a structure with a more self-regulating economic mechanism--a controlled "invisible hand" rather than the cumbersome system of the Party as directing mechanism. For Kosygin, East-West trade on a bilateral basis--rather than on the more complicated footing of some sort of agreement between the Common Market and

COMECON 31--could certainly contribute to Soviet economic development. Yet it was no priority.

He generally paid relatively little attention to East-West cooperation, often mentioning it in one and the same breath with Third World countries, or relating its effect directly to security and peace rather than to its domestic economic leverage. In accordance with the views of many of the economic leaders he represented, he primarily promoted the economic development of the Soviet Union and the socialist world (COMECON) from within 32. Shortly before the Central Committee Plenum in December 1973, undoubtedly well aware of Brezhnev's hopes of using foreign "reserves," Kosygin urged greater efficiency as being the means of fulfilling the 1974 plan, to which he added: "This in turn, presupposes the optimum use of internal production growth reserves." 33

In holding out the prospect of "new relations with other states on the basis of peaceful coexistence," Brezhnev had indeed presented a sharp contrast.

> They demand, and this was already noted at the April CPSU Central Committee plenum, a new approach to a number of problems of our economic construction, taking into consideration that our economy will participate on an increasingly larger scale in the international division of labor. 34

One can only speculate about the possible link between Brezhnev's domestic and foreign economic policy as far as the strengthening of the role of the Party is concerned. Did he intend to use economic relations as a means of bypassing the central planning agencies and ministries, as Simes concludes 35? Would direct dealings between Western businessmen and Soviet managers of "associations," as is suggested by Yanov, be possible in the centralized economy 36? There is not much evidence to support a positive answer to these questions. For one thing, economic detente lasted only a very short time and increased trade never reached--and probably could not reach--a level high enough to give any tangible leverage in domestic economic policy. Moreover, Brezhnev and the Party organization lacked the means needed to encroach upon or bypass the foreign trade agencies. Brezhnev had to use the ministries to develop and administer trade. He could not circumvent their economic leadership by means of republic and regional Party support as he had done with the restructuring of domestic economic management.

Most important of all, Brezhnev lacked political support for his idea of vastly expanding foreign trade. No one in the Politburo picked up this theme at any length or with visible enthusiasm. On the contrary, reluctance and scepticism were predominant. Some went no further than support for "convenient" economic cooperation 37, while emphatically pointing to the risks and calling for ideological vigilance. Most top leaders appeared to share Kosygin's views of the limited possibilities and benefits of trade with the West. They also saw as priority No 1 the development of the Soviet and socialist economy. More time and a still further "developed socialism" seemed to be required for sufficient confidence in equal and balanced trade with the West. A few days before the April Plenum Ustinov, who on the whole supported Brezhnev's economic policy, very carefully formulated the conditions for and consequences of trade, neatly balancing the various considerations.

> The development of relations of peaceful coexistence implies the expansion of constructive cooperation in the economic, scientific-technical and cultural fields. The opportunities for this are extended beyond measure under conditions of the swift growth of the economic potential of the Soviet Union and the entire socialist community. Awareness of the pointlessness of attempts to place obstacles in the path of developing links with the socialist countries is growing in the world. Of course, these links can only be built on the basis of mutual advantageousness and equality of rights, with complete renunciation of discrimination and interference in internal affairs (Emphasis added). [38]

Despite the limited enthusiasm of most Soviet leaders--for economic or political reasons, or both-- Brezhnev's vigorous efforts to develop trade, especially with the United States, were at first not unsuccessful. In 1972 the consequences of the bad harvest were considerably reduced at short notice by grain purchases in the US; numerous projects entailing technological, scientific and business cooperation followed the Moscow summit; and last but not least the Trade Agreement was signed on October 18. Before the parties had signed, however, Senator Jackson started his crusade against the Emigration Tax and discrimination of Soviet Jews and--at least implicitly--against Soviet-American detente. The Jackson-Vanik Amendment linking Most-Favored Nation status and severe credit restrictions to the emigration issue, was adopted by an overwhelming majority in the House in December, 1973. After a year of domestic bargaining and Senate deliberation, President Ford signed the Trade Reform Act, including the Amendment, on January 3, 1975 [39].

By this time the President's act no longer mattered. Although the official Soviet reaction came on January 10, the decision to cancel the Trade Agreement had already been taken at the December Plenum of the Central Committee in 1974. "...the word was being put out today that Brezhnev had personally decided the trade act should be

rejected and presented that decision for ratification at
the Communist Party Plenum, December 16." 40
   There were a number of reasons for the Soviets to
turn down the agreement, which Brezhnev had made valiant
efforts to save. The Nixon Administration had been unable
to tone down Jackson's irreconcilability and the issue
was one no Senator or Representative could reasonably
oppose without the risk of losing voters. Consequently,
the Administration could not respond--at least not
adequately--to the Soviets through "quiet diplomacy."
First of all, Brezhnev clearly signalled Soviet readiness
to comply--though silently--with American demands
regarding Jewisch emigration. The Soviet bureaucracy
reacted to events with almost incredible speed. Brezhnev
reportedly told Americans that the emigration tax was a
mere "bureaucratic bungle." 41
   Second, numerous signals reached the United States
about the importance of non-interference in Soviet
domestic affaris and of an--at least--unhindered formal
agreement on trade. Brezhnev told the Soviet-American
Trade and Economic Council that the Soviet Union
attached "not only economic, but, I should say, even
greater political importance" to the Agreement. At this
moment, October 15, 1974, he still appeared to be ready
to fight for his trade policy:

   Unless _timely_ concern is shown for the elimination
   of these negative factors, the further development
   of cooperation may be seriously delayed...

   We and you could very well get along without the
   further development of trade and economic relations
   with one another...

   The economic relations between our two countries
   are in their early spring. But we believe that, as
   in nature, summer will inevitably come in these
   relations--what is important is that the process
   should not be delayed too much. 42

   Brezhnev badly needed to pick up momentum in foreign
policy, quite apart from the economic significance in
itself. He would need it even more after the Vladivostok
summit with President Ford. Controversies in the Soviet
polity had reached the point where American credibility
regarding detente had become the yardstick by which to
measure Brezhnev's policy. In the end, however, the
Jackson-Vanik Amendment proved to be a most effective
means of strengthening opposition in Moscow and forcing
Brezhnev's withdrawal 43.
   In sum, the Soviet leaders were not against trade,
but against Brezhnev's unbridled enthusiasm; there were
fears that it would result in too much interdependence
or too much interference from both inside and outside the

Soviet Union. The issue of a vast expansion of foreign trade was in itself too complex and controversial a matter to allow a strengthening of Brezhnev's position. His authority as the economic leader suffered rather than benefited from it. Brezhnev stirred up opposition and antagonism in the Party on an issue of relative economic significance, and he wanted results in a very short time. The view that economic and technological aid from the West would be useful for selected priority projects seems to have been a characteristic aspect of Brezhnev's economic strategy [44]. It was not an essential component of rational development of the economy as a whole.

In the final analysis the reasons for reluctance and opposition were political, not economic. In the eyes of many Soviet leaders the economic advantages were outweighed by the political costs, both domestic and international. The issue assumed major importance because Brezhnev's persistence and pushing made it a political issue. The Central Committee was "against hasty, ill-considered" plans. The trade issue was only part of the much broader process of normalization that in the course of 1973-1974 would increasingly define the political climate in which discussion took place. This leads to the second point, the international actor and his insistence on linking economic and domestic issues or, in Soviet parlance, interfering in domestic affairs. According to Stern, Zamyatin indicated Soviet readiness to link trade with progress in arms control negotiations, but all Soviet spokesmen firmly rejected the explicit and publicized linkage envisaged by Jackson [45]. The domestic processes in both the United States and the Soviet Union substituted politics for businesslike economic relations [46]. For Brezhnev, the conduct of foreign economic policy became a liability rather than an asset in the realization of his goals, at least in the medium and long run.

BREZHNEV ON THE DEFENSIVE

Although Brezhnev's experimental domestic "muddling through," the selective, ad hoc approach he favored in foreign economic relations and his personal conduct of policy had met with reluctance and resistance, his overall strategy was still gathering momentum in early 1973. His visits to the FRG and the United States were important, even historical, events; the CSCE and MBFR talks were about to start; and the diplomatic settlement of the Vietnam war had removed an embarrassingly open target for criticism at home and from China.

But in the summer of 1973 it became apparent that the overall strategy itself was in question. The far-reaching normalization of which trade was just one part became subject to criticism which was of course couched in Marxist-Leninist terms. Detente incurred the risk that ideological differences between East and West would be neglected. It even led some observers to confuse inter-state relations with normalization between social systems. For example Inozemtsev, an advocate and important interpreter of "the fundamental reconstruction of international relations," found it "especially urgent" in 1973 to explain at great length and to correct the current mistakes about "the nature of contradictions in our era," and particularly about "the fundamental priority role of class contradictions." [47] Of course, no one doubted the fact that peaceful coexistence was linked to the ideological struggle, but one begins to wonder to what extent this was actually the case in view of the Party leader's conclusion that for the new system of international relations completely different methods and "perhaps, a different psychology are needed from those which existed previously." [48]

The different mentality, the new attitude Brezhnev had in mind still presupposed the inevitably favorable course of history, socialist unity and an unswerving loyalty to proletarian internationalism. However, as noted above, the "organic links" between Marxist-Leninist dialectical concepts are complex, if not confusing, in theory, and inconceivable and unworkable in practice. For example, how is Brezhnev's new mentality, for which "it is essential that we learn to cooperate," [49] to be reconciled with Mazurov's antithesis of the use of peace and socialist strength in order "to seriously undermine the position of imperialism in the world arena." [50] Or how can the Moscow summit deal in 1972--where the Soviet leaders agreed to put pressure on Vietnam in exchange for Soviet-US trade and cooperation-- [51] be explained in terms of socialist internationalism and solidarity? If Brezhnev's "new approach and, perhaps, new psychology" meant an equation of detente with peaceful coexistence as a principle higher than proletarian internationalism, then socialist unity was really at stake. Political debate assumed an either-or character.

By the summer of 1973, after the US-Soviet summit at which the Agreement on the Prevention of Nuclear War had been signed, assertions about a "nuclear condominium," the "nuclear diktat of the superpowers" were heard and-- as Trofimenko notes--"not only in the Western press." [52] These accusations were evidently dismissed as "absurd and provocative." However, irritation about this argument against the new Soviet foreign policy was clear and several efforts were undertaken to counter these allegations about the exclusive rights of the Soviet Union as superpower, even by Brezhnev. He assured all countries that they all had the same rights.

It is not necessary to prove that a constructive contribution from any state deserves equal respect and an attentive and favorable approach. To try to

117

counterpose a great or even super-great state to a medium-sized or small one, as some are trying to do, is totally without foundation, unnecessary and even harmful. [53]

In Tashkent two months later Brezhnev again denied several times that the Soviet Union made a distinction between the rights of smaller and larger states to deal with each other or to actively pursue international security and trade. As Izvestia explains, partly quoting Brezhnev:

> The policy of peaceful coexistence among states with different social systems and the application of its principles cannot be of a "selective" nature. These principles must extend to all states, great and small. "The watershed runs not between the large and small countries but along the line which divides the policy of peace and progress from the policy of aggression and reaction." [54]

Such assurances to the fraternal parties in Eastern Europe were certainly not given in response to doubts about the Soviet military or nuclear guarantee. The Agreement on the Prevention of Nuclear War concluded in June, 1973, did not affect the security situation in that region. Unless the East European leaders thought--unrealistically--in terms of a surprise attack by NATO, they could be quite confident that their territory would not be the main nuclear battlefield while Soviet territory was spared.

Soviet concern seemed rather to relate to East European demands for greater equality and more freedom to approach the West, particularly in the economic realm. Increased economic cooperation with the West would undoubtedly further complicate the already troublesome implementation of the "Comprehensive Program of Socialist Economic Integration." The coordination of foreign policy stressed by Gromyko would also become more complex. Moreover,

> ...the broader cooperation becomes and the more diverse the business contacts and the more intensive the exchange of material and spiritual values in relations between states with different social systems, the more insistently appeals ring out from the reactionary circles of imperialism that "the war of ideas should be carried into the territory of the enemy," that is, into the socialist countries. [55]

A report of the Crimean meeting between Brezhnev and East European Party leaders, a tradition since 1971, indicates that all these issues were discussed [56].

118

More specifically, Brezhnev admitted soon afterwards that
the participants had noted considerable reserves for the
expansion of socialist cooperation in all fields, and had
stressed the need "to raise significantly the level of
the fraternal parties' ideological cooperation." [57] The
Summer/Fall of 1973 was a period in which Soviet-American
cooperation was called "a historic shift in class (sic)
relations," [58] a Soviet achievement which was supported
and approved by all fraternal parties, while at the same
time internationalist principles were termed "norms of a
higher order" [59] and deviation from the experienced
leadership of the CPSU was feared and condemned. The
implication was that the Soviet Union should not assume
too special a position in international relations.

> A Party which rejects or underestimates the
> experience of the other detachments of the world
> communist movement and which puts national interests
> above international ones and regional goals above
> those of the world workers movement and, even more,
> a Party which pursues a chauvinist dividing policy,
> as the present CCP leadership is doing, does great
> harm to the revolutionary cause both in its own
> country and throughout the world. [60]

Brezhnev, now apparently on the defensive, attempted
to allay all possible doubts about foreign policy
continuation by assuring a Party gathering in Alma Ata
that "we are talking about not relaxing our efforts for
the realization of the Peace Program." [61]
It was also unusual for him to thank writers of
letters to Pravda and Izvestia for their support and to
present this as evidence of the correctness of the foreign
policy course, "which we should continue." [62] Furthermore,
in Tashkent the same month, he dismissed "allegations
that the concluded treaties are unsatisfactory" as a
naive view. International politics, according to Brezhnev,
required patience, a step-by-step approach and the use
of all available and created opportunities [63].
The "Peace Program" was under attack and Brezhnev was
clearly defending it. But the mounting pressure did not
yet prevent him from attempting to broaden the ground
recently gained. The process of detente was not only to
be made "irreversible," but also to be "supplemented by
military detente." The meaning of this phrase was
explained in his speech at the World Peace Congress in
October where, according to Podgorny, "Brezhnev in fact
further developed the Peace Program." [64]
Podgorny was not the only colleague in the Politburo
who sided with the Party leader at this time, particularly
on the issues of military detente and the potential
financial savings. Of no less importance was the support
he received from Suslov and Kosygin in this issue area,
to which more attention will be given in Chapter VII.

Suffice it to note here that the top leadership closed its ranks against the mounting opposition to Brezhnev's policy in general, and to its ideological and economic consequences in particular. This is not to say that the Politburo fully agreed with Brezhnev's views on detente, but in 1973 its inner circle found--for some time--common ground in the related issues of Soviet security, the relaxation of tension and the role of the economy in international relations. The question was how long the "coalition" would hold, but in 1973 Brezhnev's political leadership had a large measure of support in the Politburo. As Kommunist's comment on the December 1973 plenary meeting of the Central Committee, where the Party's "outstanding successes in the consolidation of peace" were praised, explains:

> The Plenum revealed the organic connection between our foreign and our domestic policy. This again leads us to V.I. Lenin's instruction that we are now exerting our main influence on international revolution through our economic policy. In the present international atmosphere this thought of Lenin's is filled with new historical content. [65] (Emphasis added)

Brezhnev's difficulty in reaching agreement with his colleagues was not only a consequence of their different approaches to many issues. It also seemed to stem from the steadfastness, if not stubbornness, with which he pursued various issues, as observed by Zagladin (see also Chapter III, footnote 99). An illustration of this personal trait is provided by the way he clung to an issue of limited significance in his overall strategy: the definition of relations with China. In 1972 Brezhnev proposed for the first time that Sino-Soviet relations be normalized on the basis of the principles of peaceful coexistence, that is if the Chinese leadership continued to insist on that principle [66]. Later he dropped this condition and thereupon declared that China could no longer be considered a socialist state. In June 1973 he went still further in announcing that the Soviet Union had "officially suggested to the Chinese leadership the conclusion of a treaty of non-aggression." [67]

However, these extravagant positions were neither supported nor emulated by other leaders. Kosygin, Kirilenko, Suslov, Gromyko and others [68] attributed the difficult relations with China to anti-Sovietism or to domestic problems of the Chinese leaders, not to the ideological schism. The question is, why was Brezhnev so insistent on a total break between the two socialist countries while the majority of the leaders were not ready to do so? They continued to cherish some hope of improvement, possibly after Mao's death. Should Brezhnev's uncompromising attitude be seen as another indication that he gave priority to an interstate rather than a socialist approach to international relations? It was definitely an attempt to isolate China. Whatever the reasons, the way in which Brezhnev disregarded the different and far more prudent approach of his colleagues is noteworthy. There is no doubt of the fact that he quite unnecessarily added another issue to his already beleaguered foreign policy.

THE "THEORETICAL-IDEOLOGICAL SYNTHESIS"

Perhaps the most difficult factor to determine is the impact of ideology on Soviet foreign policy. Though the vast literature on ideology in general yields considerable insight into its political function, the question about its impact has led to sharp disagreement and to far from scholarly, indeed ideological disputes. One reason is that analysis is complicated by personal beliefs and feelings of righteousness, blurring the distinction between facts and values and disguising the fact that we are all ideologists. Another reason is that Marxism-Leninism contains so many contradictions and raises so many questions. Most of these problems have not been solved; on the contrary, they are being kept alive knowingly, faithfully, or both. It is not difficult to show that Marxism-Leninism is not a science: it lacks coherence and is based on neither experience nor empirical verification [69].

But it is quite another thing to conclude--or for that matter admit--that its principles are "applied science" in the hands of a world power and of many newly-inspired regimes and--mostly young--individuals. Even though adherents can never prove the so-called "laws," in practice the Marxist-Leninist appeal is apparent and a political fact. For example, analysis of the "correlation of forces," taking into account all forces in all issue areas, does not produce laws but is--even if couched in terms of the inevitable gains made by socialist forces--a tool to measure the "balance of power." The extent to which such analysis is colored and distorted by pre-scientific or deterministic views is politically important, yet extremely difficult to ascertain.

On the one hand, one cannot label such ideological prescriptions as nothing more than rationalization of essentially pragmatic actions. Nor is it enough, let alone correct, to conclude that "policy is based on interests, not sentiment." [70] Ideology and pragmatism are no opposite concepts, since, in the final analysis, justification and legitimization of every action are based on an appeal to morals and beliefs. Even assuming that an actor is able to define the interests he "pragmatically" pursues, then nevertheless such

...interest-based beliefs are the same as all the other political beliefs, since the conception and propagation of any political belief requires at one stage or another resort to ethical norms for the public justification of a socially important satisfaction and integration of demands. 71

On the other hand, the impact of ideology should not be exaggerated. It is going too far to say that ideology "permeates all Soviet activity in international politics." True, Marxism-Leninism gives the leaders "certain long-range goals for Soviet foreign policy" and "a method of analysis." 72 But, as in the former case, such observations are not enough and do not tell us much about the significance of ideological images in the conduct of foreign policy. It is even more doubtful whether ideology provides the leaders with "a system of knowledge" and "strategy and tactics." 73 The former attribute seems to turn ideology again into a science; the latter fails to differentiate between general, well-considered plans and short-term, temporary decisions, often ordained by unforeseen events and suffering from incomplete, hasty decision-making.

The main point is that both views of the impact of ideology assume--to borrow the terms used by Seliger in his dispassionate and thoughtful work on this matter--that the "fundamental ideology" is known. Moreover, the descriptions fail to distinguish between the "fundamental and operative dimensions" of ideology 74.

With regard to the first shortcoming, the blatant contradiction between the proclaimed communist goals of equality and the political organization in the Soviet Union exemplifies the difficulty of singling out what is fundamental. "There is little in the fundamental principles and final goals of socialism and communism to justify the prolonged terrorist dictatorship of a tiny minority and the hecatombs of victims ad majorem communismi gloriam." 75

The interest in preserving the rule of this "tiny minority" is no less important than the declared morals of communism. Interests and morals are inseparable in politics, and ideology alone cannot be used as a means to illustrate that the one is more fundamental than the other. This is not to say that Soviet history has not shown a tendency to safeguard personal interests first, as happened in the period of Stalin's cult of personality. It is also true that the recovery from that period has been slow and erratic. But this cannot conceal or explain away Khrushchev's genuine beliefs nor his successors' attempts to create a communist society and to develop a political structure conducive to that end. Policy questions are "in the final analysis" derived from a formal belief system, but they are asked and answered in the context of established decision-making processes, interests, and power relationships. There is a fundamental dimension and an operative dimension in the way ideology functions and presents itself. The "fundamental dimension" of ideology is just one part of the elusive, albeit inseparable trilogy of ideology, process and power. None of these aspects can be neglected by Soviet actors without risking serious consequences for the system as a whole.

It is the Party and the ideology together that provide the system with its built-in momentum. The decline of either would force the regime to rely almost exclusively on terror, as did Stalin, or face the prospect of far-reaching transformation of the system. [76]

This interplay between the actors and ideology leads to Seliger's description of the "operative dimension" of ideology, where "technical prescriptions" have taken over the central position of "moral prescriptions." [77] Political actors do not consider all issues to be equally important. Nor are all issues brought to the political arena or under public attention. Compromises and package-deals between opponents are a real part of politics and they include morals and ethics. Some ideological issues can be used in a political controversy and acquire central importance. "Core issues would be those fundamentals which the parties themselves continue to refer to in political debate as the important issues on which they are ideologically divided." [78]

Ideology, an instrument of power in the hands of various actors, can be an advantage to the political leadership "to ensure concerted action," but also a disadvantage. Lenin can be quoted in support of a proposal, or equally well as a forceful antidote to that same proposal. In the Soviet Union, where ideology is such an explicit part of the aforementioned trilogy, the expedient use of Marxism-Leninism is apparent at an early stage and not necessarily to the benefit of the political leadership and its policy. With regard to Brezhnev's foreign policy, it therefore remains to be seen whether and to what extent "Soviet ideology gives its leaders a useful conceptual framework for dealing with many comtemporary political problems." [79] Brzezinski and Huntington's observation should be followed by the question: "Useful for whom, for which leaders?" To paraphrase Lenin: "Ideology is part of the whole, the whole is politics."

The CPSU undoubtedly enjoys "a monopolistic position." But it is no monolith characterized by adherence to a "monistic set of principles." [80] Except perhaps for a few fundamental principles--at the very least the survival of Party rule, the monopolistic position,--there is no clear "united front by the leadership, [no] unity of opinion at the top of the decision-making process." [81] Jurrjens is right in saying that communist "truth" is "resolved in Soviet ideology by the outcome of the process of power politics." But it is questionable--and therefore subjected to further investigation in the next section--whether he is right in ascribing so much authority to the Party leader and in assuming that the Party's monistic position is one of such strength:

> The General Secretary of the Party, as the primus inter pares among his colleagues in the Politburo, wields the ultimate authority in this collective body of Chief Proclaimer (or Discoverer) and Chief Interpreter of the objective laws, which determine the inevitable road mankind must follow on its way to the future Communist society. [82]

FOREIGN POLICY AND THE "THEORETICAL-IDEOLOGICAL SYNTHESIS"

As early as September 1971, Suslov praised the new foreign policy defined by the Party leader as "an out-standing contribution to Marxist-Leninist theory." [83] The campaign for a fundamental restructuring of international relations certainly needed a solid "scientific" foundation and it had to be made clear that the new foreign policy would unabatedly contribute to social progress in the world. But as tension and disagreement about the content of foreign policy grew, so too did the need to find a common ideological language. The lack of ideological clarity was giving rise to two opposing interpretations.

During the heyday of detente, for example, Zarodov, cited earlier in connection with his dogmatic approach to the Leninist type of party organization (footnote 60), insisted that Marxist-Leninists "have not departed nor will they depart one centimeter from their scientific principles." [84] Indeed his own account warrants such a conclusion. Not one single word was devoted to Brezhnev's first--historic--trip to the FRG or to the Soviet-American summit which had just taken place on American soil. Instead, his sole reference to detente was to urge the communist parties "to consider it extremely important to preserve and develop revolutionary qualities."

The problem of course was how the "organically linked" principles of peaceful coexistence and socialist or proletarian internationalism could be combined in the detente policy. The distinction between two kinds of relations--interstate and social--though repeated endlessly, could not solve the very real problem that "we communists are often asked whether this policy is compatible with revolutionary views." [85] Nor were critics and ideologists like Zarodov likely to be satisfied by gratuitous statements to the effect that the "Peace

Program" was "the concrete embodiment of the class nature of Soviet foreign policy." [86] Those who continued to insist that peaceful coexistence and international agreements "merely mark a certain coincidence of (the) will and desire to preserve peace" between East and West [87] challenged the views of the "Chief Interpreter" and undermined both his authority and the Party's monistic set of principles.

The ideological discussion apparently started soon after the "Peace Program" was launched. Zagladin, commenting on the Central Committee Plenum of April 1972, emphatically claimed "Adherence to Principle and Consistency" for the foreign policy course the Politburo had been "instructed" to carry out. But he admitted that "one cannot fail to recall that even now, of course, instances are encountered of an extremely arbitrary interpretation of the question of the socialist states' international duty. This particularly concerns the question of the policy of peace and peaceful coexistence." [88]

Zagladin deemed it necessary in this article to stress repeatedly that the new foreign policy followed the true "Marxist-Leninist line." It combined short and long-term interests and various--not only military-- methods of struggle. According to this authoritative writer and adviser of Brezhnev's, one-sidedness and reliance on one group of methods of struggle, e.g., military power, could in certain instances "jeopardize the attainment of...fundamental objectives" of socialist foreign policy. He refuted, as was "sometimes said,"

> ...that in response to one or another tough action by imperialism socialist countries, and the Soviet Union above all, for their part must have no alternative but to react in the same way: to toughen their position too. [89]

The idea underlying this article, which appeared in the early days of detente, was two-pronged: (1) peaceful coexistence was to be extended to more issue areas than just security; and (2) hard-liners should not impede the development of peaceful coexistence, as envisaged here, by unnecessary defense measures [90]. Like Inozemtsev, Zagladin defended peaceful coexistence as a principle that was favorable to social progress and in no way contradictory to its ideological counterpart, proletarian and socialist internationalism.

This theme of social progress was increasingly heard, and became the central criterion for a theoretical-ideological "synthesis." A highly important contribution in this respect came from Ponomarev, Party ideologue and head of the International Department of the Central Committee. In perfect harmony with the "objective" course of history, his argument followed two main lines:

the growing power of socialism and the exacerbating
General Crisis of capitalism. Given that framework, he
explained that the improved interstate relations had
furthered these objective developments [91]. First, he
pointed out the socio-political significance of international detente in the Western countries and concluded:
"Detente facilitates the strengthening of realistically-
minded circles in the bourgeois camp and helps to isolate
the most reactionary imperialist forces, the "war-
parties," and the military-industrial complexes." [92]

Ponomarev went so far as to say that social progress
was "impossible" without further consolidation of international detente. Likewise, the revolutionary forces
were strengthened in their struggle for peace and against
the "imperialist strategy oriented towards the admissi-
bility of war." [93] Of course the preservation of peace
by Western subscription to peaceful coexistence was also
in the interests of capitalist states. But this vital
interest of every nation should not be confused with
other essential interests of capitalism. In all other
issue areas it was socialism, not capitalism, that stood
to gain. "Detente promotes progress. In its turn
social progress promotes detente."[94]

Secondly, the socio-political development of the
capitalist countries was accompanied by antagonism
amongst themselves as well as between them and Third
World countries. Capitalist crises--energy shortages,
stagflation, unemployment--were bound to sharpen their
differences. Ponomarev viewed these simultaneous processes not simply as a "further deepening but a definite
qualitative shift" in the general crisis of capitalism [95].

The scientific-technical revolution would not and
could not "ease capitalism's wounds, increase its
viability, and give it 'second wind'." Nor would the
economic prospects of the West be any brighter as a
result of East-West relations. Such side-effect and of
course undesirable help from socialism were, according
to another theorist, of mere tactical significance, a
mere side-effect and not sufficient to save capitalism.

> Thus the policy of peaceful coexistence is by no
> means a policy of the easing of capitalist contra-
> dictions, and it is totally untrue that the social-
> ist countries can by their policy alter the natural
> development of capitalism. Of course, in the
> process of peaceful coexistence and in the course of
> the development of financial-economic relations,
> some partial difficulties can be smoothed over. [96]

Thirdly, the "Peace Program" was a graphic expression
of the fact that the communist movement had seized the
initiative in the international struggle. The resulting
agreements between capitalist and socialist countries
not only constituted recognition of the achievements of

world socialism, but also mobilized and inspired the masses in their continuous struggle. The peace offensive linked polity with society, and interstate relations with social relations. "Thus the relaxation of tension means the broadening and deepening of the front of the ideological struggle, not "peaceful coexistence" between the opposing ideologies." 97

Finally, the peace offensive also linked Soviet interests with the communist movement. Detente put the Soviet Union and Soviet communists at the center of international activities. Anti-Sovietism was becoming the pivot of bourgeois attempts to discredit socialism and to undermine socialist unity and, according to Ponomarev, "this is precisely why the communists in the fraternal parties rightly stress that the struggle against anti-Sovietism is a matter for all working people, all democrats and all patriots." 98 In this way Ponomarev arrived at proletarian internationalism and linked the Soviet leadership and example in the world with communist ideology and unity. Analogous to the essential domestic bond between Party rule and ideology, he projected an international system based on the ties between the leader Moscow and the "legitimizing" common ideology. In a perspective from Moscow he provided the international system with a "built-in momentum," to cite Brzezinski once again 99.

Can we conclude then that Ponomarev's "synthesis" solved the differences in the theoretical-ideological debate? Not at all. The discussion about "principled firmness" and "tactical flexibility" in foreign policy, and about the "objective" and "subjective" factors of social progress, could not be solved by ideology; it was itself ideology. This problem was certainly recognized in the Soviet Union. For example, foreign policy expert Kapchenko was only partly right when he said that "the foreign policy of any state is ultimately determined by objective conditions." It was, moreover, too general a statement. Kapchenko came closer to the truth when he also admitted that subjective factors such as parties, governments or statesmen played an "enormous role." But he was right on target when he actually ruined his and others' painstaking efforts to prove the objectivity of "the scientific principles of Soviet foreign policy" with the conclusion that "it is essentially in the operation of subjective factors that the operation of objective principles finds expression." 100 Ponomarev's "objective" justification of detente was of little help in that respect.

What Ponomarev's "synthesis" brought about was the ideological appeasement of both opponents and proponents of East-West interdependence. They were lured into a compromise which was badly needed to preserve the unity between Party and ideology. The "synthesis" avowed to the opponents that "a concession in the ideological sphere means departure from the class line, which inevitably leads to revisionism in theory and practice and to deformation of socialist achievements." 101

At the same time, the opponents were forced to acknowledge that a Pax Sovietica was beyond their power as long as capitalist states displayed "a certain unity" in the political and military spheres. Therefore master plans for a Moscow world center leading an ideologically united popular front were not to be considered a realistic development. For that reason, too, the relaxation of tension had to be viewed as an "objective requirement of comtemporary international life." For these Soviet actors detente "demonstrates the ground-lessness of the thesis that ideological differences make the improvement of relations...impossible." 102

Brezhnev, the "Chief Interpreter," had to witness a re-adjustment of his great theoretical contribution to Marxism-Leninism. Normalization was severely limited and the development of mutually advantageous economic relations--which even Podgorny at some point called the content of detente--dit not receive the hoped-for blessing. East-West issues remained at the fifth and lowest level on the hierarchical order of the principles of peaceful coexistence. They were recognized as a factor favoring social progress, though in a circumscribed way. The "philosophy of historical optimism" 103 which Brezhnev still acclaimed in 1973 made room at the XXV Party Congress for "principled" reasoning and for sub-ordination to communist morals and Party interests. Of course the long section in Brezhnev's speech about "The CPSU and the World Revolutionary Progress" was in part an answer to emerging Eurocommunism, but it also reflected the more general tendency to stress internationalism rather than the more liberal or moderate aspects of peaceful coexistence. The restructuring of international relations should however not be seen as "a new Brezhnev doctrine." 104

The Party leader publicly retreated because he had to avoid the risk of being accused of a lack of principles and divisive action. The clash between two different conceptions of peaceful coexistence 105 had created too tense a situation. In the theoretical-ideological debate, the strains of an "either-or" situation were removed and replaced by the more relaxed one of "both-and." The opponents and proponents of normalization could describe this process in both moderate and dogmatic terms of peaceful coexistence and proletarian/socialist internationalism.

However slight this change may seem, the new consensus--or lowest common denominator--was not a complete return to the 1960's or further back to the Cold War years. The so familiar Marxist-Leninist language of those years was counterposed by a different one. Although one encounters the irreconcilable approach

recalling that "it ought also be emphasized that the
ideological struggle...is becoming proportionately more
important," 106 other Soviet writers dared to write as if
there were no difference between interstate and socialist
relations. For example, Tomashevsky bordered on ideological ignorance, if not slander, in saying about
detente:

> Another important large-scale problem in this field
> is linked with the rise in the proportional weight
> of economic, scientific, and technical cooperation
> between the two systems. The unique feature of this
> form of the historically inevitable confrontation
> between socialism and capitalism is that peaceful
> competition not only does not rule out, but on the
> contrary, presupposes the widespread development
> of mutually advantageous cooperation among states.
> Whereas during the cold war period economic
> cooperation developed primarily within each of the
> world socio-economic systems, now, in addition, the
> significance of cooperation stretching beyond the
> bounds of each of the systems is also increasing. 107
> (Emphasis added)

In sum, the theoretical-ideological debate reflected
the dynamic political process of the 3-4 years following
the XXIV Party Congress. Ideology was not a product of
arm-chair theorists, published under the auspices of
Suslov and Ponomarev. It was an important power base
in domestic politics, an indispensable factor in legitimizing policy and communicating its content to the
Party members. However, ideology could also be used the
other way, in support of the political leadership's
policy.

CONCLUSION

Brezhnev's "great contribution to the elaboration
and implementation of the Leninist foreign policy, to the
working out above all of its most fundamental problems" 108 was not accepted gratefully by all Party
members. In particular, the basic elements of Brezhnev's
overall policy--the economic normalization that had to
serve as an important "reserve" for domestic economic
development--met with considerable opposition. Although
a number of Politburo members did not altogether share
his views, they seem to have decided to act together in
the face of growing disunity within the Party. The
fraternal parties probably joined in the debate as well,
trying to get their share of the benefits of East-West
detente. Brezhnev was thrown on the defensive at home,
perhaps decisively, when the dramatic decision of the
American House of Representatives reduced the prospects

of trade to mere symbolic proportions and dealt a painful
blow in the sensitive area of human rights in the Soviet
Union.

Whether the development of trade in the absence of
the Jackson-Vanik Amendment would have prevented the
opposition from becoming so strong is of course a matter
of speculation. The available evidence certainly
suggests, however, that the Amendment was a factor in
Brezhnev's retreat as a pushing actor in the field of
East-West detente. Extensive trade between the Soviet
Union and the United States was not likely to have been
sufficient to offset Soviet economic shortcomings, but it
would have boosted Brezhnev's authority as foreign policy
leader and perhaps have enhanced his position as economic
leader at a most critical moment in the Soviet domestic
political process.

The foregoing confirms Rosenau's general conclusion
that the way in which the domestic and foreign responsibilities of "linkage elites" or "dual politicians" are
balanced "serves both to link their policy to its
environment and to delineate the boundaries between
them." [109] The position of Brezhnev as the active and
articulate leader in domestic and foreign affairs shed
valuable light on Soviet domestic considerations and on
the disparate views on an acceptable measure of interdependence with the outside world. Furthermore, by
focussing on the position of leadership, a number of the
questions posed by Rosenau can be answered with regard
to the Soviet Union. For example, "dual politicians"
like Brezhnev appear to be "more vulnerable than their
non-linkage counterparts." [110]

This also seems to be the case with other leaders if
they hold domestic and foreign policy views which are
found together on the same side of Dallin's left-right
spectrum. Shelest, consistently on the conservative side,
and Podgorny, on the moderate side of this continuum,
may in part have been the victim of their own consistent
and rather outspoken views. Gromyko, on the other hand,
balanced his pro-detente views with reassurances of his
conservative domestic stance. Even Kosygin, notwithstanding his political weight in the top leadership,
created room to maneuver with regard to East-West trade
and diplomatic normalization. He himself may have had
reservations about Brezhnev's foreign policy, but his
position vis-à-vis the governmental organization--in some
ways his "constituency"--and his known advocacy of
domestic economic reform may further have encouraged him
to keep aloof from liberal orientations in foreign
affairs. In general, in order to reduce political
vulnerability, Soviet actors tend to share some views
with their likely opponents in either domestic or foreign
policy (see Tables IV and X) [111]. They are inclined to
avoid total isolation from coalitions in specific contested issue areas. This is a further illustration of

the tendency towards collective rule and of Ross'
conclusion that the Soviet "decision-making style...
is characterized by lowest-common-denominator or rule-by-
committee principles." 112

Obviously, Brezhnev was a highly outspoken "dual
politician" whose position became extremely vulnerable
113. This leads to the conclusion that at some point
he had to choose between his national and international
leader's role. The fluid and unstable coalition of
Politburo members was unwilling to accept or fully to
support Brezhnev's leadership, but was at the same time
unable to establish a "grand coalition" within the Party
at large. Brezhnev's foreign policy was most controversial. Moreover, his possible intention--perhaps even
attempts in the early 1970's--to use foreign policy in
domestic politics made Brezhnev's conduct of foreign
policy a clear target for a composite opposition.

Furthermore, various sections of the fragmented
centers of autonomy were driven together in their defense
of the existing institutional arrangements. Finally,
the difficulties experienced in the international context,
together with the leadership's primary concern with
domestic development, made the field of foreign affairs,
if not the most urgent, then at least the most likely
area for concessions.

By the end of 1974 the number of contested issues
had grown to the point where effective control of the
overall process, and of its direction in particular, was
extremely difficult to maintain. The events of the
preceding years had fostered opinions and arguments both
for and against groupings and the "correlations of power"
within the polity had probably become more identifiable.
For example, the Vladivostok accord between President
Ford and General Secretary Brezhnev was possible because
security had increasingly become the issue area on which
the political leadership was able to reach agreement,
though not without difficulty and, as will be argued
later, not for too long a period. The less successful
Soviet-American economic relations fell victim to
opposition which was no doubt strengthened by the successful actions of Jackson and Vanik in mobilizing a vast
majority in Washington to limit and condition Soviet-
American trade.

The December Plenum of the Central Committee decided
to review the meaning and content of detente. As in the
case of priorities for resource allocation, the opposition to the policy formulation at the XXIV Party Congress and to Brezhnev's interpretation and implementation
succeeded in redirecting the policy course along more
conservative lines. "Lenin's Approach to Compromises in
Politics" 114 resulted at this Plenum in a "synthesis"
carrying the seeds of conservatism and Soviet independence.

These soon burst into life. At the next Central

Committee Plenum in April 1975, it was not Brezhnev who delivered the report on foreign policy, but Gromyko who had the honor of addressing this Committee which no longer deemed it necessary during the remainder of the 1970's to put the subject on the agenda. In the summer of 1975 the change in foreign policy was marked by Soviet activities in Angola, a revival of her internationalist task followed up in Portugal and the Horn of Africa. The switch from Brezhnev's "personal" conduct of foreign policy to a "collective" approach to the West was also soon apparant in the SALT negotiations, where Gromyko became the most visible "executive" of the Soviet Union. Of course the Presidential elections of 1976 and the aggressive diplomacy of the new administration, especially on the human rights issue, were anything but conducive to detente. Numerous other events on both sides could be cited to illustrate the deterioration in the international situation.

That part of it which can be ascribed to the domestic process in the Soviet Union, however, to the return to Soviet intransigence and militancy, took place at the Central Committee Plenum of December 1974. Brezhnev was again fully incorporated into collective rule; the limits of detente and interdependence were defined. In sum, Brezhnev's personal conduct of foreign policy caused no significant change in the power relationship among the Soviet leaders. Brezhnev failed to free himself from the strait-jacket of collective decision-making. Henceforth foreign policy was drawn more and more into the realms of collectivity; first in the Politburo and later, as a consequence of both the agreed style of leadership and foreign policy disagreements, in a broader context. After the initial results of detente policy, Brezhnev perhaps advanced too fast, involving too many domestic and inter-national issues at the same time. Brezhnev's foreign policy, which had originally seemed to be an asset of his leadership, finally proved to be a liability for his domestic position.

Part Two:

Domestic Politics and Security Policy

5
Civil-Military Relations:
The "Societal Imperative"

INTRODUCTION

Defense policy has important domestic roots. It is not a mere function of the external situation and perceived threats, but is organized in the domestic setting and is largely determined by developments taking place there. The main actors in defense policy are subject to the political culture and the institutional patterns through which decisions are made. The military, professionally and directly involved in the organizational structure of defense, face policies and policy plans that may be inconsistent with their responsibilities. Political leaders, on the other hand, though no less concerned about national security, must reconcile various interests with one another. Their task "on the institutional level is to develop a system of civil-military relations at the least sacrifice of other social values; The achievement of this objective involves a complex balancing of power and attitudes among civilian and military groups." [1]

This objective must be achieved within the confines of the general political setting or culture as described above. The nature of security and the many specific professional problems involved, however, generate as many differences as similarities with other policies. Part II will address some of these problems and, in particular, the process of "balancing of power and attitudes" by which military and civilian demands are reconciled.

The military are the actors primarily in charge of organizing an effective, credible defense. The way they organize the means of violence is a most important asset for national security. Military professionalism is however not confined to the competence, knowledge and skills of the military; it is also dependent on the extent to which the "professional soldier" is allowed and enabled to do his job and on the measure in which his métier is regarded as essential in international relations. It is imperative for the military institution that the means of force and their organization correspond with the international military situation and its developments and that this necessity is recognized by the political leadership.

The military institutions of any society are shaped by two forces: a functional imperative stemming from the threats to the society's security and a societal imperative arising from the social forces, ideologies and institutions dominant within the society...

The interaction of these two forces is the nub of the problem of civil-military relations. The degree to which they conflict depends upon the intensity of the security needs and the nature and strength of the value pattern of society. [2]

In his thorough and penetrating framework of analysis, Huntington postulates that national security is best served by "objective civilian control." This requires that the political leadership should seek to maximize military professionalism. The leaders should make the military and their power an instrument of the state's security policies. These are divided into external (e.g., East-West), internal (e.g., avoidance of subversion) and "situational" (e.g., countering political erosion that reduces the power of the state) security policies. In none of these security policies should the military acquire political influence.

The antithesis of objective civilian control is military participation in politics: civilian control decreases as the military become progressively involved in institutional, class and constitutional politics. Subjective civilian control...presupposes this involvement. The essence of objective civilian control is the recognition of autonomous military professionalism; the essence of subjective civilian control is the denial of an independent military sphere. [3]

Thus the political and military leadership should respect each other's field of responsibility. Ideally, the boundaries of both the realm of the "professional soldier" and "the realm of political autonomy" should be known to each participant. In reality, however, these boundaries are extremely difficult to fix. Somewhere on the civil-military borderline tensions are likely to occur, the more so if one tries to encroach upon the responsibilities of the other. Huntington distinguishes two levels at which the policy process takes place: an operating level where immediate issues such as military strategy, capabilities and deployments are involved; and an institutional level where "in the long run the nature of the decisions on these issues is determined." [4]

These two levels of the policy process largely correspond with Huntington's conditions for optimizing military security, viz. maximizing both military professionalism and objective civilian control. Thus military "expertise, responsibility, and corporateness" should be allowed to develop independently and be recognized so that the officer corps can function fully at the operational-technical level [5]. At the institutional--and in particular at the ideological--level "the key issue is the compatibility of the professional military ethic with the political ideologies prevailing in society." [6] The military ethic, so it is argued at length, is "pessimistic, collectivist, historically inclined, power-oriented, nationalistic, militaristic, pacifist, and instrumentalist in its view of the military profession." [7] This "conservative realism" of the military ethic is basically similar to political conservatism. Other major political ideologies--liberalism, fascism and Marxism [8]--are more or less opposed to it or at least to some of its elements. In a society or polity where an anti-military ideology prevails, the military may--feel to--be forced into politics. As a consequence of latent or manifest subjective civilian control, military professionalism and operational-technical competence are likely to be weakened. "The generals and admirals may triumph but not the professional military ethic. The taming effect of political power makes them good liberals, good fascists, or good communists, but poor professionals." [9]

Whereas the "military mind" is taken as a constant factor, the "civilian or political mind" is considered to be the variable. Civil-military tensions may occur when the political mood changes, and this may not only lead to concrete and visible budgetary measures but also affect the military institution and its professional status itself.

The actual state of civil-military relations is both reflected in and part of the power relationship between the political and military leaders. It is at this point, however, that Huntington tries to separate the inseparable. He introduces the concept of "distribution of power" as a new element alongside professionalism and civilian and military ideology. He asserts that "the realization of objective civilian control thus depends upon the achievement of an appropriate equilibrium between the power of the military and the ideology of society." [10]

But power and ideology should not be counterposed to each another. On the contrary, ideological images and military professionalism should be regarded as important power bases. The patterns of civil-military relations can be usefully described in terms of anti- or pro-military ideology and high or low military professionalism [11]. However, Huntington's third element--high or low military political power--is not independent, but dependent on these variables.

Furthermore, the restriction of Huntington's main elements of description of civil-military patterns to professionalism and ideology is fully consistent with the distinction he makes between the functional and societal imperative and between operative and institutional policy. The functional and operative aspects of civil-military relations should primarily be examined by an analysis of the category of power bases, characterized by the actor's possession of particular qualities--physical means, knowledge, skills and wealth [12]. The extent to which the military enjoy autonomy varies according to their ability to use these power bases. This is obviously no black-and-white picture. For example, the defense budget--"wealth"--is authorized by the political leadership and is dependent on political rather than military consent. Yet large defense expenditures give the military leverage vis-à-vis other policy elites and ensure some kind of participation in questions concerning R&D and allocations of means at the industrial level.

At the societal and institutional level, the central question to be considered is which power bases the military share with political leaders. Military power is primarily defined by the degree of consensus with civilians and involves such power bases as ideological images, rights, prestige and affection. It seems useful for our understanding of Soviet security policy to examine to what extent the "civil and military mind" coincide, and how the military can use consensual power to maintain or enhance their position.

Finally, the military have a strong structural power base. They defend the most fundamental state interests. Contradictions and antagonism in East-West relations inherently ensure this power position. It is basically independent of actions of the political leadership and primarily varies with the state of international affairs. For example, the introduction of a new threatening weapons system by the adversary is quite likely to affect the military position in internal deliberations on measures to be taken. Another example is provided by the Soviet military presence in Eastern Europe or, rather, the need for it. The socio-economic system superimposed on the East European countries requires latent and sometimes manifest military power. Thus the structure or the nature of Soviet-East European relations entails domestic power for the Soviet military. It was the use of military power that "settled" the Czechoslovakian question in 1968 after political attempts had failed and the armed forces are a prominent factor in Poland today.

The foregoing elaboration of Huntington's framework of civil-military relations serves as a guide for analysis in the present and two following chapters. First, civil-military relations will be examined at the

138

institutional level by focussing on the consensual power bases. After a short description of what Soviet military doctrine includes, an attempt will be made to ascertain how the military can use these power bases to penetrate the political realm.

Chapter VI is devoted to Soviet military professional considerations and their translation into practice. Special attention is devoted to the use made by the "professional soldier" of the power bases characteristic of his responsibility.

In the final chapter, Soviet civil-military and military-professional considerations will be placed in the context of East-West relations, primarily--of course-- in the perspective of East-West arms control. A point of special interest is the way in which the dominant tendencies described above are affected by military detente. In addition, the analysis, which also takes into account the findings of Part I, will focus on the relationship between political and military detente, and in particular on the question of what considerations weigh most heavily.

WHAT DOES SOVIET MILITARY DOCTRINE INCLUDE?

Soviet views on defense, its needs and organization, are expressed in the military doctrine. The doctrine contains the rules that prescribe the set of ends, means and moments an actor should choose in various situations [13]. Sidorov defines the military doctrine as "a system of scientifically substantiated, officially approved views on preparation for and victorious conduct of war in defense of the interests of the Soviet Union."[14]

This definition first points to the political impact. The doctrine is "officially approved" and is aimed at the "interests of the Soviet Union." It is not a matter for the military alone, but one that must correspond with the views of the Party top. "The basic principles of the doctrine are determined by the political leadership of the state. Therefore military doctrine is state doctrine." [15]

Here the military and political leadership meet, setting military goals and limits. Second, the doctrine is "scientifically substantiated." It is based on Marxism-Leninism and its "scientific" principles. The fundamental "laws of war"--its essence, nature, origin, course and outcome--are formulated by the political leadership and the "laws of the armed struggle" are dependent on policy [16]. Thus the science is a military responsibility, but subject to political tenets and, quite obviously, sanctions.

In the Soviet literature military science is distinguished from military art. In the basic work on Soviet Military Strategy, Sokolovsky defines military science as

...the theory of military art whose subject is the
nature and methods of military operations of various
scopes, both in the aggregate and as applied to each
separate service of the armed forces, and each branch
of service in particular. [17]

The scopes to which Sokolovsky refers are the
tripartite hierarchy: strategy, operations and tactics.
Military art, in particular, represents the contribution
of the military to doctrine. Professionalism provides
the basis for military art. When necessary, the military
must be able to meet the requirements of an armed conflict. They must be prepared for this in theory and in
practice. "The subject of military science is the study
of the general laws of a war.... It must study the manner
in which probable enemies will unleash and conduct wars."[18]
  While art concentrates on future battle, military
science relates the art to its setting involving economics, politics and national morals. Success or failure
in a war is largely dependent on these factors. Even
though the art is very important "in itself, it will not
be sufficient to bring about the victory." [19] Military
science places military art in the political context.
Here the political leadership meets the military who, in
exercising their profession, may try to influence political goals and considerations.
  The most important military part of the doctrine is
strategy, but--as is stressed time and again--it
"occupies a subordinate position with regard to the military doctrine." Essentially, military doctrine is overall policy embracing all issue areas at all levels of
security policy. The task of military strategy is to
determine the nature and conditions of a future war so
that the military can be properly prepared and thus be in
a position to win it. It is evident that this somewhat
limited, yet enormous, task implies political questions
in addition to those of a purely military nature.
  For example, the national defense utilizes a
considerable part of the national resources and this may
be in conflict with the employment of means other elites
would like to appropriate. Similarly, with regard to
foreign policy, military strategy is a part of political
strategy. Military strategy "must determine the composition of the forces and the means necessary to accomplish
the aims placed before it." [20]
  The aims are political. In military literature
Lenin's thesis of the subordination of the military to
the political viewpoint is constantly repeated, even
though the military usually add some references to the
crucial importance of their task. According to them,
military considerations should rank high in the priorities and sometimes even be accorded the highest priority
(for example, with regard to technological developments) [21]. Yet Colonel Kozlov's description of the

serving task of military strategy is still valid. "The
objective of military strategy is the creation by military means of those conditions under which politics will
be in a position to achieve the aims it sets for
itself." 22

Thus political and military considerations are
complementary, but in the event of any conflict between
them the viewpoint of the political leadership should
prevail.

Without doubt, political primacy also applies with
respect to the content of the military doctrine. When
Garthoff defines military doctrine, he adds the following:
"Soviet military doctrine, like Soviet policy and strategy
in general, is the product of a dynamic conjunction of
ideological and pragmatic motivations." 23

Lenin's pronouncement about the inevitability of war
as long as capitalism remained in existence has generally
been accepted as a rule ever since. Capitalism, by
virtue of its nature, would certainly unleash a war
against the socialist states. Awareness of the disastrous consequences of a nuclear war, however, prompted
Khrushchev to oppose--very cautiously--this sacred dogma
at the XX Party Congress in 1956. Needless to say,
Lenin's opinion regarding imperialism was still valid
but, he added, Lenin had lived in a different epoch
without nuclear weapons. Was it necessary to go on
repeating, asked Khrushchev, that

>   ...wars are inevitable as long as capitalist
>   countries exist? We live in a time when Marx,
>   Engels and Lenin are not with us... On the basis
>   of the teaching of Marxism-Leninism we must think
>   for ourselves, analyze the present situation and
>   draw the conclusions that are useful for the common
>   cause of communism. 24

In actual fact Khrushchev abjured the ideological
concept. War between the two different social systems
could no longer be accepted as "fatally inevitable."
Just the same, though it might be true that war was not
inevitable, it was not unthinkable. The aggressive
capitalist countries could still unleash a war against
the Soviet Union. If war were to occur, the Soviet Union
would defeat the aggressor. This notion led many Soviet
analysts to question whether victory in a nuclear war
would still be possible. At the same time, Soviet
leaders had recognized since the 1950's that nuclear war
would cause enormous damage to their own country. In
that sense, most of them realized that their ideological
stand was untenable 25. Soviet literature reflected
both ambiguity and uneasiness about it. "The unleashing
of a war between nuclear powers really would be a
disaster for both." 26 But also: "The laws of history
are stronger than the laws of nuclear artillery." 27

Professor Butenko, however, stated in the same article
that the ultimate end was "the construction of communism.
But one cannot build communism quickly on ruins."
    In other words, the victory of communism would be
delayed by a nuclear war since it "would do irreparable
damage to the whole world revolutionary process." [28]
Not only was nuclear war accompanied by serious risks;
it was not a necessary condition for revolution. As the
1961 CPSU program stated: "revolutions are definitely
possible without world war." [29]
    Thus the "pragmatism" initiated by the Party leader
led to denunciation of the necessity and the inevitability of war in the advancement of communism. This
process of revision was to go further. Starting in the
early 1960's official statements and military doctrine
leaned increasingly towards avoidance of nuclear war.
Despite the "certain victory of the Soviet Union,"
Sokolovsky was well aware by the time of the third
edition of Military Strategy of the "guaranteed destruction" capability of both superpowers.

> The Communist Party makes the conclusion about the
> absence of the fatal inevitability of war in the
> modern era, when political and economic potentiali-
> ties are being created to prevent a world war,
> even though imperialism still remains on a portion
> of the earth. [30]

    The advent of nuclear weapons and the consequent
awareness of the vulnerability of the Soviet Union also
prompted reconsideration of the tenet that war was a
political instrument. Despite the conviction that the
outcome of a "just" war with the capitalist states would
be victory, war as a means to an end had to be rejected
not only because of its suicidal consequences but, it
would seem, on moral grounds as well.

> Although we are convinced of the fact that the
> capitalist order will perish as the result of a
> future war and the socialist order will conquer, we
> communists do not strive for victory in that way...
> It is anti-moral and at variance with our communist
> world view. [31]

    The Soviet Union should be able to prevent a world
war by its military power and the Communist Party should
express its disapproval and call for the prevention of
war, aiming instead at "a more realistic view" and "a
more reasonable conception of the relation of forces." [32]
    The successors of Khrushchev inherited military
doctrine as it had been developed during the decade of
his leadership. Sacred ideological motivations had been
adjusted to the requirements of the nuclear era. They
basically, though more cautiously, pursued "consequences,"

"avoidance" and his "rejection" of nuclear war as an acceptable political means. As Kosygin said in his speech to the XXIII CPSU Congress: "We communists look to the future with well-founded optimism; the aggressors can and must be curbed, a new world war can and must be prevented." At the political level, the leaders repeated on numerous occasions that the primary goal was to avoid an East-West military conflict. Declaratory policy gained credibility by the Soviet readiness to discuss the limitation of strategic weapons with the United States. Moreover, the first SALT agreements were of great significance as a visible sign that the Soviet leaders shared the view that negotiations were a means of achieving greater international security. Admittedly, SALT-I was limited in scope and raised a number of questions about certain shortcomings, while leaving the more difficult issues, including the problems of asymmetries, definition and verification with respect to many weapons systems, for future negotiations. Finally, modernization programs for offensive weapons systems remained unaffected.

Although SALT-I confirmed the strategic situation and current military developments on both sides, the Moscow agreements also paved the way for greater mutual stability. First of all by the ABM Treaty, which guaranteed mutual vulnerability; secondly, by the Interim Agreement, which was seen as an effort to establish improved parity. In addition, SALT-I was regarded by the two parties as a first step [33], the first move in a long process of bargaining, learning, trusting, fighting and compromising, both at home and abroad. SALT greatly politicized strategic matters, and the relatively stable situation made it possible to cast doubt upon the Soviet military nuclear wisdom and strategic assumptions of, say, the early 1960's. As far as the Soviet Union was concerned, the SALT process constituted a further departure from the pre-Khrushchevian views on war.

The various departures from orthodoxy did not escape the attention of the military. Like the military in the West, they were confronted with the question of how much credibility could be given to the nuclear deterrent if nuclear weapons were no longer considered to be usable [34]. The rejection of nuclear weapons as a new--indeed, revolutionary--form of military power would not only have dramatic consequences for military strategy, but would also seriously undermine ideological conceptions of war and armed struggle and of Lenin's acceptance of Clausewitz' views on "War as a continuation of politics with other means." War between the two social systems would be unlimited because of the radical socio-political changes it would bring about.

Whether and how the Soviet Union would survive formed no part of the Soviet military "laws of war," [35] but scepticism about the possibility of waging a victorious war had always been heard among the military. For example, Major General N. Sushko and Major Kondratkov had asserted in 1964 that nuclear weapons had rendered "war an exceptionally dangerous and risky tool of politics" and that it should not be used as such. They were followed by Talensky, Nikolsky, Simonjan and others, who all underlined the massive destruction that would ensue for all parties concerned [36]. This point of view still exists and still appears--explicitly and implicitly--in today's military publications.

But by no means all military authors stress this aspect. Indeed most of them continue to emphasize the "correct Marxist-Leninist understanding" and refuse to reject the use of nuclear weapons for "solely political aims." [37] Like Epishev, head of the Main Political Administration and observer of ideological matters in the armed forces, they give priority to the theoretical-ideological approach and reject the conviction of others that nuclear war would have terrible consequences. Milovidov asserts that errors made by the military should be redressed.

> Unfortunately, not all our researchers immediately adopted a creative approach to problems of war and military theory. In some works by Soviet authors there are errors, for example, in the question of the essence and consequences of a nuclear missile war. The authors of these works have treated as absolute the qualitative analysis and arithmetical calculation of the destructive power of nuclear weapons...

> A methodological error in the assessment of the correlation between war and armed struggle has been rectified also. In the course of the discussion of this question, it was decided unanimously that it is wrong to see war merely as an armed struggle, even though the latter constitutes the specific and determining feature of war. In an armed struggle, all means are subordinated to the interests of victory: politico-economic, ideological, diplomatic, and others. If war becomes a fact, the entire domestic life of the country is subordinated to its victorious prosecution and conclusion. [38]

This assessment may well be too optimistic. Unlike similar questions treated by military strategy, i.e. at the level of "the laws of the armed struggle," the problem of war and the ideological ambiguity in that respect have not been resolved. The moment Pravda stated that "the atomic bomb does not adhere to the class principle." [39] ideological clarity about the class principle in military doctrine was damaged. A schism between theory and practice appeared, and is still in existence.

While ideologists point to the inherent dangers contained in capitalist societies--including nuclear war, which they do not exclude as an instrument--the more pragmatically inclined view this instrument as nothing less than the suicide of socialism. Of course, the latter will not dispute the "class definition Lenin gave of the essence of war," and will yield to its ultimate consequences. A striking example of the dilemma is given by some military authors when they refer to the position of imperialist theoreticians and statesmen.

> Their position with respect to nuclear missile war is a dual and contradictory one. On the one hand, they regard nuclear missile war as a means of struggle against socialism and communism but, on the other hand, fear the ruinous consequences a thermonuclear war would have for capitalism. [40]

CONSENSUAL POWER BASES AND THEIR USEFULNESS

Soviet military doctrine links political and military issues and considerations. To some extent it regulates political-military relations and prescribes the hierarchical order of questions regarding political leadership and the military institution. The primacy of politics, for example, is stressed time and again and it seems--for what so general a statement is worth-- that Soviet practice follows that design. Ultimately, the Party decides and it has created a vast apparatus within the armed forces, the Main Political Administration, to promote and control military adherence to Party rule. Any dissident behavior, let alone conspiracy, runs the risk of being detected. The danger of internal intervention by military means or military subversion is remote under the present, well-institutionalized collective leadership. Unless current political practices and arrangements are seriously threatened or factional struggles lead to an appeal for military support, actual use by the possessors of the powerful means of violence is not likely to occur [41]. The Soviet military have shown no interest in seizing political power, in challenging in that way the primacy of politics and of Party rule [42].

> As members of a privileged segment of society with good bureaucratic representation, they have not had an outstanding interest that would demonstrably gain from greater political competition. So it is with the economic and intellectual realms, where for most officers the advantages of prevailing arrangements far outweigh the disadvantages. [43]

145

This rejection of Kolkowicz's widely-shared view that the Party-military relationship "is essentially conflict-prone and thus presents a perennial threat to the political stability of the Soviet state" [44] does not mean that there are no internal bureaucratic struggles or civil-military tensions. Far from it. Military doctrine formalizes "objective civilian control" only to some extent, and leaves no doubt that there is a number of areas where political and military competence overlap and even criss-cross each other. In such areas of mutual penetration "subjective civilian control" of both formal and informal processes is bound to occur and, as Janowitz has noted, supplements objective control [45].

One pertinent and consistent way for the military to ensure a say in the formulation of Soviet military policy is the cultivation of vagueness in theory and definition. Although the Party is said to define military doctrine and the "laws of war," the weight of professional considerations and military experience is constantly interjected. For example:

> The laws of war and armed struggle closely interact, intertwine and penetrate each other mutually, each in its own system as well as between systems. Therefore, a division of them into systems or groups bears an arbitrary or relative character. By virtue of this, some laws of war are in a certain sense also laws of armed conflict, since they not only determine the course and outcome of war as a whole, but also have a direct or indirect influence on the development of combat (military) operations. On the other hand, the laws of armed conflict are to one degree or another also laws of war, the more so as armed conflict comprises the chief content of war. [46]

And:

> Pointing out a certain independence enjoyed by strategy, F. Engels dit not intend to stress its independence from politics. He only warned that if policy violates or ignores the laws of military strategy, this can lead to the defeat of the army and to the destruction of the state. During the war, strategic concepts often have a reverse effect on policy. Cases even arise when the military factor acquires decisive significance. [47]

Moreover, in describing the desired organization of strategic leadership, military writings stress the importance of the unity of political and military leadership. The lesson drawn from the experience of the early days of World War II is that the Supreme Command should

146

be established well in advance. There is no doubt that, according to the military, the General Staff must assume the main responsibility for planning and, in the event of war, for decision-making and the execution of strategic actions: "practical experience serves as a criterion of truth." 48 The military not only point to their indispensable experience, but some also advocate an economic organization--essentially on a war footing--to be run by an integrated military-civilian strategic command well in advance of a military conflict. The superiority needed to win a war must--in the absolutist approach of Kulikov--be organized and prepared before it is too late, as was the case in World War II 49 when "the strategic leadership was organizationally formed about three weeks after the start of the war... Consequently, one of the lessons of the war consists of the fact that the system of strategic leadership must be thought out, worked out, and coordinated in all details ahead of time, before the start of a war." 50

Infringement upon the responsibilities of the political leadership may not go as far as Colonel Skirdo describes, but the requirements to be met by a good military commander, as he sees it, totally blur the distinction between the statesmen and his military servant:

> The wars of the present epoch, more than ever before, have turned commanders into statesmen. Fulfilling his leadership role in peacetime and training his troops for a future war, a military leader proceeds from the postulates of state policy and the socio-political essence of such a war. And from the moment of the outbreak of hostilities, he directs the entire course of the armed struggle toward the attainment of particular political goals. A military leader's world outlook and political views determine his entire activity, including that in the field of moral-political preparation of the personnel under his command. 51

At the same time, Soviet military doctrine reflects a design of civil-military relations that is aimed at assuring both a strong consensual power base and professional autonomy. On the one hand, the military emphasize the unity of Marxist-Leninist teachings and military science. On the other hand, they stress the distinction between the exclusive right of the political leadership to decide whether or not to use military power in foreign policy--certainly whether or not to go to war--and their own professional responsibility for developing "the law of the armed struggle in their interaction with the laws determining the course and outcome of the war." 52 Thus the Party is committed to the common cause expressed by the doctrine, while at the same time

147

it is kept at a safe distance when military experts use
their own language--according to <u>military science</u>. The
primacy of politics and of the Party is not questioned
and cannot be questioned. The military are dependent on
political decisions for what they get and ultimately
for how much they can say. Stalin's remark that "the
military should occupy themselves with their own business
and not discuss things that do not concern them" still
seems to be valid [53]. In return, however, the military
insist on the rights and responsibilities of the
"professional soldier."

> ...the more the political leadership is guided by
> the conclusions and instructions of military science,
> the more effective and effectual will be accepted
> their decisions and the greater will be reached
> unity of political and military leadership. V.I.
> Lenin repeatedly stressed the importance of expert
> knowledge and the role of specialists in the leader-
> ship of any matter, including the country's
> defense. [54]

For the military institution to operate effectively,
it is bound to speak with one voice, to ensure internal
unity.

> Soviet military doctrine is called upon to secure
> the unity of the thought and will of the Soviet
> soldiers not only through the community of their
> political ideology, but also through the community
> of their views on the nature of the military tasks
> facing them, the ways of their solution and the
> methods for the combat training of the troops. It
> is a sound basis for preparing the country's
> defense. [55]

The military are successful in presenting a united
front in the political arena. For example, though the
Main Political Administration (MPA) may at times be the
unwanted political watch-dog of the Central Committee [56],
it is at the same time a useful ambassador for maintaining
good relations and fostering understanding at the highest
political level. In practice, the MPA is an important
intermediary between professional and political-ideological values and interests. The military are probably
better off with these "uniformed Party watchers" than
with direct civilian supervision, for these "political
soldiers" are largely integrated and tend to side with
their professional counterparts on major issues. As
Colton illustrates,

> ...the MPA has forcefully echoed military views
> about relations with the West, the necessity of
> civilian cooperation in all aspects of the defense

effort, and the desirability of inculcating military and "military-patriotic" values in the population. 57

As we have seen, there are differences of opinion among the military. However, the 1960's en 1970's witnessed the development of a remarkably uniform military strategy, the result of a successfully enforced unity of thought and a dominant "military mind." The military academies and institutes working under the auspices of the General Staff of the Ministry of Defense and the Central Committee's MPA have succeeded in formulating one political and military doctrine for the military institution as a whole. The existence of an "officially approved" set of basic rules for Party-military relations is an important asset of the military. In a one-party system every policy elite is open to political interference of any kind. More or less formalized agreement about the elite's competence and its relation with the ultimate authority endows it with the right to defend its position more or less openly and explicitly. The military have a field of competence that can readily be distinguished from other areas of governmental activities, which puts them in a better position to draw the line than, for example, economists or industrial managers. To be sure, Party intrusions are inevitable. Military doctrine is based on Marxism-Leninism and the latter's "laws"--workable or not--must be included. Another fact the military must accept, whatever its perceived and actual disadvantage to professionalism, is Party interference at the operational level in the armed forces 58. For example, Epishev never fails to mention the ultimate subordination of the military commander. The basic principle for building a viable army is, he says, "the Communist Party leadership elevating the role and intensifying the influence of Party organizations in all aspects of the life and activities of the Army and Navy." 59

The growing number of technological complexities and of engineers with little ideological training in the armed forces have confronted the political worker with an increasingly arduous and difficult task which involves seeking accommodation with, rather than the subordination of, the military commander. Yet Party involvement has always been an impediment to the commander's independence and initiative, and constantly raises the question of who is actually in command. In the military organization edinonachalie--one-man command--is important, if not essential, for swift and effective operations, management and troop control. The commander's decisions should be taken on professional and technical grounds and should not be complicated by ideological and political considerations, and operations should not be delayed unnecessarily by cumbersome collective decision-making. This traditional problem seems largely to have been

solved in theory; in practice, friction between the Party
organizations and the commander will undoubtedly continue
to exist [60].

The disadvantages at the operational level and the
restraints of political subordination in general are
offset by the considerable advantages gained from being
tightly bound to the Soviet polity and the political
culture. First, the "scientific" Marxist-Leninist
foundation of Soviet military doctrine is a powerful
hedge against criticism of military thought on the best
approach to the security problem. For example, capitalism is aggressive, from which it follows that nuclear
weapons have changed neither the role of the military nor
the function of military power in foreign policy.
Justification of this reasoning stems directly from the
ideological roots of the doctrine. Moreover, the
"scientific status of military theory" [61] justifies the
claim that it occupies an independent place among the
sciences.

Unlike the West, where military strategy and
doctrine are regarded primarily as the province of
interested or contracted civilians [62] who may or may not
be assisted by the military, the Soviet Union relies on
a number of prestigious institutes run exclusively by
the military. Their scientific status is based on the
military expertise and experience deemed indispensable
for scientific development. As a consequence, the
"civilian layman" is virtually deprived of authority to
speak about military matters. The "scientific" foundation promotes political dependence on military advice.

Second, the "scientific" foundation provides a
reliable tool for explaining what and how much should be
allocated to defense. The needs--or costs--of military
security are not calculated by a few conspiring firebrands, but are based on sound reasoning and "laws."
The "scientific status" and the authority of "laws"
have an important function. As Lider concludes:

> It would seem laws are used as justification of
> policy which has already been carried out,
> especially justification of the continuous increase
> in military power. If such an increase is presented
> as following objective laws, it must be regarded as
> necessary and just. To take a simple example, laws
> such as that of the correlation of forces, of the
> role of armament, of the significance of surprise
> in nuclear war, etc., are presented as a justifi-
> cation of economic and military efforts, and of a
> high degree of readiness for starting military
> operations at any point of time. [63]

Third, the fact that Marxism-Leninism and military
science "both study and investigate the same object"
and "have a common ultimate aim--to prepare the country

and the army for the waging of victorious wars in defense
of the socialist country," [64] justifies this call for an
ever stronger and better defense posture at the political
level as well. This constant strengthening is "dictated
by an objective necessity." [65] A most important
consequence is that the military can postulate some
essential premises which have a direct bearing on their
operational and professional task. They concern military
superiority, an offensive strategy and the full incorpor-
ation of nuclear weapons in the military strategy.

The aim of military superiority is only part of the
overall correlation of forces. The role of the Soviet
Union is to represent and to prove the superiority of
the system. Grechko, more often than not the professional
soldier who readily "militarizes" political-ideological
tenets, asserts that this overall superiority "finds its
concentrated expression primarily in the army, in its
definite socio-political type and combat capabilities." [66]
But even disregarding these extreme views on the need for
a "militarized society," statements such as the following
are no exception: "Until disarmament has been brought
about, the socialist commonwealth is always obligated
to maintain superiority over the imperialists in a
military sense." [67]

Another most important military-strategic premise
stemming from the need to wage "victorious wars" is the
need to plan an offensive [68]. This is a definite
advantage for practically all aspects of military planning
and policy, for attack can be prepared much more readily
than defense. The attacker chooses the means--conven-
tional, nuclear, or a combination of both--the loca-
tion(s)--two, three or more main fronts--and the time and
scope of the assault--ranging from a limited surprise to
a mobilization-under-deception to an all-out attack.
The defender, on the other hand, is unable to foresee
where, when and how a military conflict will start. The
problem of military planning and preparation in a defensive strategy dramatically complicates defense and
deterrence both in theory and in practice [69]. The development of a single, comprehensive strategy is practically
impossible. At most, a number of contingencies based
on various situational factors can be foreseen and
projected as more or less likely occurrences in time of
crises. This is not to say, however, that an offensive
is a simple undertaking or that it is not hampered by
unknown variables. Certainly not. But the military
profession is in a better position to flourish and to
develop a scientific approach when the means of violence
can be organized in an offensive strategy. This is the
case in the Soviet Union, where ideological tenets and
the experience of World War II provide forceful arguments
for never changing this basic point of departure in military strategy.

Recognition of strategic defense as one of the basic
types of strategic operations of the armed forces
in a modern war means recognition of defensive
strategy as a whole--essentially an extension of the
situation at the start of the Great Patriotic War to
modern conditions...
...Strategic defense and then a counteroffensive
under present-day conditions cannot assure the
attainment of these decisive war aims [viz. defeat
of the aggressor]. This does not mean that defense
as a forced, temporary type of troop combat
operation will not have a place in a future war.
Our troops should study and master defense in order
to master all forms of military operations. But
here we are speaking of operational and tactical
defense. Strategic defense and defensive strategy
should be decisively rejected as being extremely
dangerous to the country. [70]

A third premise, one enabling the Soviet military
to actually "think about the unthinkable," rests on the
shared image of the aggressive capitalist who will use
all available means in waging war. War between the two
opposed socio-economic systems will be total in character,
and probably in scope as well [71]. Rather than being
restrained--as are many in the West--by the self-deterring
worry about crossing (first) the socalled "nuclear
threshold," the Soviet military are allowed to incorporate nuclear weapons in their thinking about defense and
deterrence. Their point of departure is rather the need
to deter any conflict, thus increasing the "conflict
threshold." Should an East-West military conflict break
out, then the Soviet armed forces must be prepared to
fight all types of war--conventional, nuclear, limited
and global--and neither party can exercise full control
over the other regarding the use of nuclear weapons.
Both sides can unilaterally cross the "nuclear threshold."
Given the total nature of a clash between the two systems
as well as the recklessness of "capitalism in its final
days," there is a great danger that nuclear weapons will
be employed once the "conflict threshold" has been
crossed [72]. Theories of "nuclear thresholds," of
"graduated" or "flexible response," are rejected by
Soviet military science. The concept of a limited war is
only "one of the methods of preparing an unlimited
nuclear war against the Soviet Union and all the socialist countries." [73]
    Again, war experience is supplemented by ideological
images of the distrustful and aggressive West, both of
which are incentives for the Soviet military to integrate
nuclear weapons in their strategic thinking. The point
here is not to dismiss doubts that also exist in the
Soviet Union about "The Absolute Weapon," as nuclear
weapons have been baptized in the West (see Chapter VII).

The point is to stress the "officially endorsed" opportunity military strategists have in arguing that nuclear weapons should be incorporated in modern strategic thought in spite of the "qualitative" or "revolutionary" change they mean in warfare. Attempts to exempt nuclear weapons from warfare as is done in the West are wrong and should not be repeated in the Soviet Union.

> Unfortunately, erroneous opinions of a similar type now and then appear also in the pages of our press. In this respect, one should point to statements of Comrade A. Bovin on the pages of some periodical publications. Thus, while he correctly confirmed that general nuclear war is unacceptable as a means of achieving a political aim, A. Bovin at the same time tolerates an outstanding methodological error. Criticizing the widely known Clausewitzian formula, the author in a number of his publications for some reason mentions not one word about the Marxist-Leninist definition of war as a continuation of policy and makes no attempt at a scientific analysis of the essence of war. [74]

The question of whether Soviet military and political leaders actually believe in these ideological images goes back to the discussion about the role of ideology in Chapter IV. Soviet military doctrine represents both values and interests, and its role in the political process and in power politics is no different from what is stated there. The argument that "the best way to deter war is to have the best weapons to fight a war" is at once a belief and a slogan protecting the interests of the military. Soviet military are apt to apply such pro-military ideological images to the formulation of military-strategic concepts. It is important to realize that these concepts call for and justify practically unlimited military demands.

Analysis should not stop at this point, however, for concepts and theories are put to the test in the political process. As Holloway rightly asserts,

> ...the study of Soviet policy on the basis of open materials, if it is to contribute to our understanding of how Soviet policy is made and of how the arms race works, must go beyond the analysis of concepts. For policy is the outcome, not of debates about concepts, but of immensely complex political and bureaucratic processes of which those debates are only a part. [75]

INSTITUTIONAL CONGRUENCE OR CONFLICT?

Soviet military doctrine undoubtedly serves the
military as an important consensus-building tool inside
the military institution as well as in their relationship
with the polity. Historical roots, ideological images,
the permitted autonomy of the "scientific" professional
realm, and the tolerated vagueness of the description of
the military right to participate in the national defense
organization reflect the consensual power base the military enjoy in the polity. These phenomena alone seem to
warrant a rejection of Kolkowicz' thesis that Party-military relations are "essentially conflict-prone."

Recognition of a civil-military connection, however,
need not lead to full agreement with Odom's conclusion
that "a more accurate assessment of the institutional
values of the two entities suggests congruence, not
conflict." 76 The Party is no clear entity. Although
many members agree with the basically "conservative-
realist" views of the military and have common interests
with them, Odom's assessment portrays political reality
in too simple a setting:

> The CPSU is not beholden unto corporate military
> interests; rather, it understands military-bureau-
> cratic requisites for ruling the Soviet-Union. It
> is not paying off the military corporate interests
> to get the marshals to behave; rather, it is
> emphasizing military power to cope with political
> realities. The marshals cannot afford the luxury
> of corporate military interests; they are in the
> same political boat with the CPSU. 77

This view disregards the political process, its
complexities and interrelationship with many other
issues, and ignores the directing role of the political
leadership. The latter formulates goals, both new and
old, which may or may not conflict with those of the
marshals. Furthermore, Odom's "institutional congruence
model," as Colton has labelled it, is heavily historical-
causal oriented. The absence of sharp Party-military
conflict in the political process today cannot be
explained by "the historical development of the Russian
Imperial state and the heritage of the multinational
empire it bequeathed the Bolsheviks." 78 One of the
reasons given by Churchward for revising his <u>Contemporary
Soviet Government</u> seems valid and sensible: "I also felt
that very often the focus, and therefore the understanding, of contemporary Soviet politics was damaged
by undue reliance on conclusions drawn from earlier
historical periods." 79

Probing Odom's challenging analysis and its meaning
for the present epoch, it seems useful to distinguish
between different levels of civil-military relations.

154

In Soviet <u>society</u>, the military institution fulfils a
number of tasks that are most useful for the political
regime, and "institutional congruence" at this level is
most forcefully argued by Odom [80]. The interest shared
by the Party and the military in fostering the patriotic-
ideological education of the people has resulted in a
formidable nation-wide youth organization on a military
footing, DOSAAF. The military are present in the schools,
universities and factories and are full-time teachers
during the two to three years of military service [81].
The "glorious armed forces"--it is stressed time and
again--provide a school for ideological training, are
ready to defend Mother Russia with their lives as in the
"Great Patriotic War," and are an example to all through
their selfless attitude to their own work and to society,
e.g., assistance with harvesting [82]. The social status
of the Soviet military seems almost untouchable in a
society where the polity draws heavily on the services
of the military institution [83]. The position of the
military organization in the political system ensures
structural power of which the military are well aware
and which is accompanied by "an unusual degree of ideo-
social consensus." [84] Khrushchev warns in his memoirs:

> We should be careful not to idolize the military.
> Among the military in the socialist countries you
> can find people who tend to regard the defense
> establishment as a higher caste. It is important
> to keep such people in check, to make sure they
> don't exercise too much influence. [85]

At the <u>political level</u>, the military position is
less clear-cut. The higher the level in the hierarchy
and the higher the stakes, the greater the military
dependence on the political process and the authorities
appears to be. Military organizational power in policy
preparation and implementation, however, can scarcely
be underestimated, and is impressive by Western standards.
Military representation and involvement in government
and administration as well as in the defense industry
is on a tremendous scale [86]. These ramifications of
military interests in the vast complex of management and
production undoubtedly constitute a major power base in
the overall defense sector. The military, in particular
the Ministry of Defense and its General Staff, play a
dominant role vis-à-vis other defense-related actors such
as the scientists and industrialists [87]. In spite of
the differences and conflicting parochial interests
that may reduce the operating effectiveness of the
defense actors in the polity, the basic commonality
of interests between the military and others--e.g.,
resource allocation, high status and pay--is likely to
guarantee a firm coalition supporting the military.
However important the organization of the Soviet-

style "Military-Industrial Complex" may be, to understand
Soviet defense policy and military influence it is
essential to examine how this sub-system fits into the
overall political system. Holloway concludes in his
study of Soviet armaments policy:

> The Soviet armaments complex should be seen not as
> a military-industrial complex in the sense of an
> alignment between military and industrial interests,
> but rather as part of a bureaucratic complex in
> which various groups, coalitions and departments
> interact and form alliances in the pursuit of
> particular policies. [88]

As the political process and relevant features of
relations within and between the Central Committee and
the Politburo have been described in Part I, only a few
additional remarks about this most important aspect of
Soviet politics will be required here. The Soviet defense
policy process does not differ significantly from the
observations made there. Thus the conservative minds of
Central Committee members, their resistance to change in
general and to alterations in power positions in particular, and their adherence to ideology as a means of
maintaining and restoring unity and of preserving--the
privileges of--the status-quo all work in favor of military demands and bear a close resemblance to the "military mind." The extremely slow pace of social, economic
and political development and the set-backs in Brezhnev's
foreign policy are no doubt advantageous to the military.
    There is one aspect, however, which is much more
to their advantage than to any other policy elite: the
lack of knowledge of Soviet actors at the level of the
Central Committee regarding the military profession. The
extreme secrecy surrounding defense policy is not only a
disadvantage for Western analysts of Soviet defense
policy; it seems to be even more detrimental to Soviet
decision-making [89]. Political discussion is scarcely
possible in a situation in which the experts enjoy a
virtual monopoly of factual and technical knowledge. A
revealing and frequently cited example of the military
guarding their secrets and, by extention, their professional autonomy, is given by Garthoff, who relates
that in the SALT-I negotiations General Ogarkov did not
wish the characteristics of Soviet weapons to be discussed in front of the Soviet civilian delegates [90].
    The Soviet delegation was led by a deputy Minister
of Foreign Affairs. If relevant information is denied
even to such a high-level official who as a negotiator
clearly requires factual military knowledge, then who
is entitled to it in the Soviet Union? It seems safe
to assume that professional autonomy is carefully
safeguarded up to a very high level in the political
hierarchy. In as far the Central Committee is involved

in defense policy, the military have little to fear. Indeed, should defense issues reach the floor in the Central
Committee, the "congruence" of values and perceptions--in
addition to the power stemming from their recognized
professional status--is likely to aid the military [91].

The top Party leadership is undoubtedly in a position
to be apprised of all information and to call on the
military for any further explanation required [92]. This
group probably includes a few secretaries of the Central
Committee, members of the Military-Industrial Commission
headed by Smirnov, and members of the Defense Council
headed by Brezhnev. Politburo members with no seat on
the Defense Council can also be considered to be well-
informed. The Politburo in plenary session will certainly review the major military projects and plans,
but its discussions are likely to cover the broader--
economic, budgetary, international--considerations, not
primarily military-strategic ones. The detailed knowledge
of military-strategic intricacies needed for participation in deliberations and decisions is the privilege of
only a small minority. The influence of even the inner
circle of defense planners and policy-makers, moreover,
seems to be limited by several factors.

First, the leadership lacks alternative sources of
information and consists of too few persons who are too
busy to make independent inquiries. "This is a group
of perhaps 20 to 25 people with ultimate authority to
make decisions based on narrowly channeled information
from monopolized origins, with limited possibility of
lower-level conflict, feed-back, or competition." [93]

Second, a most important restraint on effective
leadership is the nature of the political leadership
itself. As has been pointed out in Chapters III and IV,
"the character of the leadership is the dominant factor
that determines how the whole system operates." [94]
Brezhnev's failure to establish a strong leadership that
could guide and control the system and further political
development also affected his chances of achieving his
declared goal of saving money for "more constructive"
purposes than defense. Even though Brezhnev and some
Politburo members are in a position to deal with defense
questions, the inherent weaknesses of collective leadership and the growing dependence of the political leadership on the expedient behavior and conservatism of the
sub-top level form a safeguard for the privileged position and nurtured professional autonomy of the military
institution [95].

The foregoing analysis of the "societal imperative"
for the military institution shows how the Soviet system
and polity grant power to the military. They do not
possess much political power beyond their role as
professional advisors and architects of the national
defense, which will be discussed shortly. Soviet military power is dependent on the political process that

first and foremost involves the top leadership and the polity. Moves made by the top leadership that are adverse to military interests cannot be redressed by the military themselves [96], but are dependent on how "various groups, coalitions and departments interact and form alliances in the pursuit of particular policies" (Holloway). The result of this political process may be similar to that of "institutional congruence." The outcome may be a constantly high level of defense spending. If that is the case, the working of the system, economic growth, the international situation and other factors must also be taken into account in determining the extent to which the civilian-political mind matches the military mind.

Were we to stop at this political level, the theory of congruent mind-sets and even that of the "Garrison state" would seem a fairly representative picture of the Soviet political process [97]. However, the most critical part of civil-military relations concerns the political leadership. As already argued, and as will shortly be illustrated in the context of the resource allocation issue, a weak leadership must concede much to political pressures. Yet the Soviet leadership vis-à-vis the military in terms of political power appears to be dominant. Moreover, its policies on some major issues are contrary to military preferences. The weakness of Brezhnev's leadership does not mean that he has not succeeded in slowly but steadily reinforcing the position of the central powers regarding the individual policy elites. Brezhnev's attempt to improve the political system and Party rule and to delineate more clearly the responsibilities and rights of both Party and policy elite also affected civil-military arrangements. His Ideal, aimed at the best use of expertise and a stronger commitment of the sub-system leaders in the phase of policy implementation while reserving the right to direct and to make policy, was also applied to the military sector and resulted in some important institutional and personnel changes.

Grechko's elevation to the Politburo as a voting member in 1973 certainly implied a stronger commitment to the current policy. It is even likely that Grechko was supposed to serve in his organization as an interpreter and moderator of the proposed policy changes. If so, we cannot but conclude that the Minister of Defense failed, for he has unabatedly continued to advocate the views and interests of his military "constituency," as is evident from his words following upon an obligatory, positive assessment of Brezhnev's peace efforts:

> The danger of war remains a grim reality of our times. Under these conditions the Party and the Soviet Government proceed as before from the

inseparability of the tasks of strengthening peace
and national defense. [98]

Grechko's statements about the absolute priority
of defense—politically, socially and economically—also
reflect the military's resistance to the leadership's
policy of economizing and increasing efficiency.
According to one Western observer, the political leadership may have been very close to the decision to remove
Grechko from the Ministry of Defense shortly before his
death in April, 1976 [99]. We shall never know, but events
after his death support such speculation. The political
leadership seized the opportunity and within a matter
of days appointed Ustinov as the new Minister of Defense.
Such speed had not been possible in 1967, when Grechko
was reportedly in competition with Ustinov and won the
contest only after three weeks of deliberations. In 1976,
an apparently more determined leadership lost no time in
choosing a civilian, the first since Bulganin left this
post in 1955. This was not the only public demonstration
of civilian leadership in the armed forces. In May and
July, the promotion of Brezhnev respectively Ustinov
as Marshal of the Soviet Union followed [100]. It was also
in 1976 that the world learned about the existence of the
Defense Council, the highest body directing and supervising all defense activities, and that its head, de
facto Supreme Commander of the Soviet armed forces, was
General Secretary Brezhnev [101]. In the new Constitution
of 1977, moreover, this institutional arrangement was
legally established and the Council's composition was
placed in the hands of the Presidium of the Supreme
Soviet (Art. 121 sub 14).
Finally, the changed positions of Kulikov and
Ogarkov—both promoted to Marshal of the Soviet Union
in January 1977—within a few months after Grechko's
death should not remain unnoticed. Kulikov, Chief of the
General Staff since 1971, and Ogarkov, first deputy of
the Chief of the General Staff since 1968, are both
highly-respected professional military, which is clearly
reflected in their successful careers. Kulikov, who
by-passed his colleagues, including Ogarkov, when he was
transferred as commander of the Soviet forces in the
GDR to the General Staff in 1971, must be considered to
have been a close ally of Grechko's. In his writings
and speeches he displays the same demanding and
traditional-military stand. This may have prompted the
political leadership to transfer him to a politically
less influential post and to make use of his professional
skills by giving him the command of the Warsaw Pact
forces with the rank of Marshal. Ogarkov, as will be
shown later, seems to be more in agreement with the political leaders than Kulikov—or at least is more willing
to say so. He publicly recognizes the need for moderation given the limited resources and his attention and

efforts are indeed directed to greater efficiency in the military organization. Ogarkov's experience as a member of the SALT delegation has also enabled him to approach defense and security problems from a more international and a less "narrowly departmental" viewpoint.

To conclude, Soviet civil-military relations are different at the societal and political levels. Whereas a very high degree of "identification" occurs at the first level, "professionalism" and military dependence on political leaders characterize the latter. The degree of "congruence" decreases and institutional conflict and disagreement may increase at the higher political level.

ALTERNATIVE RELATIONS BETWEEN THE MILITARY AND SOCIETY [102]		
Level of Interaction	Level of Congruence	
	Low	High
Low	Insulation	Self-sufficiency
High	Professionalism	Identification

Here the relationship is best decribed with the aid of Colton's "participatory model." [103] In the event of conflicting views, the Soviet political leadership proceeds to the political "insulation" of the military, while preserving their professional status. According to Huntington's scheme, as applied here, Brezhnev's foreign policy moved civil-military relations towards a "lower level of congruence." His foreign policy successes were a threat because of the probable loss of "identification" with the "military mind," especially if this were to lead to second thoughts among other policy elites about military spending. However, as we have seen, detente did not last long enough to bear on the minds of the "Little Stalins." Moreover, as will be shown at the conclusion of this chapter, institutional congruence with regard to the issue of shifting resources away from military to more "constructive purposes" is an extremely strong force in favor of the military.

THE RESOURCE ALLOCATION ISSUE

By the end of the 1960's and well into the 1970's one of the main issues at stake was where to find the money for agricultural development. As argued before, the people's well-being was something the political leadership could not afford to ignore. Moreover, the uprising in Poland in December, 1970 must have given a sense of urgency to the issue even for some downright "firebrands."

The direct link between agriculture and material well-being was clear and recognized by all political leaders. It was also apparent that the "constructive purposes" to which Brezhnev referred related above all to agriculture, a constant source of anxiety in the Soviet economy. The 9th Five-Year Plan reserved about one-third of the total investment sum for agriculture-- 157.9 billion of about 500 billion rubles, an increase of about 56% over the previous plan [104] --and the privileged sectors of heavy and defense industry were to foot the bill, or were expected to do so. This came as a surprise, the more so in that it was the General Secretary who introduced and led the campaign. For Brezhnev's reputation was that of a reliable ally of the defense sector, and throughout his career he had never risked his neck. An able and shrewd politician, he was often seen as an interest broker, as someone who would certainly not be the consumer spokesman vis-à-vis the sector of traditional power. In June 1970, for example, Brezhnev was still reassuring this sector that the new Five-Year Plan

> ...envisages further sizable growth in industry, primarily in those branches that produce the means of production, ensure the economy's power-engineering base and determine scientific and technical progress. [105]

However, in 1970 Brezhnev was no doubt aware that "fundamental changes" were planned with a view to developing the consumer sector in industry ("Group B") "at increasing preferential rates compared with Group A" (heavy industry) [106]. I. Aleksandrov, writing in Kommunist of the Armed Forces, August, 1970, appeared to be very well informed about the new quinquennial investment in agriculture [107]. It is therefore quite likely that basic agreement had been reached at the July Plenum of the Central Committee, where agriculture was the main subject, or even earlier, at the December Plenum [108]. A decision to invest huge sums in agriculture is obviously not one the political leadership would have taken overnight. Nor was the apparent intention to extract at least part of the money from the military easy to put into practice. On the contrary, resource allocation was

and has remained a contested, far from settled issue [109].
For example, Kotov reported in November, 1971 that the
Central Committee Plenum had "basically" (not "fully")
approved the "drafts" for economic development.

As so often, the basic agreement reached did not
silence the opposition and the resulting compromise left
many loopholes intact. The prospect of successful
implementation and of a boost in agricultural output--"an
important prerequisite" for the growth of the consumption
fund--was to a great extent dependent on the good faith
and cooperation of all actors--to say nothing of good
weather. Characteristic of the "deal" was that all
sectors were able to claim victory. The "agriculture
lobby"--Brezhnev, Polyanski, Kulakov--had won: huge sums
would flow into agriculture, whose structure and organization would continue to be based on ideological and
agro-industrial considerations rather than on a peasant
mentality and economic criteria. The "consumer lobby"--
Kosygin, Podgorny--had taken its share: the growth rate
of the consumption fund was to be roughly 10% higher than
that of the investment fund and a more balanced economic
development would ensue. Finally, the "status-quo lobby"
could point out that in practice little had been conceded.

Kotov's explanation--like I. Aleksandrov's--in a
military publication is illustrative. He maintained that
the "structural and fundamental changes" were essential
to ensure a more balanced economic development, which in
turn was conducive to economic growth. But he hastily
added:

> Of course, this does not negate the effect of the
> economic law regarding the priority growth of the
> means of production (subdivision one) compared with
> the growth rates of consumer goods (subdivision two).
> These subdivisions characterize social production
> as a whole. They must not be identified, as some-
> times happens in speeches and even in the press,
> with groups A and B in industry. The changes taking
> place in the correlation between the latter groups
> do not mean that the increasing preferential
> (priority) growth of the means of production has
> ceased to be an economic law of expanded repro-
> duction. [110] (Emphasis added)

The changes in industry--consumer versus heavy
branches--did not affect the basic rule that "the material
and technical base of communism"--that is, the means of
production--had to be strengthened. Like I. Aleksandrov,
who stated that agriculture investments were concentrated
in "technical re-equipping" and "mechanization," Kotov
emphatically reassured the producers of the means of
production that the main investments in fact remained
unchanged. The socialist economy

162

...demands high rates for the production of the machinery and equipment necessary for <u>all sectors</u> of the national economy. At present there is an intensive process to equip agriculture technically. Capacities in the light and food industries and in branches of the services sphere are increasing at high rates. Hence the need for the priority development of the means of production. That is, subdivision one.

Thus the heavy-industrialists and the military did not have to worry immediately. The Soviet consumer had first to await production of the necessary machinery before the extended production of consumer goods could start. The prospects for the consumer were even bleaker, moreover, when the organization of production was taken into account. For the powerful industrial "Group A" was entrusted with the direct production of consumer goods, the output of which was scheduled in the Five-Year Plan to be twice that of the previous plan 112. There was little doubt about how the heavy industry managers would fix their priorities if shortages occurred or deadlines could not be met. Not surprisingly, complaints appeared in the Soviet press about the non-fulfilment of the plan for consumer goods. The ministries responsible for military production--including the Ministry of Tractor and Agricultural Machine Building 113 --and the defense industry, which had been accorded prominence in expanding consumer goods production in the Ninth Five-Year Plan 114, had little to fear as long as they were so deeply involved in the implementation of such "structural and fundamental changes."

Notwithstanding the limited threat to the predominant position of heavy and defense industry, changes--no matter how slight--were important and had to be warranted. It was hardly coincidental that so strong an appeal and such extensive explanations should appear in the military press. However, an appeal was not an order and vague compromise left room for maneuver. Opponents could ignore and even publicly contradict the proposed changes. For example, as Kotov noted, it was not always practice to distinguish between the subdivisions and industrial groups; instead, the distinction could be blurred. The Minister of Defense (Grechko) commented on the Five-Year Plan as if no change had occurred. Even though he referred specifically to the importance of "agriculture and the related sectors," he left no doubt about the right way to "improve the industrial base for developing the socialist economy."

Here, high development rates will be maintained for heavy industry, which is the foundation of the economic and defense might of the state and the basis for the further growth of national prosperity. 115

Evidence that the proposed changes were taken
seriously was provided by the First Deputy Chairman of
Gosplan, Sokolov, and the Minister of Defense Industry,
Zverev. The former not only strongly defended the
investments in agriculture, but took the offensive by
arguing that agricultural investment returns were certainly not as bad as the military and industrialists
wished the leadership to believe [116]. Zverev cited
numerous examples to prove how efficiently consumer rubles
could be used in the defense industry. Returns in sectors like drilling, railroad truck construction, power
production, or computer and automated systems technology
were even claimed to be very high. Moreover, the technological spin-off in the civilian economy was important
and should be taken into account. Finally, Zverev
claimed that the decision to raise the production of
consumer goods had "found a warm response among the working people of the defense industry" and that in 1971
"our sector will produce consumer articles worth 10 million rubles above the plan." [117] The message is clear.
At the same time, the outspoken advocacy of the Minister
of Defense Industry gave further credibility to the
genuineness of the policy plans proposed at the XXIV
Party Congress [118].

As outlined in the foregoing, the political leadership was unable to carry out these plans and the higher
consumer investments were never realized during the
Ninth FYP [119]. The attempt to reallocate resources
suffered the same fate for much the same reason: the
powerlessness of the political (collective) leadership
vis-à-vis established preferences and priorities. The
harvest disaster of 1972 was an additional setback for
agriculture and consumer interests, but this cannot be
called a decisive factor. The opposition proved to be
too strong, and in December, 1974 the Central Committee
endorsed the widespread call for "back to normal." The
official reversal of investment priority in favor of
"Group A" was a highly dramatic act of the XXV Party
Congress in 1976. "Institutional congruence" between
the Party and the military was largely responsible
for a victory which the military themselves had not been
at pains to bring about. They were not the shock forces
in the political struggle but rather the rear-guard
protecting the main body. The political strategists were
ignored by the political troops, who followed the familiar traditional patterns and refused new methods of
combat.

The implications for East-West relations were that
the Soviet military build-up was not limited by unilateral budgetary restraints. In any event, the period of
detente was too short to bring about visible changes in
Soviet weapons procurement. The set-backs in detente
with the West damaged Brezhnev's plans, but as far as the
resource allocation issue was concerned, it seems that

the "security-productionist-ideological grouping"
(Aspaturian) did not really need the deterioration in
East-West relations to repel the modest attack on its
privileges. The political "solution" was found during
the heyday of detente, and was reinforced rather than
presented by the deteriorating East-West relations. The
Soviet polity acted as it would probably have acted
anyway, and repulsed the attempt to reallocate a modest
part of its financial resources.

6
Civil-Military Relations:
The "Functional Imperative"

INTRODUCTION

During the 1970's Western, and in particular American, interest in Soviet military strategy grew immensely. Whereas in 1975 William Scott [1] may have had reason to complain about too little attention being paid to Soviet military theory, this gap was increasingly bridged and virtually filled by an avalanche of publications during the second half on the 1970's. Of course, detente and the SALT process were accountable for the general upswing of East-West and area studies. But also the important change from American strategic superiority to nuclear parity between the superpowers, and especially the fear that the continuing military build-up would lead to Soviet strategic superiority, were and continue to be phenomena that explain the increased interest in and, above all, the intense reaction to Soviet military strategy, primarily among conservatives in the United States [2].

Concern about Western security was not unfounded given the growing Soviet capabilities. The fourth generation ICBMs--SS-17, SS-18 and SS-19--deployed since 1975, were seen as a direct threat to the American land-based systems. By 1983, their accuracy will have been sufficiently increased to put, in theory, 90 per cent of the Minutemen at risk--and that with only a limited number of their total [3].

The vulnerability of the American ICBMs dramatically affected the nuclear guarantee for Western Europe, and, to make things worse, here, too, the balance shifted steadily in favor of the Soviet Union. In conventional forces, the Soviet Union had enjoyed numerical superiority since the Second World War; in the field of the theater-nuclear forces she appeared to be gaining the upper-hand as well.

"Essential equivalence" [4] allows for some imbalance in one of the elements of the Triad--e.g., conventional forces--if this can be redressed by an advantage in another element--e.g., strategic forces. It was, however, the Soviet strengthening "across the board" that under-mined essential equivalence and, consequently, the credibility of the Western deterrent and defensive capa-bility. Not one, but all elements of the Triad--stra-tegic, theater-nuclear and conventional--were shifting in favor of the Soviet Union. If numerical superiority had not yet been attained in all areas, it was felt to be a matter of time before this happened. Similar concerns were expressed about the expansion of the Soviet Navy, ever more capable of threatening NATO lines of communi-cations and of projecting Soviet power ashore both within and outside NATO's area of direct defense [5].

In general, as Soviet military capabilities increas-ingly matched the doctrinal tenets of superiority, and an offensive, war-fighting posture emerged ever more clearly, fears--and for some the conviction--grew that Soviet military strategy equalled political strategy [6]. Inten-tions were read from military capabilities, and it was argued that the Soviet military power was designed not only for influence and expansion in the world but also for direct use in East-West crises in which vital interests or state security were involved [7]. These sentiments were bound to affect the political arena.

For example, Secretary of Defense Brown explained and justified the "countervailing strategy" prescribed by Carter's "Presidential Directive No 59" as follows [8]:

> This is not a first strike strategy. We are talking about what we could and (depending on the nature of a Soviet attack) would do in response to a Soviet attack. Nothing in the policy comtemplates that nuclear war can be a deliberate instrument of achieving our national security goals, because it cannot be. But we cannot afford the risk that the Soviet leadership might entertain the illusion that nuclear war could be an option--or its threat a means of coercion--for them...

> The increase in Soviet strategic capability over the past decade, and our concern that the Soviets may not believe that nuclear war is unwinnable, dictate a United States need for more--and more selective--retaliatory options. [9] (Emphasis added)

The strategy formulated by the Carter Administration was not new; rather, it was an extension and evolution of the strategic philosophy originated back in the early 1960's. Brown rightly points to his predecessors McNamara and Schlesinger when he concludes that "the United States has never had a doctrine based simply and solely on reflective, massive attacks on Soviet cities. Instead, we have always planned more selectively (options limiting urban-industrial damage) and more comprehensively

(a range of military targets)." [10]
    Yet, this evolutionary development of strategic
thought had reached the point that the traditional
politically rather than militarily inspired view that "if
the deterrence has to be used, it will have failed" had
been left behind [11]. The "countervailing strategy" was
the most explicit Western departure from the thesis of
"The Absolute Weapon" and the engrained reluctance to
"think about the unthinkable." Western strategists had
gradually accepted and adopted the Soviet military view
in that deterrence equals defense, which McGwire
pointedly characterizes and distinguishes from the
deterrence-only view by the phrase should war come,
defense of the Soviet Union "will have failed only if her
armed forces are unable to recover and achieve final
victory." [12] Thirty-five years of Western (American)
thinking about nuclear weapons shows a transition from
"Massive Retaliation," to a more "graduated" and "flexible
response" which was extended by strategic "Limited Nuclear
Options" in 1974, and finally to strategic and theater
"Selective Employment Options" whose credibility is still
ultimately founded on a capability of massive retaliation,
presently known as "General Nuclear Response." [13] In
short, the United States has gradually adopted a
nuclear strategy that recognizes the fact that deterrence
is and can only be based on military means meeting war-
fighting requirements. There are in the Alliance today
however serious doubts about the extent to which the
American administration seeks to strengthen security by a
dramatic military build-up and a nuclear "war-fighting"
posture.
    To deter someone, obviously, is a unilateral affair.
There is no such thing as "mutual deterrence." Rather,
there may be "mutuality" in the doctrine, in the weapons
systems and in their deployment by two opposing parties.
If so, one can speak of unilateral deterrence and mutual
stability, the latter being greatly subject to the success
of arms control (Chapter VII); if not, the situation can
arise in which one party thinks it can deter certain
actions of the other, while in reality it lacks the military means. Thus, a predominant "countervalue" or
"deterrence by punishment" posture cannot be maintained
in the face of a purely "counterforce" or "deterrence
by denial" capacity. During the 1960's and 1970's the
Soviet Union corrected its strategic inferiority and
established unilateral deterrence, imposing it as a firm
reality on the West. It is "ironic," indeed, as Erickson
finds, that

    ...while we have pressed to "educate" the Soviets to
    the facts of nuclear life, it may well be that we
    shall have to do some learning and consider what is
    involved in effective unilateral deterrence. We may
    learn that it is not the contradiction in terms that

168

some believe it to be--or that it is less of a contradiction than "mutual deterrence," which is becoming badly frayed at the edges. [14] (Emphasis added)

"Mutual Assured Destruction" has long been the basis of the American deterrent. However, if the accuracy of Soviet ICBMs were to increase, and the Soviet Union were to have a number of selective options at her disposal, then, so asked President Nixon in 1970: "Should a President in the event of a nuclear attack be left with the single option of ordering the mass destruction of enemy civilians, in the face of the certainty that it would be followed by the mass slaughter of Americans?" [15]

Schlesinger's answer in 1974 in the face of the upcoming generation of Soviet MIRVed ICBMs was negative [16]. He asked for deployment of the 335 kt, Mark 12 A warhead on 300 Minutemen III in order to more flexibly put at risk about half of the Soviet hardened ICBM silos. Moreover, 400 Poseidon SLBM warheads were assigned to SACEUR in an attempt to demonstrate NATO's "strategic unity" and American willingness to extend strategic "Limited Nuclear Options" to the European theater. The "Countervailing Strategy" took this a firm step further by the employment of a most flexible posture for countering a wide range of Soviet options.

Among the many questions about the validity of American nuclear deterrence theory--its deductive nature, "ethnocentric" restraints and biases, arguable rationality, limitations of time, and knowledge of one's own military-technological capacity and strategic policies--[17] Soviet military theory and practice are crucial ones. Some basic assumptions of the countervailing strategy are based on an interpretation of Soviet military professionalism. Soviet military writings and operational activities are used as indicators of, and, most importantly, as a justification for, Western defense measures. It is worth to note that under the present administration doubts about Soviet adherence to a war-fighting and war-winning strategy or even doctrine have given way to rather affirmative statements in this respect.

However, military strategic theory, even if it were one single entity agreed upon by all the military, and military capabilities, even if the missions assigned to them were cristal-clear, are important to but insufficient for an understanding of Soviet security policy and cannot be relied upon in formulating Western security policy. The growth of Soviet military power and the development of strategy must be seen in historical, international-political and domestic perspective.

169

THE DOCTRINE PUT INTO PRACTICE

Khrushchev's strategic design--see the next section--
certainly determined the direction of the Soviet defense
posture during the 1960's. But domestic and international
factors, rather than his theory and the political-military
debate generated by his ideas, were responsible for the
lightning pace of the military build-up and its generous
financial foundation. The realization of a military
superpower requires more than a theoretical design and the
victory of a military rationale over Khrushchev's largely
political viewpoint.

The basis for today's tremendous Soviet military
power was to a great extent laid during the early 1960's.
In spite of Khrushchev's efforts to reduce military
expenditure the defense budget was reviewed in 1961 and
sharply increased--officially--from 11.9 to 16 per cent
of the total state expenditures. This decision was
prompted mainly by international events, above all
Kennedy's new budget and military-strategic plans.
Regardless of Khrushchev's political position at the time,
the Kremlin leaders would probably still have decided not
to further relax Soviet military efforts [18]. The drastic
expansion of American strategic procurements would have
soon made clear the fact that the Soviet Union was fated
to hold an inferior position for years to come. The last
bit of credibility for Khrushchev's "minimum deterrent"
was erased. One consequence was the substantial increase
in funding for Soviet military development [19].

Initially, Khrushchev's successors decreased the
military budget somewhat, and strategic-weapons procurements proceeded at the same slow pace. During the period
1964-1966 the ICBM force increased only from 200 to 300
launchers, allowing the United States at that point a
three-to-one missile lead. The Soviet Union was to
suddenly produce a tremendous output and about double her
ICBM strength in 1967. Why such a dramatic departure and
why after only two years of the new regime's rule?

First, and quite importantly, the Soviet Union was
not able technically to build a reliable second-strike
force until the mid-1960's [20]. Khrushchev had not only
bluffed about the number of missiles available to
retaliate to an American first attack, he had also gross-
ly exaggerated--or been too optimistic about a swift
improvement in--missile performance. The first-generation
missiles showed technical and operational shortcomings
that considerably diminished their chances of survival.
In order to build a credible deterrent, no matter what
its size, the Soviets would first have to improve their
missiles. The expensive and very frequent fuel changes
that were needed, the long preparation time, the
vulnerability of above-ground installations, and their
limited accuracy offered reasons enough to delay large-
scale production, and remedying these faults turned out

to be a time-consuming operation. In the meantime, the
Cuban adventure in 1962 revealed Soviet concerns about the
lack of credibility of their existing deterrent. By
placing some of the redundant European medium-range
missiles in Cuba, Khrushchev would have substantially
enhanced Soviet capabilities vis-à-vis the United States.
This strategic and economic short-cut failed, however,
demonstrating instead the sad reality of the strategic
balance. The Soviet Union had to await the necessary
improvements before she could deploy a credible second-
strike force.

The slow Soviet quantitive growth until 1967
reflected priority concentration on the development
of second-strike characteristics (hardened silos,
mobile launching pads, initial ABM endeavours, etc).
The consequent effecting of strike survival
expectations mitigated Soviet vulnerability, and
gave her a security she had not possessed since
the war. 21

Secondly, the technical obstacles being removed, the
new leaders who came into power in 1964 had to make the
political decision. To be sure, during their first years
military insistence on "at least parity" with the United
States intensified, but the Brezhnev-Kosygin regime
had different priorities, notably agriculture and consumer
improvements. According to Erickson, Brezhnev reassured
the military in early 1965 that the leadership was
interested in restoring Soviet credibility through an
effective offensive-defensive build-up, but that such an
endeavour must be a long-term, disciplined and efficiently
conducted effort, unlike Khrushchev's vascillation. In
fact, the military were asked to recommend a strategy,
undoubtedly one aimed at strategic equality 22. But the
ultimate decision would only be taken after the leadership had settled down and agreed among themselves on a
number of issues.
Thirdly, during the same period, Soviet attitudes
towards the United States became more hostile, primarily
because of the ever-deeper American involvement in
Vietnam. This is not to say that any bilateral arrangement concerning the strategic balance would otherwise
have been more likely. The obviously inferior Soviet
position itself precluded any arms negotiations with the
United States. It is quite possible that this clear
inferiority in itself helped to convince the leadership
that it must set high strategic goals and that the
Vietnam War was only used as an excuse. But as Zimmerman
outlines in detail, a more traditional, harder line
dominated the domestic scene during 1966-1967, replacing
the post-Cuban, moderate course of Khrushchev's last
years. Several groups of interested parties, among them
the military, found mutual support in an anti-American

policy. "For them, the war in Vietnam was not an isolated event, but evidence that the United States confronted Soviet interests in revolution in every corner of the globe." [23]

In other words, during these years a number of elements dovetailed, enhancing the desire for capabilities enabling a self-reliant, independent foreign policy vis-à-vis the capitalist superpower. As yet the Soviet Union was no more than a continental power and had only required the potential status of a superpower, but the decision to match American strategic power was apparently made in 1966 [24]. The foremost priority given to the build-up of the ICBM force resulted in numerical parity with the United States in 1969. The enormous output slowed only after numerical superiority was established and the prospect of a SALT ceiling had become clear.

As to the Submarine Launched Ballistic Missiles (SLBM), a definite acceleration in deployment began in 1969. Land-based missiles had previously been given priority, but an awareness of their vulnerability as well as a mastering of the technology necessary to build long-range SLBMs in larger submarines led the Soviet Union to base a greater part of her deterrent in the high seas [25]. In 1969, the first Y-class submarines became operational; these had sixteen tubes, instead of the three in the previous types, each tube containing the 1750-mile-range SS-N-6 that replaced a far shorter-range missile. In 1972, this capacity was again improved with the SS-N-8 which exceeded a range of 4000 miles and allowed the Soviet Union still wider geographic options to strike from. The tremendous production of submarines-- eight to ten yearly, each equipped with twelve to sixteen SLBMs--simply erased the inferior ratio with the United States and brought "at least parity" in only four to five years. This constituted a revival of the early 1960's emphasis on the increased role of submarines and a consistent implementation of the strategic design regarding submarines as a minimally vulnerable deterrent.

The SALT-I Interim Agreement of 1972 sealed the established strategic parity, although qualitative differences existed which had to be taken into account. The larger numbers for the Soviet Union, however, were not unacceptable for the United States, since the Agreement would be reviewed in five years and no serious imbalance was anticipated in that period. Thus, for five years the United States accepted numerical inferiority in ICBM/SLBM launchers that were superior due to the acquired MIRV technology [26].

Important as SALT-I was, the omission of current technological developments dramatically undermined its military significance. "In military terms," the SALT agreement only confirmed existing developmental trends [27]. Indeed, the movement away from quantitative competition was well underway at the time of SALT-I.

Most obvious was the MIRV technology that enabled each party a multiplication of targets without any increase in the number of launchers, the very item of strategic weaponry limited by SALT-I. By the time the Interim Agreement was to expire, the United States would achieve the capability of striking about 7,700 separate targets with its missile forces and another 6,000 with its strategic bomber forces. These prospects were not unknown in 1972. On the contrary, they formed the very motivation for American military planners to go along with SALT-I. American MIRVs were fully tested and ready for deployment. Even though a major reason for MIRVed missiles had basically disappeared with the conclusion of the ABM Treaty which assured penetration of offensive missiles, the United States Joint Chiefs of Staff insisted on MIRV deployment. At the same time, their position was considerably strengthened by the Soviet refusal until late 1974 to cover MIRVs.

On the Soviet side, MIRV systems had not been tested before the Moscow summit, and a ban on this technology was, therefore, highly unlikely. MIRV technology might not have been developed at all had SALT started before the American tests in 1968, but the Soviet Union was definitely unwilling to grant permanently to the United States this technological inequity 28.

The Soviet Union started MIRV-tests in 1972-1973 for three new ICBMs, SS-17, SS-18 and SS-19. All three were deployed in 1975, and the continuing test program led to marked improvements in missile accuracy. When these new systems were fully deployed, the IISS concluded as early as 1974, "the Soviet ICBM throw-weight would increase from the present 6-7 million pounds to 10-12 million pounds and would be able to deliver some 7000 separately-targeted warheads in the MT-range." 29

TABLE V: FOURTH GENERATION SOVIET ICBMs 30)									
	SS-17			SS-18				SS-19		
	MOD 1	MOD 2	MOD 3	MOD 1	MOD 2	MOD 3	MOD 4	MOD 1	MOD 2	MOD 3
MIRV	4	1	4	1	8-10	1	10	6	1	6
MT	0.75	3.6	0.75	24	0.55 0.8	20	0.5	0.55	4.3	0.55
CEP (NM)	0.24	0.23	0.24	0.23	0.23	0.19	0.14	0.19	0.21	0.14
RANGE (KM)	10,000	11,000	10,000	12,000	11,000	16,000	10,000	9,550	10,100	9,550
NUMBER	150			308				300		

At sea, the Soviet Union, by the strengthening of
her surface fleet, had come increasingly to challenge
American world-wide naval dominance. In spite of the
earlier Khrushchev-inspired feelings that surface ships
were outdated and of no use except for an expensive
showing of the flag, and despite the actual priority
given to submarines, the fleet had grown considerably
and enhanced Soviet military sea-power [31]. But one should
look for the significance of its expansion in a peacetime
rather than wartime role. Of course, its growth and
qualitative--nuclearized--improvements actually mean
increased military power in an armed conflict, but, unlike
other forces, the Navy can be used everywhere in peace-
time, indeed "show the flag." [32] Apart from the felt need
in the past for distant, military support, the enlarged
"reach" of influence symbolized by this fleet enhanced the
perceived status and role of the Soviet Union as an
emerging superpower. The expansion of the Navy served
Soviet military, political and deterrent capabilities and
was to bring the Soviet Union on an equal footing with
her rival in all these respects.

Admiral of the Fleet of the Soviet Union Gorshkov
published a series of articles in 1972 in which he
described these tasks, which were not in themselves new
but which had only recently become feasible for the
Soviet Navy [33]. He assessed, of course, the significance
of submarines but also stressed the need for surface
ships, therewith indicating his desire for a more
"balanced," general-purpose Navy. Gorshkov explicitly
pointed out a number of reasons why the Soviet Union
should be a mighty sea-power--the continuation of a long
tradition, the contribution to Soviet prestige, the role
as counterweight to American aggression, the advantageous
use in the past of imperialist sea-power, the protection
of the merchant and fishing fleet and in turn their
potential role in the defense of the country, and so
forth. As in other cases, Khrushchev's one-track
approach was not completely rejected but was complemented:
the priority of submarines was maintained, but, as soon
as circumstances would allow, the albeit suppressed but
not absent interests in a multi-purpose Navy would
resurface.

> We, while giving priority to the development of
> submarine forces, believe that we have a need not
> only for submarines, but also for various types of
> surface ships. The latter, in addition to giving
> combat stability to the submarines, are intended to
> accomplish a wide range of missions both in peacetime
> and in war. [34]

The building of two aircraft carriers in the 1970's
and the introduction of new equipment below the high-
strategic level certainly corresponded with Admiral

174

Gorshkov's design for the Navy. This build-up of both submarine and surface strength suggests a departure from Soviet "defensive naval traditions" towards the deployment of a "truly high-seas navy for operation anywhere." 35
   Gorshkov would repeat his basic arguments in The Sea Power of the State (1976), but would also add to the Navy's role. For example, he no longer confined the task of the Navy to sea denial, offensive strategic (second-strike) missions and disruption of NATO's lines of communication, but stressed Anti-Submarine Warfare (ASW) and found a new war-fighting role in the "theater of military operations" (TVD) 36, the "Fleet against Shore." Whereas the naval battlefield had traditionally been a separate one, the Navy should now assume in-theater responsibilities.

   Today, a fleet operating against the shore is able not only to solve the tasks connected with terri- torial changes but to directly influence the course and even outcome of a war. In this connection the operations of a fleet against the shore have assumed paramount importance in armed conflict at sea, governing the technical policy of building a fleet and the development of naval art. Confirmation of this is that in the USA atomic-powered missile submarines are assigned to the strategic forces and all other ships to the general-purpose forces. 37

   However, Gorshkov was speaking not so much about strategic, retaliatory missions but at the expansion of the operational war-fighting role of naval forces.

   Thus, the traditional operations of fleet against fleet which, since ancient times, have been characteristic of the struggle against sea communi- cations of the opposing sides, are now being used in a new, decisive sphere--operations of a fleet against the shore. This trend in the operational and strategic use of the fleet is becoming increas- ingly prominent and assuming the features of the main field of operations of a fleet, governing all others at all operational levels. 38 (Emphasis added)

   This leads us to the Soviet military effort in the European theater, first of all to her nuclear forces. In Tables VI, VII and VIII different categories of Theater Nuclear Forces (TNF) for NATO and the Soviet Union are given. Weapons systems covered by SALT agreements are excluded, but French and British systems are counted in order to present a more complete picture of the nuclear balance in Europe. An estimate of systems targeted against China is, in a number of cases, subtracted from the total Soviet inventory. It must be borne in mind that the figures by no means represent an exact picture.

175

	NATO					
SYSTEM	TYPE	IOC a)	RANGE (KM)	NUMBER OPERATIONAL	ESTIMATED NUMBER AVAILABLE FOR NUCLEAR ROLE IN EUROPE	
					PERCENTAGE	NUMBER
A I R C R A F T	F-111 E/F	1969	2000	156	100 %	156
	FB-111 A b)	1969	2000	66	100 %	66?
	VULCAN B 2 c)	1960	3000	48	100 %	48
	BUCCANEER S 2 d)	1962	1500	62	100 %	62
	MIRAGE IV A (FR)	1964	1200	37	100%	37
M I S S I L E	SSBS S2/S3 (FR)	1971/ 1980	3000	18	100%	18

TABLE VI: NUCLEAR AND DUAL-CAPABLE DELIVERY VEHICLES OF GROUND AND AIR FORCES HAVING A RANGE OF 1000 KM OR MORE

a) Initial Operational Capability
b) Based in the United States. FB-111 carry 'Short-range attack missiles' (SRAM) with a range of 160 km
c) This UK bomber will be replaced by Tornado fighter-bomber with a shorter range
d) UK medium-range bomber
e) These medium-bombers can launch dual-capable ALCMs of the following types: AS-2 (range 40-185 km), AS-4 (range 300-450 km), AS-5 (range 150 km) and AS-6 (range about 600 km)

Sources: see General author's note, p. 242

176

WARSAW PACT					
ESTIMATED NUMBER AVAILABLE FOR NUCLEAR ROLE IN EUROPE		NUMBER OPERATIONAL	RANGE (KM)	IOC	TYPE
NUMBER	PERCENTAGE				
170	80	215	2500	1955	TU-16 BADGER C/G e)
100	80	125	2750	1962	TU-22 BLINDER B e)
72	80	90	4000^{+}	1974	TU-22 M BACKFIRE B e)
160	50	320	1750	1974	SU-19 FENCER
180-240	60 - 80	300	1900	1959	SS-4
			3500	1961	SS-5
168	60	280	4000^{+}	1977	SS-20

SYSTEM	TYPE	IOC a)	RANGE (KM)	NUMBER OPERATIONAL	ESTIMATED NUMBER AVAILABLE FOR NUCLEAR ROLE IN EUROPE	
					PERCENTAGE	NUMBER
A I R C R A F T	A-6E INTRUDER b)	1963	2000	120		20-70
	A-7E CORSAIR c)	1970	850	244		48-168
	F-UK PHANTOM d)	1966	1000	14	100 % ?	14?
	ETENDARD IV M (FR)	1974	1000	48	100 %	48
S L B M s	POLARIS A3	1969	4500	64	100 %	64
	M-20 (FR)	1973	4500	80	100 %	80
S L C M s (Range more than 50 KM)						

TABLE VII. MARITIME NUCLEAR AND DUAL-CAPABLE WEAPONS SYSTEMS

a) Initial Operational Capability
b) Dual-capable strike aircraft; ten A-6Es on each American carrier
c) Dual-capable attack aircraft; 24 Corsairs on each carrier
d) Dual-capable aircraft, based in UK. Nuclear role is uncertain
e) See footnote e) of TABLE VI
f) SS-N-3 deployed on Echo II, Juliet and Whiskey class submarines and Kresta I and Kynda surface ships
   SS-N-12, main weapon system of Kuril class aircraft carrier (8 each) and of Echo class submarines
   They can be aimed at both land and sea targets (Assumption here: 50/50)
g) SLCM deployed on Charlie and Papa class submarines
   (Assumption: 100% against sea targets)
h) SLCM deployed on Nanuchka patrol-vessel and Sarancha hydrofoil craft
   (Assumption: 100% against sea targets)
i) SLCM deployed on Kirov cruiser and Oscar class submarine
j) 7 Hotel class SSBN, of which 6 carry SS-N-5 SLBMs, are counted under SALT II ceiling

Sources: See General author's note, p. 242

WARSAW PACT					
ESTIMATED NUMBER AVAILABLE FOR NUCLEAR ROLE IN EUROPE		NUMBER OPERATIONAL	RANGE (KM)	IOC	TYPE
NUMBER	PERCENTAGE				
120	50%	240	2500	1955	TU-16 BADGER C/G e)
20	50%	40	2750	1962	TU-22 BLINDER B e)
35	50%	70	4000^{+}	1975	TU-22M BACKFIRE C e)
57	100%	57	1300	1963	SS-N-5 j)
190	50%	380	300-500	1961/ 1979	SS-N-3/SS-N-12 f)
—	—	130	55	1970	SS-N-7 g)
—	—	130	100	1969	SS-N-9 h)
20	50%	40	360?	1980	SS-N-19 i)

179

SYSTEM	NATO					
	TYPE	IOC a)	RANGE (KM)	NUMBER OPERATIONAL	ESTIMATED NUMBER AVAILABLE FOR NUCLEAR ROLE IN EUROPE	
					PERCENTAGE	NUMBER
A I R C R A F T	F-4 PHANTOM b)	1962	720	464	40 %	185
	F-104 STARFIGHTER c) F-16	1958 1981	990	318 Unknown	40 %	125
	JAGUAR d)	1973	720	200 +	20 %	40
	MIRAGE III E e)	1971	700	29	100 %	29
M I S S I L E	PERSHING I f)	1962	350 - 600	180	100 %	180

TABLE VIII. NUCLEAR AND DUAL-CAPABLE DELIVERY SYSTEMS OF GROUND AND AIR FORCES WITH RANGE OF 350-1000 KM

a) Initial Operation Capability
b) In service in air force of USA, FRG, Greece and Turkey. Air defense aircraft (Phantom FG 1/2) not included
c) In service in air force of FRG, Italy, Netherlands, Turkey, Belgium, Greece and Norway
d) Deployed by UK and France
e) Deployed by France
f) Deployed in FRG
g) Weapons systems of Non-Soviet Warsaw Pact countries not included
h) SS-22 replaces SS-12 Scaleboard

Sources: see General author's note, p. 242

WARSAW PACT					
ESTIMATED NUMBER AVAILABLE FOR NUCLEAR ROLE IN EUROPE		NUMBER OPERATIONAL	RANGE (KM)	IOC	TYPE g)
NUMBER	PERCENTAGE				
33	33 %	100	650	1959	SU-7 FITTER A
466	33 %	1400	900	1971	MIG-23/27 FLOGGER
200	33 %	600	600	1974	SU-17 FITTER C
450	33 %	1450	650	1970	MIG-21 FISHBED
100?	100 %	100?	± 400	1962	SSC-1
100 - 120	100 %	100 - 120	± 850	1969	SS-12 SCALEBOARD
			900 $^+$	1978	SS-22 h)

181

They merely illustrate the balance of nuclear forces. The estimates of dual-capable systems that actually have nuclear roles are no more than calculated guesses. For instance, although some aircraft are technically capable of delivering nuclear bombs, only a limited number of pilots are trained and certified for nuclear missions. Similarly, many Soviet sea-based systems can be used against land as well as sea targets. This further complicates the assessment of Soviet systems having a nuclear mission in the European theater.

Finally, the lower limit of the range of Theater Nuclear Forces is set at 350 km. Again, this is an arbitrary choice, for the significance of nuclear weapons--i.e., whether they are strategic or tactical--cannot be based exclusively on their range. But the inclusion of artillery and other so-called dual-capable "battlefield weapons" would complicate the picture even further. Moreover, the overall picture would not be changed significantly. The fact remains, however, that the method used is speculative and somewhat arbitrary and the tables must be regarded as an illustration of the balance of Theater Nuclear Forces only.

The tables show that the Soviet Union enjoys a clear superiority both quantitatively and qualitatively. For example, if we compare the weapons systems with a range of more than 1000 km for both sides, the Western forces are outnumbered by roughly 940 systems. The 369 aircraft and eighteen--French--missiles of the West are overwhelmed by the roughly 750 aircraft and 580 missiles of the Soviet Union. If, in addition to these unequal arsenals, the maritime systems and those with a range of 350-1000 km are counted, the "correlation of forces" is even worse. On the Western side, we count 364 maritime aircraft (and about 60 "European" aircraft in reserve), roughly 782 tactical dual-capable aircraft (and about 228 "European" dual-capable aircraft), and 180 Pershing I missiles: a total of about 1,200 weapons systems. The Soviet arsenal, on the other hand, consists of about 4,500 systems: approximately 350 maritime aircraft, 3,550 aircraft of the tactical air forces, 157-177 missiles and over 500 cruise missiles [39].

Of course, the military significance of numbers should not be exaggerated. But the discrepancy is striking and--what is more--the numbers are important in arms control negotiations.

No matter how far SALT or START will be extended into the "grey area," the West will be in an extremely diffi-cult bargaining position. NATO may decide to deploy additional systems, but it is highly unlikely that the Alliance can equal Soviet numerical power [40].

The East-West qualitative differences are perhaps even more serious. Whereas for NATO the pre-launch survivability (PLS) of the weapons systems has declined, the Soviet Union has drastically enhanced her defensive forces, particularly by the deployment of effective Surface-to-Air Missiles. The PLS of Soviet forces, therefore, has been enhanced. Another important qualitative factor is the Probability-to-Penetrate (PTP) of the weapons systems. Here again, the operational capability of Soviet forces is far superior to that of NATO. For instance, the comparison between systems of both sides given in Table VI shows that precisely those systems with a very high PTP--missiles--are not deployed by NATO, while the Soviet Union has at its disposal large numbers of M/IRBMs. The old SS-4 and SS-5 are being replaced by the SS-20, of which some 280 are now deployed. The SS-20 has an increased range and is equipped with 3 MIRVed warheads. The accuracy of the re-entry vehicles is much greater than that of the SS-4 and SS-5 (SS-20: Circular Error Probability of 200-300 meter).

These characteristics enable the Soviet Union to strike against any target in Western Europe, including air bases for NATO's dual-capable aircraft, naval bases for submarines and the French ICBM force. The deployment of the SS-20, therefore, cannot be considered a simple replacement of older systems. Politically, the SS-20 is no doubt the most visible weapon development in the Soviet Union; militarily, it is another practical expression of Soviet military theory and an important element in the growing discrepancies between the operational capabilities of NATO and the Soviet Union [41]. The overall increased flexibility in options of the Soviet Union, merely highlighted by the SS-20, prompted NATO to modernize its LRTNF. In order to deter Soviet "Selective Employment Options," it was necessary to show NATO's political determination and ability to make a decision by which the credibility of NATO's military capabilities will be visibly enhanced.

This brings us to the ground forces [42], previously the heart of the Soviet defense but whose predominance is now being challenged by the Strategic Missile Forces. Traditionally, a soldier-dominated system succeeded in maintaining the numerical strength of Soviet ground forces, and the figures on Soviet strength in Central and Northern Europe have not varied much, now numbering roughly 350,000 men. However, the increase of and qualitative improvement in European theater armaments must be noted. For example, increases in Warsaw Pact tanks amounted to 14,000 in Central and Northern Europe in 1970 and continue to rise in spite of the established Soviet superiority of almost three-to-one over NATO. The Warsaw Pact now counts over 20,000 tanks of which more than 13,000 are Soviet. Another striking feature in the build-up of the theater forces is the heavy emphasis on increased mobility, greater firepower, flexibility through significant expansion of air-transport capacity, and improvement of logistical performance. Indeed, aside from maintaining total manpower, the Soviet armies in Eastern Europe have been able to improve considerably the ratio of advanced equipment and weapons [43]. This is illustrated by comparing the strength of the Soviet tank division in 1965, 1975 and 1979.

TABLE IX: SOVIET TANK DIVISION STRENGTH					
	1965	1975	(%) 65-75	1979	(%) 65-79
PERSONNEL	8500	11000	(+ 30)	12000	(+ 41)
ARTILLERY	60	96	(+ 60)	108	(+ 80)
TANKS	333	344	(+ 4)	415	(+ 25)
ANTI-TANK WEAPONS	0	428		724	
APC/AFC (modern)	60	120	(+100)	175	(+200)
AIR-DEFENSE WEAPONS (modern)	40	359		451	

Of particular importance is, of course, the nuclearization of the ground forces. Although there is still speculation in the West about the nuclear capability of Soviet artillery (152 mm and 180 mm) [44], the nuclear capability of short- and medium-range missiles (Frog, Scud and Scaleboard) is a clear fact.

Moreover, as will be dealt with below, the fear that "any armed conflict would inevitably develop into a global nuclear-missile war," [45] is not shared by all officers and is notably absent among members of the ground forces. According to them, technology now provides nuclear options that do not inevitably escalate into global war. Their call for the preparation of "any future war" has always included tactical nuclear warfare, but the "nuclearized" conventional forces are no longer regarded as part of a deterrent capable of little more than a massive, indiscriminate use of nuclear weapons. On the contrary, these have acquired a war-fighting capability. As Grechko proudly asserted in 1971 in describing the role of the forces:

> The operational and tactical missile units comprise the basis for the firepower of the Ground Troops. This is a qualitatively new branch of arms which is the basic means for employing nuclear weapons in combat and operations. The missile troops are capable of hitting any targets located at ranges of from several score to many hundreds of kilometers with great accuracy and dependability, using nuclear

184

ammunition. As a result of the nuclear strikes, entire <u>enemy subunits and units as well, located in the enemy rear</u> can be instantaneously wiped out. In terms of their combat properties, the missiles of our Ground Troops are not only not inferior to the foreign ones, but surpass them in terms of a number of important indexes. 46 (Emphasis added)

Grechko's 1971 assessment of Soviet TNF capabilities was probably too optimistic, representing rather a shopping-list for the coming decade. But many of his plans are now being realized. SS-20 deployment began in 1977, Frog is being replaced by the SS-21, and the SS-22 and SS-23 are the successor-models for the Scaleboard and Scud missiles. Although uncertainty exists about the deployment of Soviet nuclear-capable artillery, there is no doubt but that Grechko has lobbied for it since the 1950's 47. Given the successes scored by the insistent military, the odds are that--if not already, then some day--his wishes will come true. By the same token, although Gorshkov's projected "fleet against shore" may initially have stirred opposition from other rival services of the armed forces, the replacement of the SS-N-3 by the SS-N-12 and the latest medium range SLCM, the SS-N-19, suggest that the Admiral's view prevails, giving the Soviet Navy a modern in-theater war-fighting capability.

In sum, the Soviet military build-up "across the board" is impressive and has clearly shifted the military balance in its favor. Its financial priority was established in the very early 1960's and was maintained throughout the decade in order to catch up with the United States and to ensure theater superiority. Attempts to reduce the defense burden failed, and weapons procurement and modernization continued unabated during the 1970's. Both international events and the domestic process played major roles in accounting for the sustained Soviet build-up.

WAR-FIGHTING, DETERRENCE...OR WHAT?

The concept of superiority is rooted in Soviet ideological thinking and is applied to nuclear weapons according to orthodox military--almost battlefield-- norms. The situation of rough parity brought with it serious doubts about nuclear warfare, but not for all strategists. Strategic superiority goes hand in hand with the acquisition of war- fighting capabilities, and these ideas continued to hold sway. Minister of Defense Grechko maintained such views and suggested a counterforce strategy for the European theater. Regarding strategic weapons he spoke not about deterrence but about "re-straining the aggressor" by the "strength of destruction and annihilation" of the Strategic Missile Troops.

The Strategic Missile Troops which comprise the
basis of the military might of our Armed Forces
have the mission of destroying the enemy nuclear
attack means, large groupings of enemy troops and
military bases, destroying the military-industrial
installations, disorganizing state and military
administration, and the work of the rear services
and transport of the agressor. [48]

This fits with Schlesinger's and Brown's views on
Soviet targeting doctrine and can surely serve as the
justification for a countervailing strategy. The
capabilities for selective options may still have fallen
short at the time Grechko wrote but these shortcomings
are not likely to last forever.

The Communist Party and Soviet Government have given
unflagging attention to the qualitative development
of the Strategic Missile Troops...

As a result of this, the Strategic Missile Troops
have recently developed significantly and have
become even more powerful. [49]

Grechko's remarks about the nuclearization and war-
fighting power of the ground troops and the flexibility
and selectivity of options available to them are no less
significant. Grechko did not mention "massive strikes"
or "retaliatory blow" or any other term indicating a MAD
strategy as the objective. On the contrary, he no longer
saw an all-out war as the only scenario for an East-West
conflict, unlike the cautious remarks made about this in
the sixties. It is noteworthy that he accepted the
feasibility of a "flexible response" and "limited war"
in Europe, even though he did not use these Western terms.
General Kulikov, Chief of the General Staff under Grechko,
magnified on this theme in 1973.

The nuclear missiles currently at the disposal of
the strategic, operational, and tactical leadership
groups provide them with great independence in
choosing the methods of combat action. The dependence of strategic successes on operational results
and of operational successes on tactical results
has changed under these conditions. There is now
the possibility of directly influencing the course
and outcome of operations and of war as a whole by
using the powerful resources at the disposal of the
higher headquarters. Now, strategic leadership can
determine not only the goals and missions of combat
operations and the procedures for using strategic
reserves but, in a number of cases, also operational

reserves. However, by using its own resources, it can also strive to accomplish strategic missions before operational or tactical missions are accomplished. [50]

It was this influential soldier, second only to Grechko, who drew particular attention to the need for war-winning capabilities and for a modern and sophisticated organization to that end.

Therefore, Kulikov called upon military science to solve as quickly as possible some "key problems," above all those concerning the introduction and use of modern technology and keeping pace with rapid military-technical developments.

Their successful solution depends greatly on the level of organization and leadership in military-scientific work. The main consideration in supervising this important sphere of military activity is to ensure the high quality of theoretical research, the <u>timely</u> application of its results. It is precisely towards this end that the combined efforts of all commanders, staffs, political organs, military academies and military-scientific enterprises are <u>currently</u> directed. [51] (Emphasis added)

To the extent that leaders such as Grechko and Kulikov, backed by large segments of the military, had a say in the organization of the armed forces and Soviet strategy, there can be little doubt but that the trend would be towards a war-fighting capability. For them, as for Erickson, the essence of Soviet military doctrine is "that technological innovation has been assimilated into the Soviet military tradition without surrendering either the import of the "military" (operational) factor or the notion of the primacy of politics, the principle enunciated by Clausewitz." [52]

However, the Soviet "war-fighting" and their version of proper military doctrine represent just one side of the shield. As in our discussion of political-ideological tenets of Soviet military doctrine, questions of military-strategic matters did not go undisputed, nor were they endorsed in a one-time political or military debate. Here, too, it is necessary to go back to the Khrushchev era.

In January 1960, Khrushchev outlined his strategy before the Supreme Soviet. His radical plans entailed that

- nuclear forces would constitute the main element in Soviet strategy;
- consequently, the armed forces would be reduced by roughly one-third from 3.6 million to 2.4. million;

187

- a future war would be nuclear and short. The
initial period would be decisive [53].

Khrushchev clearly chose for the modernists as
against the traditionalists [54]. The Supreme Soviet
adopted a strategy in which the nuclear forces would play
the main role, but the advocates of large armies were
vocal in their opposition to the corollary conclusion that
ground forces be reduced [55]. As they saw a conflict with
the West, nuclear and conventional forces would be closely
interconnected and both would be essential. In no case
should the strengthening of one be accomplished at the
expense of the other. After all, traditionalists argued,
the advocates of a simple nuclear deterrent cannot
demonstrate any proof of its validity or boast of any
experience, a highly respected principle in Soviet military history [56].

When President Kennedy announced his first defense
budget in 1961, he no doubt put a valuable argument in
the hands of Khrushchev's opponents. In any case, the
policy proposed by the Party leader was abandoned that
same year. At the XXII Party Congress Minister of Defense
Malinovsky announced "in response to the intensified
practical preparations for war being made by the Western
countries with the 'Berlin crisis' as the pretext":

> The reduction of the armed forces that had been
> planned and was in process was temporarily halted;
> defense expenditures were increased somewhat; the
> regular demobilization from the army and navy to the
> reserve of noncommissioned officers and men who had
> completed their tour of active service was tempor-
> arily put off; nuclear weapons tests are being
> conducted. [57]

These set-backs to Khrushchev's defense policy by no
means diminished the significance of his "historical
report," as Malinovsky put it. "The report...contained
a penetrating analysis of the nature of modern war;
this analysis became the basis of Soviet military
doctrine." [58] (Emphasis added)

Khrushchev's conception of Soviet strategy in the
nuclear age did indeed need further development, if not
correction, on some major issues. Malinovsky as Minister
of Defense was probably in the right position for an
attempt to cautiously compromise between the different
factions. Committed to his profession and his colleagues
and, at the same time, well aware of the speedy demotion
of his predecessor, Zhukov, after he had displayed too
much independence from the Party, Malinovsky took a
rather conciliatory position. He agreed with Khrushchev
on the nature of a future war and the primacy of the
Strategic Rocket Troops, on the special importance of the
initial phase of a war, and on the danger of a surprise

attack.[59] But he also stressed the significance of a mass army[59]. "We also believe that under modern conditions any future war would be waged, despite the enormous losses, by mass, many-millions-strong armed forces."[60] And of particular importance for future Soviet strategy are his following remarks:

> Although nuclear weapons will hold the decisive place in a future war, we are nevertheless coming to the conclusion that final victory over an aggressor can be achieved only <u>through combined operations by all branches of the armed forces</u>...

> For our armed forces (the five and a half years since the XX Party Congress P.V.) has been a period filled with important events related to rearmament with new and up-to-date equipment and the <u>extensive introduction of nuclear missiles</u> in the forces...

> On the basis primarily of the extensive introduction of these weapons in the forces, <u>all the old branches</u>, so to speak, of the armed forces have been greatly improved in the past few years.[61] (Emphasis added)

Malinovsky not only underlined the need for large armies, he also assigned nuclear weapons "of various types and purposes" to all their branches. The armed forces should respond to any aggressor through <u>combined operations</u>. He was apparently not attracted by a "massive retaliation" strategy in view of the very modest Soviet forces vis-à-vis American strategic capabilities and sought greater flexibility in the force structure and build-up. It may be that a theory of general purpose forces had not yet been fully elaborated and agreed upon—let alone made technically possible—but its basic elements were formulated; the "minimum deterrent" strategy was seriously criticized and sufficient manpower had been secured. "The Khrushchev years saw the creation of the practical and theoretical nucleus on which more extensive General Forces would rely, and from which they eventually emerged."[62]

With regard to the strategic nuclear forces, the traditionalists never contested their importance, and everyone recognized their prime role in Soviet strategy, especially in the correlation of forces with the United States. Their priority, however, was not allowed to be at the expense of conventional forces for reasons that were not always clear in the beginning and would seem to have stemmed from a mere desire for superiority. But the military merits of conventional forces were heralded with increasing frequency after Malinovsky's allusions at an early hour to a "flexible response" strategy. Conventional forces, equipped with nuclear weapons, were seen as an indispensable part of the deterrent in Europe.

Should deterrence fail, these forces must win the battle in Europe.

The publication of <u>Military Strategy</u> in 1962 may have been an effort to arrive at or enhance consensus in military affairs, for one could not speak of a clearly unified view on the "best" strategy at this time. The military no doubt resented Khrushchev's far-flung interference in military affairs. Critics of the Party leader and his modernist advisors demanded attention for their philosophy by pointing out that military doctrine cannot be thought out "by a single person or group of persons." [63] The authors of <u>Military Strategy</u> included in their text traditionalists' views such as the need for a mass army and for "serious preparation for a protracted war." But they also warned of the danger of traditionalism, especially among the ground forces. They took issue with "certain authors" who saw no essential changes in the "strategic offense and strategic defense in the theaters of military operations" (TVD). According to the military collective, led by Sokolovsky: [64]

> This is an incorrect concept of the method for conducting a modern war. This is the result of a reappraisal of the experience of the past war and of the mechanical conversion of this experience to modern conditions.

And the second edition continues:

> The error of such a point of view is that it minimizes the role of strategic nuclear rocket weapons, underestimates its tremendous combat possibilities and, therefore, is oriented toward the ground forces and the usual methods of conducting war. The imperialists by no means intend to conduct a war against the socialist countries with ground forces. They are counting on nuclear, primarily strategic, weapons. [65]

Thus, we arrive at a new "type of strategic operation," in which not the ground troops but nuclear rockets play the main role. The ground forces are necessary to "destroy the remaining groups of enemy troops, occupy enemy territory, and protect their own territory."

> The fulfilment of these tasks requires strategic operations of the Ground Troops; however the nature of these operations has changed compared with the last war. Now it is not a case of the Strategic Rocket Troops--the basic means for conducting a modern war--timing their operations with those of the Ground Troops, but just the opposite, i.e., the Ground Troops should utilize to the fullest extent

the results attained by the Rocket Troops for a
rapid fulfilment of their tasks. [66]

Nuclear rocket attacks against objectives within
enemy territory, mainly against their nuclear
devices, will create conditions favorable for the
operations of other services of the Armed Forces.
At the same time the Strategic Rocket Troops, long-
range aviation, and rocket-carrying submarines will
strike strategic objectives in the theaters of military operations as well, destroying simultaneously
both enemy troop units, including reserves, and the
bases of operational-tactical nuclear devices,
communications, the military control system, etc. [67]

The ground forces were apparently pressured not only
to defend their position and prestige vis-à-vis the other
branches but also to review their basic strategic
concepts. Their traditional predominance was not only
threatened by the newly established strategic rocket
forces and Khrushchev's heavy emphasis on nuclear weapons,
but they were also asked by their colleagues--more
cautiously though--to adopt an essentially new way of
strategic thinking. For example, the meaning of defense,
taken quite literally by the traditionalists, was
seriously undermined, for "it is difficult for the strikes
by the Rocket Troops to qualify as offensive or defensive
in nature, regardless of whether troops are on the
offensive or the defensive on the ground." [68]
As in the West, the nuclear dilemma has not been
solved in the Soviet Union. Most revealing in this
respect is the third edition of Military Strategy which
admits that--as of 1968--there were "polemics" about
the type and nature of strategic operations. The authors
formulate the problem very clearly:

In essence, the argument is about the basic method
of conducting future war: will it be a land war
with the use of the nuclear weapon as a means of
supporting the operations of the ground troops, or
a war that is essentially new, where the main means
of solving strategic tasks will be the nuclear
rocket weapon. [69]

Three years later, in a key publication for the
1970's Grechko gave his answer, which unswervingly
supported the traditionalist view.

In recent years, Soviet military science has been
enriched by new theses and conclusions on the
possible character of modern war...

A war can begin with the use of either nuclear
weapons or conventional means of attack. Different

variations are possible in using all types of
weapons available to the enemy. For this reason,
all the types of Armed Forces and branches of arms
are developed, improved, and equipped with the most
modern means of combat in accord with the requirements of their coordinated use in modern combat, in
operation and war as a whole. 70 (Emphasis added)

However, these "new theses" were not presented " in
recent years," but at least a decade earlier. But they
could finally be realized technologically and economically. Soviet military theory had moved from an extremely
high priority on strategic missiles to a general purpose,
flexible strategy, in which multi-million-men armies had
found a fully integrated role. The ground forces had
successfully secured their internal position and their
strategic significance in the defense of the Soviet
Union.

The foregoing observations lead to a conclusion
which is often too readily foregone in Western literature:
namely, that the war-fighting posture advocated by these
military experts concerns a "land war" and obviously the
European TVD 71. Unlike the American meaning of "strategic" which more or less equals "intercontinental,"
Soviet military doctrine considers a strategic operation
as one of decisive importance for the course and outcome
of a war in one or more TVDs.

Strategic operations in Europe are very different
from intercontinental ones. They require different
weapons and armed services, and their various targeting
doctrines may have little in common. Political goals,
or geopolitical motives, and the prospect of victory in
a nuclear war between the superpowers are of a different
order. "The various theaters of military operations
play by no means identical roles. And consequently there
will be essential differences in the strategic mission,
the forces, and the various theaters, and in the ways in
which they are used." 72

Military strategy rightly calls a nuclear (intercontinental) missile war "essentially new." The most
direct and concentrated military confrontations and the
major latent, unforeseeable instabilities and tensions
between East and West have, since World War II, concerned
the European theater. This situation and the foregoing
observations on the persistent and powerful position of
the ground forces help explain that

> ...despite the increasing emphasis given under
> Khrushchev to the strategic missile forces and to
> the influence of strategic nuclear operations on the
> outcome of a future war, there was still a strong
> disposition to focus on the familiar problem of
> European theater warfare. 73

The Soviet armed forces must be prepared to fight all types of war, including a "limited war" in Europe, with or without the use of nuclear weapons. Indeed, scenarios of selective nuclear options are envisaged by Soviet military writers. For example, Colonel Shirokov, discussing the targeting of the economic-industrial capacity, focusses on some "critical links of the economy" and their effect on production potential as a whole.

Even the destruction of individual plants that are especially important has had a great effect on the output of certain types of military production. For example, it is sufficient to destroy a few enter- prises producing transistors in order to restrict extremely the production of missiles for all branches of the armed forces. And even strikes on area objectives are directed at that portion of the target which is of vital importance to a country or a coalition of countries. In determining these tar- gets, application should be made of the industrial branch principle and the selection of the critical link in the economy. [74] (Emphasis added)

On the other hand, limited war in Europe is seen as extremely dangerous, since

...the war would hardly be waged very long with the use of tactical nuclear weapons only. Once matters reach the point where nuclear weapons are used, then the belligerents will be forced to launch all of their nuclear power. Local war will be transformed into a global nuclear war. [75]

Others also exclude the possibility of avoiding escalation from conventional to nuclear war in an East- West military conflict. Trofimenko, acting as the devil's advocate and understandably using Americans as example, explains:

American leaders and theoreticians are nowadays forced to acknowledge the untenability of the theory that some kind of clearly visible "watershed" exists between conflict in general and nuclear conflict. They have in fact come to recognize that the most effective means of preventing nuclear war is not the artificial construction and fixing of one set or another of "thresholds" in military escalation but the renunciation of the use of force in any form and of the threat of force. It was this change of attitude which made it possible to conclude the Soviet-American agreement on the prevention of nuclear war, which L.I. Brezhnev called a document of historic significance. [76]

The third edition of <u>Military Strategy</u> outlines extensively the dangers of escalation, and most changes from previous editions occur in the chapter on "the military strategy of the imperialist countries." The writers point to the "most critical problem confronting the military leadership of the USA and NATO" that follows from the uncertainties and unknown inherent in the use of nuclear weapons [77]. Accordingly, the 1968 edition denounces NATO's "flexible response" strategy by saying that it might "raise false hopes that a military conflict in Europe can be kept within local bounds and not allowed to develop into a big war with use of all means of extermination."

> ...such a war must be "limited" only with relation to the United States; for the other European countries of NATO, whose territories will be fully embraced by a "limited" war, it will be an unlimited "total" war with all the consequences. [78]

In short, uncertainties about the consequences of a war in the European TVD are tremendous, but this view is not accepted by the "professional soldiers," above all of the traditional army men who have continuously insisted on the feasibility of victory and the need to consistently work out a conventional and/or nuclear offensive in all details [79].

As has been pointed out, the war-fighting scenario for the transatlantic TVD is a different chapter, and statements about a Soviet-American nuclear war are essentially different from those analyzed above. Contrary to the popular belief that the war-fighting doctrine also includes the American continent, it must be pointed out that explicit references to this in Soviet literature are very difficult to find. Rather the vast majority of political and military authors state time and again that a global nuclear war amounts to suicide and cannot be fought with any prospect of victory. "No country can set itself the aim of defeating the enemy at the cost of its own destruction." [80] Doubts about nuclear war in Europe are great, but intercontinental nuclear exchanges are flatly rejected. Semeiko, for example, comments on Schlesinger's Limited Nuclear Options as follows:

> One cannot fail to take into consideration not only the fact that nuclear weapons are weapons of mass destruction <u>irrespective of the scale of nuclear strikes</u>, but also the fact that, having begun as a limited exchange of strikes, a nuclear war can reach unlimited proportions much more rapidly than a war in which conventional weapons are used. [81] (Emphasis added)

194

This military staff member of the Institute of the
USA and Canada condemns Schlesinger's doctrine not only
because of fears of counterforce strategy but, above all,
because of its "desire to legalize the use of nuclear
weapons." [82] Such plans bypass the "problem of the
fundamental inadmissibility of a nuclear war." [83]
Another prominent military strategist and contributor
to all three editions of Military Strategy, Larionov,
points to the "tremendous distance between bellicose
plans and their implementation." [84] According to him, the
improvement of nuclear weapons, their accuracy and
flexibility of targeting should never lead to a situation
in which this "tremendous distance" is narrowed down to
dangerous margins of uncertainty and insecurity for
either side. SALT-I guaranteed penetrability and
vulnerability--two basic requirements for unilateral
deterrence--and it provided a dynamic, but relatively
stable, strategic balance. This result could only be
threatened if one seeks "a way out of the current
situation of nuclear restraint by broadening the usability
of nuclear weapons and finding methods which could
supposedly prevent the disastrous consequences of nuclear
conflict." [85]

Milshtein and Semeiko, two prominent Soviet
strategists of the SShA Institute, are apparently opposed
to any attempt to improve deterrence by increasing the
capability of destroying more efficiently, more selectively or more extensively. For them, the idea of
improving deterrence in this way rests on the fallacious
presumption that defense is enhanced. The vulnerability
of the attacker is guaranteed as long as launch-upon-
warning and launch-upon-attack [86] are possible and the
survival of submarines, bombers and dual-capable aircraft
can be maintained. Defense with a capital "D" is not
possible. Deterrence and defense at this level are both
absolute, and this situation cannot be changed by more
usable intercontinental nuclear weapons.

While quoting Western sources extensively on the
subject, they raise serious doubts about the possibility
of conducting "surgical strikes" against "military targets
without hitting nearby cities and centers at the same
time." The assumption of rational decision-making under
circumstances of a limited nuclear exchange is similarly
dealt with and dismissed as an illusion. The attempt
à la Schlesinger to describe and estimate the course of
limited nuclear conflict is vehemently rejected as
"simply a means of making the prospect of a nuclear
conflict more acceptable." [87] The concepts and theories
of deterrence and war-fighting capabilities should not be
further confused by the seemingly less "absolute"
destruction by more accurate and lower-yield weapons.
"The quest for ways of making 'limited' use of nuclear
weapons both strategically and tactically is fraught with
dangerous consequences." [88]

Flexibility may be carried to the point that no distinction can be made between a first-strike and a general-nuclear-response posture. Fears in the United States about Soviet intentions in this regard were unambiguously addressed by Brezhnev in a timely speech a few days before the inauguration of President Carter.

Of course, comrades, we are improving our defenses. It cannot be otherwise. We have never neglected the security of our country and the security of our allies, and we shall never neglect it. But allegations that the Soviet Union is going beyond what is sufficient for defense, that it is striving for superiority in armaments with the aim of delivering a "first-strike", are absurd and utterly unfounded... I want to re-emphasize, that the Soviet Union has always been and continues to be a staunch opponent of such concepts. [89]

Indeed, although Mutual Assured Destruction is not officially and explicitly mentioned, Soviet confidence vis-à-vis the United States is based on its retaliatory power. Deterrence is the main task of intercontinental weapons. "They must keep the aggressor in check by the threat of inevitable retaliation." [90]
William Scott is correct when he concludes that Soviet leadership had formulated the doctrine and strategy by 1962 and that basically little has changed since. Khrushchev's "minimum deterrent" was untenable, but the basics of "deterrence by punishment" are still present. The counterforce doctrine was first launched by McNamara in 1962 and it is noteworthy that the second edition of Military Strategy, appearing in 1963, immediately seizes the opportunity of incorporating this deep-rooted Soviet military thinking in the standard work on military strategy. A purely countervalue posture could not be maintained. Soviet intercontinental missiles would accordingly follow the trend, and this development

...which can be tied clearly to the American ICBM programme was the shift in Soviet targeting philosophy from one of area devastation to a primary emphasis on counterforce point targeting. The initial trend in Soviet warhead development was to ever larger sizes. The 6-MT SS-7 and -8, whose warhead was probably tested in 1958, the missile being deployed in 1961-1962; the 18-MT SS-9 whose warhead was tested in September 1961, the missile being deployed in 1966; and weapons in the 25-100 MT range, whose development was claimed in 1961 but which did not go into production. The trend was then broken abruptly, and the 1.5-MT SS-11 began deployment in 1966. At the same time the production of ICBM rose from about 50 to 200 a year and ran for

196

five years at this rate thus roughly matching the Minuteman build-up. 91

As noted earlier, technological developments, particularly the improvement of missile accuracy and MIRV technology, are fully incorporated in the Soviet fourth-generation ICBMs. But Table V also shows a continuation of "heavy" and most likely countervalue variants of the SS-18 and SS-19. Moreover, the Soviet Union was ready to limit its counterforce capability in SALT-II by agreeing to limitations on the MIRVing potential of these missiles. Soviet actors cannot and do not deny a counterforce capability, but they add--on historically verifiable grounds and on (geo-) politically sound arguments--that this is a response to declared American policy and weapons-acquirement decisions.

The Soviet armed forces have always been defensive, or deterring, especially if one turns to the military-political doctrines for their use. All systems of strategic arms suited for <u>counterforce</u> options were adopted by the Soviet Union <u>only after</u> they had been procured and deployed by the <u>United</u> States. The Soviet missiles that are now the subject of so much concern in the West were built <u>in reaction</u> to another U.S. thrust forward in the arms race. 92 (Emphasis added)

Whereas the Soviet "professional soldier" has strongly influenced both theory and practice with regard to the war-fighting capability in the European TVD, he has encountered an intransigent political leadership that, since Khrushchev's "historical report," has shown disbelief of and restraint in applying traditionalist "battlefield norms" to the intercontinental theater. Significantly, Grechko's two major publications in the 1970's do not contain the slightest reference to a detailed description of war-fighting on the intercontinental level. The subject is hardly mentioned; apparently it is not to be entrusted to this and any other representative of the "land war school."

The Soviet strategic aim is to neutralize, not to defeat, the United States at the highest strategic level. The central concern, again, is Europe, where the Soviet Union seeks as much freedom as possible to fight and win a war, should this become inevitable 93. By putting the military, industrial and human resources of the United States at risk, it tries to decouple the allied theaters and undermine, at least, the credibility of the American nuclear guarantee.

Superiority in the relationship of forces of the higher level creates favorable conditions for the successfull military actions of lower levels, and

197

the possibility of supplying the superiority of
forces in the military actions of a lower level
contributes to the change in the relationship of
the forces of the higher level. [94]

For the Soviet Union, the question is whether
nuclear superiority vis-à-vis the United States is
feasible; this will be examined in the next chapter. For
the United States and its allies the disputed and elusive
problem of coupling and decoupling has always been there
and is a vexed one well before questions about strategic
superiority are in order [95]. Parity or essential equivalence at the highest level combined with Soviet in-
theater superiority seriously threatens European security.
Schlesinger's and Brown's "extended deterrence by denial"
of strategic operations in Europe is an important attempt
to increase credibility by coupling the threat of "General
Nuclear Response" to Allied and European options available
to deter Soviet Selective Nuclear Strikes and a conventional and/or nuclear offensive. To raise uncertainty
in the Soviet mind remains the key. It is Western Europe
that should be aware of the gradually decreasing uncer-
tainty--largely the consequence of vastly superior Soviet
forces, if not of the doctrine itself--of the Soviet
Union at the lower, European-strategic level [96]. American
strategic-nuclear strength or the "countervailing
strategy" cannot make up for West European defense
weaknesses.
     In conclusion, the Soviet "professional soldier"
has developed a comprehensive and consistent military
strategy. He has fully employed the professional autonomy
allotted to him by the Soviet polity. International
events have underlined rather than undermined the
opportunity to put this doctrine into practice. "It is
hardly possible to reproach the professional military
in any country for carrying out professional duties",
as Trofimenko puts it, "but politicians' activities can
and must be evaluated." [97] As shown before, after parity
was reached, the Soviet political leadership failed to
constrain military expenditures unilaterally. How it
has tried to reduce the defense burden by means of bi-
and multilateral negotiations is the subject of the next
chapter.

7
Soviet Views
on Security and Arms Control

INTRODUCTION

Reactions to SALT and MBFR are ones of mixed feelings and disappointments. Proponents of national or international security in East and West alike can point to many failures and few successes. Both sides can explain these according to numerous factors and each from his own viewpoint. These explanations are in one way or another likely to underscore the technical and political complexities of arms control. These two aspects, of course, cannot be separated in reality. Neither can one be said to be more important than the other. One thing should be clear, however. If political will is lacking the many technical problems will never be solved; desirability of arms control is an absolute necessity. Once the security problems are actually negotiated, the conflicting views, interests and approaches of the various actors involved surface.

The question of whether international security must be strengthened may be answered positively, but the problems of how, by which means and to what extent remain sources of contention, both within and between political and military circles. For example, are confidence-building measures more important or more feasible than limitations on military "hardware?" Which proposals are negotiable and which are not? How does the process of political detente--say, in the diplomatic and economic areas--relate to military detente? Which one comes first in the opinion of the actors? In this chapter Soviet views on the "Peace Program" "for curbing aggressors and averting a new world war, a program of struggle for the triumph of the principles of peaceful coexistence of states irrespective of social systems" [1] will be examined, and the complexities of the political-military processes outlined.

SOVIET SECURITY: CONCERNS AMIDST CONFIDENCE

"Complete self-confidence--this is the dominating feature of the foreign policy section of Brezhnev's report--" so concludes Kommunist from the foreign commentaries, and the journal adds considerable "evidence" to underscore this "correct" conclusion [2]. Soviet confidence in the international situation stems from a large number of facts, all pointing to increased Soviet influence and the decline of Western power. More specifically, this widely acknowledged phenomenon involves the changed "correlation of forces" in favor of Soviet power, on the one hand, and the Western crisis and the end of military, nuclear blackmail on the other. The Soviet Union is consistently and successfully substituting a "system of international security" for the degenerated, doomed policies of capitalism.

> The change in the correlation of forces in favor of socialism...served to strengthen the cause of peace and international security. This is convincingly evidenced by shifts in Soviet-American relations and by a healthier situation in Europe, particularly in connection with ratification of treaties between the USSR and the FRG and Poland and the FRG. [3]

That the "general crisis of capitalism continues to intensify" is an ideological slogan, but one that gained in substance during the Western recession in the 1970's. In this respect, broad Soviet consensus is established, particularly regarding the United States. The Vietnam-trauma, Watergate, the devaluation of the dollar, increasing dependency and so forth, to some extent underscore Arbatov's 1971 observations on "the far-reaching consequences on the moral-political atmosphere in the country" and "the lack of relevance to the contemporary situation in the world of US foreign policy." [4]

Yet, despite the fact that these and other expectations are partially coming true, the United States is still regarded as the leading and formidable power, posing the most important obstacle and the greatest threat to the Soviet Union. The new correlation of forces may have forced the United States and the West to recognize "the illusion about the omnipotence of America," but Soviet strategists can say little more than that. The Soviet Union is willy-nilly forced to deal with the evil opponent, primarily because "the significance of Soviet-American relations is determined by the fact that they exist between the two largest states in terms of their military might." [5] There is no doubt in the Soviet mind that the significance of military power will not decrease and that military competition will continue to be pursued by the imperialists [6].

Although the entire experience of the past years speaks of the futility of the attempts to achieve its foreign policy aims with the help of military force, the U.S. Government has directed its <u>chief</u> efforts not to resolving questions in dispute with the help of negotiations but to improving its <u>military machine</u> and to the quest for ways of extending the latter's "applicability" (through the utilization and strengthening, as envisaged by the "Nixon doctrine," of the military potentials of the allies, the introduction of new types of weapon and tactics, and so forth). 7 (Emphasis added)

There is enough reason for moderate confidence about the improved "correlation of forces." One need not be a fanatic "hawk" to recognize the potential threat--at the least--stemming from American power and to conclude, as Brezhnev does, that "without large defense expenditures we and our economy would move ahead far more quickly." 8 The defense burden is undoubtedly tremendous, and many recognize it as such. But political leaders such as Brezhnev, Suslov or Ustinov time and again stress that the criterion for the extent of the defense budget is the threat to the Soviet Union, not the economic cost. Analysts also point to the fact that "American politicians' and strategists' hopes of 'economically exhausting' the Soviet Union by imposing on her a rapidly developing contest in the military sphere" 9 always have been and will remain idle. Moreover, adds Arbatov, such efforts "have the effect of a boomerang for the United States themselves," as testified to by the pessimistic forecasts of economic growth 10.

This brings little solace to most in the Soviet Union where the deep-rooted conviction and consensus exist that Americans are exercising a "position-of-strength foreign policy." Even though Trofimenko notes "an extremely fundamental change of views by American political and military leaders" 11 in nuclear policy, testified to by the agreements and understandings of the first half of the 1970's, the basic attitude remains characterized by mistrust and the expectation that America will use its superiority 12. For example, President Nixon's concepts of "sufficiency" and "realistic deterrence" are received suspiciously. New strategic concepts are seen as mere "adaptations" of American imperialism to new world realities. 13

The imperialist nature and the inherently dangerous dynamics of the capitalist system cannot change. Thus Trofimenko explains the impossibility of "a cardinal break" of the "realistic deterrence" strategy with previous ones in terms of the nature of capitalism.

The US military-political strategy is embodied not only in the already developed strategic armaments

but also in those systems which still do not
actually exist "in the flesh," that is, in metal,
and which will become realities only in several
years' time. But they have already been ordered,
and industry is working on them. Therefore, a
fundamental change in theory, so radical that some
of the previous systems would become unnecessary,
is virtually impossible under the conditions of a
capitalist economy. [14]

The less ideological and more factual part of
Trofimenko"s analysis also demonstrates that the United
States does not intend to change. The era of qualitative
competition impelled Nixon's "new definition of strength,"
but it was equally aimed at the maximalization of military power in international relations.

Proceeding from the formal recognition of the
strategic equality and parity of the US and the
USSR, this strategy nonetheless does not want to
come to terms with the fact of this equality and
is aimed at searching for crafty, devious ways to
nonetheless achieve for the United States some military advantages over the USSR. Thus, the "realism"
of the new strategy is reduced to modification of
imperialist strategy and to attempts to combine
certain "realities" which cannot be combined, while
keeping unchanged its expansionist foreign policy
aims and philosophy of force. [15] (Emphasis added)

Larionov sees strategic sufficiency as a concept
that is defined in a meaningless way, at least for arms
control. The United States was forced to refrain from
open advocacy of superiority, but, according to Larionov,
the "philosophy of intimidation" and the "position of
strength" policy are still maintained by military means.
Sufficiency as characterized by Nixon, i.e., "a political
concept in the broad sense," is misleading. This is
exemplified, for instance, by strategic reinforcements
through MIRVs. Unlike McNamara's quantitative, "cost-
effectiveness" criterion for sufficiency, giving at least
some basis for assessment, Nixon's concept attempted to
"satisfy the hawks and placate the doves simultaneously."

Making "sufficiency" into an "absolute" technical
criterion does not limit the growth of strategic
arms and, in this sense, the concept of "strategic
sufficiency" is highly subjective and indefinite.
It creates broad scope for any steps and measures
on the part of the administration. [16]

Events in the following years operated to reaffirm
the concern of Larionov and others. SALT-I was used by
Secretary of Defense, Laird, as a tool to assure

congressional support for further development of MIRVs and development of the Trident submarine and the B-1 strategic bomber. Traditional and persistent doubts about American "good" intentions as to sufficiency and strategic capabilities were also raised by Laird's successor, Schlesinger. His plans once more exposed the painful fact that parity at the time was still an objective, not a reality, for the Soviet Union. The flexibility of options Schlesinger envisaged were very remote possibilities for the Soviet Union in 1974. Despite Schlesinger's declared primary aim of reinforcing the credibility of nuclear deterrence and his most carefully formulated assurances regarding a (first) use of nuclear weapons [17], Soviet reactions unanimously condemned his statements as military and political devices.

> Known influential circles in the United States that are opposed to the easing of tensions, representatives of the military-industrial complex in the Congress...are trying to poison the atmosphere of the talks and to sow seeds of mistrust between the two sides. The militarists of the 1970's pin large hopes on regaining, if only in the future, the former strategic superiority of the United States by way of qualitatively perfecting weapons and developing new parameters of their use in order to bring pressure to bear on the socialist countries. [18]

Today, similar complaints and fears are voiced with regard to American strategic programs, which are alledgely designed to shift the balance considerably in favor of the United States during the second half of the 1980's [19]. Economic and technological inferiority forces a number of actors to temper somewhat their optimism about the actual state of strategic parity and to recognize serious concerns amidst the confidence. American and Western defense measures, if deemed necessary and indeed taken, painfully underline Soviet vulnerabilities and its perpetual second position in the era of the Scientific-Technical Revolution (STR). As shown before, the major conditions for a sustained Soviet military effort are present: the recognition of an ever-continuing competition with the West, preferential treatment as to financial and human resources, and the establishment of a powerful position for the defense sector in the overall system [20]. Moreover, the unsuccessful attempt to develop "mutually advantageous economic cooperation," foregoing greater interdependence and ultimately Soviet participation as an economic superpower, has slowed if not undermined the momentum of military policy [21]. The Soviet Union is still on her own in maintaining her status as military superpower, and must function without the economic and technological benefits or assistance that Brezhnev sought in order to smooth domestic problems.

Aside from the economic aspect of Brezhnev's strategy for the 1970's, the system's improvement qualitatively--as intensive growth, greater efficiency, rapid introduction of the results of STR--and the relaxation of international tension formed two interrelated impulses which bore on military policy as much as on other policy fields. On the one hand, arms control agreements could to some extent relieve the defense burden; on the other, improvement in the military organization corresponding with the requirements of scientific-technological competition with the West was of no less concern. To be sure, the military sector can be said to be one of the forerunners in Soviet technological development and to represent a large part of the overall "scientific potential." [22] But assertions about a far better performance in this sector than in the civilian sector must be treated with great caution. Difficulties so commonly ascribed to the Soviet system as a whole exist also in realizing its "military potential." Personal involvement at the highest political level, priority at different stages of R&D and procurement, and the advantage of a "consumer" orientation in military R&D cannot completely eliminate endemic Soviet problems [23]. Concerns in this respect are voiced even among the military. This will be briefly illustrated.

For example, all four factors which Lomov mentions as important for technological development pose major difficulties in the Soviet Union. These factors "are the presence of a statewide plan of scientific develop- ment, its fulfilment, the conformity of this plan to the highest level of world science, and the focussing of this plan on solving the fundamental problems confronting the nation's scientific forces." [24]

These requirements are only met to a degree in the Soviet Union, while the omnipresent condition which Lomov evidently must mention--"obligatory condition of the more and more profound mastery of Marxist-Leninist ideology and the dialectic materialistic method"--has hindered rather than facilitated scientific development. A "unified plan" dependent on political rather than scientific-technical initiative, elaboration and coordination is still hampered by "the chronic tension between autonomy and control that continues to characterize the regime's basic and anomalous perspective on the role of the scientist in Soviet society." [25]

Furthermore, the autonomous--political--center can only follow a limited number of priority projects. As long as these fall mainly in one sector some progress is possible. But the complexity of a modern, "developed socialist" state which increasingly faces labor shortage and moderate growth makes such progress extremely difficult, both politically and technically. Under conditions of limited resources and increasing demands of the overall, civilian economy, a choice must be made.

Most military actors do not leave any doubt about their own choice. Yet others are aware of Soviet limits and restraints and of the fact that better overall scientific potential also affects their own sector. The theme of unlimited allocations stressed by Grechko, Kulikov and others, finds a detractor in Colonel Bondarenko who links defense needs to "characteristics of the scientific potential" of the enemy.

The need for more accurate quantitative indicators is conditioned by the fact that it is important from the military viewpoint to know not simply the fatherland's scientific potential possibilities of themselves but to know without fail what these are compared with scientific potential of states opposed to us in the military respect. 26

Bondarenko is quite clear about the state of affairs in his country and about the need to draw the right conclusions regarding the apparently well-entrenched preference for preponderance.

The rapid growth rates of the external and quantitative indicators of science indicate that development is still proceeding through extensiveness... It is not hard to understand that the development of science cannot long continue along this path. Sooner or later, a development path of intensiveness will gain the upper hand. 27

Uncertainty about required capabilities vis-à-vis the opponent is not the only necessary index of one's own needs. Even a rough calculation tells Bondarenko enough about the Soviet extensive approach in science itself and the accompanying waste, apparently an exceedingly serious matter in the military sector as well. The Soviet "scientific potential" is insufficient to match that of the opponent, and this includes, even in particular, the military capacity.

The above facts make the problem of increasing the efficiency of science and scientific research activity exceptionally acute. This task is particularly urgent in the field of military matters. Here, as nowhere else, an extremely accurate correlation between the scientific and the practical needs of military building is required. 28 (Emphasis added)

Another problem for military men like Bondarenko is the very concept and priority of "scientific potential." Aside from the ideological disadvantages mentioned earlier, the Soviet system has shown many signs of inertia and inherent resistence to change, including

military-scientific developments. Khrushchev and
Malinovsky were at pains to institutionalize the notion
of the primary role of nuclear weapons; Brezhnev and some
of his military experts were and still are confronted with
a dawning recognition of the central role of scientific-
technological progress in a modern society with limited
resources. Despite the recognition by many people
concerned with defense in the early 1960's that quality
is of the utmost importance, many of their colleagues
in the 1970's still think in terms of quantity when
dealing with power and growth. Brezhnev's radical
advocacy of a qualitative, intensive approach in Soviet
thinking met a rather slow response. Even in the defense
sector, it was largely external developments--like the
MIRV technology--that significantly bolstered the case
of the modernists, highlighting the widening qualitative
gap between the superpowers [29]. Bondarenko's insistence
on the extremely "urgent and acute" need for change in
1971 clearly illustrates this [30].

Even the late Minister of Defense Grechko does not
seem to have fully appreciated the implications of the
technological era. In his major publication in 1971, about
the armed forces of the soviet state, he stressed the
essential significance of Soviet economic growth in
general, of which the scientific potential was merely one
aspect [31]. Whether his seeming obtuseness was genuine or
stemmed from ideological rigidity in divining the future
of Soviet military power is hard to say, but the fact is
that Grechko nowhere takes an explicitly "progressive"
stance on the main issue of arms competition: technology.
Instead we find outspoken conformity with the laws of
dialectical materialism. One cannot but doubt the
validity and usefulness of conclusions such as the
following of Rutkov:

> The problems connected with military and military-
> economic maintenance...only arise and exist in the
> socialist system in connection with external factors,
> and are nor of a self-sufficient nature. For this
> reason, quantitative and qualitative indicators in
> this area can only be regarded...in relation to
> corresponding indicators on the opposing side...
> With the given magnitude of our military and mili-
> tary-economic power, the degree of its relative
> superiority will increase in proportion to the
> degree to which the imperialist military machine
> and its economic base are affected by contradictions
> and disorders. [32] (Emphasis added)

Of course, modernists respect these ideological
tenets, but the main thrust of their writings maintains
the central role of STR as the major determinant of
"the military might of the country," [33] and the importance
of scientific-technological development is not always

understood. To the extent that modernist thinking is incorporated in Soviet defense planning, this dates from rather recent years.

Soviet preoccupations concern not only the attitude of top military advisors, but also problems in the military organization at large. Coordination, innovation and application of new methods are essential <u>at all levels</u>. Extensive attention has been paid to what Marshal Zakharov called in 1965 "An Urgent Demand of the Time: On Further Raising the Scientific Level of Military Leadership." Khrushchev angrily noted the ignorance about modern weapons--even their existence--among officers in the early sixties [34]. In 1974, the leadership was warned of the danger of inadequate information and the exclusion of the lower levels.

> It is incorrect to present the increasing role of science in strengthening the defensive capability of the country as a unique problem "of a higher order" reserved only for strategic questions of military development and therefore of interest only to the higher circle of the officer corps, its intellectual and theoretical center. The development of the Soviet Armed Forces shows that science is permeating the entire life of the troops to an ever greater degree. [35]

In 1976, Deputy-Chief of the General Staff Kozlov urged "the active participation of a wide range of generals, admirals and officers in the organization of military-scientific work." He insisted that they discuss "really topical questions" and that the results be incorporated "in good time" in theoretical works and practical activities [36]. His chief, Ogarkov, showed the same concern about attitudes that were slow to change. In 1971, prodding his colleagues to master as quickly as possible "the new propositions and conclusions concerning the possible nature of modern warfare," he also warned that "one must not think that we have already accomplished and learned everything." Elsewhere he addressed, as had Sokolovsky before him, traditionalist currents in the armed forces and pointed out to them the new approach and methods advanced by Brezhnev at the XXIV Party Congress.

> The nature and scale of modern tasks makes it impossible to remain content with the established forms and methods, even though they have been of good service in the past. <u>Applied to military art, this means that it is impossible to approach the assessment of possible future battles simply by using the yardstick of past battles</u>. [37] (Emphasis added)

207

In sum, the Soviet Union faces shortcomings in the crucial area of military science and technology. Russian pride and its desire to equal the West are known and, indeed, can hardly be underestimated. It seems safe to contend, however, that military leaders are aware of Soviet technological inferiority. Soviet "military-scientific potential" is catching up with the United States but is not leading the way. The strategic and conventional build-up is no doubt impressive, but R&D and the defense industrial sector cannot but be affected by the basic weaknesses of the Soviet system [38]. Within the military, traditionalism, extreme secrecy, and a conservatism in the face of change impede Soviet efforts to effectively compete with the West, particularly the United States. Achieving change in the system and in people's attitudes toward the system is a slow painful process, as Soviet leaders are well aware, and this can only weaken the Soviet position in the East-West rivalry.

Soviet desire for arms control negotiations, above all with the United States, stems, therefore, from both external military strength and internal economic and technological weakness. At the strategic level, sufficiency must take precedence over superiority, not only for the political but also for the military leadership. As dealt with earlier, strategic parity is sufficient, given the "correlation of forces" in the European theater, and an all-out technological race with the United States is not an enviable prospect for the Soviet Union.

> The Soviet Union's defense potential should be sufficient to deter anyone from disturbing our peaceful life. Not a course aimed at superiority in armaments, but a course aimed at their reduction, at lessening military confrontation; that is our policy. [39]

Naturally, Brezhnev in no way alludes to Soviet inferiority, nor does he indicate any respect for the American and Western potential. He says, rather:

> We do not set ourselves the goal of achieving military superiority. We also know that this very concept becomes meaningless given the existence of the present enormous arsenals of stockpiled nuclear weapons and delivery means for them. [40]

Although Brezhnev does not use the words Mutual Assured Destruction, they are clearly implied. At the same time, he draws the conclusion: there must be strict equality or we cannot but improve our defense. Arms control can succeed only if both sides recognize this. In his usually shrewd manner, Brezhnev accommodates all parties. On the one hand, he as usual reassures his audience that the "defense is reliable and that it will continue to be at the required level." [41] On the other hand, he sides to a degree with those who are skeptical about the applicability of military power and who rule out its actual use. "To count on a new world war, therefore, is becoming increasingly meaningless... The military machine, absorbing immense human and material resources, is being brought to its peak." [42]

He sees military-technical improvements and innovations as still possible, but contends that their effect will yield no important military advantage. Insofar as military power can be used, it will be in the political-diplomatic realm, not in an East-West military conflict. Continuing "useless" weapons and doctrinal development only highlight the contradiction "existing between the developing processes of political detente in the world and the major lagging behind in terms of military detente." [43] It is precisely by entering negotiations that military power can be used to exert influence and be converted to diplomatic and economic advantage. The stronger party yields, the weaker one wields power in linkage politics. Soviet determination to maintain "at least" parity is probably the only effective lever for gaining favorable concessions in other fields.

Military leaders are not always against such a use of military power, either. It is interesting, and significant, that Kulikov's successor, General Ogarkov, shows confidence in the present deterrent and sees the present levels as sufficient.

> A general shift has occurred in favor of the relaxation of international tension, the positions of peace have been consolidated and a move has been made in the direction of reducing the danger of the outbreak of world thermonuclear war. [44]

Although Ogarkov does speak about the necessity of further strengthening and maintaining what has been achieved, he does not advocate Kulikov's "total" view. The latter wrote in Izvestia on the occasion of the 56th anniversary of the armed forces and navy:

> There is no more reliable shield for peace and the security of the people building a communist society than our army and navy...
>
> The peace policy...relies on the unity of the Soviet people rallied around the communist party, on their devotion to Lenin's ideas on the building of the new society, and also on the might of the armed forces. Therefore, the strengthening of the state's defense capability and of the combat might of the Army and Navy is a vitally important nation-wide

task. 45

The question of "how much is enough" is never
clearly answered in the military press, but former calls
for superiority, etc., have lessened and here and there
the word sufficiently even shows up. For example, in a
generally very military-orthodox article, it is asserted
that "the forces of peace now have sufficient power to
prevent the outbreak of a new world war by their energetic, coordinated actions." 46
Whether the Soviet leadership has prevented the
defense burden from increasing at the same rate as during
the 1960's is a matter of speculation. As a general rule,
it can be said that the growth of Soviet defense
expenditures follows the rate of economic growth. NATO's
assessment is that "between 1970 and 1979, Soviet defense
spending increased at a real annual average rate of
about 4%." Given the declining economic growth, this
means that the defense share will have risen from 11 to
12 per cent to "between 12 and 13 per cent by the end of
the decade." 47 In the light of Soviet military effort
in terms of weapons procurement and R&D, these estimates
seem to be much closer to reality than Brezhnev's
assurances of Soviet budgetary reductions or Ogarkov's
claim in 1973 that "the relative share of military
expenditures is diminished." 48 This does not mean,
however, that attempts by the political leadership to
economize in the defense sector have not taken place.
Both Soviet political and military sources point to that
fact. However, domestically, Brezhnev's strategy also
largely failed in this respect. Defense policy is even
more pressing than Brezhnev's domestic plans in general
and is dependent on "the international situation" as
predicted at the XXIV Party Congress. In the security
issue area, political leadership is more and more
conditioned by the results of arms control negotiations,
above all SALT. Presently, Soviet perspectives on arms
control with the United States cannot be optimistic.
Yet, the domestic strait-jacket can be loosened a little
bit only if there is a strengthening of international
security.

EQUAL SECURITY: HOW TO STRIKE THE BALANCE?

International security and arms control were neither
the only nor the major reason for normalization of East-
West relations. They formed just one part of a broader
political framework, which was primarily determined by
domestic considerations. Arms control, like military
might, is a means in international politics, not a goal
in itself. The active pursuit of detente, however, led
to a situation in which defense policy became ever more
important. Along with the East-West arms control

210

negotiations, some Soviet political leaders, who had never before contested defense priorities, gradually reviewed their positions. For example, Suslov, known for his firm stand on relations with the West and his support for the "glorious armed forces," became a supporter of a policy aimed at a new international power structure. At a time when Brezhnev badly needed support from his colleagues, Suslov suggested that military security was sufficiently guaranteed and that the time had come to determine "scientifically" the direction in which the peace-loving foreign policy of the Soviet Union should go. In November 1973, he said:

> The Soviet Union's foreign policy is based on an allround analysis of the international situation and the correlation of forces at each time and in each section. (Emphasis added)

He totally omitted the usual praise of the military and the role of military power in international relations, pointing to other issues instead.

> The switch in the development of international relations toward detente and mutually advantageous cooperation had deep objective roots. Its primary foundation is the basic change in the balance of forces in the international arena to the benefit of world socialism and, above all, the fast growth of the economic potential and political prestige of our country. [49]

Even though Trofimenko's conclusion that "long-term strategic decisions in the present-day environment cannot be other than decisions directed at demilitarizing politics," [50] was not be considered realistic by Soviet political leaders, they do seem to have reached the conclusion that arms control is desirable (see Table X). For the reasons outlined above and also because of Western insistence on military detente as a precondition to other forms of detente, Soviet political leaders have increasingly come to realize "that peaceful coexistence-- with continued political and ideological competition--is the preferable alternative to an unrestrained arms race and to recurring high-risk politico-military confrontation." [51]

As in the West, arms control is a disputed issue, above all with regard to the question as to whether and how national security is strengthened by its results [52]. But the experience of the 1970's has also demonstrated consistency and consensus in the Soviet approach to East-West arms control. As a general rule, it can be concluded that it is the political leadership which prevails in the decision-making. The military are advisors, whose power to influence the substance of the negotiations lies in their professional knowledge and expertise [53]. They have no say in the ultimate decision on arms control and the acceptance of a negotiated "package." As in military doctrine, the decision to use military power in foreign policy is a political prerogative. Once the "employment of means" in overall Soviet foreign policy is determined, military strategy and professional considerations regarding "the attainment of objectives" enter the game [54].

For example, the ABM Treaty definitely worked against traditional ideas of war-fighting and positive assessments of defense engrained in Soviet military strategy. Surprisingly, it was the Soviet Union that by 1971 insisted that ABMs be included in an agreement. Prior to this the Soviet negotiators had been very reluctant to even discuss defensive systems [55].

Apparently, the feeling had gained ground that defense was not always "good" but might in fact be destabilizing, triggering a new and very costly arms race. Furthermore, the former offensive imbalance had been redressed, and American defensive efforts--limited but far more extended and elaborated than Galosh--were now seen as most unwelcome. As Larionov indicated as early as 1970:

> ABM defense means, although they still do not have the capability of fulfilling the function given to them--that is, to guarantee defense from nuclear missile attack by the enemy--already act as the stimulus for the next stage of interdependence, when the effectiveness of the ABM system still being created is counterposed by the superior effectiveness of the means of counter-action (MIRVs), and so forth, ad infinitum...

> This cycle of the arms race will bring no solution to US security problems, but on the contrary, will help to destabilize the situation and lead to unrestricted competition between offensive weapons systems and to the complication of the entire arms complex, which it will be increasingly more difficult to control. [56]

The doubtful effectiveness of missile defense, reinforced by developments in offensive weaponry, was a major reason for the change from the "good" to the "bad" image of ABM in the Soviet Union. The system would soon be described as a "threat" to equal security, fit only for the plans "of those who contemplate the possibility of unleashing aggression," and serving to maintain the "illusion of unleashing a war unpunished." [57] With the prohibition of ABM by SALT-I, however, "deterrence by punishment" was guaranteed. The Soviet military view that "defense must be erected, no matter what the cost" was abandoned [58].

Soviet political determination to continue the SALT process is attested to by the evolution of the SALT-II agreement. Re-occuring delays for American domestic political reasons and the considerable changes in the 1974 Vladivostok agreement as proposed by the new Carter Administration in March 1977, undoubtedly complicated the position of Brezhnev and others in favor of SALT [59]. Kornienko's remark to Warnke is revealing as to the importance of the compromise reached and the bureaucratic rigidity even within the top leadership.

"What are you trying to do--kill SALT?" asked one Soviet official in private conversation with his American counterpart. Gromyko's deputy Georgy Kornienko took Paul Warnke aside and admonished him "You shouldn't have disregarded the fact that Brezhnev had to spill political blood to get the Vladivostok accords". [60]

From the viewpoint of the Soviet military, the SALT-II agreements can be--and probably are--seen as a sacrifice of hard-won advantages without much of a return in political-military currency [61]. A Soviet "hawk" may argue that American Forward Based Systems are painfully absent, and the advantage of the Soviet "heavy" ICBMs is significantly reduced by the limitation on the number of MIRVs of the SS-18 and SS-19, while the United States is free to deploy a modern heavy missile. The numerical advantage, conceded to the Soviet Union in SALT-I in order to off-set qualitative and operational confines of ICBMs and SLBMs, respectively, no longer exists, whereas the Soviet Union has even to dismantle some 250 ICBMs and has no cruise missiles to fully exploit the 1320 MIRV-ceiling. The United States is allowed to expand its missile force and to arm 120 strategic bombers with ALCMs. With regard to modernization and technological competition, the United States is not restrained in any of its existing programs, except for unconfirmed but possible plans to deploy conventional cruise missiles. A Soviet opponent of SALT may also point to the prohibition of the SS-16 or any new mobile, land-based intercontinental missile for the duration of the Treaty. Given these facts it is difficult to see how the new administration expects to get a "better" agreement in START. Of course, many arguments can be put forward to counter Soviet military objections [62]. The point here, however, is to illustrate that Soviet leaders are willing to make concessions and to accept restrictions which run counter to Soviet military-strategic thinking. One may even speculate that among the military themselves a gradual shift in thinking is taking place. In any case, Ogarkov's strong public endorsement of SALT-II is markedly different from Kulikov's cool appraisal of SALT-I in

1972 63.

A second important feature of the Soviet approach to arms control is its comprehensiveness. Unilateral disarmament measures and weapons limitations are out of the question. Strategic stability can only be achieved by taking into account the many complexities and differences between East and West. "A unilateral approach to the more complete limitation of the number of strategic offensive arms would, in many US evaluations, hardly be productive because of qualitative differences in the strategic weapons systems. It would seem hard to disagree with this." 64

Furthermore, the Soviet arms control approach is to a large extent integrated in overall policy. Unlike in the West, where arms control is seen by some as an end in itself and by others as "an unnatural act," 65 Soviet "national security policy has incorporated disarmament policy rather than being seen as in conflict with it." 66 The threat to Soviet security is assessed globally and, like the military-strategic input, considered that way. For example, the MBFR negotiations concerning the Central European theater are linked to the broader strategic and political situation. From the very outset of MBFR, the Soviets have maintained that "the correlation of conventional forces cannot be separated from the correlation of tactical and strategic nuclear forces, and the regional balance in Central Europe cannot be separated from the all-European and global balances." 67

In addition to the omission of American FBS, the exemption of French nuclear and conventional forces from the Euro-strategic equation is undoubtedly regarded a serious asymmetry. A Soviet military planner is not likely to disregard the special relationship between France and NATO and its strategic meaning. Indeed, French moves towards the Alliance are followed with suspicion. Pronouncements such as those of General Méry and President Giscard d'Estaing in 1976 are noted immediately and draw disapproval from the highest level. I. Aleksandrov was quick to regret the departures from the independent Gaullist line and moves toward the integration of France in an "expanded security zone" and "participation in forward line combat." 68

Furthermore, Soviet comment does not fail to point to the long land frontiers for their defense, "not only in the West, but also in the East en the South." 69

Nor do Soviet analysts agree with the Western view that "the geographic factor" is advantageous to the Warsaw Pact. On the contrary, the West is said to enjoy considerable advantages such as "the presence of NATO countries' military bases close to the socialist states' borders, the location of large continents of US troops in Europe near the region of reduction and the economic and mobilization capabilities of the Western European countries." 70

Finally, Western insistence on the reduction of ground forces exclusively and, moreover, in unequal numbers, is seen as an attempt to gain "one-sided military advantages." There is no justification for requiring asymmetrical reductions, since the manpower strength is roughly the same in East and West, as is documented by extensively quoted Western sources [71]. Soviet criticism of limiting the negotiations to the question of manpower, particularly of the ground forces, is well-founded. No military planner in either East or West assesses the European balance of forces without taking into account the air forces, conventional weapons systems and nuclear-capable systems of primary importance on the battlefield [72]. In 1973, five days before the opening of the talks, Brezhnev outlined to the World Peace Congress the Soviet Union broad approach. He added that if Western proposals were aimed at disturbing the existing balance of power, "the whole question will become a bone of contention and an object of unending dispute." [73]

Seven years later, the positions of the two parties have changed only marginally. The talks are still deadlocked, for neither side accepts the other's basic approach. Aside from many other factors such as stubbornness in the so-called "data-discussion," the fact of MBFR being hostage of the SALT process, and technical complexities, Caldwell's conclusion about MBFR points to the basic problem: "Mutual force reductions have suffered from the outset because of a conflict between the Soviet's global and comprehensive perspective and NATO's fractional and restrictive one." [74]

This basic difference of approach continues to be a complicating factor in East-West arms control. In the talks on Long Range Theater Nuclear Forces (LRTNF) in Europe that started in November, 1981, the Soviet Union demands the inclusion of FBS and will probably insist on a comprehensive future SALT agreement. NATO and the United States, on the other hand, have proposed in Geneva that first of all the 572 Pershing II missiles and GLCMs are subject for negotiation. In the so-called "zero option" the Soviet counterpart of these land-based systems are primarily the SS-20, SS-4 and SS-5. There is no indication that the Western preference for a selective, step-by-step and system-by-system approach to arms control is changing. For example, Leslie Gelb-- as well as others--concludes, on the basis of rich experience in arms control: "Arms restraint talks with Moscow should be fashioned to move in small steps to do what can be done and to reach agreement expeditiously." [75]

Gelb is probably right, for the complexities and asymmetries involved in TNF arms control are too many and too great to be dealt with in a comprehensive manner. Whether arms control agreements contribute to international security is a value judgment, not a technical-mathematical matter. The geographic, qualitative and doctrinal asymmetries demand from political leaders in East en West judgments that go beyond the current quantitative comparisons and military-technical considerations. Therefore, a selective an step-by-step approach seems to be the "best" if not the only approach. A short digression on TNF may be useful to illustrate this.

The TNF weapons systems presented in Tables VI, VII and VIII do not lend themselves to comparison, because of their variable characteristics and capabilities. They clearly rule out a mere continuation of the quantitative approach to arms control. The great variety of systems precludes a simple counting process. Factors such as what the systems actually can do and are planned and deployed for must be taken into consideration.

First, it is characteristic of most LRTNF that they have a multi-role capacity. They can be used in both tactical and strategic roles--e.g., cruise missiles, fighter bombers--and, moreover, in a conventional as well as nuclear role--e.g., dual-capable aircraft.

Second, these weapons systems have a multi-mission capacity. For instance, modern dual-capable sea- and air-launched cruise missiles as currently deployed by the Soviet Union can be used against naval as well as land targets (the sea-based SS-N-3, SS-N-7, SS-N-12, SS-N-19, and the ACLMs AS-2 through AS-6). These weapons are assigned to the Soviet navy, but they pose a threat to large parts of Western Europe, and to a lesser extent, to coastal areas of the United States. Soviet superiority in maritime weapons systems is not limited to quantitative aspects, however. On the contrary, most disturbing are the qualitative differences with NATO's forces. While the Soviet Union has enhanced the pre-launch survivability (PLS) and the probability to penetrate (PTP) of its nuclear systems, NATO has increasingly been confronted with a greater vulnerability of its own systems, particularly with regard to the PLS of aircraft-carriers and the PTP of aircraft. Soviet maritime nuclear systems may come to play an even greater role in the East-West nuclear balance should arms control measures exclusively restrain other so-called "grey-area" weapons, e.g., land-based missiles. Missions previously assigned to air and ground forces could be transferred to maritime forces. Thus the "grey-area" would not disappear but simply be moved to sea.

Third, long-range systems are characterized by their multi-theater capacity. This is clearly the case with naval and air forces, but the new mobile land-based systems, such as SS-20 and cruise missile, also defy arms control measures limited to a specific geographical area. The possibility of rapid redeployment of these weapons seriously undermines the validity of a regional arms control agreement. It is therefore, that the United

216

States has proposed a global limitation on land-based LRTNF.

However, a more or less selective approach, although much easier to formulate, is not easy to negotiate. For example, LRTNF with a range of more than 1000 km include missiles and aircraft, and the negotiations face most of the difficulties outlined above.

Moreover, the--omnipresent--quantitative disadvantage of NATO is also a serious problem in this selective package. NATO's inventory consists of the 572 planned missiles and the F-111 and A-6 aircraft. The Soviet side numbers the SS-4, SS-5, SS-20 and the SS-N-5 missiles, the Backfire, Badger and Blinder bombers and the Fencer fighter-bomber. If launchers were the counting unit, the Soviet Union would number some 1740 systems against 848 American FBS. If NATO systems are included, the Western inventory would be about 1200. If the parties were to agree about the number of systems available for a nuclear role in Europe, as estimated in the Tables, these ratios would be roughly 1100: 750 and 1100: 1120. Thus, there is only rough parity, if the Soviet Union does not further increase her forces, the LRTNF modernization program is included, the China factor is taken into account, and the three Western nuclear powers agree about a range of complex qualitative factors--a highly unlikely matter, if negotiable at all.

If deliverable warheads were made the counting unit, the discrepancy in numbers would increase because of the three MIRVs of the SS-20. Moreover, Soviet bombers (Backfire, Badger and Blinder) can be reloaded with one or two stand-off weapons (A-2, A-3, A-4 or A-6). The reload-capable stand-off bomber force is far more effective than the fighter-bomber carrying nuclear bombs, since the survivability of the latter is highly questionable. Also in this respect NATO is at a considerable disadvantage, for the air forces--lacking stand-off weapons--must penetrate the dense air defenses of the Soviet Union.

The selection of one particular range is obviously arbitrary. The Soviet Union, moreover, might insist on a lower range, thus adding to NATO's disadvantages. Western Europe is vulnerable to most medium-range weapons striking from non-Soviet Warsaw Pact countries. At the same time, all NATO systems capable of reaching the Soviet Union would be subject to limitation and reduction. A range floor of, say, 800 km would include all dual-capable NATO aircraft.

The most serious shortcoming of this approach, however, would be that all American TNF in Europe would be subject to limitation without the West being granted some say in Soviet developments with regard to all SLBMs and SLCMs on both submarines and surface ships. Similarly, land-based ballistic missiles (Scud/SS-23, Scaleboard/SS-22) would continue to threaten large parts of the European continent. Neither their modernization nor their possible increase could be raised by the West in arms control negotiations.

To conclude, even though the Soviet comprehensive approach to arms control seems more attractive in theory, the numerical differences and, above all, the geographic asymmetry between Eastern and Western forces in Europe make it extremely difficult to strike a mutually acceptable balance and to determine what is "equal security."

MILITARY POWER, ARMS CONTROL AND FOREIGN POLICY

Equal security is defined differently in East and West, but before international negotiators meet each other in the conference room, most of the positions taken there have been determined at home. Arguments for and against a given proposal have already been heard. One important group of contributors is the Soviet military, and most of them are "skeptical about and generally hostile to arms control." [76] Aspaturian's conclusion-- reached about fifteen years ago--about the Soviet military attitude remains largely accurate.

> In general, the professional military has resisted troop cuts and reduced military expenditures; is skeptical of disarmament and arms control measures; is more prone to view U.S. intentions as implacably aggressive; is more concerned with the possibilities of preventive war by the United States; has consistently supported a large military establishment, demanded greater defense expenditures and more advanced military weapons; and has with equal constancy called for vigilance, preparedness and readiness to fight any type of war from a local conflict to all-out thermonuclear war. [77]

It is not surprising, therefore, that new initiatives regarding arms control can only come from other quarters and, as has been shown, only from the top political leadership. Soviet military theory shows an almost total indifference to arms control and a total lack of professional concept and framework [78]. Arms control negotiations threaten the Soviet military with the loss of their virtual monopoly of knowledge, with interference from Party leaders and bureaucrats such as those from Foreign Affairs, and with the risk of having their professionalism and efficiency assessed. Finally, of course, the military are concerned about the Soviet strategic and defense posture.

The establishment of the United States Institute (SShA), headed by Arbatov, and the expansion in 1969 of political-military studies in the Institute of World

218

Economy and International Relations (IMEMO) by a new
Division are a reflection of a felt political need for
more channels of information [79]. Moreover, the heads
and staff members of the divisions concerned include
such prominent military writers as Larionov, Kulish,
Milshtein and Semeiko. It is worth noting that Larionov
left the United States Institute in 1974 and returned to
the General Staff to head, as is believed, its arms
control section. The fact that these military
representatives of political institutes can publish
independently from their (former) professional colleagues
and that even "civilian strategists" such as Arbatov and
Trofimenko can publicly contradict some basic tenets
of military strategy are indicative of significant
developments in the Soviet system of secrecy and professional autonomy.

Their impact must not be overestimated, however.
First, a distinction must be made between the specific,
technical issues of arms control and the general policy
questions, for the "division of labor" in military
strategic matters is also predominent in arms control
policy. The military dominate the former while neither
civilian nor military scholars are supposed to deal with
specifics. In the formulation of arms control policy
by the various departments, a similar situation exists.
During SALT-I, officials from Foreign Affairs "were kept
almost totally ignorant of both qualitative and
quantitative characteristics of Soviet ABM and strategic
forces."

> However, when it came to the issue of the formula-
> tion of the general Soviet approach to SALT-I, the
> foreign policy establishment played an equal, if not
> more important, role than the military-industrial
> complex. [80]

As noted before, mutual respect is displayed up to
the highest level. Military considerations were
decisive for the rejection of the American proposals
in March and June-July, 1974. Kissinger's "conceptual
breakthrough" concerning a limitation of throw weight
of MIRVed missiles and Nixon's attempt to limit MIRVed
missiles were discussed in Politburo meetings--for one
of which Grechko flew back from the country--and were
unacceptable because the Soviet MIRV test program had
not yet been completed. The military gave the green
light in October of that year, after they were sure
deployment could start--in 1975--and that the Soviet
Union could speak as an equal of the United States in
Vladivostok [81].

Second, military considerations are important and
indeed respected. The following example illustrates
how military opposition led to the political correction
of a proposal made--apparently too hastily--by the

General Secretary, personally.

In June 1971, Brezhnev--totally unexpectedly-- declared Soviet readiness to discuss the matter of American and Soviet fleets "cruising about for long periods far from their own shores." [82] His initiative was understandable at the time, for Brezhnev was eager to advance his foreign policy plans. But the idea ran counter to the widely advocated political and military role of a high-seas Soviet navy. It is not surprising, therefore, that Brezhnev's remarks met a cold reception. The phrases were never quoted, nor did he again repeat them. Most strikingly, in the July issue of Morskoi Sbornik, Grechko stood up for the interests usually defended by his colleague Admiral Gorshkov. The Army Marshal once more stressed the military, political and prestige role of the Soviet navy.

> (The Okean maneuvers) showed the entire world the enhanced might of the Soviet Union as a world naval power, whose fleet the imperialists cannot help but take into consideration...
>
> It is not only for maneuvers that our fleet enters the oceans. Our ships sail the oceans and seas in varied areas--wherever the security and state interests of the Soviet Union require...
>
> The Soviet navy is a symbol of the fraternity of peace-loving peoples. In recent years, our warships have made scores of official visits to countries in Europe, Africa, Asia and America, and everywhere Soviet seamen are welcomed as honored guests, sincere friends, as envoys and defenders of peace. [83]

It is no surprise that the case was closed and only surfaced again in 1974 after the proposal had been essentially altered. Brezhnev then said: "We consider it useful to reach an agreement on the withdrawal from the Mediterranean Sea of all Soviet and American ships carrying nuclear weapons." [84]

On this occasion the Party leader got support. Admiral Gorshkov hailed Brezhnev's renewed initiative in an interview with Pravda one week later and Brezhnev would--perhaps one should say was allowed to--repeat the proposal several times, for instances, at the XXV Party Congress [85].

Consensus had apparently been established about the important role of sea-denial and power projection of the navy and, at the same time, about the most threatening aspect of the American fleet: its nuclear capability. The new proposal only affected the Soviet-American nuclear balance near the European theater and pointedly omitted Soviet non-nuclear capabilities to "project military power." The essential difference with the previous proposal was the exclusive restraint on the American capability--or threat--to cross the Soviet territorial threshold in a conflict in the European theater. Had this proposal been accepted by the United States, Soviet military preponderance would have been enhanced and a strategic-nuclear confrontation with the United States removed a little further.

Thus, military considerations--whether made explicit or not--are respected and incorporated in the Soviet approach to arms control. Furthermore, even though some top military leaders may be inclined toward a positive attitude to arms control, the vast majority still appear to be "skeptical and generally hostile." Despite the inclination of some military leaders to recognize the validity of political arguments pointing to Soviet geographic and numerical advantages and technological and economic benefits, the preservation of both the military domestic position and a strong, in more than one respect superior defense posture continues to be valued by most as the highest priority.

Proponents of arms control in the Soviet Union are understandably cautious in advancing their views [86]. Seriously hampered by incomplete information--or even by a total lack of factual knowledge--they are even more vulnerable vis-à-vis the powerful politico-military complex. Although their views, if implemented, will bear on military-technical matters, they deal with arms control in broad, political terms. But this is only one reason for their political rather than military analysis. As mentioned before, the Soviet approach is political. Military power is seen as one instrument of foreign policy, and arms control is regarded as a means rather than a goal in itself.

This is not to say that fear of nuclear war is not as important a motive in the East as in the West or that genuine concern about nuclear warfare is absent. There may or may not be differences with the West as to the political-moral acceptability of nuclear weapons and their use. There is, however, a difference with regard to the Western tendency to view arms control as a separate issue and as a relatively more important one than others in East-West relations.

Few of the "arms control community"--if one may call it that--in the Soviet Union share the view of Milshtein and Semeiko who called arms control "that salient which decisively influences relations in all other spheres." [87] It was exceptional that a Politburo member, Suslov, referred to SALT as the most important of the Soviet-American agreements. Kissinger and Nixon were understandably amazed when Podgorny intervened during the 1972 negotiations with Brezhnev and Kosygin and contradicted his superior-ranking colleagues by saying that arms limitations were more important than

trade 88. Such revelations, however infrequent, show
that there is belief in and importance attached to the
effectiveness of agreements on the limitation of the
arms race. As Arbatov has often stressed, new and more
arms are "useless" and restraints on their development
and deployment must also be assessed in terms of their
military relevance for a more stable strategic balance.
These analysts maintain that technical improvement of the
arsenals is "politically senseless and unbelievably
costly on the economic plane." 89
    A more common and a different approach is
Trofimenko's. He is skeptic about the military effectiveness of arms control agreements and, rather, emphasizes the contribution of military detente to political
detente.

> Without measures to eliminate mutual terrors and
> fears and without the limitation of the scale and
> speed of strategic arms building, it is impossible
> either to establish genuine mutual trust or to have
> a prospect of strengthening peaceful relations
> between the USSR and the United States in other
> spheres. 90

Trofimenko's attitude is not only different with
regard to the impact of arms control on military detente,
but he also denies that the arms race is politically
senseless. He is clearly against the arms race and doubts
whether it is decisive in the overall military balance,
but he does not dismiss the political importance of
changes in military power. For example, he concludes
about Schlesinger's design to improve the flexibility
in strategic options:

> All the talk of Pentagon officials about
> "retargeting" such missiles does not at all repre-
> sent some sort of objective information as to the
> intentions and proposed tactical military use of
> American strategic forces, being publicized for the
> information of the general public. Instead, it is,
> on the contrary, a specifically designed attempt
> to exert psychological pressure upon the other
> side, i.e., an attempt to derive if not a direct
> military-technical gain then, at least, a conceptual,
> psychological advantage over the opposition. 91
> (Emphasis added)

Second, because of the political significance of
military power, the arms control process is regarded as
both a political undertaking and a political responsibility. In fighting the "technological imperative" of
the arms race, "only solutions in the political sphere
relying on the firm will for peace of the broadest
people's masses can be a real 'anti-bomb'." 92

In an excellent article, Trofimenko elaborates on the principles guiding SALT. He fully recognizes the many asymmetries between Soviet and American military-technical policies and the resulting military postures. However, he questions the American tendency to teach strategic affairs and to base the talks on an entirely American approach. This "proved to be the principal stumbling bloc" in 1974. Trofimenko questions the usefulness of the American, predominantly "military-technical," solutions to the problem of international security. In his view, SALT-I is: "An Important Action," [93] but no more than that. The most important understanding between the Soviet Union and the United States was that

> ...the agreements be based primarily upon what, in principle, are political decisions. This lifted the debate above the narrow technical considerations and emphasized the close correlation between a military and political detente...
>
> (Such an approach) helped both superpowers to break away from the restrictions of petty practicality, of "technical logic," and to cut through the Gordian knot of individual problems which, for a long time, appeared insoluble. The acceptance of political solutions resulted also in solving the sacramental question as to where to begin: with the establishment of mutual confidence or with measures postulating an absolute lack of confidence-measures which, however, would be unable to generate confidence. [94]

Arms control is, according to this view, not a matter for technicians but for politicians. An attempt to separate military and political detente and to leave arms control to the military "can result only in disarmament problems becoming buried in innumerable committees and sub-committees of experts, inevitably retarding the entire normalization process." [95] This Soviet observer evidently knows the working of bureaucratic politics, the more so when political leadership is lacking.

A third--and to this author somewhat questionable-- approach is an almost total reliance on the political process and on an exclusively political contribution to military detente. This is the view taken by IMEMO's analyst of European security and MBFR, Proektor, when he writes that "any measure for military detente without the corresponding political prerequisites is doomed to fail." [96] He does not deny the importance of the large military forces concentrated in Central Europe, but he stresses that it is "primarily the fact of their function and the political and military concepts of the states which condition this function" [97] which must be considered the main problem and focus of arms control.

Political antagonism--obviously ascribed to NATO--not
the military presence itself is the basic problem.

> The struggle for a detente in which military
> antagonism would play an ever smaller part, is an
> important component of the policy of peace pursued
> by the socialist countries. The view inherent in
> the Western supporters of a military-militarist
> (Voenno-militaristsky) approach to security--the
> view according to which security is insured only
> by military might, by a show of strength, and also
> by mutual recognition of an "equilibrium of power"
> both now and in the future--is extremely narrow.
> It does not accord with the variety of the era and of
> ways of insuring peace. It invariably contributes
> to the growth of the military factor. [98]

The fact that Proektor uses the word "mutual" in
this context may indicate an awareness of the action-
reaction game the "militaristsky" on both sides play to
insure continuously high defense appropriations. In
that case, his argument contains the message for political
leaders on both sides that they must get a tighter grip
on military programs. This would align Proektor with
Trofimenko's view that "long-term strategic decisions
in the present-day environment cannot be other than
decisions directed at demilitarizing politics." [99] If
this is not the case, then the naivity of his extreme
reliance on political leaders and the political process
is suspicious and--given Proektor's knowledge and military background--may be tantamount to deliberate
deception.
In East and West alike, political leaders are not
by definition "better" or more morally inspired than
military leaders, nor does negotiation which is
predominantly political in nature give greater assurance
for success than negotiations based on technical
considerations. For example, Richard Burt concludes
about the experience of the Arms Control and Disarmament
Agency in Washington:

> As arms control moved from being a diplomatic
> experiment to being a central fixture of US
> foreign policy in the last 15 years, ACDA has been
> displaced by units within the Pentagon, the State
> Department, and the National Security Council.
> The result is that in order to justify its existence,
> the agency has had to become ever more doctrinaire
> in its adherence to the primacy of arms control.
> This has created unnecessary bureaucratic frictions,
> and in many cases it has curiously reduced the
> influence of the agency. [100]

There is no reason to assume that the situation in Moscow during the early 1970's was any more conducive to expansive "diplomatic experiment" than the situation in Washington ten years before. Exclusive emphasis on the political-diplomatic aspect of the arms control process is unrealistic given the Soviet domestic "correlation of forces." Trofimenko and other "arms controllers" are cautiously trying to pave the way for a somewhat greater political-diplomatic and international-oriented input in Soviet security policy. They praise summitry and its impressive and important results but carefully avoid any suggestion that arms control is a goal in itself, prevailing over military-strategic, ideological or other considerations.

Political leaders in the Soviet Union are, like Trofimenko, very much aware of the complementary role of military detente. In 1973, at a time when Brezhnev needed support, Suslov, Gromyko, Podgorny, Kosygin, Andropov and Republic Party secretaries repeatedly underlined the General Secretary's call for "supplementing political detente with military detente." It was clear to them that detente with the West, particularly in economic areas, was not possible without concrete arms control agreements.

As Table X shows, the diplomatic area, dominated as it is by ideological precepts poses a major stumbling bloc in the Soviet policy of normalization. Despite the arguments for arms control, Soviet leaders are reluctant-- to say the least--to abandon "communist diplomacy," even if practiced selectively and not in direct relations with Western powers. Except for the Minister of Foreign Affairs, it is only Podgorny and he alone who explicitly links diplomatic and security issues of foreign policy. He was exceptionally straight-forward in December 1973, when he explained "the principle of indivisibility of peace."

> This is a concise, yet very comprehensive and meaningful formula. First and foremost this formula means that all developments in the world are interconnected and to a certain extent interdependent... The efforts to strengthen peace and security, in whatever part of the world they are undertaken and whatever problem they affect, are, therefore, inseparably linked and indivisible.
> 101

Podgorny reminds his audience of the horrors of the Second World War which "cry out to the conscience of the living" and applauds the positive changes in Europe, while expressing his hope for a similar development in Asia. Next, he formulates a condition for diplomatic relations that is similar to Western views and stripped of Soviet ideological tenets.

	I	II	III
BREZHNEV	+	[+ +]	+
ANDROPOV	+	+	+
GRECHKO*	[- -]	+	- -
GRISHIN	- —→ +	-	- -
GROMYKO	+ +	-	[+ +]
KIRILENKO	-	-	[- -]
KOSYGIN*	+ +	+	[- -]
MAZUROV*	-	-	- -
PODGORNY*	+ +	+	[+ +]
SUSLOV*	+ —→ + +	-	- -
USTINOV	+	[+]	-
(Secr. bloc)	+	-	-

+ +   positive
 +   moderately positive
 −   unsympathetic
– –   negative
[ ]   dominant issue for the leader

SOURCES: Speeches 1970 - 1976

* Grechko died in 1976; Podgorny lost his membership in 1977, Mazurov in 1978; Kosygin died in 1980, and Suslov died in 1982.

Unilateralism versus bi- and multilateralism is schematically presented for the security, economic and diplomatic issue areas. The views on cultural-ideological normalization are obviously negative and are not separately presented. However, they are clearly reflected in the priority of communist diplomacy. The views of only a limited number of Politburo members are analyzed, since those who are not involved in foreign policy seldom distinguish between the issues in their speeches. The views of Grishin and other Party secretaries are shown as one bloc, but their stand is based on a considerably smaller number of speeches. The marks (-) and (--) represent the view that favors the status quo to a greater of lesser degree. Proposed changes in the direction of greater East-West bi- and multilateralism are indicated by (+) and (++). Like Table IV, this Table should be considered to be no more than an illustration of the positions of persons and groupings as seen by the present author. It is his interpretation of the selected speeches.

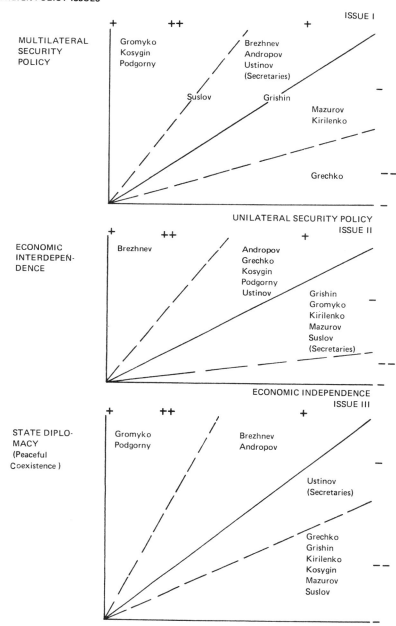

ISSUE I

MULTILATERAL
SECURITY
POLICY

+   ++   +

Gromyko
Kosygin
Podgorny

Brezhnev
Andropov
Ustinov
(Secretaries)

Suslov   Grishin

−

Mazurov
Kirilenko

Grechko   − −

UNILATERAL SECURITY POLICY

ISSUE II

ECONOMIC
INTERDEPEN-
DENCE

+   ++   +

Brezhnev

Andropov
Grechko
Kosygin
Podgorny
Ustinov

Grishin
Gromyko
Kirilenko
Mazurov
Suslov
(Secretaries)

−

− −

ECONOMIC INDEPENDENCE

ISSUE III

STATE DIPLO-
MACY
(Peaceful
Coexistence)

+   ++   +

Gromyko
Podgorny

Brezhnev
Andropov

−

Ustinov
(Secretaries)

Grechko
Grishin
Kirilenko
Kosygin
Mazurov
Suslov

− −

COMMUNIST DIPLOMACY (Proletarian Internationalism)

If we are really to build firm peace with a
lasting prospect for fruitful and all-embracing
cooperation between states, then the democratic
principles born by the practice of international
relations should be observed in the strictest
manner. 102   (Emphasis added)

Finally, he once more points to the ineffectiveness
of military power for the attainment of nationalistic
foreign-policy goals. "The situation in the world is
such that any attempt to achieve self-interested aims
through the use of crude force inevitably is doomed to
failure." 103
     The "Basic Principles of Mutual Relations" and the
"Agreement on the Prevention of Nuclear War," signed
by Nixon and Brezhnev in 1972 and 1973, are often said
to be the most important results of Soviet-American
detente. In light of the foregoing, this is not
surprising.
     They form the "new code of conduct" of states
following the principles of peaceful coexistence. They
are "the great victory for the Soviet foreign policy
line in international relations." 104 Peaceful
coexistence, which acknowledges East-West competition,
implies military detente and, according to Andropov,
should free East-West relations of "military rivalry."
If this is successful, normalization in other fields
is likely to follow and, indeed, is feared by many.
Andropov assures those who fear normalization that the
new foreign policy is no threat to either internal or
external security, but it is clear from his words in
1976 that he regrets that "the easing of international
tension itself continues to be an object of sharp
ideological struggle. There is perhaps no other question
causing so much debate and argument today." 105
     He does not make clear whether he is speaking of the
situation nationally or internationally or both. After
the prospect for a significant economic detente was
eliminated in 1974-1975, diplomatic detente was the next
victim. The leadership was able to continue military
detente with the West but was unable to supplement this
process of international security with military restraint.
Significantly, Brezhnev was "relieved" of his duties to
lead the arms control efforts which were now assumed
by Gromyko as an executive of the collective leadership.
     To conclude, Soviet military power is first of all
assessed in terms of national security based on military-
professional considerations. But the political leadership attempted to determine where war preparation should
stop and at the same time sought ways to turn military
power into political currency at home and abroad 106.
Brezhnev declared Soviet readiness to link progress in
arms control negotiations with the expansion of Soviet-
American trade but failed 107. At the same time, the

West insisted on concrete arms control results and demanded Soviet "good behavior" and cooperation in diplomatic relations. This proved to be too high a price for many Soviets. The political insecurity endemic to the Soviet system outweighed confidence in its military security [108].

Arms control measures were not likely to reduce the role of military power, but they could alter its role in international relations and in domestic politics. Therefore, national security and military policy was to reflect "the spirit of the entire policy" of the Soviet Union, viz. normalization. "This and only this is the crux of the matter." [109] It was precisely a lack of this new spirit or, in Brezhnev's words, of "a new mentality" that impeded arms control progress. A huge and continuing military effort and "bad behavior" devaluated the political currency derived from the demonstrated Soviet willingness to pursue arms control. Soviet proponents of detente have pointed out at length the need for a simultaneous and parallel "normalization" in various areas.

In the end, arms control alone cannot keep alive the process of detente. As far as the Soviet Union is concerned, her domestic political and economic problems cannot be solved by detente, the less so if detente is confined to military affairs. However unresponsive to Soviet problems Western policies may have been and may be in the future, what is imperative are Soviet domestic changes and reassessments of the "irreproachably correct" Soviet international behavior [110]. Without these, arms control, the last and increasingly threatened element of detente, may also fall victim to the weaknesses of Soviet collective leadership.

Conclusions

From the viewpoint of international relations theory it seems that Soviet declared readiness in the early 1970's to seek "normalization" and "mutually advantageous cooperation" with the West was a natural and rational step. The emerging superpower had taken care of "its own safety," and the changed correlation of forces had brought confidence in Soviet power. This allowed greater attention for and activity in the "diplomatic system"--to use Aron's terms. Moreover, the international climate had changed appreciably and was by the time of the XXIV Party Congress in 1971 conducive to new approaches to East-West relations and to the creation of further strongholds in the political world structure.

An analysis of Soviet diplomatic-strategic behavior during the early 1970's may also reveal some domestic rationales for the new foreign policy, notably the decline of economic growth, the need for Western technological assistance in the era of the Scientific-Technological Revolution, and the evergrowing defense burden. Indeed, the "Peace Program," the Soviet blueprint for detente, appeared to be a rationally designed and comprehensive policy plan linking a number of domestic and foreign strategic goals. On the international plane, the Soviet Union was to become a committed actor; domestically, the Soviet leaders intended to strengthen the national power base and to exploit opportunities stemming from normalization and "mutually advantageous cooperation." Beyond these conclusions the rational actor model is of little help for our understanding of Soviet foreign policy. Nonetheless, little as it may add to our knowledge of the Soviet Union, the conclusion that the Soviet Union was willing to become a committed international actor denoted an important, if not fundamental, development in Soviet diplomacy.

Another question of no less importance--and one which tends to be overlooked by the "Grand Strategy model" builders of international relations--is whether foreign policy motives were primarily of a diplomatic-

230

strategic nature or whether their origins were more
domestic-political. The new foreign policy undoubtedly
carried superpower ambitions. It was also an expression
of Russian pride and of a desire to be recognized as an
equal by the Western great powers, above all by the
United States. But this does not appear to have been the
main motivation for the major architect and advocate of
the "Peace Program," General Secretary Brezhnev.
International strategic-diplomatic advances were not the
principal concern or pivotal element of the normalization
of relations with the West. Soviet readiness to become
a committed international actor stemmed first of all
from domestic factors and in this respect from weakness
rather than from strength. Apart from military security,
the Soviet system was vulnerable and this fact, though
not publicly admitted, was recognized by the Soviet
leadership.

By the end of the 1960's the system was seriously
threatened by immobilism and by undirected rather than
directed political-economic development. One way to
spur on domestic development was the use of foreign
"reserves"--which Brezhnev expected to be substantial,
to say the least. At the same time, foreign policy
successes were probably seen as advantageous to domestic
political authority and a boost to the domestic leadership of both the Party and the Party leader. Successful
implementation of the "Peace Program" would cut both
ways.

The considerations prompting Brezhnev and his
followers to formulate this domestic and foreign "policy
package," however, constituted at the same time the
basis on which opponents were to build their main
objections. Brezhnev's "daring new plans," as Podgorny
called them, and his political ambitions soon became
the "core issue" and the Achilles' heel of the proposed
strategy for--limited--change. Soviet vulnerability to
Western influence might be acceptable to him, but others
perceived it as a threat to political sovereignty.
Some felt that the Soviet systemic weaknesses might be
overcome by international competition and interdependence;
others believed that the Soviet Union would incur
revisionism and reform undermining both socialist
achievements and the hard-won power positions of many
actors.

Soviet views on change, both international and
domestic, must be seen against the background of a
pervasive sense of political insecurity. For many,
normalization was likely to invite uncontrollable
capitalist inroads into the socialist system. By the
same token, Soviet actors may have been alarmed by
Brezhnev's seriousness and determination to improve the
domestic situation. His most important objective was
the re-establishment of a genuinely leading Party and he
left no doubt that he--in true Leninist style--was

going to play the main role as Party symbol, example and inspirer and that he expected his comrades to play the supporting roles.

The crucial question for the years following the XXIV Party Congress was whether the political leadership--Brezhnev and supporters--would be strong enough to implement the "agreed policy." Policy initiative and design in the Soviet Union originate at the top, but cooperation, evaluation and judgment involve various and indeed different actors. The Soviet political leadership may be seen as the "acting man" and "producer of effects;" one, however, that is bound to have restraints imposed upon it by other actors and by the inseparable political variables of the nature of power relations, the political process, and the content of the proposed policy.

Since the fall of Khrushchev in 1964, the Soviet polity had been at pains to prevent the re-emergence of a "personality cult" and the personal insecurity contingent on the rule of a "supreme leader." One of the few points characterized by complete unanimity among Party members was the prevention of personal rule. Under the Brezhnev-Kosygin regime political security was indeed carefully safeguarded. No-one could force his view or decision upon others by the use of crude power. A most important feature of the power relationship between Soviet actors was its mutuality. The formulation and implementation of policy required consent. The initiator had to form a coalition with some committee members and seek the support of others by convincing and pursuading them. Soviet decision-making is collective decision-making; the decision is a compromise in which all actors can recognize some of their wishes and by which their power positions are to a great extent respected.

Brezhnev's policy package bore all the marks of collective decision-making. He personally had come a long way from his staunch advocacy of heavy industry and defense priorities to his new role of major spokesman for consumer interests and military moderation. In this way Brezhnev had moved some distance from old-time coalition partners like Kirilenko and Grechko and closer to more moderate and economy-oriented leaders like Kosygin and Podgorny. In foreign policy a similar pattern can be distinguished.

Although the General Secretary on the whole respected the policy package or collective mandate, he nonetheless vigorously pursued the issues to his own liking. Whereas the Party leader made concessions to more moderate leaders on some issues--e.g., decentralization, consumption, arms control--he led the Party apparatus in a militant campaign for Marxist-Leninist political development at home, while seeking foreign "reserves" in order to avoid domestic reform.

Brezhnev personally encroached upon the responsibilities of Kosygin and insisted on Party rule in government and society. Brezhnev's international appearance and his growing image as a statesman were to underline his leadership and to reinforce the thrust of domestic politics.

The simultaneous pursuit of "Left"--domestic--and "Right"--international--policies brings to mind Dallin's observation concerning the instability of "reciprocal linkage." Brezhnev, imprisoned by collective leadership and the consensual power relationship, was forced to base his power on conflicting views and he was dependent on the support of a complex mix of opposed groupings. The policy package and the energetic, pushing conduct of the Party leader antagonized both those who were inclined to accept greater interdependence, but resisted increased Party intrusion, and those who opposed far-going normalization, but welcomed his domestic proposals (see Tables IV and X). Political leadership, however, cannot be sustained--let alone strengthened--when it has to switch sides continuously.

In the end, persistent disagreement in the Soviet polity impeded the implementation of the policy--"agreed" or not. Moreover, the political opponents did not yield to one another and it was inevitable that the polity would have to find an ultimate arbiter. Then the Soviet political system, lacking a popular vote, turned to the level of decision-making where the lowest common denominator could be found: that of the Central Committee and its Secretariat. The outcome of that process was predictable: the restoration of unity could not but prevail over a solution to the issues at stake. The collective device was "Back to Normalcy."

It may be the fate of comprehensive policy plans in general, but the policy package presented at the XXIV Party Congress found too many actors and policy elites in its way and involved too many different issues at the same time. As a consequence, the "Peace Program" fell into the hands of people who, unhindered by knowledge or understanding, were led by rigid ideological images. Brezhnev's foreign policy failed because it became "the main problem of domestic policy." Despite the fact that a number, if not the majority, of Politburo members closed ranks in 1973 in support of the besieged "Peace Program," the steadily enlarged collective leadership decided to restore unity at the expense of the active pursuit of normalization of East-West relations. Detente was not completely halted; nor were all the domestic plans abandoned. However, the driving force was neutralized and the autonomy of the sub-systems was largely preserved.

In the course of the 1970's, it became increasingly clear--to the Soviet leaders as well--that "mutually advantageous cooperation" had to be "supplemented by military detente." Contrary to Brezhnev's expectations and hopes, it was not trade but arms control which became the backbone of detente. The West insisted on concrete arms control measures and expected from the Soviet leadership military restraint and limitation of the impressive military build-up.

This is not to say that military detente was an unimportant part of the "Peace Program." From the outset the "relaxation of international tension" had been recognized by Brezhnev as a prerequisite for East-West normalization. But he considered military detente to be a means to political, and above all economic, ends rather than an end in itself. Indeed, like other parts of the policy package, Soviet security policy in the 1970's must be evaluated in the context of the overall policy process, decision-making and power relationships. Foreign policy emerged as a core issue in the course of the overall political process.

The basic features of Soviet politics in general were also present in the area of Soviet security policy. Thus vulnerability in a military sense found its expression in a definite high-threat perception on the part of Soviet actors. Even though the Soviet Union could be confident as regards its military security, Western, above all American, technological and economic capabilities and Soviet systemic weaknesses affecting the military organization as well, were matters of real concern to both political and military leaders. Furthermore, the weaknesses of collective leadership had a similar impact on defense policy, as was exemplified by the abortive attempt to reallocate defense resources for agricultural consumption purposes and by the effective role of ideology as a power base to legitimize the status quo. The military themselves did not possess the power to influence the outcome of these political questions. Nor can it be concluded that the Soviet military sought political responsibilities. Rather, the greater autonomy of the sub-systems, acting in concert--deliberately, incidentally or both--confronted the political leadership with tremendous difficulties in its directing and controlling task.

The complex of political-economic-military linkages, which had grown strongly, points to an overwhelming weight of military considerations in Soviet domestic and foreign policy without any corresponding weight of the military themselves in the political process. The Soviet military do not play a dominant role. Instead, the high "military rationale" in Soviet policy must be sought in the "autonomy of the political realm." The "societal imperative" of the military institution is firmly internalized in the Soviet polity.

The direct political influence of the military stems primarily from their monopoly of technical and strategic knowledge and expertise. The "functional imperative" is to a large extent respected by the political leadership and the military enjoy considerable professional autonomy. Moreover, Marxism-Leninism provides useful themes and "laws" for the military to underscore the political-military unity of their thinking. At the same time the military emphatically point to the responsibilities of the "professional soldier." Marxism-Leninism is also used to derive some basic military-operational premises--the planning of the offensive, the goal of superiority, and adherence to a "deterrence-through-defense" rather than a "defense-through-deterrence" nuclear strategy.

The successful implementation of the "Peace Program" and the conclusion of arms control agreements might have undermined both military imperatives in various respects. Detente might have led to drastic changes in images of the West; agreements might have constituted convincing reasons for reducing defense expenditure; arms control negotiations might have threatened the near-monopoly of the military expert.

It must be concluded, though, that military-technical considerations have continued to play a dominant role in Soviet approaches to arms control. Many military security concerns are shared by political-strategic analysts. For example, most will agree with the military objections to MBFR, that these talks do not address a number of essential problems and concerns. Whether these and other concerns stem from professional-military considerations or are voiced by actors stressing a global, comprehensive and, above all, political approach, the argument can hardly be mistaken by the Soviet polity.

Besides the monopoly of knowledge and the common adherence to ideology as important power bases, the Soviet military enjoy other advantages compared with their Western counterparts. First, numerical superiority in practically all categories of weapons systems gives the Soviet military a comfortable position in arms control negotiations. The present mostly quantitative approach to arms control works in their favor. Second, geographic factors--e.g., the separation of the US and Western Europe, the limited space in Western Europe-- form a tremendous complication for the West in formulating an arms control proposal that contributes to the strengthening of Western security. A third asymmetry favoring the Soviet Union is the difficulty experienced by Western sovereign states in finding common solutions and approaching the Soviet Union with closed ranks.

The political leadership may point out these advantages to the military and underline possible spin-offs of military detente in other issue areas. At the same time, arms control negotiations serve to strengthen the Party with regard to defense matters and to counter the "Garrison State syndrome" that--officially or actually--affects the thinking of most military and quite a few Party members. Indeed, detente runs counter to the civil-military coalition dominated by the "military mind" as defined by Huntington.

A most dangerous situation in East-West relations would arise if the "civil and military minds" were to fuse and assume the world outlook and strategic considerations of the latter. A "grand coalition" of political and military leaders of the stamp of Kirilenko and the late Marshal Grechko, supported by an autistic, dogmatic polity that seeks unilaterally guaranteed security behind the "Iron Curtain," could transform the present East-West competition into downright confrontation. Current Soviet indifference to East-West relations could change to a deliberate challenge to the West far beyond the Soviet-Afghan border.

If the Soviet tendency to advocate in extremis a war-fighting capability, to subscribe to the usefulness of military superiority and to lean towards the ever greater militarization of the domestic socio-economic system meets with no opposition whatsoever, East-West security is likely to worsen, quite probably to the detriment of the West.

First, there is reason to doubt whether the Western democracies are willing to devote still greater sums to defense. The West can perhaps outrun the Soviet Union economically; but it would choose the virtually sole issue area where the Soviet system can sustain fierce competition and where the leaders are politically in a superior position to most Western leaderships. It is highly questionable whether President Reagan will succeed in convincing the Congress that the US defense budget should - and can - increase so dramatically as the proposes. The idea of strengthening security by spending more money on more weapons is still less appealing in Europe. Even now, in spite of the ongoing Soviet military build-up and military superiority in Europe, West European governments have difficulty in meeting the military requirements agreed upon by the Alliance as a whole. Some European governments even have to cope with popular peace movements demanding unilateral steps like budgetary cuts or weapon reductions.

Second, from the military-strategic point of view a still further enhanced Soviet war-fighting capability deployed in the European theater cannot but weaken West European security. The ability to defend Western Europe is being questioned today, largely because of the military and geo-strategic advantages of the Soviet Union referred to in the foregoing. To the extent that increased Soviet capabilities will strengthen confidence and reduce the number of uncertainties in the mind of the Soviet planner, the credibility of West European defense will decrease. This in turn is bound to affect Western determination sooner or later in both the political and the military sense. Unlike their approach to the intercontinental--American--theater, for which there is no conceivable war-fighting and war-winning strategy, the Soviet military have developed such a strategy in detail for the European theater. Moreover, they have been quite successful in gradually deploying the military posture that corresponds with Soviet military theory. Soviet military capabilities have undeniably grown impressively, and there is no evidence whatsoever that the Soviet Union will ever allow itself to fall behind in that area.

As long as there is a tendency to favor the Soviet foreign policy embodied in the "Peace Program" however, there are ways of maintaining a relatively stable military balance, of negotiating, and of influencing Soviet behavior to a greater or lesser degree. Far-going militarization of Soviet foreign policy and East-West relations need not become reality. To be sure, fundamental differences and East-West competition--not least in the military sphere--will remain. Yet, as has been stressed several times, the question is not whether antagonizing developments will take place, but to what extent they can be allowed to occur. Our distaste for the Soviet system, the Soviet conflict-prone approach to the West, and the Soviet systemic bias against change in the highly militarized domestic and international system are not the only factors to be taken into account in Western assessments.

There are Kremlin leaders who recognize the weaknesses of the system and seek the potential benefits of normalization. There are leaders who are concerned about Soviet economic stagnation and are ready to take the risks stemming from greater interdependence. There are political and military leaders who are aware of the danger of competing war-fighting strategies and of the economic burden of defense. Although they will never say so, some leaders probably admit to themselves that Marxism-Leninism is a poor guide for East-West relations but at the same time--often regrettably--an effective political means of preserving the status quo and established domestic power positions.

Brezhnev introduced a number of changes when he launched the "Peace Program." Ten years of implementation have seen limited success and many failures, certainly from Brezhnev's point of view. His domestic economic policy in no way benefited from economic cooperation and trade, as he had hoped; his conduct of foreign policy enhanced his political authority for only a short period of time; he was forced to temper his drive for normalization. The conduct of foreign policy was taken over by a much more cautious, ideology-prone collective leadership that did not eschew foreign military assistance detrimental to detente, that decided to invade Afghanistan, and that has continued the Soviet military build-up.

Arms control negotiations did not significantly strengthen international military security. The relatively stable military situation of the end of the 1960's was maintained, that is, on the basis of Mutual Assured Destruction. Military breakthroughs were not regarded as upsetting the balance dramatically, yet ongoing unilateral defense efforts seriously hampered bilateral determination of security. The Soviet Union energetically pursued the goal of absolute equality, which involved extensive military programs aimed at national security. This, in turn, set in motion a major campaign in the United States for strengthening American national security and constituted the principal reason for NATO's TNF modernization.

On the other hand, the Soviet Union was committed to East-West arms control and indeed showed its determination in that respect. Brezhnev and others became aware of the Western view that political detente is a function of military detente rather than vice versa. He even concluded in 1976 that "all other successes...may lose their meaning" if SALT failed to yield results. (Pravda, January 18) Although not pursued as priority issue, arms control became a crucial issue. The importance of East-West relations and arms control was reflected in the Soviet Union by some personnel and institutional changes in the field of security policy, but--like other plans and policies--they took place at an extremely slow pace.

Obviously, the set-backs suffered by Brezhnev's policies cannot be ascribed to domestic factors alone. A most serious blow to Brezhnev's position and to the implementation of detente policy was the adoption of the Jackson-Vanik Amendment. First, the time in which the subject was discussed coincided with the heated Soviet domestic debate. The timing could hardly have been worse. Second, the explicit linkage of trade with the human rights of Soviet Jews could not have failed to provoke a negative reaction.

Finally, Soviet actors fully accept the fact of East-West conflict and competition. Although many protest against Western defense policies are heard, military competition is regarded as normal. The question is not whether East and West should have a credible defense and modernize their forces, but rather to what extent. There are many reasons why the Soviet Union is ready to be a committed international actor. Most of these reasons seem to be even more compelling in the 1980's than they already were in 1971. The Soviet leadership has slowly come a long way from its autarchic tendencies, its drive for military superiority, and its predominant concern for national security to some form of interdependence, military "essential equivalence" and concern for international security. The "Peace

238

Program" at least achieved this. Western policy should avoid strengthening the opposite tendency, for Soviet security is also our security.

Notes

General author's note. The figures for weapons systems and the East-West military balance have been compiled from a variety of publications. The number game is complex, much more than a matter of simple counting. A major problem is what is counted, and by whom. Are weapons systems or warheads selected? Are the categories that are compared in fact comparable? The analyst not only has to contend with methodological problems, but is totally dependent on the publication of governmental intelligence which, according to the former Secretary of the US Defence Intelligence Board, Cordesman, entails many uncertainties and intended as well as unintended biases. (Preface of Imbalance of Power) There is no need to share Disraeli's cynical view that "There are lies, damn lies, and statistics" to concede to sceptics the questionable value and accuracy of numerical comparisons of military strength. The difficulties mentioned in any case explain the discrepancies between the various data sources. This obviously also implies that no more than relative importance can be attached to the present author's judgment in compiling his figures of military strength.

Besides articles published in a wide variety of newspapers and journals, the data are borrowed mainly from the following publications:

> The Military Balance. Yearly published by the International Institute for Strategic Studies, London; John M. Collins, American and Soviet Military Trends since the Cuban Missile Crisis, Washington D.C. 1978; John M. Collins and Anthony H. Cordesman, Imbalance of Power: An Analysis of Shifting US-Soviet Military Strengths and Net Assessment Appraisal, San Rafael 1978; Tactical Nuclear Weapons: European Perspectives, Stockholm International Peace Research Institute, London 1978; Aviation Week and Space Technology, Air Force, Soviet Aerospace and other periodicals.

INTRODUCTION

1. Rosenau's observation regarding "construction paradigms
   that more adequately account for the changing structures
   of world politics" is of no less significance for the study of Soviet foreign policy.

   The question of how much change constitutes basic
   change is more a conceptual than an empirical question; the empirical attempts to measure change have
   not yielded such clear-cut and convergent findings as
   to promote widespread agreement on whether fundamental
   transformations are at work.

   James N. Rosenau, "Muddling, Meddling and Modelling: Al-
   ternative Approaches to the Study of World Politics in an
   Era of Rapid Change," Millennium: Journal of International
   Studies, Autumn 1979, p. 133.

2. Studies and wargames conducted as early as 1955 (Operation
   "Sage Brush" in Louisiana, and "Carte Blanche" in Western
   Europe) showed that "limited" tactical nuclear wars would
   result in the death of millions of people.
   cf. Jeffrey Record, U.S. Nuclear Weapons in Europe: Issues
   and Alternatives, The Brookings Institution, 1974, pp. 10-
   11; Alain C. Enthoven and K. Wayne Smith, How much is
   enough? Shaping the Defense Program 1961-1969, New York
   1971, Chapter 4; George W. Rathjens, "The Dynamics of the
   Arms Race," (April 1969) in Arms Control: Readings from
   Scientific American; San Francisco 1973, p. 185, where he
   calculates U.S. fatalities in several hypothetical nuclear
   exchanges. Various scenarios for limited nuclear attacks
   on both the United States and the Soviet Union are described in The Effects of Nuclear War, Congress of the
   United States, Office of Technological Assessment, Washington D.C., 1979.
   It is hard to disagree with what Kissinger contended in a
   major statement, "Detente with the Soviet Union: The Reality of Competition and the Imperative of Cooperation" to
   the Senate Committee on Foreign Relations, September 19,
   1974.

   Paradox confuses our perception on the problem of
   peaceful coexistence; if peace is pursued to the ex-

243

clusion of any other goal, other values will be com-
promised and perhaps lost; but if unconstrained rivalry leads to nuclear conflict, these values, along with
everything else, will be destroyed in the resulting
holocaust.

Reprinted in Survival, January/February 1975, pp. 35-42.

3. Of the many publications of Thomas Wolfe, the following
    are worthy of special mention:
    Thomas Wolfe, The SALT Experience: Its Impact on U.S. and
    Soviet Strategic Policy and Decision-making. RAND R-1686-
    PR, September 1975; Thomas Wolfe, Military Power and So-
    viet Policy, RAND P-5388, March 1975.
    Matthew P. Gallagher and Karl F. Spielmann Jr, Soviet
    Decision-making for Defense: A Critique of U.S. Perspec-
    tives on the Arms Race, New York, 1972; Karl F. Spielmann,
    Analyzing Soviet Strategic Arms Decisions, Boulder Co,
    1978; Edward L. Warner III, The Military in Contemporary
    Soviet Politics: An Institutional Analysis, New York 1977;
    the numerous publications of David Holloway should also be
    mentioned.

4. The so-called "Team B," a number of scholars gathered to-
    gether under chairman Professor Richard Pipes of Harvard
    University. By the same token, it is questionable whether
    scholars should take an active part in such "anti-SALT"
    lobbies as the Committee on the Present Danger. cf. Arthur
    M. Cox, The Dynamics of Detente, How to End the Arms Race,
    New York 1976.

5. For a concise, lucid review of "theories" treating the
    arms race as a mere particular consequence of the "action-
    reaction" process, a conspiracy of the "Military-Industri-
    al Complex" or the result of "human madness," see John
    Garnett, "Disarmament and Arms Control Since 1945," in
    Laurence Martin (ed.), Strategic Thoughts in the Nuclear
    Age, London 1979, especially pp. 198-206.

    Hedley Bull's comment on ideas such as reliance on a world
    government or rejection of military power as a foreign po-
    licy instrument is still worth mentioning. He calls it

        ...a corruption of thinking about international relations,
        and a distraction from its proper concerns. The fact
        is that we are where we are, and it is from here that
        we have to begin. There can only be a relative securi-
        ty.

244

Hedley Bull, <u>The Control of the Arms Race</u>, New York, 2nd edition, 1965, pp. 26-27.

6. Political science must be based on a recognition of the interdependence on theory and practice, which can be attained only through a combination of utopia and reality.

E.H. Carr, <u>The Twenty Years Crisis, 1919-1939; An Introduction to the Study of International Relations</u>, 2nd edition, London 1946, p. 13.

7. Morris Janowitz, <u>Military Conflict: Essays in the Institutional Analysis of War and Peace</u>, Beverly Hills 1975, p. 23.

8. Kenneth E. Boulding, <u>Conflict and Defense: A General Theory</u>, New York 1963, p. 335.

9. H. Butterfield, <u>History and Human Relations</u>, London 1951, p. 21; quoted by Garnett, <u>op.cit.</u>, p. 199.

10. Henry Kissinger in conversation with Walter Laquer, <u>The Times</u>, December 19, 1977.

11. Kanet, referring to Hanna Arendt's <u>The Origins of Totalitarianism</u>, Chapters 11 and 12; Roger E. Kanet (ed.), <u>The Behavioral Revolution and Communist Studies</u>, New York 1971, p. 6.
cf. Robert Conquest in 1977 about the Soviet leaders as a product of Russian history:

> The basic point...is that it isn't a matter of their having "opinions".... They are simply soaked in their tradition.... Brezhnev has enough ideology to get along and the rest is soaked into his bones.

<u>Hearings Before the Subcommittee on Europe and the Middle East of the Committee on International Relations</u>, House of Representatives, Washington D.C. 1978, pp. 191-192.

12. A. Dallin, "Biases and Blunders in American Studies on the U.S.S.R.," <u>Slavic Review</u>, September 1973, p. 565.

13. The definition of "policy elites" is borrowed from Brzezinski and Huntington: "Groups whose scope of activity is directly dependent on the allocation of national resources and which are directly affected by any shift in the institutional distribution of power." Zbigniew Brzezinski and

Samuel P. Huntington, <u>Political Power USA/USSR</u>, New York 1966, p. 196.

14. Alexander Dallin has pointed out the usefulness of applying the literature of political development and taking it as a point of departure for analysis of Soviet policy. He mentions five general trends: 1) a tendency towards political participation; 2) integration at the level of the nation-state; 3) priority of attention on the domestic, rather than foreign, arena; 4) greater reliance on "authoritative institutions" in foreign affairs; and 5) the totalitarian ability to override and distort undesired tendencies in political development.
Alexander Dallin, "Soviet Foreign Policy and Domestic Politics: A Framework for Analysis," in Erik P. Hoffman and Frederic J. Fleron (eds.), <u>The Conduct of Soviet Foreign Policy</u>, Chicago 1971, pp. 37–38.

15. Dan Smith, <u>The Defence of the Realm in the 1980s</u>, London 1980, p. 31.

16. For example, the knowledge of Senators Nunn and Jackson-- and their staffs--or Representative Les Aspin is no different from that of "professional soldiers." Many civilians in the Pentagon are involved in top level decision-making. In fact American strategy has largely been developed, and has in many cases actually been given direction, by civilians, e.g., Schlesinger, Kissinger, Brown.

17. See Vernon V. Aspaturian, "Internal Politics and Foreign Policy in the Soviet System," especially pp. 526-531 ("Who 'benefits' in Soviet society from international tensions?"), in Vernon V. Aspaturian (ed.), <u>Process and Power in Soviet Foreign Policy</u>, Boston 1971.

18. Andrew C. Janos, "Interest Groups and the Structure of Power: Critique and Comparison," <u>Studies in Comparative Communism</u>, Spring 1979, p. 8.

19. Samuel P. Huntington, <u>The Soldier and the State: The Theory and Politics of Civil-Military Relations</u>, New York 1957.

20. cf. Nils H. Wessell, "Soviet Views of Multipolarity and the Emerging Balance of Power", <u>Orbis</u>, Winter 1979, pp. 785-812; Arbatov explicitly points to the danger of a return to the Cold War situation because of the "much greater number of participants in international relations," some of whom may possibly be playing "imprudent and irresponsible games," above all China.

G. Arbatov, "U.S. Foreign Policy at the Start of the 1980s," SShA, No 4, 1980, p. 50.

21. Stanley Hoffman, "An American Social Science: International Relations," Daedalus, Summer 1977, p. 58. He continues:

> ...we need to examine in far greater detail the way in which the goals of states have originated, not (or not only) from the geopolitical position of actors, but from the play of domestic political forces and economic interests; or the way in which statesmen... also wanted their moves abroad to reach certain objectives within; or the way in which external issues have shaped domestic alignments and affected internal battles.

CHAPTER I

1. William Welch, <u>American Images of Soviet Foreign Policy</u>,
   New Haven 1970, p. 174.

2. Welch, <u>Ibid.</u>, p. 27. The studies Welch refers to are Jan
   F. Triska and David D. Finley, <u>Soviet Foreign Policy 1917-</u>
   <u>67</u>, New York 1968; Adam B. Ulam, <u>Expansion and Coexistence:</u>
   <u>Soviet Foreign policy, 1917-73</u>, New York, 2nd edition 1974.

3. <u>Ibid.</u>, p. 179.

4. <u>Ibid.</u>, p. 187.

5. See Lucian W. Pye, "The Confrontation between Discipline
   and Area Studies" and Alfred G. Meyer, "Comparative Politics and its Discontent: The study of the U.S.S.R. and
   Eastern Europe," in Lucian W. Pye (ed.), <u>Political Science</u>
   <u>and Area Studies: Rivals or Partners?</u>, Bloomington 1975,
   pp. 3-22 and 98-130. Scientific progress seems to be hampered rather than served when academic discussion and
   sound criticism turn into a "dialogue des sourds" and
   self-righteousness. The sharp controversies of the 1960s
   during the "Behavioral Revolution" raised much dust in the
   academic world, but one wonders whether the goals would
   not have been reached otherwise. This movement explicitly
   required scientific research techniques and a methodological rigor that had been neglected by traditional approaches.

    > Because they are impressionistic, unique and fail to
    > classify events and conditions according to explicit
    > and rigorous coding rules, we cannot be sure that our
    > descriptions are comparable. (1)

   Knowledge should be made transmissible and verifiable, a
   goal that is certainly not "revolutionary" in scholarly
   endeavors, but apparently had not fully penetrated in the
   social sciences.

    > The historian and political scientist will typically
    > look at large numbers of facts, constantly reappraise
    > and rearrange them in his mind, and then, on the basis
    > of what <u>may</u> have been a highly disciplined sequence of
    > mental calculations, come up with an interpretation of
    > them. But no one else will ever <u>know</u>; we may find his

interpretation plausible or even compelling, and we may be persuaded or put off by his reputation, but no one could consciously reproduce his intellectual processes. In sum, both imagination and rigor are necessary, but neither is sufficient. (2)

On the other hand, the value of history be recognized: "the understanding of past events and problems can be part of a learning process that assists us in understanding present events and problems." (3) It seems a positive development that the debate on "what is scientific," the "blessings" of quantitative methods, or of "scientific value relativism" calmed down in the 1970s. (4) Moreover, awareness of the limits of rigorous scientific models in the social sciences and a lesser measure of theoretical pre-occupation have perhaps increased the chance of more attention being paid to analyses useful for the policy makers. Sometimes it is regrettable, but understandable, that policy makers and government officials so easily dismiss academic output. Scientific endeavor should aim at theoretical improvement, but pay equal regard to social relevance. One can only hope that political science will not follow economics, which in many respects has fallen victim to "quantifiers" and has largely lost its original bonds with the social sciences.

(1) J. David Singer, "The Behavioral Science Approach to International Relations: Payoff and Prospects," in James N. Rosenau (ed.), International Politics and Foreign Policy, New York 1969, p. 66.
(2) Ibid., p. 67.
(3) Klaus Knorr, "Introduction: On the Utility of History," in Klaus Knorr (ed.), Historical Dimensions of National Security Problems, Lawrence, Kansas 1976, p. 3.
(4) For the issues mentioned cf. Arnold Brecht, Political Theory: The Foundations of Twentieth-Century Political Thought, Princeton 1959; Rosenau (ed.) op.cit.; James N. Rosenau, The Science of International Relations, New York 1975; Hedley Bull, "International Relations: 'The Case for a Classical Approach'," World Politics, April 1966; J. David Singer (ed.), Quantitative International Politics, New York 1968; Frederic J. Fleron (ed.), Communist Studies and the Social Sciences, Chicago 1969; Oran R. Young, Systems of Political Science, Englewood Cliffs, 1968; Discussion about "The Study of International Relations," Oost-West, June 1970 (in Dutch).

6. Rosenau (ed.), International Politics, p. 457.

7. Morton H. Halperin, Bureaucratic Politics and Foreign Policy,

Washington D.C. 1974, p. 5.

8. Alfred G. Meyer, "U.S.S.R. Incorporated," Slavic Review 20, 1961, pp. 369-376.

9. T.H. Rigby, "Crypto-Politics," Survey, January 1964, pp. 183-194, reprinted in Fleron, pp. 116-128; Janos, op.cit., p. 13; see also Jerry E. Hough, "The Bureaucratic Model and the Nature of the Soviet System," in Hough, The Soviet Union and Social Science Theory, Cambridge 1977, pp. 49-70.

10. Arnold L. Horelick, A. Ross Johnson and John D. Steinbruner, The Study of Soviet Foreign Policy: A Review of Decision-Theory-Related Approaches, RAND, Santa Monica 1973, p. 2; cf. A.H. Brown, Soviet Politics and Political Science, New York 1974.

11. Graham T. Allison, Essence of Decision: Explaining the Cuban Missile Crisis, Boston 1971, p. 249.

12. Ibid., p. 251.

13. Horelick et al., op.cit., p. 50.

14. Idem.

15. Jan F. Triska's Review of "Interest Groups and Soviet Politics," in Journal of International Affairs, No. I, 1972, p. 115.

16. cf. Aspaturian, Process and Power, pp. 62-63.

17. Robert Conquest, Power and Policy in the U.S.S.R., London 1962; Michel Tatu, Power in the Kremlin from Khrushchev to Kosygin, New York 1968. (French edition, Le Pouvoir en URSS, Paris 1967)

18. For example, the Analysis of the USSR's 24th Party Congress and 9th Five-Year Plan, edited by Norton T. Dodge, notes no particular changes or indications of proposed change (Cremona Foundation, Mechanicsville, 1971). Widespread and bipartisan Western assessment of the possible genuineness of the need for East-West cooperation and of the severe Soviet economic situation occurs in the course of the second, rather than the first half of the 1970s. cf. initiation of NATO "East-West Study" by President Carter in 1977; appearance of numerous studies and articles in the press about problems of energy and labour

force shortage, various CIA "Research Aides" and so forth. Most studies concern capability analysis, based on economic performance, Soviet statistics and the Gosplan outlook. Policy analysis, notably since the Central Committee Plenum in December 1969, could have given these insights in Soviet future economic problems years before.

19. The following discussion about the Backfire bomber illustrates the nature and role of intentions in the political process. They are persistent: the Backfire issue remained for a long time a major obstacle in SALT despite "general" agreement not only on the bomber's peripheral capabilities, but also on Soviet intentions. Yet doubts still prevail somewhere in the intelligence community in America and agreement on the Backfire reached in SALT-II does not seem a definite settlement. They are enigmatic and uncertain: intentions are not known but are inferred from other indicators, allowing no more than a "calculated guess." Intentions also have central, political significance: capability and policy-analysis are to a large extent used according to the intentions ascribed to the other party. As the illustration shows: the Backfire may or may not have the capability to reach the United States, but it is a Soviet bomber that may readily be able to do so. Soviet intentions may suggest--for others even imply--that goal.

> Mr. BUSH: Mr. Chairman, on the question of the Backfire, I still am not happy with the way I think this is coming out on the differences concerning Soviet intentions between CIA and the Air Force, or anybody else in the community. I have community responsibilities.

> Chairman PROXMIRE: I simply picked up the assertion that there were some differences of opinion in the intelligence community on the Backfire bomber, and I wanted to know what that was. And I think we have made that clear; that there is no difference op opinion on the number; there is no difference of opinion on how rapidly it is being produced, and there is a difference of opinion simply on what it would seem to be like, given the nature of the bomber. In other words, it is extremely effective in its peripheral mission. On an intercontinental mission it is less effective.

> Mr. BUSH: To the degree that there is a difference, it could be on intention. I think the record is coming out a little more black and white than these differences may be (.....)

Representative BROWN of Michigan: What indicators of intention are there that are reliable at this point in time on the Backfire?

Mr. BUSH: Well, construction at forward bases would be one, or readiness of forward bases, or ability to make forward bases ready to receive the Backfire from which it could do a round-trip mission. It is a very hard thing to estimate.

Representative BROWN of Michigan: It is fair to say that what you are both doing is making a calculated guess without much to go on?

Mr. BUSH: When we get into intention, unfortunately that is what we are dealing with, yes, sir.

Mr. FIRTH: And there is agreement on the intention that it is primarily a peripheral weapon at this point. And that is where the deployment has been so far.

Hearings before the Subcommittee on Priorities and Economy in Government of the Joint Economic Committee, Washington 1976, pp. 72-73.

20. Rationality should be understood here as the attempt to pursue the "best" result of an actor's calculations. Sidney Verba concludes that despite such limiting factors as 1. human frailty, 2. deviations from the rational model, 3. collective decision-making, 4. inconsistency in the set of goals, 5. imperfect acquisition of information and 6. coincidence of more decisions at one time, "the assumption of rationality within theories of international relations may still be a useful assumption...(and it will, of course, be more useful if its limitations are made explicit than if they are ignored)." Sydney Verba, "Assumptions of Rationality and Non-Rationality in Models of International Systems," in Harold K. Jacobson and William Zimmerman (eds.), The Shaping of Foreign Policy, New York 1969, p. 201; see also, Raymond Aron, Peace and War, A Theory of International Relations, New York 1966, p. 16: "The theory of international relations starts from the plurality of autonomous centers of decision, hence from the risk of war, and from this risk it deduces the necessity of the calculation of means." See for "policy analysis" as against "capability analysis" Harold and Margareth Sprout, "Environmental Factors in the Study of International Politics," in Rosenau (ed.), op.cit., pp. 41-56. For example, (p. 48)

All the probabilistic models with which we are here
concerned carry an assumption that the environed unit
is capable of choosing among alternatives. But that is
not equivalent to assuming that all choices which, by
definition, are possible choices are equally probable
choices. The essence of such a model is that some
choices are more probable than others. With respect
to policy-making and the content of policy decisions,
our position is that what matters is how the policy-
maker imagines the milieu to be, not how it actually
is. With respect to the operational results of decisions, what matters is how things are, not how the policy-maker imagines them to be.

cf. Triska and Finley, Chapter III, op.cit.; Hoffmann and
Fleron, Jr. (eds.), Part III, op.cit.

21. As stated in the "General Author's Note," assessments of
capabilities are difficult and remain arbitrary. A more
serious shortcoming is, however, to stop the analysis of
defense and foreign policy at the point of description of
military output. Explanations predominantly based on military writings, facts and figures, seriously neglect the
overriding fact that "ultimately it is political rather
than strictly strategic or fiscal considerations that may
be said to have determined Soviet reactions to nuclear
weapons and shaped the content of Soviet nuclear strategy."
(p. 29). In spite of his apparent acknowledgement of this
widely shared view, Pipes regrettably and almost exclusively nonetheless selects orthodox, military statements in
order to demonstrate "Why the Soviet Union Thinks It Could
Fight and Win a Nuclear War," (Commentary, July, 1977).
Instead of honoring the confessed rule of the "primacy of
politics" and complementing his in other respects valuable
research with policy analysis, Pipes—to mention only one
example of a rather common phenomenon—derives not only
foreign policy content, but even intent from military statements. No matter how well some parts fit together in the
case of military doctrine, the main question whether—and
if so, to what extent—Soviet "military doctrine is indicative of intent" (p. 34) is not addressed, let alone answered by Pipes. Not a single political leader is mentioned,
not one political motive indicated. As Brodie observes,
the word "Why" in the title

> preempts the prior question whether some entity called
> the Soviet Union thinks as he says it does. The appro-
> priate question is: "Who in the Soviet Union thinks
> they can fight and win a nuclear war?"

253

Bernard Brodie, "The Development of Nuclear Strategy," International Security, Spring 1978, p. 72.

22.　The "doubtful art of quotation" has long characterized not only the Kremlinological literature but a good many other scholarly works on Soviet foreign policy as well. In varying degrees the impression is created that Soviet communications more or less accurately reflect Soviet behavior.

Charles Gati, "History, Social Science and the Study of Soviet Foreign Policy," in Hoffmann and Fleron, p. 12.

23.　William E. Odom, "A Dissenting View on the Group Approach to Soviet Politics," World Politics, July 1976, p. 567.

24.　Ibid., p. 545.

25.　Zbigniew Brzezinski, "Preface," in Lenard J. Cohen and Jane P. Shapiro (eds.), Communist Systems in Comparative Perspective, Garden City 1974, p. XX.

26.　Carl J. Friedrich and Zbigniew Brzezinski, Totalitarian Dictatorship and Autocracy, Cambridge, Mass. 1956, pp. 9-10. See for a concise comment, Jerry F. Hough and Merle Fainsod, How the Soviet Union is Governed, Cambridge, Mass. 1979, pp. 518-522.

27.　Dimitri D. Simes, "The Soviet Invasion of Czechoslovakia and the Limits of Kremlinology," Studies in Comparative Communism, Spring-Summer 1975, p. 179.

28.　Frederic C. Barghoorn, Politics in the USSR, Boston 1972, pp. 312-313; cf. L.G. Churchward, Contemporary Soviet Government, 2nd edition, London 1975; Hough and Fainsod, op.cit., describe the distribution of power (Chapter 14) in a less formal way, giving ample attention to various--pluralist--power centers below the top committees of the Communist Party. For this view see, in particular, Jerry F. Hough, The Soviet Prefects, Cambridge, Mass. 1969.

29.　T.H. Rigby, "Crypto-Politics," in Fleron, p. 124.

30.　For an example of how difficult it is to argue convincingly that the "interest group" approach fits the Soviet political setting, see Donald R. Kelley, "Group and Specialist Influence in Soviet Politics: In Search of a Theory," in Richard B. Remnak (ed.), Social Scientists and Policy Making in the USSR, New York 1977, pp. 111-119, the section under the heading "The Group Interaction and Organizational Process Model." For example, he mentions as "the basic premise" of this model that "policy making occurs in an essentially nonhierarchical setting characterized by institutional pluralism." (p. 111), but admits that "even the most devoted advocates...do not deny the considerable potential for party intervention on virtually all policies regarded as politically sensitive." (p. 112) Moreover, the model is seriously undermined by adding that "the party itself is frequently far from unified or homogenuous on most policy-related questions," (p. 113), and that various networks cut across "the formal distinction between apparatus and nonapparatus posts to create a never clearly defined relationship of partial dependence and partial hostility." (p. 115)

31. Janos, op.cit., p. 19-20.

32. Jan F. Triska, loc.cit., p. 113.

33. Brzezinski and Huntington, op.cit., p. 193.

34. Joseph LaPalombara, "Monolithics or Plural Systems: Through Conceptual Lenses Darkly," Studies in Comparative Communism, Autumn 1975, pp. 326-327.

35. David Silverman, The Theory of Organizations: A Sociological Framework, London 1970, pp. 215-216.

36. The following rests heavily on the conceptualization of Carl J. Friedrich, Man and His Government: An Empirical Theory of Politics, New York 1963, especially Part II, "The Dimensions of Power and Justice," pp. 159-284.

37. Ibid., Chapter X.

38. cf. Theodore H. Friedgut, Political Participation in the USSR, Princeton 1979.

    The activity of the Soviets represents an attempt to promote closeness of regime and citizens, the creation of face-to-face politics in which civil society and political society, community and regime, can merge. (p. 322)

39. Samuel P. Huntington, Political Order in Changing Societies, New Haven 1968, p. 91.

40.   It has been said many times recently by such well-known
        dissident figures as A. Solzhenitsyn, V. Mazimov, A.
        Sakharov, V. Bukovsky, and others, especially those
        who have now emigrated, that Marxism is not believed
        in any more in the USSR, and that even young students
        in secondary schools do not believe it and "laugh
        about it...." This, however, is simply not true....
        The major part of the Soviet intellectual community
        still frankly remains within the framework of the Mar-
        xist ideology, but it tries to adopt the Marxist ana-
        lysis of modern society to the changing realities and
        to favor more liberal, reformist ideas of socialism.

        Zhores A. Medvedev, Soviet Science, Oxford 1979, p. 168;
        cf. A. Sakharov's letter to The New York Times (Internatio-
        nal Herald Tribune, June 13, 1980).

41.   Stephen White, Political Culture and Soviet Politics, Lon-
        don 1979, p. 189. For a different view on the attention
        of the Soviet political leadership and of the analyst for
        the "power of society" and the creation of a "Rechtsstaat"
        see William E. Odom, "Comment" on Janos, loc.cit., Studies
        in Comparative Communism, Spring 1979, pp. 23-25.

42.   Friedrich, op.cit., p. 175.

43.   Ibid., p. 171.

44.   Huntington, Political Order, op.cit., p. 79.

45.   cf. Friedgut, op.cit., pp. 322-325.

46.   Friedrich, op.cit., Chapters XII, XIII, XIV.

47.   Definitions and concepts as developed by G. Kuypers in
        Grondbegrippen van Politiek [Basic Concepts of Politics] ,
        Utrecht 1973, are elaborated and/or translated in English
        by R.Th. Jurrjens, The Free Flow: People, Ideas and Infor-
        mation in Soviet Ideology and Politics (forthcoming, Sijt-
        hoff, Leiden). Quotes are taken from Jurrjens' Ph.D. manu-
        script.

            Power bases comprise all those more or less durable
            factors on which the power of an actor is based, and
            by which he maintains or enlarges his power (p. 58).

        The eight power bases mentioned are enumerated by Jurrjens,
        p. 58.

48. See Hough and Fainsod, op.cit.; Hough, op.cit.; Paul Cocks, see next footnote.

49. Kelley, op.cit., p. 126; see Paul Cocks, "Retooling the Directed Society: Administrative Modernization and Developed Socialism," in Jan F. Triska and Paul Cocks (eds.), Political Development in Eastern Europe, New York 1977, pp. 53-92; Cocks, "Science Policy and Soviet Decision Making: PPBS comes to the Kremlin," paper presented at A.P.S.A. convention, San Fransisco, September 2-5, 1975.

50. Idem.

51. Col. Trevor N. Dupuy, "Civilian Control and Military Professionalism: A Systemic Problem," Strategic Review, Winter, 1980, pp. 40-41.

52. "X" [George F. Kennan] , "Sources of Soviet Conduct," Foreign Affairs, July, 1947; James N. Rosenau, "Pre-theories and Theories of Foreign Policy," in R. Barry Farrell (ed.), Approaches to Comparative and International Politics, Evanston 1966, pp. 27-92.

53. cf. Stanley Hoffman, footnote 21 of the Introduction above.

54. Rosenau, in Farrell, p. 75.

55. Welch, op.cit., p. 27 (footnote 29), where he refers to Rosser (Englewood Cliffs, N.J. 1969), and pp. 185-187, where he refers to Jan F. Triska, "A Model for the Study of Soviet Foreign Policy," American Political Science Review, March 1958, pp. 64-83. Triska proposes that Soviet policy be viewed as made up of five components: "ideology, strategy, operational direction, tactics and propaganda," ideology being "the essence of the matter." (Welch, p. 185)

56. Morton Schwartz, The Foreign Policy of the USSR, Domestic Factors, Encino, Ca. 1975, p. VI.

57. Aspaturian, op.cit.; Brzezinski and Huntington, op.cit.; Alexander Dallin in Hoffman and Fleron, pp. 36-49; and Dallin, "Domestic Factors Influencing Soviet Foreign Policy," in M. Confino and S. Shamir (eds.), The USSR and the Middle East, Jerusalem 1973, pp. 31-58.

58. Dallin distinguishes in dichotomic form:

left	right
Goal-orientedness (utopianism)	Pragmatism
Optimism	Pessimism
"Red" (partisanship)	"Expert" (rationality)
Transformation	Stability
Monolithism	Pluralism
Politics	Economics
Mobilization	Normalcy
Heavy Industry	Consumer goods
Uneven ("breakthrough") development	Even development
Central command economy	Market economy
Cultural revolution	Traditional persistence
Tension-management	Consensus-building
Dialectic ("The worse, the better")	Linear ("The better the better")
Centralization	Decentralization
Violence	Gradualism
Three-class alliance strategy	Four-class alliance
Inevitability of international conflict	Avoidability of conflict
Voluntarism	Determinism

Dallin in Hoffman and Fleron, p. 45; cf. Aspaturian, Process and Power, especially Chapter XV, "Internal Politics and Foreign Policy in the Soviet System"; and Aspaturian, "Moscow's Options in a Changing World," Problems of Communism, July-August 1972, pp. 1-20, vide p. 6.

59. Aspaturian, Ibid.; Dallin, Ibid.

60. Hannes Adomeit, "Soviet Foreign Policy Making: The Internal Mechanism of Global Commitment," in Hannes Adomeit and Robert Boardman (eds.), Foreign Policy Making in Communist Countries: A Comparative Approach, Guilford 1979, p. 37.

61. Ibid., pp. 35-37.

62. Kuypers, op.cit., Chapter I; Jurrjens, "Introduction," op.cit.

63. Jurrjens, op.cit., p. 16, translated from Kuypers, op.cit., p. 274.

64. Kuypers, Ibid., pp. 267-271.

65. Rosenau in Farrell, p. 31.

66. Rosenau, "Muddling, Meddling and Modelling," loc.cit., pp. 130-144.

67. Ibid., p. 140; cf. The discussion in Millennium by Steve Smith, "Brother, can you Paradigm? A Reply to Professor Rosenau," Millennium: Journal of International Studies, Winter 1979-1980, pp. 235-245.

68. cf. Henry A. Kissinger, "Domestic Structure and Foreign Policy," in Rosenau, International Politics and Foreign Policy, pp. 263-267; Halperin, op.cit., Chapter IX and XIII; Allison's summary of organizational concepts, op.cit., p. 256.

69. Horelick et al., Decision-Theory-Related Approaches, p. 53.

70. Halperin, op.cit., p. 28.

71. Erickson concludes, for example
        It is not...institutional change but shifts in person-
        nel--"key" officers who redefine the role and function
        of their positions--which must of necessity command
        close attention in order to make better sense of what
        is loosely called "policy...."
    John Erickson, "The Reshaping of the Soviet Military Com-
    mand 1965-1970," in Amos Perlmutter and Valerie Plave
    Bennett (eds.), The Political Influence of the Military;
    New Haven 1980, p. 196.

72. Dallin in Confino and Shamir, p. 38.

73. Karl F. Spielmann, Analyzing Soviet Strategic Arms Decisions, Boulder, Co 1978, p. 41.

74. Alexander Dallin, "The Domestic Sources of Soviet Foreign Policy," in Seweryn Bialer (ed.), The Domestic Context of Soviet Foreign Policy, Boulder 1981, pp. 335-408. cf. William Zimmerman, "Issue Area and Foreign Policy Process: A Research Note in Search of a General Theory," American Political Science Review, December 1973, p. 1208.

75. Ulam, Expansion and Coexistence, p. 729.

76. Triska and Finley, op.cit., p. 127.

77. Zimmerman, loc.cit., p. 1204.

78. cf. Rosenau in Farrell, p. 73.

79. Zimmerman, loc.cit., p. 1204-1207.

80. cf. Talcott Parsons' "four functional prerequisites for any social system: 1. the maintenance or reproduction of its own basic patterns; 2. adaptation to the environment and its changes; 3. the attainment of whatever goals the system has accepted or set for itself and 4. the integrating of all the different functions and subsystems within it into a cohesive and coordinated whole." Karl W. Deutch, The Nerves of Government, New York 1966, pp. 116-117.

81. An issue area is conceived to consist of

> ...(1) a cluster of values, the allocation or potential allocation of which (2) leads the affected or potentially affected actors to differ so greatly over a) the way in which the values should be allocated or b) the horizontal levels at which the allocations should be authorized that (3) they engage in distinctive behavior designed to mobilize support for the attainment of their particular values.

Rosenau in Farrell, p. 81.

82. Franklyn Griffiths, "A Tendency Analysis of Soviet Policy-Making," in H. Gordon Skilling and Franklyn Griffiths (eds.), Interest Groups in Soviet Politics, Princeton 1971, p. 369.

83. Zimmerman, loc.cit.,p. 1212.

84. Griffiths, op.cit., pp. 335-379; see also his Genoa plus 51: Changing Soviet Objectives in Europe (Toronto 1973), where he applies the "tendency analysis." For a critique, see A.H. Brown, op.cit., pp. 72-74.

85. For example, Eran asserts that "the indications of close personal relations between Inozemtsev on the one hand and Suslov and Ponomarev...on the other hand, make sense." Oded Eran, The Mezhdunarodniki: An Assessment of Professional Expertise in the Making of Soviet Foreign Policy, Tel Aviv 1979, p. 240. There are other reported links as indicated here, e.g., between Brezhnev and Arbatov.

86. cf. Zhores A. Medvedev, The Rise and Fall of T.D. Lysenko, New York 1969; Zhores A. Medvedev, op.cit.

87. Arbatov goes on to say about these "unsuccessful, dogmatic and vulgar writings":

In particular, this concerns works which from alleged-
ly Marxist positions reject modern genetics, the theory of relativity, cybernetics and some other major dis-
coveries, and also the vulgar works of some economists
and sociologists who interpreted problems of the economy, socio-political relationships and culture of the
modern world superficially, without a knowledge of life.

And in the footnote, he further explains why this experience
has done harm to the Soviet Union.

Works of this kind were damaging, of course, not only
because they provided the arguments for slanderous
fabrications by bourgeois propaganda. The main thing
was that they were detrimental to Soviet science and
for some time held up the development of some of its
branches. Besides, the authors of these works masked
their own dogmatism, torpid thinking or simply lack
of knowledge with lofty ideological considerations,
with "concern" for the purity of Marxist-Leninist theory. (Emphasis added)

Georgi Arbatov, The War of Ideas in Contemporary International Relations, Moscow 1973 (English edition), pp. 137-
138.

88. Based on his research of the Soviet historical record, Eran
concludes that

...one cannot foresee any development of Soviet foreign
policy research in the direction of more autonomy from
the regime or depoliticization of any sort. The regime
is unlikely to be interested in this kind of development. And the leading scholars of that community, who
have gained a privileged position through their services, would hardly want to give up that role. It is probable, therefore, that the operational conception of
Soviet foreign policy research, as well as of the social sciences in general, will remain for a long time
to come very different from the Western conception of
academic endeavor.

Eran, op.cit., p. 276.

89. Griffiths, op.cit., p. 358.

90. Ibid., p. 371.

91. See footnote 21.

92. Dallin, in _Bialer_ op.cit.

93. Jerry Hough, "The Soviet System: Petrification or Plura-
    lism?", _Problems of Communism_, March-April 1972, p. 45.

94. Aron, "Introduction," op.cit. Comparing the behavior of
    the diplomat with that of an economist or a soccer player,
    Aron says of the former: "This behavior has neither a goal
    determined as that of the soccer player (to send the ball
    across the line) or even an objective, in certain condi-
    tions rationally definable by a maximum, like those of
    economic subjects."

95. _Ibid._, p. 17. cf. footnote 20, above.

96. Stanley Hoffman, "An American Social Science," loc.cit.,
    p. 52.

97. Griffiths calls attention to changes over time and urges
    comparison of the "tendencies" and efforts "to characte-
    rize the difference between policy at the outset and
    conclusion," op.cit., p. 371.

98.   During the latter part of the post-World War II years,
        particularly in the Western world, the words "arms
        control" and "disarmament" acquired technical meanings.
        Though the two terms are used rather loosely in both
        official and private writings (including this text),
        it is helpful to clarify their technical meanings.
        "Disarmament" involves the reduction or the elimina-
        tion of armaments or armed forces. "Arms control" or
        "arms limitation" involves limitations on the number
        or types of armaments or armed forces, on their deploy-
        ment or disposition, or on the use of particular types
        of armaments; "arms control" also encompasses measures
        designed to reduce the danger of accidental war or to
        reduce concern about surprise attack. Although the
        terms are generally thought of in connection with in-
        ternationally agreed undertakings, they can also be
        applied to unilateral actions of states. Postwar nego-
        tiations have involved efforts at both arms control
        and disarmament, but most agreements actually achieved
        have technically been measures of arms control.

        John H. Barton and Lawrence D. Weiler (eds.), _International
        Arms Control_, _Issues and Agreements_, Stanford 1976, p. 3
        fn. 1.

99. This definition is borrowed and only slightly different
    from J.I. Coffey's in _New Approaches to Arms Reduction in_

Europe, Adelphi Paper No. 105, IISS, London 1974, p. 1.
The only difference concerns adaptation to our term "political sovereignty" that embraces his "economic viability and political independence." Most importantly, the
implications of the definition as Coffey explains, are
fully subscribed to: the definition is (1) a "minimum
concept," (2) "differentiates between specific objectives
essential to security," (3) "Does not set up perfectio-
nist requirements," (4) "concentrates on inhibiting the
use of force," and (5) "extends to perceptions of security."

100. cf. Morton Schwartz, Chapter I: "Capabilities," op.cit.

101. An example is the Carter Doctrine and the (immensely com-
plicated) creation of a Rapid Deployment Force. For a
short discussion of "The Uses of Military Power," see
Klaus Knorr, The Power of Nations: The Political Economy
of International Relations, New York 1975, Chapter V.
Also, Klaus Knorr, On the Uses of Military Power in the
Nuclear Age, Princeton 1966. For a Soviet discussion of
the use of military force in international relations, cf.
Voennaya Sila: Mezhdunarodnye Otnoshenia, Voennye Aspekty
Vneshne-Politicheskykh Kontseptsy S.Sh.A., Moscow 1972.

102.   The game of strategy can, like music, be played in
      two "keys." The major key is direct strategy in which
      force is the essential factor. The minor key is in-
      direct strategy, in which force recedes into the
      background and its place is taken by psychology and
      planning. Naturally, any strategy may make use of
      both these keys in various degrees....

      André Beaufre, An Introduction to Strategy, New York 1965,
      p. 134.

103. K.J. Twitchett, "Strategies for Security: Some Theoretical Considerations," in Kenneth J. Twitchett (ed.), Reflections on Survival and Stability, Oxford 1971, p. 16.

104. Ibid., p. 18.

105. Erich Fromm, "Paranoia and Policy," New York Times, December 10, 1975.

106. Presidential elections in the United States are illustrative in this respect. In 1976 President Ford dropped the
word "detente" when he was rather successfully attacked
on that subject by Republican opponent Ronald Reagan.
During the same year, Kissinger and his aid Sonnenfeldt

263

were vigorously attacked on the policy or doctrine concerning American-Soviet "one way" relations and the So-
viet-East-European "organic" relationship. In 1979/1980,
President Carter's foreign policy was beleaguered by presidential contenders as well as by many other politicians
for many reasons. But, again American-Soviet relations
suffered from emotions, erratic decision-making and over-
reactions. A disappointed former Director of the Bureau
of Political-Military Affairs of the Department of State
describes Washington's political climate as follows.

What the State Department believes is negotiating
with an adversary, the White House insists is bargaining with the devil. What the diplomat sees as
a concession to give fluidity to a frozen situation
politicians may call appeasement.

Leslie H. Gelb, "Diplomacy vs. Politics," New York Times,
April 22, 1980; cf. Leslie Gelb, "A Decade of Arms Control: A Half Glass Full?," Foreign Policy, Fall 1979.

107. Robert Conquest, "A New Russia? A New World?," Foreign
      Affairs, April 1975, p. 493.

108. Convergence is not meant here as the result of "objective"
      systemic changes, for instance caused by technology.

109. cf. Marshall Shulman, "Toward a Western Philosophy of Co-
      existence," Foreign Affairs, October 1973, pp. 36-39;
      Ulam, Chapter XIII, op.cit. For a critical assessment,
      see Lawrence L. Whetten, Contemporary American Foreign
      Policy, Lexington 1974; and especially Theodore Draper,
      "Detente," Commentary, No. 6, June 1974; Theodore Draper,
      "Detente or Appeasement," Commentary, No. 2, February 1976.
      For the defendent's case, see Henry Kissinger's major
      speech about detente before the Senate Committee on For-
      eign Relations, September 19, 1974, reprinted in Survival,
      January/February 1975, pp. 35-42; and Helmut Sonnenfeldt,
      "The Meaning of Detente," Naval War College Review, Sum-
      mer 1975.

110. Clemens summarizes the aspects of "The Balance of Inte-
      rests" as follows:

Essential: 1. Mutual satisfaction that the proposed
arms control will enhance the basic interests of each
side as perceived and defined by its own government,
based on security and other considerations. 2. Sufficiency (as conceived by each party) in the forces

regulated-despite or because of the proposed controls. 3. If the agreements cover forces central to the strategic balance, there must be parity if not symmetry. 4. Credible second-strike forces must remain after the agreement, and not just a delicate balance of terror that could be upset by marginal accretions by either side. 5. Accords on peripheral areas of military competition, however, are attainable without parity or symmetry, and many have been concluded. 6. If there is neither parity nor symmetry, agreements are still possible if each side--for its own reasons--believes that they enhance particular objectives.

Helpful: 1. Parity or symmetry in the forces to be regulated facilitates agreement but is not essential, since trade-offs are possible in other domains. 2. Recognition and action by both sides at roughly the same time ("in-phase") to promote parallel interests.

Harmful: 1. A sharp imbalance in the forces to be controlled which is the weaker party is determined to redress--either through mutual agreement or through unilateral actions--and which the other party is determined to preserve. 2. Insistence by either party on absolute "equality" in some domain, regardless of asymmetries or trade-offs that may make the proposed agreement advantageous to both sides. Such equality could theoretically be achieved by agreements reducing the forces of the stronger party or by permitting the weaker side to build to that same level: or by unilateral policies without any agreements.

Walter Clemens, The Superpowers and Arms Control, Toronto 1973, pp. 58-59.

111. Knorr, The Power of Nations, p. 208. Knorr distinguishes 13 "major properties of international interdependence," Ibid., pp. 208-210.

112. See William E. Odom, "The 'Militarization' of Soviet Society," Problems of Communism, September-October 1976, pp. 34-51, vide p. 50, fn. 76. The concept of "The Garrison State" is Laswell's (American Journal of Sociology, January 1941; cf. World Politics and Personal Insecurity, New York 1935). This concept denotes the situation in which political leaders are very strongly influenced by military views in their decisions because of the tense, threatening environment. War preparation becomes a constant feature in the polity as if it were a besieged

garrison. The "garrison state" may be continued even though external threats have diminished. This aspect will be dealt with later.

113. Morris Janowitz, op.cit., pp. 27-28.

114. Ibid., pp. 35-42.

115. Kuypers distinguishes six characteristics of means:

effectiveness	:	the degree a means contributes to the achievement of a chosen goal;
alternative applicability	:	the number of goals that can be served by a means;
total efficacy	:	the positive minus negative effectiveness of a means toward all goals for which it is used;
efficiency	:	the effectiveness of a means toward one chosen goal minus its negative side-effects as compared to an alternative means for the same goal;
indispensability: (necessity)		a means without which a goal is not attainable in a given situation, regardless of the combination of available means;
sufficiency	:	a means by which a chosen goal can be achieved without the use of other means.

Kuypers, op.cit., pp. 44-55. (transl.)

116. Jerome H. Kahan, Security in the Nuclear Age, Washington 1975, especially Part II, "The Search for Stability."

117. Christoph Bertram, "SALT II and the Dynamics of Arms Control," International Affairs, October 1979, p. 566.

118. C.G. Jacobson, Soviet Strategy, Soviet Foreign Policy, Glasgow 1974, p. 16.

119. Christoph Bertram, The Future of Arms Control (Part II): Arms Control and Technological Change, Elements of a new Approach, Adelphi Paper 146, London 1978, p. 19; cf. Bertram (ed.), Part I, Adelphi Paper 145, London 1978. John Collins also suggests a different approach to sizing force levels. He illustrates the difference between the quantitative and a comprehensive approach as follows:

266

Superiority and parity...are oriented exclusively on
Soviet holdings, without regard for real US requirements. Sufficiency, a better standard, concentrates
on what this country can do despite Soviet opposition,
not on what each side has.

Collins explains in footnote 47:

Superiority is a force planning concept which demands
markedly greater capabilities of certain kinds than
those possessed by opponents. Parity/essential equivalence is predicated on particular capabilities that
are approximately equal in overall effectiveness.
Friendly and enemy numbers need not jibe in either
case, but statistical strengths tend to be overempha-
sized, because friendly force levels depend on the
extent of enemy deployments. By way of contrast, sufficiency as a force-sizing criterion calls for adequate abilities to attain desired ends without undue
waste. Superiority thus is essential in some circumstances; parity suffices under less demanding conditions; and inferiority (qualitative as quantitative)
sometimes is acceptable.

United States/Soviet Military Balance: A Frame of Reference for Congress, Washington D.C. 1976, p. 26.

120. Ibid., p. 28.

121. cf. Colin Gray, "Who's Afraid of the Cruise Missile,"
Orbis, Fall 1977.

122. Fred C. Iklé, "Can Nuclear Deterrence Last out the Centu-
ry?," Foreign Affairs, January 1973; reprinted in Robert
J. Pranger, Detente and Defense: A Reader, Washington
1976, pp. 424-442, vide p. 441.

123. Garnett, in Martin, p. 217.

CHAPTER II

1. B. Ponomarev, A. Gromyko, V. Khostov (eds.), History of
    Soviet Foreign Policy 1945-1970, Moscow, English edition
    1974, p. 555.

2. Aspaturian, Process and Power, p. 929.

3. By the same token, the war in the Middle East in 1967
    dealt the Soviet Union a humiliating blow in one of its
    most prestigious realms: its military force. The Soviet
    Union found itself in the losers' camp that would undoubt-
    edly want more expensive military support in return for
    political influence that was moderate and volatile at the
    most. Soviet influence in this region varied widely accor-
    ding to the degree of American involvement. It depended
    much less on Soviet appeal than on its financial and mili-
    tary resources. Nor could the Soviet position in the Viet-
    nam war be called wholly enviable. The nuclear stalemate
    of the two superpowers precluded any assertive action on
    the part of the Soviet Union. Beyond military help to
    North-Vietnam, the Soviet Union could do very little with-
    out incurring a serious risk of direct confrontation with
    the United States. On the other hand, American military
    involvement in Vietnam was an ideological impediment to
    Soviet freedom of action in developing Soviet-American
    relations along more desirable lines. The Soviet Union
    could take little action with respect to friends or foes
    without harming the relationship. In any case the Soviet
    leaders were hardly in a position to take action against
    imperialism and foreign intervention after the invasion
    of Czechoslovakia which had at least called a halt to the
    relative prestige gains accruing from the growing anti-war,
    anti-American sentiment.
    cf. R.D. McLaurin, The Middle-East in Soviet Policy, Le-
    xington 1975, pp. 144-151; R.E. Kanet and D. Batry, Soviet
    Economic and Political Relations with the Developing World,
    New York 1975, Chapter III.

4. Peking Review, No. 17, April 24, 1970.

5. Another consequence is that Soviet prestige and influence
    among its fraternal parties will be continuously challenged,
    if not damaged, from within the socialist world itself.
    The smaller socialist countries are provided with an op-
    tion to choose sides with either one of the contenders for

ideological leadership. Furthermore, open hostilities between the Soviet Union and China, going as far as military
confrontation, mean a considerable weakness in Soviet dealings with the West. In 1967 at the Conference of Communist
and Workers' Parties of Europe Brezhnev lamented:

> The events in Vietnam remind us again of how vital is
> the task of strengthening the unity of the world com-
> munist movement. It is clear that if it were possible
> to support Vietnam in agreement with and jointly with
> China, the task of ending United States aggression
> would be considerably eased. (Pr., April 25, 1967)

But at the next international communist gathering in 1969
Brezhnev instead spoke about Chinese revisionism, hegemo-
nism, militarism and the loss of the socialist class content of its foreign policy by helping the West.

> Naturally, the imperialists are making use of Peking's
> present foreign-policy orientation as one of their
> trump cards in the political struggle against world
> socialism and the liberation movement. (Pr., June 8,
> 1969)

6. Ulam, op.cit., p. 749.

7. I. Aleksandrov, "Road Without a Future," Pr., April 7,
   1980. (CDSP, No. 14, pp. 1-5) For example,

> The role of imperialism's accomplice and junior part-
> ner--that is the price Peking has to pay for the cour-
> se it has taken, one of alignment with the imperialists
> and forming blocs with them and with their policy of
> aggression and war, and also for its one-sided orien-
> tation toward economic and military assistance from
> the capitalist states. This new role is causing an-
> xiety and concern in the developing countries, since
> Peking has recently claimed and continues to claim
> leadership among these nations. (CDSP, p. 4)

8. cf. Henry Kissinger, Chapter IV, "First steps towards China,"
   White House Years, Boston 1979.

9. Aspaturian, op.cit., p. 915; cf. Michel Tatu, op.cit., pp.
   532-539.

10. Uri Ra'anan, "The USSR and the 'Encirclement' Fear: Soviet
    Logic or Western Legend?," Strategic Review, Winter 1980,
    pp. 44-50; Even Professor Richard Pipes becomes discrimina-
    tive in this respect. Asked whether in arming Peking (which

Pipes favors) the United States would "run the risk of provoking a dangerous Soviet response--perhaps even an attack on China?," he answers:

> I don't normally worry much about Soviet anxieties, but in the case of China the Russians are indeed extremely sensitive--almost irrationally so. An all-out campaign by the United States to arm China could trigger a violent response from them. Therefore, an American policy of selling arms to China must be carefully calibrate. In this instance, we should put ourselves in the Soviets' shoes and ask: Will a specific weapon worry Moscow only to the point where it says the situation may get out of hand, so let us stop? Or will the Soviets say the situation has already gotten out of hand, and so we had better strike while we may? There's a fine line there. A broad spectrum exists between doing nothing and doing too much.

Interview in U.S. News and World Report, July 21, 1980, p. 27.

11. John Dornberg, Brezhnev, The Masks of Power, London 1974, p. 238; Similar conclusions are drawn by Robert C. Horn, "1969, Year of Change in Soviet Foreign Policy," paper presented at the Annual Meeting of the Western Slavic Association, San Diego, February 19-21, 1976.

12. cf. Edward Crankshaw, "Where Khrushchev Left Off," Survival 1970, pp. 374-375; Michel Tatu, "The Future of the USSR," Interplay, May 1969.

13. Pr., June 28, 1968.

14. Warsaw Pact "Declaration," Pr., July 9, 1966. (CDSP XVIII, no. 27)

15. This is not to say that Nixon-Kissinger or Brandt-Scheel were completely free to choose their policies, nor that East-West relations were the only considerations leading to them. Actually a number of facts facing them abroad and at home were the joint cause and practicable point of departure. A changed attitude towards the East fitted other relations and largely originated from the logic of the situation. In the German case, disillusionement with postwar foreign policy aiming at German reunification, the unsuccessful attempt of the Kissinger-Brandt "Grand Coalition" to solve the German question with Poland and

Czechoslovakia while bypassing the Soviet Union, and the
changing, possibly weakening, military commitments of the
United States in Europe, were all facts in need of answers. Electoral victory enabled Brandt to abandon the
CDU/CSU's traditional policies and to implement the "Ostpolitik" that was even more vigorously supported by his
new coalition partner, the FDP. Public support was of
no minor significance for the new foreign policy. "Ostpolitik" was approved by the electorate and the slim majority coalition "was to take the fullest advantage of
a favorable public opinion in domestic politics. "(1) Thus
both situational and purposeful factors played their role
in the new German foreign policy.
(1) Josef Korbel, <u>Detente in Europe: Real or Imaginary?</u>,
Princeton 1972, p. 204.

16. Podgorny, <u>Pr.</u>, November 7, 1969.

17. Gromyko, <u>Pr.</u>, July 11, 1969.

18. Communiqué of the Brandt-Brezhnev meeting, <u>Pr.</u>, September
     19, 1971.

19. The developments of the 1960s had accumulatively led to
     a new situation in which the following questions required
     an answer:

          1. A need to cut down American commitments overseas
          in response to the evolution of public opinion. This
          meant in the first place bringing the Vietnam war to
          an end, but also implied an intention of restricting
          intervention in local situations and cutting down
          direct American participation in maintaining stabili-
          ty in different parts of the world;
          2. The creation of a stable international system which
          would take into account the new power centres of a
          more diversified world. However much the United States
          might wish to diminish her international responsibili-
          ties, she could not avoid the task of adapting the old
          balance of power between two blocs to a more complex
          situation;
          3. The creation of a new relationship between the Uni-
          ted States and her principal allies in Western Europe
          and Japan. In practical terms this implied not only
          revivifying the security content of the alliances, but
          also finding solutions for the numerous problems cre-
          ated by the economic and technological interdependence
          of those advanced industrial societies lying outside
          the Communist bloc;

4. The continuation of the dialogue with the Soviet Union in the hope of simultaneously lowering tension between the two superpowers and placing restraint upon exercise of Russian power.

A. Hartley, American Foreign Policy in the Nixon Era, Adelphi Paper no. 110, London, pp. 15-16.

20. Helmut Sonnenfeldt, "The Meaning of Detente," loc.cit., pp. 3-4.

21. Ibid., p. 4.

22. cf. Marvin Kalb and Bernard Kalb, Kissinger, New York 1975, p. 123.

23. cf. Lawrence T. Caldwell, Soviet Attitudes to SALT, Adelphi Paper No. 75, London 1971; Marshall D. Shulman, "SALT and the Soviet Union," in Mason Willrich and John B. Rhinelander (eds.), SALT: The Moscow Agreements and Beyond, New York 1974.

24. For Ambassador Thompson's mission and Kosygin's reaction then and later that year in Glassboro, see Newhouse, Chapter 2, especially pp. 86, 89-91, 94-95. Gromyko reiterated Soviet readiness in his Supreme Soviet speech (Pr., July 11, 1969) and at the U.N. in meetings with Secretary of State Rogers in September.

It was probably on October 20 that Ambassador Dobrynin told President Nixon of his Government's readiness to begin talks.

Caldwell, op.cit., p. 9. However, Moscow's weighing of pros against cons remained puzzling for the U.S.

Neither in 1968, nor again in 1969, did Washington really know why Moscow had opted for SALT.

John Newhouse, Cold Dawn; The Story of SALT, New York 1973, p. 107.

25. Pr., June 28, 1968.

26. Pr., July 11, 1969. (CDSP XXI, No. 28, p. 8)

27. cf. Shulman, who wrote as early as 1966:

It is no longer sufficient--if indeed it ever was-- for the leaders of either country to define their

policies simply by reference to the other....
...We have now passed into a stage whose main characteristic appears to be a differentiation between the limited field of maneuver in the still decisive but largely stabilized European theater, and the traceless movement of revolutionary conflict in the underdeveloped areas, complicated by the Chinese effort to establish its influence by militant policies.

Marshall D. Shulman, Beyond the Cold War, New Haven 1966, pp. 31-32.

28. Triska and Finley, op.cit., p. 127.

29. Aspaturian, op.cit., p. 915.

30. Pr., March 31, 1971. (CDSP XXIII, No. 12, pp. 2-13, No. 13, pp. 1-7, No. 14, pp. 1-12) Further references to and quotes from Brezhnev's speech are from this publication.

31. These paragraphs relate to (1) the class struggle under capitalism; (2) the World Communist movement; and (3) the national liberation movement. At the XXIV Congress they were united in one paragraph, thus deviating from Brezhnev's speech at the previous congress. (Pr., March 29, 1966)

32. Robin Edmonds, Soviet Foreign Policy 1962-1973: The Paradox of Super Power, London 1975, p. 167 (Conclusion); cf. Kanet and Batry, op.cit., about the selectivity and pragmatism of Soviet policy towards the Third World.

33. William Zimmerman, Soviet Perspectives on International Relations 1956-1967, Princeton 1969, p. 282.

34. Soviet News, published by the Soviet Embassy in London, called it the "Peace Programme" in its translation in the issue of March 31; cf. Pr., April 13, 1971. Initially the press mostly ascribed this term to foreign sources. By summer 1971 some Politburo members were referring it by this name, e.g., Kirilenko and Podgorny in their election speeches in June.

35. Pr., June 12, 1971. (FBIS, June 14, p. J 9)

36. Idem.

37. Medvedev, Soviet Science, p. 139.

38. Ibid., pp. 149-150.

39. Paul Cockle, "Analyzing Soviet Defence Spending: the De-
    bate in Perspective," Survival, September-October 1978,
    pp. 218-219.

40. The "Budapest Appeal" by the Warsaw Pact countries inclu-
    ded for the first time the U.S. and Canada as partici-
    pants in an European security conference. Pr., June 27,
    1970.

41. NATO's strange request that the success of the conference
    be ensured in advance is simply confirmed by the "Peace
    Program." However, the earlier Communiqué of the Politi-
    cal Consultative Committee of the Warsaw Pact had angrily
    noted in this respect:

    ...a broad basis has been laid for mutual understand-
    ing and for ensuring that the conference will have
    positive results....
    ...There are no reasons whatever for delaying the
    convocation of the conference or for making any kind
    of preliminary conditions.

    Pr., December 3, 1970. Besides, in this communique--is-
    sued only three months before the XXIV Congress--MBFR
    was not mentioned or referred to at all.

42. cf. Gertrude E. Schroeder, "Consumption in the USSR--a
    Survey," in Bornstein and Fusfeld, The Soviet Economy--
    A Book of Readings, Homewood 1974, 4th edition, pp. 286-
    298.

43. See Radio Free Europe Research, April 5, 1971.

44. For instance, Brezhnev's address to the International Con-
    ference of Communist and Workers' Parties, Pr., June 8,
    1969.

45. Sydney I. Ploss, "Soviet Politics on the Eve of the 24th
    Party Congress," World Politics, October 1970, p. 67.

46. Radio Moscow in English to Great Britain, May 29, 1971.
    (FBIS, June 2, 1971)

47. Radio Moscow Domestic Service in Russian November 25,
    1971. (FBIS, November 30, 1971)

48. cf. T.H. Rigby, "The Soviet Leadership: Towards a Self-

Stabilizing Oligarchy?," <u>Soviet Studies</u>, October 1970, pp. 188-190.

49. Kosygin mediated in the Pakistan-India conflict in 1965, and in the Middle-East in 1967, travelled to France, Britain and the U.S. in 1967, and seemed in charge during the initial stages of SALT. Brezhnev conducted SALT from early 1971 on; he met Brandt in September, Pompidou in October, etc.

50. cf. Brezhnev's unusual attention for domestic economic problems before an international audience at the Conference of Communist Parties in 1969.

51. cf. Gregory Grossman, "From the Eighth to the Ninth Five-Year Plan," in Norton T. Dodge (ed.), <u>Analysis of the USSR's 24th Party Congress and 9th Five-Year Plan</u>, Maryland 1971, pp. 54-66.

52. <u>Pr.</u>, March 31, 1971.

53. <u>Pr.</u>, April 10, 1971. (<u>CDSP</u>, Vol. XXIII, No. 17, pp. 21-29)

54. <u>Ibid.</u>

55. Resolution "On the International Activity of the CC of CPSU after the 24th Congress of the CPSU," Radio Moscow TASS, International Service in English. (<u>FBIS</u>, November 24, 1971, pp. J2-3)

56. Brezhnev met East-European Party leaders in the Crimea (<u>Pr.</u>, August 3, 1971) and in these months he also visited Hungary, Czechoslovakia, Yugoslavia and the G.D.R.

57. See article, "The First Results," <u>Novoye Vremya</u>, No. 41, 1971.

58. <u>Kr. Zv.</u>, October 12, 1971, editorial.

59. <u>Kr. Zv.</u>, November 2, 1971; cf. <u>Pr.</u>, July 31, "The Reliable Defense of the Fatherland," in which reference is made to "The constant strengthening of the Soviet Armed Forces combat capability." This editorial refers to the Congress Resolution and not to the "Peace Program." Brezhnev's speech is quoted only once, with the passage that was repeated in many military writings: "Everything created by the Soviet people must be reliably defended." An editorial in <u>Pravda</u>, August 28, headed "The Path to

Disarmament," is very different from that of July 31. It views disarmament, that had been accorded "a special place in the 'Peace Program'" as an "increasingly realistic and feasible" goal that would "promote the strengthening of confidence in interstate relations." This editorial is very much in line with Brezhnev's policy.

60. Of course not all Soviet leaders were equally involved in foreign policy. Nor were their speeches always printed or reported in full, which complicates the analysis. For example, Kirilenko's election speech was reported in Pravda and Leningradskaya Pravda (both June 2, 1971), but only the latter commented on his foreign policy remarks in detail, including his positive approach to SALT and MBFR. Yet apart from disarmament, Kirilenko sounded reluctant, or even tough about any further extension of East-West relations. The term "Peace Program" was not regularly used by Politburo members; indeed, shortly after the Congress most leaders made no mention of the program at all. Katushev, in his speech on Lenin's 101st birthday (Pr., April 23), did not refer to foreign policy, even though he was Secretary of the Party's CC in charge of Communist bloc relations. At the Congress, Defense Minister Grechko did not devote one word to Brezhnev's foreign policy plans. (Pr., April 3) Foreign Minister Gromyko, who supported many of Brezhnev's ideas, likewise desisted from mentioning Brezhnev's program. It was not until September that Gromyko gave a very Brezhnevite speech about foreign policy and the "Peace Program" in the U.N. General Assembly. Politburo member Shelest not only consistently ignored the "Peace Program," but also argued in the opposite way, stressing ideological vigilance, defense strengthening and the like. (cf. Kommunist, No. 12, 1971, pp. 14-31. Soviet foreign policy and the anti-imperialist struggle "will continue to be pursued consistently and relentlessly." (p. 14) No change is envisaged by Shelest)

61. Trud, June 30, 1971. Shelest also typically referred to the Congress resolution at the Georgian Jubilee in May 1971, despite Brezhnev's presence and his remarks about MBFR negotiations on that occasion. Zarya Vostoka, May 15, 1971.

62. Resolution "On the International Activity....," FBIS, November 24, 1971.

CHAPTER III

1. T.H. Rigby, "The Soviet Leadership," loc.cit., p. 187.

2. Dornberg, op.cit., p. 209; cf. Tatu, op.cit., p. 521.

3. Leonard Schapiro, The Communist Party of the Soviet Union, 2nd edition, New York 1971, p. 628; cf. Jeremy Azrael, "The Party and Society" in Allen Kassof (ed.), Prospects for Soviet Society, New York 1968. Azrael has written:

> In the short and medium run, at least, the decisive variable is not the disembodied "logic" socio-economic maturation but the character of the emergent political leadership. (p. 71)

4. Pr., December 19, 1976. The birthday greetings were signed by the Central Committee, the Presidium of the Supreme Soviet and the Council of Ministers; see for references to Brezhnev's leading role in the formulation and implementation of foreign policy the election speeches of Politburo members, June 1974.

5. For instance, Podgorny told his audience during the celebration of Brezhnev's 70th birthday:

> Leonid Ilych Brezhnev's anniversary is not merely a notable date in his life. It is a major event for the Party and the state, for the entire Soviet people, who rightly see him as their recognized leader. (Emphasis added)

And about Brezhnev's political strategy:

> This strategy--a strategy of construction and peace-- was embodied most fully in the Reports of the CPSU Central Committee to the XXIII, XXIV and XXV Party Congresses, in your speeches at plenary sessions and in other works that are a major contribution to the treasure house of Marxism-Leninism.

Pr., December 20, 1976.

6. This is McAuley's explanation for Stalin's ascent to power in the 1920s. Mary McAuley, Politics and the Soviet Union, Middlesex 1977, p. 115.

7. <u>Pr.</u>, December 20, 1976. (<u>CDSP</u>, No. 51, p. 23).

8. Rigby, "The Soviet Leadership," <u>loc.cit.</u>, p. 190.

9. Baibakov's report of the 1970 economic plan stated that shortcomings in the economic reform were "largely due to the failure of enterprise and ministries to fully use the opportunities opened by the economic reform." <u>Pr.</u>, December 17, 1969; cf. <u>Soviet Economy Forges Ahead, Ninth Five-Year Plan 1971-1975</u>, Moscow 1973, written by a group of Gosplan officials. They claim:

> All these shortcomings stemmed from the fact that full advantage was not taken of the economic reform and some of its aspects had yet to be further specified and developed. (p. 214)

See also Gregory Grossman, "From the Eight to the Ninth Five-Year Plan" in Norton T. Dodge (ed.), <u>Analysis of the USSR's 24th Party Congress and the 9th Five-Year Plan</u>, Maryland 1971, p. 62; Alec Nove, <u>The Soviet Economic System</u>, London 1977.

10. <u>Pr.</u>, June 8, 1969. (<u>CDSP</u>, No. 23, p. 14)

11. Michel Tatu, "The Future of the Soviet Union," <u>Interplay</u>, May 1969, p. 4.

12. <u>Pr.</u>, June 8, 1969. (<u>CDSP</u>, No. 23, pp. 15,16)

13. Brezhnev, <u>Ob Osnovykh Voprosakh Ekonomicheskoi Politiki KPSS na Sovremennom Etape</u>, Moscow 1975, Vol. I, p. 417.

14. Cocks, "Retooling," <u>loc.cit.</u>, p. 66 (see next footnote).

15. For the most penetrating analysis of the indeed "comprehensive" plans for modernization and development outlined by Brezhnev since the XXIV Party Congress, see the works of Paul Cocks. He explains the goals of the "systems approach" intended to be applied to the Soviet system as a whole, the attempt to enhance and to introduce sophisticated tools of analysis and planning, and the motives that led to the Kremlin's adoptation of a systems approach. Paul Cocks, "Science Policy and Soviet Decision-Making: PPBS comes to the Kremlin," paper presented at the APSA Annual Meeting San Francisco, September 2-5, 1975; "The Policy Process and Bureaucratic Politics," in Paul Cocks et al., <u>The Dynamics of Soviet Politics</u>, Harvard 1976, pp. 156-178; "Retooling the Directed Society: Administrative

Modernization and Developed Socialism" in Jan F. Triska
and Paul Cocks, Political Development in Eastern Europe,
New York 1977, pp. 53-92; "Science Policy and Soviet
Development Strategy" in Alexander Dallin (ed.), The XXV
Congress of the CPSU: Assessment and Context, Stanford
1977, pp. 39-52; "Rethinking the Organizational Weapon:
The Soviet System, in a Systems Age," World Politics, Ja-
nuary 1980, pp. 228-257.

16. A. Rumyantsev, "Management of the Soviet Economy Today"
in Soviet Economic Reform: Progress and Problems, Moscow
1972, p. 21. A Kommunist editorial in 1971 spoke out
strongly in favor of consumer priority and argues that
it is both possible and desirable.

> Under conditions of mature socialism the Soviet nation
> is capable of concentrating still greater forces and
> assets on the solution of tasks connected with a fun-
> damental improvement in the people's well-being....
> ...This is the main task of the ninth Five-Year Plan:
> In determining it, the Party also proceeded from the
> premise that raising the working people's well-being
> is an increasingly urgent prerequisite for rapid pro-
> duction growth....
> ...[The workers' attitude and productivity depend] to
> a considerable extent on the people's living standard
> and on how fully their material and spiritual require-
> ments can be satisfied. (Emphasis added)

Kommunist, No. 16, 1971, pp. 3-11, editorial.

17. Idem.; cf. Erik P. Hoffman, "Soviet Views of 'The Scientific-Technological Revolution'," World Politics, July
1978, pp. 615-644.

18. Grossman, loc.cit., p. 63. Doubts about planning feasibility are also apparent in the description of the work for
the Ninth Five-Year Plan by the Gosplan collective, Soviet
Economy Forges Ahead, pp. 214-227.

19. See, for example, the account of two former officials of
the central planning in Moscow, Albina Tretyakova and Igor
Birman, "Input-Output Analysis in the USSR," Soviet Studies,
No. 2, April 1976, pp. 157-186. A familiar pattern of Soviet articles (about planning) is a description of what
is to be done to improve the system. Much less space is
devoted to comments of what has been done, except for the
defense of the basic achievements of centralized, quantitative planning. cf. N. Baibakov, "The Further Improvement
of Planning is a Most Important National Economic Task,"

Planovoye Khozyastvo, No. 3, 1974, pp. 51-53; Resolution "On Improving Planning and Strengthening the Economic Mechanism's Influence in Enhancing Production Efficiency and Work Quality," _Pr._, July 29, 1979; I tak dale.

20. Rumyantsev, _loc.cit._, p. 20.

21. _Planovoye Khozyastvo_, (No. 4.,1973) announced that Gosplan was already working on the 1976-1990 economic development plan.

22. Brezhnev avoids the word "economic reform," referring rather to the "improvement of the economic mechanism," cf. Cocks, "The Policy Process," _loc.cit._, p. 172.

   A major aim of the drive to form science and production associations is to concentrate managerial responsibility and authority for the research and development process as a whole, to centralize decision-making in order to achieve greater unity and order and to eliminate endless wrangling and delays that can occur at every stage of the cycle....
   ...Recent efforts have centered particularly on finding more effective ways of integrating research and development planning with general economic planning.

23. Cocks, "Retooling," _loc.cit._, pp. 62-66.

24. Cocks, "The Organizational Weapon," loc.cit., p. 228.

25. Brezhnev told the XXV Party Congress:

   V.I. Lenin pointed out that when a correct policy and a correct line have been worked out, success depends primarily on organization. We have such a policy and such a line. Hence the decisive element is organization--that is, the further improvement of economic management in the broadest sense of the term.

   _Pr._, February 25, 1976. (_Current Soviet Policies VII, The Documentary Record of the XXV Congress of the CPSU_, Columbus 1976, p. 22). This compilation from CDSP translations is hereafter indicated as "XXV," _CDSP_.

26. cf. Galkin, Director of a metallurgical combine, who told the XXV Congress that "economic managers are especially pleased" with Brezhnev's proposals for management reform.

   They _impel_ executives at all levels, from the USSR State Planning Committee and the branch ministries

to the enterprises, to do some deep thinking about
how to improve all operations of the economic mechanism.
Actually, the upper echelon of our country's economic
leadership is...often loaded down with petty questions
of current operations. Many of these questions could
be resolved at lower levels, frequently on the local
level. (Emphasis added)

"XXV," CDSP, p. 65.

27. V. Shcherbitsky, "Party Organizations and the Improvement
of Economic Management," Kommunist, no. 6., 1973, pp.
19-33; cf. Alec Nove, op.cit., p. 80.

28.   The improvement of the management tiers is not only
a matter for the planning and economic organs. It
needs the special concern of the party committees.
To whom to entrust the leadership of a complex, how
to organize more rationally the restraining and economic studies of management personnel, increase their
responsibility, find positions for those who have
been released from jobs and how the primary party
organizations should act under the new conditions--
these and many other questions must merit the constant attention of the party committees.

Pr., May 23, 1975, editorial, "The Production Association."

29. The Soviet Prefects, esp. Chapters IV and V.

30. Hough and Fainsod, op.cit., p. 444. With regard to a number of possible conflictual situations they conclude

        In all of these conflicts the relevant Central Com-
mittee departments and sections are likely to be supporting the ministry they oversee and opposing the
Central Committee departments and sections (and ministries) on the other side of the issue. (p. 446)

31. K. Varlamov, "Democratic Centralism is the Principle of
Economic Management," Pr., April 5, 1974.

32. Moscow 1977, p. 265. At the XXV Party Congress Brezhnev
used the euphemism "subject of repeated discussion" to
indicate the rivalry between Party and government bodies.
("XXV," CDSP, p. 22) This confrontation was in fact the
second major one in his career as General Secretary. When
he and Kosygin took over the Ministries were reinstated

281

and assumed under Kosygin's leadership the major role in
economic policy. Moreover, the Economic Reform of 1965
brought the Ministries, according to Grossman, a great
deal of power in economic planning. Brezhnev apparently
fought an uphill fight during the first years of his
leadership. The Party "generalists" were kept from too
much interference in the work of the economic "specialists." cf. Tatu, op.cit., Gregory Grossman, "Comment,"
Survey, Winter/Spring 1969, p. 167.

33. Pr., November 28, 1974.

34. "XXV", CDSP, p. 50. cf. Pr., May 23, 1975. The editorial
     states that

          ...other Ministries also plan to achieve a conside-
          rable saving from the improvement of the organizatio-
          nal forms of leadership. However, this work is by no
          means proceeding well everywhere.... There are at-
          tempts to avoid reducing the numbers of the ministry's
          central apparatus, to preserve main administrations
          and to create an excessively large number of middle
          tier subdivisions, although the production associa-
          tions are becoming the centers of operational leader-
          ship.

35. Tatu, op.cit., pp. 429-460: "The Lobbies"; cf. Skilling
     and Griffiths (eds.), op.cit. for relations between the
     Party and interest groups. For example, Judy describes
     the position of economists who lean toward economic ra-
     ther than ideological considerations for development.
     They are hindered in two ways in their belief

          ...that analytical economics is fully compatible with
          rational humane socialism. It is not compatible, how-
          ever, with the unfettered exercise of power by a
          small minority such as the party apparatus. Percep-
          tion of this may cause the apparatchiki to limit or
          reverse the trend toward freedom of discussion and
          advocacy among Soviet economists. Another dogged ally
          of conservatism is the economic illiteracy of the
          Soviet political leadership. ("The Economists," p. 250)

36. It is not surprising that Podgorny, in particular, should
     insist on a clear division of work and responsibility,
     since his "constituency," the Soviets, is the weakest
     amidst Party and Government organs.

37. cf. Ken Jowitt, "Inclusion and Mobilization in European
     Leninist Regimes," World Politics, October 1975, pp. 69-96.

38. V. Shcherbitsky, "The Sources of Responsibility," _Pr._, August 31, 1973. The Ukrainan First Secretary lists a number of successes of the "harmonious system for training and retraining leading cadres" that had been created throughout the country. He stresses not only economic and technical training, but also the importance of the selection and training of those gifted with capacities for leadership. cf. I. Kapitonov, "The Development of Intraparty Democracy in the CPSU," _Problemy Mira i Sotsializma_, No. 11, 1973.

39. cf. Zhores Medvedev about "political control of promotion in science and education," _op.cit._, pp. 180-194; Shcherbitsky complaints that economic and Soviet organs and specialists play safe and transfer too eagerly their responsibilities to Party members and committees. _Idem._

40. cf. Cocks, "Retooling," _loc.cit._, pp. 73-79.

41. _Sotsialisticheskaya Industria_, October 18, 1978.

42. A declared goal of economic reform. See _Soviet Economic Reform_, p. 5, and Chapter IX, "The Economic Reform and the Development of Socialist Emulation," pp. 229-247.

43. See Brezhnev's speeches in _Pr._, March 15, and June 14, 1974. Shcherbitsky asserts that greater technical and economic knowledge in the cadres is very important and necessary, but

> ...it is little for a leader to know production technology and to understand economics; it is extremely necessary for him also to have good organizational skills and to be a true leader of the masses....
> ...The personal authority of the leader and his ability to rally the collective and create a business-like creative atmosphere is a guarantee of successful work in any sector.

_Pr._, August 31, 1973.

44. Ken Jowitt, "An Organizational Approach to Political Culture in Marxist-Leninist Systems," _American Political Science Review_, September 1974, p. 1176.

45. Cocks, "The Organizational Weapon," _loc.cit._, p. 251.

46. _Pr._, June 5, 1977. Brezhnev's formulation was virtually identical to that used by Kosygin when he vigorously defended the economic reform in 1970. _Pr._, June 11, 1970.

47. _Pr._, June 18, 1977. Efforts to enhance the role of the Soviets continue, at least formally and legally. For example, a law on the basic powers of territorial and regional Soviets was approved in June 1980. The law aims at increasing the responsibilities of local government and strengthening the connection between economic and social development and between industrial and territorial management. See _Pr._, July 4, 1980, Editorial "The Increasing Role of the Soviets."

48. Friedgut, _op.cit._, p. 322. He too recognizes a tendency towards greater democratization.

> There appear to exist pressures in the Soviet Union for movement into a stage of adaptation in which detailed, all-embracing Party control and the centralized monopoly on political power would give way to a more balanced distribution of forces composed of functional groups, intellectual critics, and participating citizens, all exercising some initiative in the determination of social priorities within an overall framework of Communist Party power. (p. 325)

Similar conclusions were drawn by an eye-witness in the scientific community, Medvedev, _op.cit._, pp. 180-186.

49. Reports from the Soviet Union do not offer an optimistic picture of the future. The chance of transforming the 15 million-strong vanguard, or for that matter the hundreds of thousands of Party secretaries, into an inspiring, morally loyal and unselfish army, gaining respect and trust on the victorious way towards communism, seems very dim, if not hopeless. Solzhenitsyn's description of the Party member, Rusanov, in _Cancer Ward_, for instance, or Yanov's slashing attack on the secretaries' economic management add up to the inevitable conclusion that there is a real gap between Party and population. The "new Soviet man" seems to have learned to live two different lives at the same time: one official and one personal. Western accounts, like those of attentive and sharp observers like Kaiser and Smith, also amount to the same impression. A unique and in fact dramatic story is the experience of two loyal and still faithful French communists who went to work and live in the Soviet Union, but after several years returned in disillusion with a feeling of repugnance for the first socialist state.
Alexander Solzhenitsyn, _Cancer Ward_, New York 1969, especially Chapter XIV, "Justice"; Alexander Yanov, _Detente after Brezhnev: The Domestic Roots of Soviet Foreign Policy_,

Berkeley, Ca. 1977; Robert G. Kaiser, Russia: The People and the Power, New York 1976; Hedrick Smith, The Russians, New York 1976; Nina and Jean Kéhayan, Rue du Prolétaire Rouge: Deux Communistes Francais en URSS, Paris 1978.

50. Paul Cocks, "The Rationalization of Party Control," in Chalmers Johnson (ed.), Change in Communist Systems, Stanford 1970, p. 189.

51. Schapiro, op.cit., p. 629.

52. cf. leading articles in Pravda on the 90th and 100th birth-day of Stalin, December 21, 1969 and 1979.

53. "The Effective Force of Leninist Principles of Party Lea-dership," Kommunist (editorial), No. 16, 1974. (FBIS, No-vember 25, 1974, p. R 8); See Kapitonov, candidate member of the Politburo and Central Committee Secretary, who confirmed the strengthened collective role.

> Graphic and convincing evidence of the development of collective, genuinely democratic methods of lea-dership is the further raising of the role of the CPSU Central Committee plenums.

I. Kapitonov, "The Development of Intraparty Democracy in the CPSU," Problemy Mira i Sotsializma, No. 11, 1973. (FBIS, November 20, p. R 2)

54. Ibid., p. R 6.

55. Ibid., p. R 8.

56. cf. Hough and Fainsod, op.cit., p. 455-466; Jacobson, op. cit., p. 176. They have gathered together the available evidence on the frequency, length, and content of the Central Committee sessions which "suggest that the Central Committee has played a minor role in the Soviet political system in the Brezhnev period (p. 465)." On the other hand, they also point to the "bargaining" position of the Central Committee vis-à-vis the General Secretary. By and large, however, no sweeping conclusions should be drawn. Given the paucity of information, "it is almost impossible to describe the work of the Central Committee and the meaning of membership in it." (p. 459)

57. cf. Dallin, XXV Party Congress, Tables on pp. 109-110; Jerry F. Hough, "The Brezhnev Era," Problems of Communism, March-April 1976, pp. 1-17; Robert E. Blackwell Jr.,

"Cadres Policy in the Brezhnev Era," Problems of Communism, March-April 1979, pp. 29-42.

58. Robert V. Daniels, "Participatory Bureaucracy and the Soviet Political System" in Dodge, op.cit., p. 77; cf. Daniels, "Office Holding and Elite Status; The Central Committee of the CPSU" in Cocks et al., Dynamics, pp. 78-80.

59. Ibid., p. 78.

60. See Hough and Fainsod, op.cit., pp. 460-510.

61. Pr., May 27, 1975.

62. Idem.

63. Pr., April 3, 1971. Kirilenko asserts that the "Central Committee and its Politburo are occupied daily with foreign policy questions and are devoting much attention to their resolution." Pr., June 12, 1974.

64. V.V. Zagladin, "Unflagging Will to Peace," New Times, No. 51, 1976, p. 5.

65. cf. Hough and Fainsod, op.cit., Chapter XI, "The Central Committee Secretariat and Apparatus," Chapter XII, "The Leading Party Organs," especially pp. 455-466.

66. Ibid., p. 443.

67. "XXV," CDSP, p. 23.

68. "The Ministry Party Committee," Pr., November 28, 1974 editorial.

69. "Communists of the Ministries," Pr., January 28, 1980.

70. Pr., November 28, 1979. Kirillin, head of the criticized State Committee for Science and Technology, was the first victim. He was relieved from his duties "in accordance with his request." Pr., January 23, 1980.

71. Reprinted in Pr., November 23, 1977. Brezhnev informed the congress about the mini-purge of 347,000 Party members, 2.3% of all members.

    Important results of the exchange are an increase in the mutual exactingness of Communists toward one another and the creation in Party organizations of an atmosphere of intolerance toward violations of the Statutes.

"XXV," CDSP, p. 23. Grishin announced that in 1974, one year after the exchange began, about 70% of the Moscow Party members had received new cards. For the remaining 30%, Grishin sounded rather threatening:

> We are faced with the task...of making fuller use of this important organizational and political measure to further improve the activities of party organizations.

Moskovskaya Pravda, March 15, 1974.

72. "XXV," CDSP, p. 25.

73. Quoted in Pr., December 28, 1973.

74. Yanov, op.cit.

75. F.F. Petrenko, "Freedom of Discussion and Criticism: A Fundamental Principle of the Life and Activity of the CPSU," Voprosy Istorii KPSS, No. 4, 1974, pp. 96-108. (FBIS, May 24, pp. R 1-R 17)

76. Ibid. (FBIS, P. R 13)

77. For example, Ustinov, Moscow Domestic Service, April 20, 1973. (FBIS, April 23); Romanov, Leningrad Domestic Service, May 28, 1974. (FBIS, June 11); Grishin, Moskovskaya Pravda, March 15, 1974; Solomentsev, Pr., June 5, 1974.

78. Radio Riga Domestic Service, December 23, 1973. (FBIS, January 3, 1974)

79. cf. Dornberg, op.cit.; R. Judson Mitchell, "The Soviet Succession: Who, and What Will Follow Brezhnev?," Orbis, Spring 1979, pp. 9-34. Counting the heads of supporters and opponents is common in press reports about reshuffles after Plenums and Congresses.

80. Erickson comments that the military influence after Grechko's promotion was "likely to be a tactical move on the part of Brezhnev to assure his position with regard to the whole of his detente policy." J. Erickson, "The Soviet Military, Soviet Policy and Soviet Politics," Strategic Review, Fall 1973, p. 29.

81. Grishin, First Secretary of Moscow Gorkom since 1967, had been a candidate member since 1961, when he was Chairman of the Trade Unions; Kunaev, First Secretary of Kazakhstan, since 1964, Shcherbitsky since 1965. When he succeeded Shelest as First Secretary of the Ukraine in 1972, he was already a full member of the Politburo. Romanov, First Secretary of the Leningrad Gorkom since 1970, became a candidate member of the Politburo in 1971.

82. Shevardnadze received this status in 1978, but his predecessor in Georgia, Mzhavanadze, had been a candidate member since 1957. Shevardnadze seems simply to have been honored according to the status of his office. Rashidov, First Secretary in Uzbekistan, has been a candidate member since 1961.

83. B. Milner, "Special-Program and Specific-Purpose Management: Experience, Problems and Prospects," Pr., June 1, 1979; cf. Shcherbitsky, who in advocating Party leadership claims that

    ...the Party committees and the primary Party organizations, whose basis is built on the territorial-production principle, are not connected with narrow departmental and sector interests.

    Kommunist, No. 6, 1973, p. 20; see also Romanov's speech to the XXV Party Congress, Pr., February 26, 1976; The Gosplan collective cited earlier admits that

    ...the right combination of territorial and sectoral planning is perhaps the most important and urgent problem in improving the planning of the country's economy.

    Soviet Economy Forges Ahead, pp. 226-227.

84. M. Vasin and Y. Zakharov, "The Broad Horizons of the Associations. Report from the Leningrad Obkom Plenum," Pr., April 20, 1973.

85. Idem.

86. Leningrad Domestic Service, May 28, 1974. (FBIS, June 11, 1974, p. R 11); cf. Grishin, Moskovskaya Pravda, March 15, 1974. Grishin lauds Brezhnev's "great personal contribution to the formulation and implementation of the party's domestic and foreign policy." He adds the following about the December 1973 plenary session of the Central Committee:

> Comrade L.I. Brezhnev defined the chief directions
> for further improving the management of the national
> economy. These are improvement of the organizational
> structure of economic management, improvement of plan-
> ning and the strengthening of economic incentives.
> The city party organization must raise the standard
> of party leadership of the economy and insure the ac-
> tive participation of party organizations and commu-
> nists....

87. Radio Moscow Domestic Service, February 21, 1974. (FBIS, February 22, 1974, p. R 3)

88. See Sovetskaya Belorussia, November 15, 1973; Pr., June 13, 1974; Pr., July 6, 1978.

89. For example, Gerhard Wettig, "Entwicklungen der Sowjeti-schen Rüstungspolitik," Berichte des Bundesinstituts für Ostwissenschaftliche und Internationale Studien, Cologne, No. 57, 1974, p. 26.

90. See Pr., November 7, 1973; Pr., June 12, 1974.

91. cf. Brezhnev's speeches in Pr., June 12, 1971; Pr., June 15, 1974, Pr., November 28, 1978; and his speeches at the more recent Fall plenary sessions of the Central Committee.

92. Pr., December 16, 1974. Kosygin, who was no doubt aware of the imminent decision of the Central Committee in De-cember, strongly defended the need for social and economic development and emphatically opposed further defense out-lays in his speech in Frunze. (Pr., November 3, 1974) For example, referring to both the bad relations with China and the worsening relations with the United States, he emphasized that the Party's policy was not dependent on temporary fluctuations or on "transient factors." The Par-ty's task was to improve Sino-Soviet relations and to make detente "steady and irreversible."

> The Party Central Committee and the Soviet Government
> will continue to do everything necessary so that the
> Soviet people will be able to enjoy the benefits of a
> peaceful life and extensive international cooperation.
> Our people have not only earned this, they have won
> this right for themselves at great costs.

93. Pr., December 20, 1976.

94. cf. Brezhnev's and Kosygin speeches. See especially D.

Valovoi, "Improving the Economic Mechanism," <u>Pr.</u>, November 10, 11 and 12, 1977.

95. Nove, <u>op.cit.</u>

96. Cocks in <u>Dallin, The XXV Congress</u>, p. 52.

97. <u>Pr.</u>, November 7, 1974.

98. Podgorny, <u>loc.cit.</u>

99. Suslov, <u>Pr.</u>, December 20, 1976. Zagladin also referred to the "General Secretary's modesty, his reluctance to draw attention to his own services, his labours." Interestingly, while stressing the collective decision-making process, he also mentioned some other personal characteristics of Brezhnev.

> Add to this personal initiative, perseverance and determination to carry out decisions in the correctness of which he is convinced, plus the ability to convince others of the soundness of one or another conclusion.

Zagladin, <u>op.cit.</u>, p. 5; for a different view see Jerry F. Hough, who suggests that "perhaps Brezhnev has really not sought a great deal more" than universal love, gratitude and deep respect. It seems to the present author that Hough underestimates Brezhnev as a "struggler" who is however smart enough to switch to a debate and to offer concessions when coercive power proves to be unsuccessful. "The Brezhnev Era," <u>loc.cit.</u>, p. 7.

CHAPTER IV

1. cf. Samuel P. Huntington, <u>Political Order in Changing Societies</u>, New Haven 1968, Chapter VI, "Reform and Political Change."

2. When Brezhnev assumed responsibility for East-West relations in 1971 the division of labor in foreign policy brought Kosygin the Middle East and less important West European countries, while Podgorny was in charge of relations with most of the Third World countries. <u>New York Times</u>, October 26, 1971.

3. <u>Pr.</u>, April 4, 1971. Gromyko demanded that the Politburo "must function constantly and precisely...for the international situation never stands still." It was therefore necessary to "construct everything" so as to ensure that the highest interests "were sufficiently safeguarded."

4. Gromyko, <u>Izv.</u>, January 11, 1972.

5. Concern for the firm institutionalization of foreign policy decision-making and implementation was expressed by Chetverikov, even though he used the Washington setting and Kissinger's problems. S.B. Chetverikov, "Organizational Problems of Foreign Policy," <u>SShA.</u>, No. 8, 1974, pp. 28-34.

6. <u>Izv.</u>, March 31, 1974; cf. <u>Pr.</u>, August 20, 1973, editorial.

7. <u>Pr.</u>, April 28, 1973.

8. B. Vesnin, <u>Novoye Vremya</u>, May 11, 1973, pp. 4-6.

9. <u>Le Monde</u>, September 14, 1973.

10. Gromyko at the XXIV Party Congress, <u>Pr.</u>, April 4, 1971.

11. V.A. Zorin, <u>Osnovy Diplomaticheskoi Sluzhby</u>, Moscow 1977, p. 82.

12. Vesnin, <u>Ibid.</u>, p. 4.

13. V. Gantman, "A Policy that is Transforming the World," <u>Kommunist</u>, No. 7, 1973, pp. 27-41.

14. M. Tatu, "Decision-making in the USSR" in R. Pipes (ed.), Soviet Strategy in Europe, New York 1976, p. 62.

15. Kommunist, No. 7, 1973, editorial, p. 5.

16. See Dornberg, op.cit., p. 264, about campaigning after the CC Plenum of November 1971. The prominence of the foreign policy issue was also apparent from Kirilenko's October Revolution Speech. Contrary to the tradition, he started with a lengthy evaluation of foreign policy before turning to domestic policy and economics, and to commemoration of the 1917 Revolution. Pr., November 7,1973; Kapitonov, Problemy Mira i Sotsializma, No. 11, 1973, pp. 12-18; Leningradskaya Pravda, April 29, 1973.

17. A. Lomako, "Relaxation and the Ideological Struggle," Sovetskaya Latvia, December 29, 1973.

18. cf. R.A. Medvedev, "The Problem of Democratization and the Problem of Detente," a Samizdat article, parts of which appeared in New York Times, November 17, 1973.

19. Brezhnev referred at the XXV Party Congress to the April 1973 plenum as the one where "the formulation of questions of our state's foreign economic activity...was very important." "XXV," CPSU, p. 24.

20. Pr., March 21, and December 22, 1972.

21. cf. Kissinger, White House Years, pp. 1151-1152, p. 1213. At the Moscow summit in 1972 it was Podgorny who insisted that SALT was more important than commercial ties. After a while Kosygin switched sides, leaving Brezhnev on his own on the trade issue.

22. Pr., May 22, 1973.

23. These descriptions of the meaning of detente, which were practically identical to Kissinger and Sonnenfeldt's views of detente, were used for example by Kommunist, "In the Mainstream of the Struggle for Peace and the Peoples' Security," No. 10, 1973, pp. 4-15, editorial; Gantman, loc.cit.; N.N. Inozemtsev, "Socialism and International Economic Cooperation," Pr., May 16, 1973; Inozemtsev, "On the Nature of Contradictions in our Era," Problemy Mira i Sotsializma, No. 9, 1973, pp. 35-45; G.A. Arbatov, "U.S. Foreign Policy and the Scientific and Technical Revolution," SShA., No. 11, 1973, pp. 3-16.

24. Arbatov, _Ibid._, p. 3; Boris Vesnin commented on the new course:

> It is of course possible to dispute the completeness or incompleteness of the lessons of the recent period. It is of course incomplete. But it does perhaps reflect the chief thing, namely, that the epoch when the dominant tune in the arena of world politics was the saberrattling of the imperialist states has irretrievably sunk into the past. The time of Mars--the god of wars--has passed. His place is now occupied by other figures, in the front ranks of whom is the god of trade--Mercury.

Vesnin, _loc.cit._

25. Brezhnev at the World Peace Congress. _Pr._, October 27, 1973.

26. Gantman, loc.cit.; Inozemtsev, _Pr._, May 16, 1973; D. Tomashevsky, "The Leninist Principles of Foreign Policy in Action," _Pr._, July 4, 1973.

27. cf. Franklyn Griffiths, _Genoa plus 51: Changing Soviet Objectives in Europe_, Toronto 1973; E. Chossudovsky, "Genoa Revisited, Russia and Coexistence," _Foreign Affairs_, April 1972, pp. 554-577; _SShA._, editorial, "A Base for Developing Soviet-U.S. Relations," No. 7, 1972, pp. 3-6.

28. cf. Franklyn D. Holzman and Robert Legvold, "The Economics and Politics of East-West Relations," _International Organization_, Winter 1975, pp. 275-320; George D. Holliday, _Technology Transfer to the USSR, 1928-1937 and 1966-1975: The Role of Western Technology in Soviet Economic Development_, Boulder, Co. 1979; Elizabeth K. Valkenier, "The USSR, the Third World, and the Global Economy," _Problems of Communism_, July-August 1979, pp. 17-33.

29. Holzman and Legvold, _Ibid._; Alec Nove, _East-West Trade, Problems, Prospects and Issues_, Washington D.C. 1978; Franklyn D. Holzman, _Foreign Trade under Central Planning_, Cambridge, Mass. 1974.

30. Press Conference in Stockholm, April 5, 1973. _Novoye Vremya_, No. 15, 1973; cf. _Planovoye Khozyastvo_, No. 3, 1973.

31. Kosygin opposed economic relations confined to EEC-COMECON.

The Soviet Union would not agree with this approach,

since it attaches great importance to vigorous bilateral relations with Western countries.

Izv., July 7, 1973.

32. See Kosygin, election speech, Pr., June 13, 1974. In contrast to Brezhnev, who believed there were unlimited
domestic resources for exploiting the benefits of vastly
expanded trade, Kosygin referred to "optimism (which) is
based on a sober calculation of our real possibilities."

33. Sovetskaya Belorussia, November 15, 1973. (FBIS, November
23, p. R 9)

34. Brezhnev in Tashkent, September 24, 1973. Moscow Domestic
Service. (FBIS, September 25, p. R 12)

35. Dimitri K. Simes, Detente and Conflict, Soviet Foreign
Policy 1972-1977, Washington D.C. 1977, p. 50.

36. Yanov, op.cit.

37. Shelepin, Pr., June 4, 1974.

38. Moscow Domestic Service, April 20, 1973. (FBIS, April 23,
p. J 13)

39. The most complete account of the domestic political process connected with the Jackson-Vanik Amendment is by
Paula Stern, Water's Edge, Domestic Politics and the Making of American Foreign Policy, London 1979.

40. Washington Post, January 16, 1975, quoted by Stern, op.
cit., p. 181.

41. Stern, op.cit., p. 65. Readiness to deal with the emigration issue was evident from the clear signals given at
various moments when Soviet-American relations improved.

SOVIET JEWISH EMIGRATION
MEASURED BY ARRIVAL IN ISRAEL

	1967	1968	1969	1970	1971	1972	1973	1974	1975
January	----	----	----	----	108	3,004	2,500	2,365	899
February	----	----	----	----	71	1,796	2,751	1,581	890
March	----	----	----	----	636	1,977	2,174	1,726	525
April	----	----	----	----	1,578	2,945	2,821	1,579	708
May	----	----	----	----	1,049	2,804	2,171	1,222	477
June	----	----	----	----	1,138	3,070	1,929	1,230	648

July	----	----	----	----	661	2,163	2,240	1,293	448
August	----	----	----	----	524	2,061	2,660	1,318	627
September	----	----	----	----	995	2,128	3,065	1,092	624
October	----	----	----	----	1,328	2,840	4,200	1,384	673
November	----	----	----	----	1,835	3,760	3,814	1,214	673
December	----	----	----	----	3,000	3,120	3,039	864	904
TOTALS (Israel)	1,412	379	2,902	1,044	12,923	31,568	33,364	16,868	8,295

Arrivals elsewhere (United States)   543   1,451   3,490   5,426

TOTAL (all countries)   32,122   34,805   20,358   13,721

Total to U.S. 1972-
September 30, 1976   15,323

Emigration to U.S.
and to Israel 1972-
September 1976   109,985

Ibid., Appendix I, pp. 217-218.

42. Pr., October 16, 1974.

43. Moreover, Jackson's presidential aspirations were not furthered, the Nixon administration was handicapped and last but not least, the Soviet Jews were not helped at all. See Stern, op.cit., "Conclusion," pp. 195-213.

44. cf. Cocks in Dallin, p. 44.

45. Stern, op.cit., p. 84.

46. Holzman and Legvold, op.cit., conclude:

> ...both Secretary Kissinger and Senator Jackson feature the political instrumentalism of the East-West economic relationship, and both protect the subordination of economics to politics. The Soviet Union, in contrast, has a certain incentive for keeping the two spheres apart. (pp. 294-295)

At this point the authors still treat the Soviet Union as one actor in international relations. When they describe the Soviet domestic process and its impact on East-West relations, their conclusion comes very close to the one reached here.

47. N.N. Inozemtsev, "On the Nature of Contradictions in our

Era," Problemy Mira i Sotsializma, No. 9, 1973, pp. 35-45.

48. Pr., September 20, 1973.

49. Pr., October 27, 1973.

50. Leningradskaya Pravda, June 5, 1971.

51. H. Kissinger, White House Years, pp. 1144-1148. The major concession Kissinger had to bring home from his secret trip in April, 1972 was the Kremlin's agreement to put pressure on Vietnam in the peace talks. Brezhnev indeed conceded. Shelest, who had to pay for his opposition, was right from the socialist point of view.

52. Kr.Zv., July 24, 1974.

53. Brezhnev in Kiev, Moscow Domestic Service, July 26, 1973. (FBIS, July 27, p. J 11)

54. Izv., September 28, 1973; see also, on the same subject, Pr., September 28. Both articles were editorials.

55. M. Mitin, "International Relations and the Ideological Struggle," Kr.Zv., November 22, 1973.

56. Pr., August 1, 1973. Similar friction may have occurred at the Crimean meetings a year before. But there were no high level reactions as in 1973; the Soviet press merely stressed the importance of consent (cooperation) with Soviet foreign policy.

57. Pr., August 16, 1973.

58. V. Korionov, "A Class, Internationalist Course," Pr., July 20, 1973; cf. I. Aleksandrov, "The Interests of Peace and Socialism," Pr., August 7, 1973; Pr., August 20, 1973, editorial.

59. Kr.Zv., September 13, 1973. Later in 1973 there were more references to socialist unity as the subject of the Crimean meeting, see Pr., December 30, 1973, editorial.

60. K. Zarodov, "The Leninist Doctrine and the Party of Today," Pr., July 10, 1973.

61. Pr., August 16, 1973.

62. Pr., and Izv., September 7, 1973.

63. <u>Pr.</u>, September 23, 1973. cf. Vernon, who detects in Brezhnev's speech at the XXV Party Congress "an element of defensiveness...suggesting that in part he was answering critics, external or internal, who were attacking him and the policy of peaceful coexistence as being 'soft on capitalism'." Graham D. Vernon, "Controlled Conflict, Soviet Perceptions of Peaceful Coexistence," <u>Orbis</u>, Summer 1979, pp. 283-284.

64. Riga Domestic Service, December 26, 1973. (<u>FBIS</u>, January 3, 1974)

65. <u>Kommunist</u>, No. 1, 1974, p. 53.

66. <u>Pr.</u>, March 21, 1972.

67. Speech in Tashkent, <u>loc.cit.</u>

68. Podgorny, for example, assessed Sino-Soviet relations as follows:

> There is a certain logic in the fact that the Maoists have found themselves in the same camp with the most reactionary circles of imperialism. This is the logic of anti-Sovietism. It has led the present Chinese leaders to an absurd and primitive scheme: all that is good for the Soviet Union is bad for China, and all that is bad for the Soviet Union is good for China....
> On the condition that the PRC leaders give up the policy of anti-Sovietism, we are already, as before, to build relations with China on the principles of peace, cooperation and good-neighborliness.

Riga Domestic Service, December 26, 1973 (<u>FBIS</u>, January 3, 1974, p. R 14); cf. Kosygin, <u>Pr.</u>, June 13, 1974, So-vetskaya Pravda, November 15, 1973.
An indication that I. Aleksandrov could be the pseudonym for someone close to Brezhnev is given by the similar wording used in discussing various issues. This is especially true of his comment on Sino-Soviet relations and his insistence that Brezhnev's line had been adopted by the Central Committee in April 1973.

> At this year's April plenum of the Central Committee our party again confirmed its immutable striving for a normalization of relations with the PRC on the principles of peaceful coexistence.

The Resolution of the Plenum had however pointedly avoided
the term "peaceful coexistence," while explicitly mentioning "the anti-Soviet course." The formulation of the Resolution is more likely to have been the agreed approach,
similar to that of other Soviet leaders. The Resolution
stated:

> The plenary meeting stresses that the stubborn strug-
> gle of the leadership of the People's Republic of
> China against the unity of the socialist countries
> and the world communist movement, against the efforts
> of the peace-loving states and peoples seeking a re-
> laxation of international tensions as well as Peking's
> anti-Soviet course injure the cause of peace and in-
> ternational socialism. The plenary meeting reiterates
> the resolve of our party, in its relations with China,
> to continue to carry out the line of the 24th CPSU
> Congress.

I. Aleksandrov, "In the Interests of Peace and Socialism,"
Pr., August 7, 1973. Resolution "On the International
Activities....," April 27, 1973. (FBIS, April 27, p. J 2)
The latter formulation is also used in editorials on the
Plenum. See Pr., April 28, 1973; Kommunist, No. 7, 1973,
p. 11.

69. cf. Rosser, op.cit., Chapter I; Triska and Finley, op.cit.;
     V. Kubalkova and A.A. Cruickshank, Marxism-Leninism and the
     Theory of International Relations, London 1980; For a
     highly cynical, but not incorrect, treatment see the
     various publications (in Dutch) on Marxism-Leninism by
     Karel van het Reve, especially his Geloof der Kameraden
     [The Comrades' Faith]. The most convincing way to check
     the flaws and rambling is, of course, to force oneself
     to peruse the pages of The Fundamentals of Marxism-Leni-
     nism, which is published by Progress at an--understandably
     --low price.

70. Schwartz adds, moreover: "This is particularly true of
     the nonromantic, highly pragmatic regime currently occu-
     pying the Kremlin." Even though one can agree with his
     conclusion that "secularization" is substantial, he goes
     much too far in down-playing the role of ideological ima-
     ges. For example, he postulates that

> ...there is considerable evidence that such ideologi-
> cal constructs as the international class struggle,
> proletarian internationalism, and their several de-
> rivatives are of little actual significance in the

formulation (not to mention the day-to-day conduct) of Soviet foreign policy.

Schwartz, op.cit., p. 110.

71. Martin Seliger, Ideology and Politics, New York 1976, p. 151.

72. Rosser, op.cit., p. 67.

73. Idem.

74. Seliger, "Basic Linkages," Chapter III, op.cit., pp. 91-121. The fundamental dimension is no different from the operative dimension in its elements, but in the centrality of its moral and technical prescriptions. In the former case "deduction prevails over evidence, doctrine over practice, principle over precedent and ends over means." The operative dimension is more characterized by the reversed order of these considerations. (p. 111) Ideology serves as justification, legitimization and coordination of political action and is a means to attain, maintain or expand power. The use of ideology in politics involves both dimensions, and may serve both "the cause" and self-interests to a greater or lesser degree. Ideology is subject to change in the political process.

> The function of ideology affects the structure of the ideological argument inasmuch as at least temporary compromises over principles are demanded by the mere involvement in political action and by the objective to mobilize as much support as possible (or desirable) for a programme of action. Compromises cause ideology to bifurcate into the purer, and hence more dogmatic, fundamental dimension of argumentation and the more diluted, and hence more pragmatic, operative dimension. In the latter, morally based prescriptions are often attenuated, or have their central place momentarily occupied by technical prescriptions. The tension between the two dimensions gives rise to the question of the sincerity of the valuations which are advanced, whereas out of the interaction between the two dimensions, which normally signifies an increase of ideological pluralism, arises the challenge of ideological change. (p. 120)

75. Ibid., p. 201.

76. Zbigniew K. Brzezinski, Ideology and Power in Soviet

299

Politics, Revised edition, New York 1967, pp. 76-77.

77. See footnote 74.

78. Seliger, op.cit., p. 213.

79. Brzezinski and Huntington, op.cit., p. 409.

80. With respect to the relationship between a principle
and its environment, one may speak of a monistic principle if it is accepted that no other principle should
be tolerated within a system.... One may refer to a
monopolistic principle if it is accepted that the
principle should be adhered to by every subject in a
system.

Jurrjens, op.cit., p. 41.

81. William B. Husband, "Soviet Perceptions of U.S. 'Positions-
of Strength' Diplomacy in the 1970s," World Politics, July
1979, pp. 495-517, vide 496.

82. Jurrjens, op.cit., p. 185.

83. Report of the Conference on the XXIV Party Congress and
the development of Marxist-Leninist theory. Pr., September 30, 1971.

84. Pr., July 10, 1973.

85. Brezhnev to the World Peace Congress, Pr., October 27,
1973.

86. Izv., March 31, 1974, editorial.

87. Mitin, Kr.Zv., November 22, 1973. He interprets Brezhnev's
speech in his own militant way, insisting that it "shows
that very important significance now attached to the question of the correct understanding of the principles of
peaceful coexistence and a correct attitude toward them."
A similar interpretation of peaceful coexistence is given
by Petrov, presumably a pseudonym. The only field for negotiation and agreement is the security issue area.

There is no doubt that the class struggle between the
two systems--capitalist and socialist--will continue
in the economic, political, and ideological spheres,
for the world outlook and class aims of socialism and
capitalism are opposite and irreconcilable.

V. Petrov, "Internationalism of the CPSU's Foreign Policy," Pr., December 21, 1973.

88. V. Zagladin, "Adherence to Principle and Consistency," Novoye Vremya, No. 22, 1972. (FBIS, June 1, 1972, p. A 3)

89. Ibid. He also tells those who want to rely primarily on military power and follow an "inflexible" course in foreign policy:

> It is understandable that any international situation that arises, even more so an acute situation, requires that the socialist states react on a flexible, current basis. However, the experience of past years has shown full well that an inclination here toward a circumstantial approach (under the influence of emotion or any other reasons) merely adds self-limitation to current present-day interests and refusal to take long-term prospects into consideration are never of benefit. (p. A 4)

90. Only a skillful combination of different--military, political, and diplomatic--methods of struggle has enabled the heroic people of Vietnam and their leadership to achieve in the liberation struggle such enormous successes which we are now observing.

The combination of principled firmness and tactical flexibility has given the Cuban leadership an opportunity of recently breaking through the isolation with which imperialism vainly tried to encircle Cuba. And it is possible to cite an infinite multitude of such examples.

In other words, the strength of socialist policy has never laid in primitiveness and stereotype, and even less in an identical repetition of the modes and methods used by the class enemy, but always in its own activeness and in the differentiated combination of various methods of action aimed in the final analysis at the same target.

Any one-sidedness in policy and the same kind of reliance on one group of methods of struggle as upon another group can in fact lead only to the improvement of the possibilities of socialist foreign policy and to the diminution of the effectiveness of its actions. And in certain instances such one-sidedness can jeopardize the attainment of this policy's fundamental objectives.

301

Idem.

91. B.N. Ponomarev, "The World Situation and the Revolutionary Process," Problemy Mira i Sotsializma, No. 6, 1974,
pp. 3-10. Reprinted in his Izbrannoe, Rechi i Stati (Selection of Speeches and Articles), Moscow 1977, pp. 528-
542.

92. Ibid., p. 531.

93. Ibid., p. 532.

94. G. Shakhnazarov, "Peaceful Coexistence and Social Progress,"
Pr., December 27, 1975.

95. Ponomarev, op.cit., p. 535.

   This is the first time that critical processes in the
   economy and factors linked with the profound political
   crisis both within individual imperialist countries
   and also in the system of present-day capitalist interstate relations have been so closely intertwined
   in a single package and been spurring each other on
   so forcefully. (pp. 534-535)

96. A.I. Sobolev, "Problems of the Strategy and Tactics of
the Class Struggle at the Present Stage," Rabochy Klass
i Sovremenny Mir, translated in Strategic Review, Fall
1975, p. 105.

97. Ponomarev, op.cit., p. 539.

98. Ibid., p. 540.

99. The comparison between the Soviet domestic model and Soviet thought on the future world order is argued most
forcefully by Judson Mitchell, who observes that the
"exclusive conceptual framework for all Soviet thought
on politics and society dictates the ultimate domination
of the world by a single social structure" (p. 374). The
Soviet approach to the integration of East-European socialist countries, is according to him, identical to the
approach to nationality policy in the Soviet Union. The
theoretical approach to the restructuring of international relations is based on the steadily growing power of
the Soviet Union and internationalism in an essentially
"zero sum" framework.

   Given the Soviet Union's weight in the process and

its interest in restructuring, the dominant Soviet
social structure is identified with all world revolutionary forces, specifically with those whose actions tend to diminish the weight of the Soviet's
chief competitor in the world balance. (p. 389)

Although Mitchell's analysis of the theoretical approach
to the restructuring of international relations is probably not far off the mark, if at all, for a number of
Soviet political actors, he certainly seems to be wrong
in calling this master plan "a new Brezhnev Doctrine."
The extent to which Soviet leaders adhere to or believe
in these long-term Marxist-Leninist constructs is unknown
and may vary widely. Brezhnev's behavior and his conduct
of foreign policy at home and abroad point, however, to
a radically different view on the development of international relations. R. Judson Mitchell, "A New Brezhnev
Doctrine; The Restructuring of International Relations,"
World Politics, April 1978.

100. N. Kapchenko, "The Scientific Principles of Soviet Foreign Policy," International Affairs, October 1977, p. 82.

101. Major-General Ye. Sulimov, "The Scientific Nature of the
Foreign Policy of the CPSU," Kr.Zv., December 20, 1973.

102. N. Kapchenko, "The Foreign Policy of Socialism and the
Restructuring of International Relations," Mezhdunarodnaya
Zhizn, No. 3, 1975, pp. 3-14.

103.   The long years of the cold war have left their traces
        in the minds of professional politicians and others.
        These are prejudice, suspicion, insufficient knowledge,
        even an unwillingness to become familiar with the
        true position and opportunities of others. It is ob-
        viously not easy to change one's outlook in such mat-
        ters, but it is essential that this be done. It is
        essential that we learn to cooperate. Our philosophy
        of peace is the philosophy of historical optimism.

     Pr., October 27, 1973.

104. Mitchell, loc.cit., see footnote 99.

105. See for an excellent analysis of the differences between
Stalin's and Khrushchev's conceptions of peaceful coexistence, Paul Marantz, "Peaceful Coexistence, From Heresy
to Orthodoxy," in Cocks et al., Dynamics, pp. 293-308.

106. _Kr.Zv._, November 22, 1973.

107. D. Tomashevsky, "Toward a Radical Restructuring of International Relations," _MEMO_, No. 1, 1975, pp. 3-13. (_FBIS_, February 3, p. A 19)

108. Gromyko, _Pr._, June 11, 1974.

109. James N. Rosenau (ed.), _Linkage Politics_, New York 1969, p. 13.

110. _Ibid._ Rosenau suggests

> ...additional questions about the role of leadership that can fruitfully be subjected to further research: What are the costs linkage elites pay within their national roles for continued attention to and performance of the demands of their international roles? What are the domestic rewards for such behavior?.... Does instability in the international system jeopardize dual politicians in the national system?

111. Table X, Chapter VII, p.p.226-7 contains the likely views of Politburo members on some foreign policy issues, including Soviet security, and compares their views on domestic and foreign policy issues.

112. Dennis Ross, "Coalition Maintenance in the Soviet Union," _World Politics_, January 1980, pp. 261-262.

113. cf. Rosenau, _Linkage_, p. 13.

114. Article by L.M. Spirin, _Voprosy Istorii KPSS_, No. 11, 1974, pp. 14-29. Spirin's interpretation of peaceful coexistence contains all the "organic links" with internationalism. Detente is strictly confined to security issues and arms control. In the final analysis, the reader is left with the firm impression that Spirin's "compromise" in foreign policy inclines heavily towards the priorities of socialist unity and internationalism; indeed, as a "pledge of the _triumph_ of peace and _social progress._"

CHAPTER V

1. Huntington, <u>The Soldier and the State</u>, p. 2.

2. <u>Idem.</u>

3. <u>Ibid.</u>, p. 83.

4. <u>Ibid.</u>, pp. 1-2, vide p. 2.

5. <u>Ibid.</u>, pp. 7-18.

6. <u>Ibid.</u>, p. 86.

7. <u>Ibid.</u>, p. 79. Huntington summarizes military conservative realism as follows:

> The military ethic emphasizes the permanence, irrationality, weakness, and evil in human nature. It stresses the supremacy of society over the individual and the importance of order, hierarchy, and division of function. It stresses the continuity and value of history. It accepts the nation state as the highest form of political organization and recognizes the continuing likelihood of wars among nation states. It emphasizes the importance of power in international relations and warns of the dangers to state security. It holds that the security of the state depends upon the creation and maintenance of strong military forces. It urges the limitation of state action of the direct interest of the state, the restriction of extensive commitment, and the undesirability of bellicose or adventurous policies. It holds that war is the instrument of politics, that the military are the servants of the statesman, and that civilian control is essential to military professionalism. It exalts obedience as the highest virtue of military men. The military ethic is thus pessimistic, collectivist, historically inclined, power-oriented, nationalistic, militaristic, pacifist, and instrumentalist in its view of the military profession. It is, in brief, realistic and conservative.

8. <u>Ibid.</u>, pp. 89-94.

9. <u>Ibid.</u>, p. 95.

10. *Ibid.*, p. 94.

11. *Ibid.*, pp. 96-97.

12. See Chapter I.

13. cf. Jurrjens, *op.cit.*, p. 39.

14. Col. P. Sidorov, "Foundations of the Soviet Military Doctrine," Soviet Military Review, September 1972, p. 14. A similar definition is given by V.D. Sokolovsky (ed.), Military Strategy, third edition translated by Harriet Fast Scott, p. 38. All further references to the third edition relate to this translation. Soviet Military Strategy, New York 1975.

15. Sokolovsky, *op.cit.*, 3rd ed., p. 38.

16. cf. Julian Lider, The Political and Military Laws of War, Westmead, England, 1979, pp. 47-60.

17. Sokolovsky, *op.cit.*, 3rd ed., p. 7.

18. Lt-Gen. Zavizion, "The Subject of Soviet Military Science," Kommunist of the Armed Forces [KVS], No. 12, June 1973.

19. Bulganin, quoted by R.L. Garthoff, Soviet Military Doctrine, Glencoe 1953, p. 13.

20. Sokolovsky, *op.cit.*, 3rd ed., p. 8.

21. cf. Maj-Gen M. Cherednichenko, "Economics and Military-Technical Policy," KVS, No. 15, August 1968, pp. 11-13; John R. Thomas, "Soviet Foreign Policy and Military," Survey, Summer 1971, p. 139, concerning military opposition to the Soviet-German Treaty.

22. Col. S. Kozlov in Military Thoughts, November 1954, p. 23. Quoted in R.L. Garthoff's Soviet Military Policy, New York 1966, p. 128.

23. Garthoff, Soviet Military Doctrine, p. 25.

24. *Pr.*, January 22, 1960.

25. For instance, Khrushchev, speaking about the Cuban crisis, *Pr.*, December 13, 1963. Also Kosygin: "For humanity, if it is to continue to exist, nuclear weapons are not necessary....," *Pr.*, February 11, 1967.

26. I.E. Tamm, *International Affairs*, No. 3, 1961.

27. A.P. Butenko, *Kommunist*, No. 4, 1961, p. 50.

28. *Pr.*, October 27, 1965.

29. CPSU Program of 1961, p. 33. The opposition of the hard-liner Molotov to the phrase was rejected. Molotov's opinion was that further progress towards communism without the most serious political conflict (war) with the imperialist countries was impossible. *CPSU report XXII Congress, Part II*, Moscow 1961, p. 352.

30. Sokolovsky, *op.cit.*, 3rd ed., p. 384.

31. *Pr.*, November 7, 1957.

32. Khrushchev, *Pr.*, November 1, 1959.

33. Obviously SALT-I was limited in scope and indeed gave rise to numerous criticisms of its shortcomings. But the omissions and the existing imbalance could hardly reduce the paramount significance of SALT-I, namely that

> ...while the United States and the Soviet Union are entirely unable to disarm each other by a first strike against strategic forces, each has within its armoury a number and variety of both delivery vehicles and weapons capable of destroying any conceivable combination of second strike targets within the other's territory. The SALT treaty on ABM systems, by permitting a level of ABM deployment which, at least in the case of cities, is little more than symbolic, perpetuates that fact, while the interim agreement on offensive missiles embodies a mutual recognition of it.

The Military Balance 1972-1973, London 1972, p. 86.

34. Janowitz speaks of "the crisis of the military style of life." Indeed nuclear weapons and their potential of unacceptable destructiveness have generated an inescapable crisis of professionalism.

> For the military profession, the overriding consideration is whether a force effectively committed to a deterrent philosophy and to peacekeeping and the concept of military presence can maintain its essential combat readiness.
> To the detached outside observer, this problem hardly appears insoluble, but to the professional officer it

is a central and overriding preoccupation. Does deterrence carry with it the seeds of its own destruction? Will such a strategy, especially under a par-
liamentary system, maintain combat readiness without
any combat experience or an equivalent?

Morris Janowitz, Military Conflict: Essays in the Institutional Analysis of War and Peace, London 1975, p. 43.
(Reprinted from World Politics, July 1974, "Toward a
Redefinition of Military Strategy in International Relations")

35.   [The] three purposes of war-survival activities--
       deterrence of war, and, if that fails, victory and
       preservation of the nation--involve the important
       role of war-survival capabilities in the conceptual
       framework of military theory. However, while war-
       survival measures have acquired a central place in
       Soviet strategic thinking and constitute a major
       element in its military preparedness, the problem,
       unlike others of the same order and importance, has
       not been reflected in conceptual considerations and
       generalizations and in law-like statements.

       Lider, op.cit., p. 196.

36.   cf. N. Talensky, International Affairs, No. 4, April 1962,
       p. 24. N. Nikolsky, Today's Fundamental Questions--the
       Problem of the Abolition of War, Moscow 1964, p. 381.
       Gen. R. Simonjan, Soviet Military Review, No. 1, 1969,
       pp. 50-52; cf. M.P. Gehlen, The Politics of Coexistence,
       Bloomington 1967. Th. Wolfe, Soviet Strategy at the Cross-
       roads, Harvard 1964.

37.   cf. Col. E. Rybkin, KVS, No. 17, 1965, pp. 50-52; Lt-Col.
       I. Grudinin, Red Star, July 21, 1966.

38.   Major-Gen. A.S. Milovidov, "A Philosophical Analysis of
       Military Thought," Kr.Zv., May 17, 1973, translated by
       the U.S. Air Force and printed in Selected Soviet Mili-
       tary Writings 1970-1975, Volume II of the series A Soviet
       View, p. 71. (Hereinafter Series A Soviet View)

39.   Pr., July 14, 1963.

40.   Marxism-Leninism on War and Army, Moscow 1972, p. 47.

41.   cf. Timothy J. Colton, Commissars, Commanders, and Civi-
       lian Authority; The Structure of Soviet Military Politics,

308

Harvard 1979, Chapters 10 and 11.

42. Conditions under which the present civil-military "acco-
     modation" and military "autonomy" could lead to "praeto-
     rianism" are enumerated by Perlmutter. He concludes:

     > In any case, in the absence of Leninist legitimacy
     > and Stalinist brutality, a future conflict between
     > a single-party system and a huge military organiza-
     > tion may not be resolved without violence, although
     > it is not a very likely option.

     Amos Perlmutter, The Military and Politics in Modern Times,
     London 1978, p. 84. See also John R. Thomas, "The Soviet
     Military as a Force for Change," in Dodge (ed.), pp. 19-
     25.

43. Colton, op.cit., p. 284.

44. Roman Kolkowicz, The Soviet Military and the Communist
     Party, Princeton 1967, p. 11; cf. The works of Raymond
     Garthoff and Thomas Wolfe, who also point to Party-mili-
     tary competition and conflict, although--one should add--
     they do not focus primarily on the problem of domestic
     political control, but rather on the friction between
     political and military views on how to deal with the ex-
     ternal threat. The internal dimension of Party-military
     conflict is examined, for example, by Herbert Goldhamer,
     The Soviet Soldier, Soviet Military Management at the
     Troop Level, New York 1975; and by Michael J. Deane,
     Political Control of the Soviet Armed Forces, New York
     1977.

45. See Morris Janowitz, The Professional Soldier, New York
     1960; Janowitz, Military Conflict, loc.cit.

46. V.Ye. Savkin, The Basic Principles of Operational Art and
     Tactics, Moscow 1972. (Series A Soviet View, No. 4, p. 87)

47. Sokolovsky, op.cit., 3rd ed., p. 19.
     This passage in the first edition of Military Strategy
     (1962) stressed even more the role of the military in
     the formulation and conduct of wartime policy. This ex-
     aggeration was corrected in the second (1963), and re-
     mained the same in the third edition (1968). The original
     text reads

     > If policy violates or ignores the laws of military
     > strategy, this can lead to the defeat of the army
     > and to the destruction of the state. In wartime,

therefore, strategic considerations often determine
policy. (Emphasis added)

Translation of the first edition, fully analysed and annotated by H.S. Dinerstein, Leon Gouré and Thomas Wolfe,
New York 1963, p. 104.

48. Colonel M.P. Skirdo, The People, the Army, the Commander,
Moscow 1970 (Series A Soviet View, No. 14, p. 86).

49. cf. the monumental work by John Erickson, The Road to
Stalingrad; Stalin's War with Germany, Volume I, London
1975.

50. V.G. Kulikov, "Strategic Leadership of the Armed Forces,"
Voenno-Istorichesky Zhurnal, No. 6, 1975, p. 14.

51. Skirdo, op.cit., p. 136.

52. Marxism-Leninism on War and Army, p. 394.

53. Quoted by Colton, op.cit., p. 255.

54. Gen. V. Ivanov, "The Scientific Principles of the Leadership of the Defense of the Socialist Fatherland," KVS,
No. 16, 1969, p. 12. Quoted by Deane, op.cit., p. 213.

55. Marxism-Leninism on War and Army, p. 392.

56. cf. William T. Lee, "The 'Politico-Military-Industrial
Complex' of the USSR," Journal of International Affairs,
No. 1, 1972, p. 80. There is no Central Committee Secre-
tary supervising the military organization.

57. Timothy J. Colton, "The Party-Military Connection: A Participatory Model," in Herspring and Volgyes, op.cit., p.
60; cf. Dean, op.cit., "The Zakharov-Yepishev Debate,"
pp. 201-204.

58. Goldhamer, op.cit., finds a great number of constraints
on Soviet military effectiveness (pp. 321-332). He concludes in his study that the Soviets are not ten-feet
tall, but adds:

> We have no wish or intention to persuade that the So-
> viet military is shot through with great weaknesses
> and subject to so many constraints that its operatio-
> nal effectiveness is seriously compromised. We wish
> only to caution the reader against accepting uncriti-
> cally some current images of the Soviet soldier and

the Soviet military and to provide him with some
considerations that both explain observable deficiencies and suggest the possible existence of others
that are not so readily discernable. (p. 334)

59. <u>Kr.Zv.</u>, March 2, 1973.

60. The problem in modern armed forces is stated by Col-Gen.
Yefimov as follows.

> The Soviet armed forces have reached a qualitative
> stage in their development where the demands on com-
> bat readiness and troop mobility are increasing, and
> in order to reach the level of the new demand the
> army and navy must be an efficient, well organized
> organism and must have a high standard of organiza-
> tion and discipline in each of its links. All this
> creates a need for the further strengthening of
> one-man command and the raising of command cadres'
> responsibility.

The solution found is to put the emphasis on the Party-
political conscience of the commander or his "responsibility." As usual, the professional and Party requirements are said to be combined organically, that is, in
a Party manner.

> Soviet one-man commanders are a new type of a military
> leader. They organically combine profound knowledge
> of Marxist-Leninist theory with sound military, engi-
> neering and technical knowledge, high moral-political
> qualities with combat organizational capabilities,
> and the functions of a leader with the functions of
> an educator of subordinates. Our commanders are true
> sons of their people. They worthily and selflessly
> perform their duty to the socialist fatherland and
> toil honestly to raise the combat capability and com-
> bat readiness of the USSR armed forces.

("One-man Command and a Commander's Responsibility," <u>Kr.
Zv.</u>, September 5, 1974; <u>FBIS</u>, September 19, pp. V 1 and
V 6.)
The solution, or rather accommodation, stemmed from the
need for unity among the military, especially as the Sino-
Soviet conflict and SALT emerged (Deane, <u>op.cit.</u>, Chapter
VII) as well as from the compelling desire and mutual in-
terest of the Party and the military to find a compromise
in a Party manner.

> The Party's acceptance of the need to develop edinona-
> chalie and initiative in the officer corps could be
> interpreted as a concession to the military strength
> as an institution. Conversely, the military's accep-
> tance of edinonachalie on a Party basis could be
> interpreted as a concession to the Party strength.
> There may have been an institutional compromise over
> edinonachalie. But it is also possible that the Party
> and the military both view this "compromise" as the
> most effective means for maximizing combat strength.

Christopher D. Jones, "The 'Revolution in Military Affairs'
and Party-Military Relations, 1965-1970," Survey, Winter
1974, p. 95.

61. Lider, op.cit., p. 55.

62. For example, those working in corporations like RAND, BDM,
    Brookings and Hoover Institutions, those who are private
    councelors and active in lobbying groups such as The Com-
    mittee on the Present Danger, and those with an academic
    position often practice "shuttle-scholarship" between
    Washington and their places of employment.

63. Lider, op.cit., p. 170.

64. Marxism-Leninism on War and Army, p. 394.

65. A.A. Grechko, "A Trusty Guard for Socialism," Pr., Febru-
    ary 23, 1972.

66. A.A. Grechko, On Guard for Peace and the Building of Com-
    munism, Translated by J.P.R.S., No. 54602, December 2,
    1971, p. 28.

67. Kr.Zv., September 19, 1963, quoted by Gehlen, op.cit.,
    p. 84.

68. An example of how the offensive is worked out in detail,
    is given by A.A. Sidorenko, The Offensive, Moscow 1970.
    (Series A Soviet View, No. 1)

> The Leninist ideas of the decisive role of the offen-
> sive in armed conflict find reflection in Soviet mili-
> tary doctrine which considers the offensive as the
> basic type of combat actions of troops....
> ...The decisive role of the offensive in the attain-
> ment of victory predetermines the importance of its
> profound study by all personnel of our army and the
> working out of the most effective methods of smashing

the enemy.... (p. 3)

69. For an excellent analysis of the problem of defensive--
deterrence--strategy, see Alexander L. George and Richard
Smoke, _Deterrence in American Foreign Policy, Theory and
Practice_, New York 1974, especially Chapter XX, "Response
Theory."

70. Sokolovsky, _op.cit._, 3rd ed., pp. 283-284.

71.
> The center of gravity of the entire armed combat un-
> der these conditions is transferred from the zone of
> contact between the adversaries, as was the case in
> past wars, into the depth of the enemy's location,
> including the most remote regions. As a result, the
> war will acquire an unprecedented spatial scope.

Ibid., p. 210.

72.
> The basis of the modern defense, according to the
> opinions of NATO military theorists, is made up of
> the massed employment of nuclear weapons....

Sidorenko, _op.cit._, p. 51. Sidorenko's view is not totally unsupported in the West. NATO's strategy of "flexible
response" assumes strong conventional forces, backed up
by tactical nuclear weapons, in order to establish a high
"nuclear threshold." Western military have pointed out,
however, that the conventional strength has become an
increasingly serious question. Indeed, the trend over
the last decade leaves ever less scope for a flexible conventional defense. The 1970s, in particular, witnessed
an immense strengthening of the Soviet conventional forces, a trend which was more detrimental to NATO than during the 1960s about which The Military Balance 1972-1973
says that "the numerical pattern over the years so far
has been a gradual shift in favour of the East" (p. 92).
Moreover, NATO's strategy, especially in the West European view, is primarily based on deterrence by nuclear
weapons, that is, on the threat of the use of nuclear
weapons in an early stage of a military conflict. Strategic Survey 1972 concludes that "in a real way, West European members of NATO have depended upon a margin of conventional inadequacy to deter attack" because of their
disinclination "to find the material resources for full-
scale conventional defense" (p. 19).

73. Sokolovsky, _op.cit._, 3rd ed., p. 64.

74. Col. Ye. Rybkin, "The Leninist Concept of War and the Present," KVS, No. 20, 1973, p. 26, quoted by Deane, op. cit., pp. 252-253.

75. David Holloway, "Strategic Concepts and Soviet Policy," Survival, November-December 1971, p. 369.

76. William E. Odom, "The Party-Military Connection: A Critique," in Herspring and Volgyes, p. 32.

77. Ibid., p. 48.

78. Idem.

79. L.G. Churchward, Contemporary Soviet Government, fully revised second edition, London 1975, p. XVIII. To be sure, historical analyses and analogies shed light on the causes of present situations, but history is no substitute for the study of the political process and causality overlooks the finalistic nature of politics. (cf. Carr, Chapter 4, "Causation in History," and Chapter 5, "History as Progress") The study of recurring themes and deep-rooted institutional characteristics is indispensable for our knowledge of the present, but it tells us little about the goals set today by the different political actors involved; a defeated political program of today may be the dominant current of tomorrow.

> The historian must not underestimate the opposition; he must not represent the victory as a walk-over if it was touch-and-go. Sometimes those who were defeated have made as great a contribution to the ultimate result as the victors. These are familiar maxims to every historian. But, by and large, the historian is concerned with those who, whether victorious or defeated, achieved something.

E.H. Carr, What is History?, 1961, Penguin edition, p. 126.

80. W.E. Odom, The Soviet Volunteers, Princeton 1973; "The Militarization Soviet Society," Problems of Communism, September-October 1976, pp. 34-51, reprinted in Herspring and Volgyes, pp. 79-104; "Who Controls Whom in Moscow?," Foreign Policy, Summer 1975, abridged version reprinted in Survival, November-December 1975, pp. 276-281.

81. cf. Odom, in Herspring and Volgyes, p. 98; see also Martin van der Heuvel, De Militair-Patriottische

Opvoeding van de Sovjet Jeugd, [The Military-Patriotic Education of Soviet Youth], The Hague 1979.

82. For example, Grechko repeatedly stressed the total fusion between military institution and society.

> We are also proud of the labor feats of our military youth. Comrade L.I. Brezhnev, general secretary of the Central Committee of our party, spoke very warmly of the soldiers' contribution to the 1973 harvest in his speech at the CPSU Central Committee December (1973) plenum. The aid which the soldiers have rendered and continue to render in resolving national economic tasks is one of the manifestations of the blood ties and firm, indissoluble unity of the army and people....
> ...I would particularly like to dwell on the formation of Komsomol members to standards of behavior in public places and outside the unit. The Soviet soldier is singled out not only by his elegant, beautiful uniform, military bearing and carriage but by the loveliness of his soul. Soviet people look with love and pride at the soldier primarily because they have become accustomed to seeing in him a model of good behavior, courtesy, modesty and immediate readiness to come to their aid in misfortune.

Kr.Zv., March 14, 1974. (FBIS, March 19, p. V 8)

> Soviet military building is a part of overall state building in our country. It is implemented on a scientific basis under the Communist Party's direct leadership, with regard to the objective laws to the development of socialist society and the requirements of strengthening the Soviet state's defense capability....
> ...The transformation of the Soviet state into a nationwide state, the further consolidation of the alliance of the working class and peasantry, the unity and friendship of the peoples in our country, and the formation of a new historical community of people --the Soviet people--have expanded still further the social and moral-political basis of the unity of the army and people and intensified the influence of the party and the popular masses on the entire process of military building. The Soviet people are vitally interested in consolidating the combat might of the armed forces--the loyal defender of their socialist achievements.

315

Grechko, "The leading Role of the CPSU in Building the Army of Developed Socialist Society," Voprosy Istorii KPSS, No. 5, 1974. (FBIS, May 30, p. A 1 and A 9)

83. The military enjoy a status that is difficult to attain for them in other jobs. Aspaturian speaks of "social degradation" and "déclassement" of officers who were demobilized under Khrushchev. Khrushchev's plans in 1960 to further reductions were commented upon by Minister of Defense, Malinovsky, who noted that "the demobilization of 250,000 officers will be accompanied by various difficulties." Only 35% of officers previously demobilized had found "civilian occupations commensurate with their previous military positions, while nearly two thirds had to assume lower skilled jobs as ordinary workers." Aspaturian, Process and Power, pp. 538-539.

84. Ibid., p. 520.

85. Khrushchev Remembers, The Last Testament, Vol. II, Boston 1974, p. 618.

86. For example, the obituary of first deputy chairman of the USSR Gosplan since 1961, V.M. Ryabikov, revealed that this "major organizer of industry" was engineering Colonel General. "V.M. Ryabikov made a great contribution to the development of industry and the strengthening of the country's defense capability and to the improvement of national economic planning." Signed by all members of the Politburo, Ministers and military top leadership. Pr., July 22, 1974.
Another example is the organization of the defense industrial sector, which delivers a considerable part of its output to the civilian sector.

    1. The Ministry of Defense Industry, concerned with the production of classical armament, such as tanks, artillery, and small arms.
    2. The Ministry of Aviation Industry, whose field of competence is indicated by its title.
    3. The Ministry of Shipbuilding Industry, whose field of competence is also indicated by its title.
    4. The Ministry of Electronics Industry, concerned primarily with the production of components and parts for assembly by other defense-related industries.
    5. The Ministry of Radio Industry, concerned with the production of all the electronic systems needed by the armed forces, such as radar and communications equipment.

316

6. The Ministry of General Machine Building, which came into existence in 1965 and is believed to be concerned with the production of strategic missiles.
7. The Ministry of Medium Machine Building, which is believed to be the administrator of the Soviet atomic energy and the custodian of the country's nuclear weapons stockpiles.
8. The Ministry of Machine Building, which came into existence in 1968 and whose functions are believed to relate to either military or space hardware.

Gallagher and Spielmann, op.cit., pp. 19-20.

87. cf. Gallagher and Spielmann, op.cit.; Spielmann, "Defense Industrials in the USSR," Problems of Communism, September-October 1976, reprinted in Herspring and Volgyes, pp. 105-122; David Holloway, "Technology and Political Decision in Soviet Armaments Policy," Journal of Peace Research, No. 4, 1974, op. 257-279; Arthur J. Alexander, Decision-Making in Soviet Weapons Procurement, Adelphi Paper No. 147-148, London 1978/1979; Edward L. Warner III, The Military in Contemporary Soviet Politics, An Institutional Analysis, New York 1977.

88. Holloway, "Technology and Political Decision...," p. 273.

89. cf. Milton Leitenberg, "Soviet Secrecy and Negotiations on Strategic Weapon Arms Control and Disarmament," Bulletin of Peace Proposals, No. 4, 1974, pp. 377-380.

90. Raymond L. Garhoff, "SALT and the Soviet Military," Problems of Communism, January-February, 1975, p. 36. He also reports that "Marshall Grechko in 1969 ordered the Soviet delegation to provide no quantitative or qualitative information on Soviet military and technical capabilities."

91. The issue of resource allocation is of course essential for the continuation of the position of the military. Alexander may be on target with his "estimate of the proportional influence of the specified class of forces on aggregate defense expenditures, holding each of the others constant":

History culture and values	40-50 per cent
Internal politics and personalities	20-30 per cent
International environment, threat and internal capabilities	10-30 per cent

```
               Doctrine                        5-10 per cent
               Organizations and decision-making   10-20 per cent

          Alexander, op.cit., p. 43.
```

92. cf. Gallagher and Spielmann, op.cit., Chapter II, "The
     Political System."

93. Alexander, op.cit., p. 26.

94. Gallagher and Spielmann, op.cit., p. 27.

95.   When the top leadership is strong and vigorous, the
         system is well designed to implement its will, and
         the defense problem tends to fall into place as mere-
         ly one, albeit a most important one, of the various
         problems that occupy the attention of the decision-
         makers. When strong and comprehensive leadership is
         lacking, considerations of political expediency tend
         to fill the vacuum. In this situation, various mem-
         bers of the Politburo are likely to vie with one
         another in demonstrating concern for the defense of
         the country and in laying claim, a consequence, to
         the loyalty of the groups and institutions within
         the regime whose interests are served by this orien-
         tation.

         Ibid., p. 33.

96. Military representation in the Central Committee is not
     overwhelming, although it may in some cases tip the
     scales.

Congress	XXII 1961	XXIII 1966	XXIV 1971	XXV 1976	XXVI 1981
Elected military (percentages)					
Full members	8.0	7.2	8.3	6.9	7.2
Candidate members	11.0	11.0	8.4	7.2	7.9

97. Odom, "The Militarization....," loc.cit., fn. 76, p. 104.

98. Kr.Zv., June 5, 1974. (Election speech for Supreme Soviet
     seat)

99.   The political leadership may have already decided be-
         fore the end of February to remove Grechko from the

Ministry of Defense. As late as Armed Forces Day in
1976, the speeches of the top military men reflected
the fact that Grechko was either unwilling or unable
to moderate the public exhortations of his military
colleagues for a harder "anti-imperialist" line and
for greater military build-up.

Deane, op.cit., p. 269.

100. Pr., May 9, 1976; Kr.Zv., July 31, 1976.

101. Pr., May 9, 1976.

102. Samuel P. Huntington, "The Soldier and the State in the
1970s," in Andrew J. Goodpaster and Samuel P. Huntington, Civil-Military Relations, Washington D.C. 1977,
p. 23. One should rather read "polity" for "society" in
the case of Soviet civil-military relations.

103. Colton, "Commissars...."; Colton, "The Party-Military
Connection: A Participatory Model," in Herspring and
Volgyes, pp. 53-75.

104. Kosygin's report to the XXIV Party Congress, Pr., April
7, 1971.

105. Pr., June 13, 1970. (CDSP, No. 25, 1970, p. 9)

106. F. Kotov, deputy chief of a Gosplan section, "Structural
Changes in the Country's Economy," Kr.Zv., November 30,
1971. Kotov mentions "an average annual growth rate of
group B of 8.25 per cent for consumer goods; means of
production rates will increase annually by an average
of 7.9 per cent."

107. I. Aleksandrov, "A Militant Program for an Accelerated
Upsurge in Agriculture," KVS, No. 17, 1970, pp. 33-41.

108. According to Lawrence T. Caldwell, Soviet Attitudes to
SALT, Adelphi paper, No. 75, London 1971, p. 14.

109. cf. Werner G. Hahn, The Politics of Soviet Agriculture,
1960-1970, Baltimore 1972, especially pp. 225-251 about
the discussion in 1970; cf. I. Karlyuk and N. Lagutin,
"Agriculture and the Country's Economic Potential,"
published in the newspaper of the main resource contenders, the military daily Krasnaya Zvezda, in 1973 (April
5). The authors deemed it necessary to stress several

times that the conclusion of the XXIV CPSU Congress was "of lasting importance: the increasingly wide-spread use of the country's <u>overall economic potential</u> is becoming a <u>prerequisite</u> for the successful fulfilment of the outlined program for the development of agriculture."

110. Kotov, <u>op.cit.</u>

111. <u>Ibid.</u>; At the XXIV Party Congress Brezhnev also emphatically explained the difference between the national subdivisions and industrial groups while pointing out the continued adherence to socialist economic principles.

112. <u>Ibid.</u>; Brezhnev told the Congress that 42 per cent of the output of heavy industry flowed into the civilian economy.

113. According to Lee, <u>op.cit.</u>, p. 74.

114. <u>TASS</u>, December 3, 1971. (<u>FBIS</u>, December 6) Complaints about heavy industry enterprises not fulfilling consumer good plans were numerous.

115. Grechko, "On Guard....," <u>J.P.R.S.</u>, p. 16. Later publications by Grechko express the same priority and desire for economic development.

116.   Soviet agriculture creates about one-third of the national income which is the main index of the national economic plan. It provides for 30 per cent of the income of the state budget. About 75 per cent of the turnover tax is related to the sale of agricultural products and their processing; and the turnover tax makes up around 40 per cent of all the state budget income.

    T. Sokolov, <u>Ekonomika Selskogo Khozyaistva</u>, No. 2, 1971, quoted in <u>Radio Free Europe Research</u>, April 28, 1971, p. 4.

117. S.A. Zverev, "The Possibilities of the Sector," <u>Izv.</u>, July 7, 1971.

118. Brezhnev thus supported Kosygin's economic views as to the issues of resource allocation, consumer priority and a greater degree of decentralization.
In these issues he moved to the right of the political-economic spectrum. In return, however, Brezhnev demanded

the strengthening of the Party as manager and controller, and priority treatment for certain projects in industry, especially in "those sectors of heavy industry which determine the aspect of technical progress--the electrical engineering, machine building, and chemical industries," according to Kotov. (Ibid.) Kotov further explains:

> These leading sectors will enjoy preferential development not only in relation to other sectors in group A but also to group B. In fact, whereas the former group's output will increase 46.3 per cent and the latter's 48.6 per cent over the five-year period, the output of the machine building and chemical industries will increase 70 per cent. The producer goods which are technically most advanced will be developed still more rapidly. Thus, the output of plastics will increase twofold, instruments twofold, and machine tools with numerically programmed control 3.5 times.

Another example of how to compromise and to put off basic decisions.

119. The realized percentages in the Ninth Five-Year Plan for group A and B were:

	Group A	Group B
1971	7.8	7.7
1972	6.8	5.7
1973	8.2	5.7
1974	8.4	7.0
1975	7.9	6.5

Michael J. Deane and Mark E. Miller, "Science and Technology in Soviet Military Planning," Strategic Review, Summer 1977, p. 79.

CHAPTER VI

1. William F. Scott, "Soviet Military Doctrine and Strategy; Realities and Misunderstandings," Strategic Review, Summer 1975; cf. Scott, Soviet Sources of Military Doctrine and Strategy, New York 1975.

2. Public resistence to SALT increased considerably after 1974-1975, and SALT and the detente process became a major issue in the 1976 presidential elections. In 1977 and 1978, the SALT-II agreement, although far from completed, was openly discussed and criticized in great detail. In 1979, serious doubts existed whether the Senate would ratify the Treaty, and the Soviet invasion in Afghanistan reduced its chances to zero.

3.   The Soviet Union has developed greatly improved guidance systems for their SS-18 and SS-19 ICBMs. These systems demonstrate accuracies less than the lethal radius of the SS-18 and SS-19 mirved warheads, even against very hard targets like ICBM silos. Therefore, when large numbers of these guidance systems are introduced into their ICBM force, our silos will no longer protect our ICBM force and no feasible improvement in hardening will restore their ability to survive a mass attack of SS-18s or SS-19s. More generally it is clear that fixed, hardened basis for any high-value target will not be a viable option in the 1980s. (Perry's testimony, p. 19)

Two 0.6 MT yield warheads of the SS-18 (CEP 0.15 nm) give a 90% probability of destroying one American ICBM silo (see Table V). An increased CEP (0.08 nm) would provide a Single Shot Kill Probability (SSKP) of 90%. In the first case, in theory, about 200 to 300 SS-18 and SS-19 would suffice to put at risk the 1000 Minuteman silos. With the increased CEP this number could be significantly reduced, thus keeping a significantly larger number of ICBMs for a "General Nuclear Response." cf. Collin S. Gray, "Soviet Rocket Forces," NATO's Fifteen Nations, Febr/March 1978; Aviation Week and Space Technology, June 16, 1980, Special Issue Strategic Forces; "Strategic Missile Counterforce Capability; United States versus the Soviet Union," House Armed Services Committee Study, Washington D.C., December 20, 1977, p. 20. Dr. W.J. Perry: "The FY 1980 Department of Defense Program for Research, Development and Acquisition," Washington D.C., February 1, 1979; Edward N. Luttwak, <u>Strategic Power: Military Capabilities and Political Utility</u>, Center for Strategic and International Studies, Washington D.C. 1976.

4. "Essential Equivalence" means for the Western forces that

 - Soviet strategic nuclear forces not become usable instruments of political leverage, diplomatic coercion, or military advantage;
 - nuclear stability, especially in a crisis, is maintained;
 - any advantage in force characteristics enjoyed by the Soviets are offset by U.S. advantages in other characteristics; and
 - the U.S. posture is not in fact, and is not seen as, inferior in performance to the strategic forces of the Soviet Union.

H. Brown, <u>Department of Defense Annual Report, FY 1979</u>, Washington D.C. 1978.

5. P.H. Nitze and L. Sullivan, Jr., <u>Securing the Seas, The Soviet Naval Challenge and Western Alliance Options</u>, Boulder, Co. 1979.

6. Pipes, "Why the Soviet Union Thinks....," <u>loc.cit.</u>, Paul N. Nitze, "Strategy in the Decade of the 1980s," <u>Foreign Affairs</u>, Fall 1980, pp. 82-101; Joseph D. Douglass, Jr. and Amoretta Hoeber, <u>Soviet Strategy for Nuclear War</u>, Stanford 1979.

7. cf. Lawrence L. Whetten (ed.), <u>The Future of Soviet Military Power</u>, New York 1976; Leon Gouré, <u>et al.</u>, <u>The Role of Nuclear Force in Current Soviet Strategy</u>, Coral Gables, Florida 1975; Peter Vigor, <u>The Soviet View of War, Peace and Neutrality</u>, London 1975.

8. Conditions for the countervailing strategy are

 - to survive a well-executed surprise attack;
 - to react with the timing needed, both as to promptness and endurance, to assure the deliberation and control deemed necessary by the National Command Authorities;
 - to penetrate any enemy defenses; and
 - to destroy their designated targets.

H. Brown, <u>Annual Report FY 80</u>, p. 77; cf. <u>Annual Report FY 81</u>.

9. H. Brown, Speech at the Naval War College, Annapolis, August 20, 1980.

10. Ibid.; cf. Graham T. Allison and Frederic A. Morris, "Armaments and Arms Control: Exploring the Determinants of Military Weapons," Daedalus, Summer 1975, pp. 99-129, esp. Table 1, "US Strategy and Forces, 1961-1968."

11. Michael McGwire, "Soviet Military Doctrine; Contingency Planning and the Reality of World War," Survival, May-June 1980, p. 108.

12. Ibid.; cf. Leon Gouré, "Soviet Military Doctrine," Air Force Magazine, March 1977, pp. 47-50; John Erickson, "The Chimera of Mutual Deterrence," Strategic Review, Spring 1978, pp. 11-17.

13. Flexibility in options stems from the (Schlesinger's) rule "To deter an option means to have an option." A selective employment capability of nuclear weapons is first of all necessary for a response in kind and scope and, second, forms, a means of "deliberate escalation" to indicate the defender's resolve and the possible, ultimate escalation to "General Nuclear Response."

14. Erickson, "Chimera," loc.cit., p. 16.

15. Richard M. Nixon, U.S. Foreign Policy for the 1970s, A Report to Congress, Washington D.C. 1970.

16. Annual Defense Report FY 1975, Washington D.C. 1974.

17. cf. Robert Jervis, "Deterrence Theory Revisited," World Politics, January 1979, and the study he reviews: George and Smoke, op.cit.; Lawrence Martin, "Changes in American Strategic Doctrine, An Initial Interpretation," Survival, July-August 1974, pp. 158-164; for a discussion about ethical and strategic considerations regarding Schlesinger's doctrine, see Robert A. Gessert and J. Bryan Hehir, The New Nuclear Debate, Council on Religion and International Affairs, New York 1976.

18. cf. M.P. Gehlen, The Politics of Coexistence, Bloomington 1967, pp. 80-81.

19. cf. C.G. Jacobson, op.cit.; Thomas Wolfe, op.cit.

20. Wolfe, Ibid., pp. 182-183.

21. Jacobson, op.cit., p. 92.

22. John Erickson, Soviet Military Power, reprinted in Strategic Review, Spring 1973, pp. 4-5.

23. W. Zimmerman, Soviet Perspectives, p. 238.

24. cf. Erickson, "Military Power," loc.cit.; Jacobson, op. cit.; Wolfe, op.cit.

25. The first edition of Military Strategy reveals either an inability or an unwillingness to view submarines as "the most stable means for the use of missiles." It says, "Actually these weapons are vulnerable" and points at ASW and the vulnerability of the bases of submarines 3rd ed., p. 290.

26.

SALT-I CEILINGS ON OFFENSIVE SYSTEMS

MODERN SUBMARINES			LAUNCHERS		ALLOWED CONVERSION
United States	44	SLBM	max.	710	
			actual	656	+ 54
		ICBM	max.	1054	1000
			actual	1054	
Soviet Union	62	SLBM	max.	950	180 SS7 & SS8
			lower		+ 30 SLBM H-Class
			limit	740	or
		ICBM	max.	1618	210 SS7 & SS8
			actual	1527	(+ 91 new "holes")

As to the Soviet forces, a major concern of the Americans was a possible conversion of "light" ICBMs into "heavy" ones such as the huge SS-9 with a 20-25 MT warhead. Therefore, they insisted that the agreement prohibit a modernization of older ICBM resulting in heavier missiles than the largest "light" ICBM deployed after 1964--meaning the SS-11, which has a warhead yield comparable to the United States Minuteman. Limited by such provision, the Soviet Union was thus free to convert the 210 SS-7 and SS-8 into SLBMs, up to a total of 950.

With regard to the SLBM force, a similar restraint on modernization was worked out. The 30 SLBMs on older Soviet nuclear submarines (H-class) would not be counted against the 740 SLBMs, but their placement on "modern" submarines would be counted against the upper limit of 940 SLBMs.

That decision would then decrease the permitted conversion of the SS-7 and SS-8 from 210 to 180. The Soviet 34
short-range SLBM on diesel-powered submarines (G-class)
were not included in any limitation. Finally, the agreed
inequality between "modern" submarines was based on operational capacity. Assuming a readiness at any time of
40% and 60% of Soviet and American submarines, respectively, the operational number would be about the same.

27. Jacobson, op.cit., p. 11.

28.   It's clear now that Moscow would have turned down any
        proposal to ban MIRV testing. Option C was speedly
        rejected in Vienna. Yet had the Russians responded by
        asking the United States to drop onside-inspection as
        the price for their acceptance of the proposal, al-
        most certainly Washington would have felt obliged to
        acquiesce. But the Soviet interest lay elsewhere.
        Just as the United States leadership was determined
        to sustain MIRV, so Moscow was determined to master
        the technology.

        John Newhouse, op.cit., p. 181.

29. The Military Balance 1974-1975, p. 4.

30.   "Special Report; Modernizing Strategic Forces," Aviation
        Week and Space Technology, June 16, 1980. The "Kill Pro-
        bability (KP) of N missiles against silos of a given
        "hardness" is $N \times Y^2/3 \times \frac{1}{(CEP)}2$. (Y= warhead yield; CEP=
        Circular Error Probable, indicating the circle within
        which at least 50 per cent of the warheads will fall)
        However, certainty about destroying the target is also
        dependent on a number of attrition factors, i.e., availa-
        bility, reliability, pre-launch survivability (PLS) and
        --in case of a Ballistic Missile Defense system--probabi-
        lity to penetrate (PTP) of the weapons systems.

31.   Gone were the days when the heavy cruiser and the
        battleship were the backbone of a navy...We made a
        decision to convert our navy primarily to submarines.
        ...Thus we fundamentally changed the strategy and
        composition of our navy. I take full responsibility
        on my own shoulders. I have no desire to conceal that
        I threw my weight to the side of the younger cadres
        in the navy and helped them overcome the resistence
        of the older officers who couldn't bring themselves
        to admit that not only was the submarine much cheaper
        to build and operate--it was also a much more formi-

dable and effective weapon. I now recall that when we were considering Gorshkov for commander in chief of the navy, we counted it very much in his favor that he was a former submarine captain.

Khrushchev Remembers, Vol. II, p. 29. Gorshkov has been C-in-C of the Soviet navy since 1956. He replaced Admiral Kuznetsov, who was a staunch supporter of a surface navy. During the past 25 years Groshkov has contributed as has no-one else to the creation of a formidable navy, including a strong surface fleet. It is believed that twelve huge battleships are programmed. One of this Kirov class is on sea trial.

32. cf. Jacobson, op.cit., pp. 128-137; Bradford Dismukes and James M. McConnell (eds.), Soviet Naval Diplomacy, New York 1979.

33. Gorshkov's articles were translated from Morskoi Sbornik and published by the U.S. Naval Institute, Red Star Rising at Sea, 1974.

34. Ibid., p. 131.

35. Strategic Survey 1972, London 1973, p. 4.

36. Teatr Voennikh Deistvy, A particular territory,...., within whose limits a known part of the armed forces of the country (or coalition) operates in wartime, engaged in strategic missions which ensue from the war plan. A theater of operations may be ground, maritime, or intercontinental.

     Dictionary of Basic Military Terms, Series A Soviet View, No. 9, p. 220.

37. S.G. Gorshkov, The Sea Power of the State, (Moscow 1976), New York 1979, p. 221.

38. Ibid., pp. 221-222.

39. cf. Justin Galen, "Tactical Nuclear Balance," Armed Forces Journal International, December 1977, January 1978; J. Schlesinger, The Theater Nuclear Force Posture in Europe, Washington D.C. 1975; Planning U.S. General Purpose Forces, The Theater Nuclear Forces, Congressional Budget office, Washington D.C. 1977.

40. cf. R. Metzger and P. Doty, "Arms Control Enters the Gray

Area," *International Security*, Winter 1978-1979, pp. 17-52. Gregory F. Treverton, "Nuclear Weapons and the 'Gray Area'," *Foreign Affairs*, Summer 1979, pp. 1075-1089. ("Yet, alas, negotiations in the gray area are not attractive," p. 1087)

41. H. Hoffman, "SS-20 Multiplies USSR Nuclear Superiority," *NATO's Fifteen Nations*, December-January 1978-1979, pp. 42-48.

42. The best description of development of the ground forces is found in Erickson's publications, e.g., *Soviet Military Power*, loc.cit.; "The Ground Forces in Soviet Military Policy," *Strategic Review*, Winter 1978, pp. 64-79; "Trends in the Soviet Combined-Arms Concept," *Strategic Review*, Winter 1977, pp. 38-53.

43. John Erickson, "The Soviet Military, Soviet Policy and Soviet Politics," *Strategic Review*, Fall 1973, p. 28. Moreover, the production rate of most weapons systems exceeds the present ratio of military strength between NATO and the Warsaw Pact. This means an ongoing worsening of the conventional balance for NATO for the foreseeable future.

44. Jeffrey Record assumes dual-capable 203 mm howitzer, *U.S. Nuclear Weapons in Europe, Issues and Alternatives*, Washington D.C. 1974, p. 39; The IISS calls it possible; Collins, op.cit., affirms this possibility; the 152 mm is reported to be dual-capable, *Tactical Nuclear Weapons, European Perspectives*, p. 232.

45. For example, Malinovsky, see Wolfe, op.cit., pp. 451-458.

46. Grechko, *On Guard*, J.P.R.S., p. 33.

47. *Khrushchev Remembers*, p. 55.

48. Grechko, *On Guard*, J.P.R.S., p. 32.

49. *Ibid.*, pp. 32-33.

50. V.G. Kulikov, "The Soviet Armed Forces and Military Science," *Kommunist*, No. 3, 1975, *Series A Soviet View*, No. 11, p. 105.

51. V.G. Kulikov, "Soviet Military Science Today," *Kommunist*, No. 7, 1976, p. 47; cf. Erickson's analysis of this article in "Trends," loc.cit. Kulikov is indeed asking for

modern, improved combined-arms forces (p. 51), and, like Grechko, he claims unlimited resources for the "sacred" duty to defend the homeland.

> In order to repulse a possible aggressor, it will not only be necessary to deploy the millions of men in the armed forces, but also to mobilize all the country's economic resources for the achievement of victory. (p. 46)

52. Erickson, "The Chimera," loc.cit., p. 15.

53. Pr., January 15, 1960. (CDSP, Vol. XII, No. 2, pp. 3-23)

54. Wolfe, op.cit.; Gehlen, op.cit.

55. Khrushchev had also other reasons in mind--economic benefits of 16 to 17 billion rubles, propaganda effects and hope for a Western reciprocal action. However, these arguments merely formed the frosting in Khrushchev's new receipt for a sound base for the defense cake. Questions primarily arose regarding statements about the priorities and sufficiency of the proposed defense structure.

> On the basis of [economic, technological, etc.] successes, our scientists, engineers and defense industry workers have built new types of modern armaments that correspond to the latest word in science and technology. This enables us to reduce our armed forces without harming the country's defense capacity....
> ...The Soviet Union has stockpiled the necessary number of atomic and hydrogen weapons....
> ...In our time a country's defense capacity is determined not by the number of soldiers it has under arms, the number of men in uniform. Aside from the general political and economic factors,..., a country's defense capacity depends to a decisive extent on the firepower and means of delivery it has.
> ...Of course, all countries would suffer in one way or another in the event of another world war. We too would suffer heavy misfortune; our territory is enormous, and the population is less concentrated in large industrial centers than in many other countries. The West would suffer incomparably more....

Pr., January 15, 1960. (CDSP, Vol. XII, No. 2, p. 10) In his memoirs, Khrushchev would repeat his economic motive.

I devoted all my strength to the rearmament of the
Soviet Union....
...However, we were taking a risk by allocating so
much of our resources to the military sector. Once
we reached a point where we had what it took to defend ourselves and deter our enemy, we readjusted
our economy. We recognized that if our people didn't
have potatoes we couldn't expect them to shout "hooray" all the time--and if they did shout "hooray,"
it would be in a rather weak voice. We began to economize on our military expenditures.

Khrushchev Remembers, pp. 611-612.

56. The authors of *Military Strategy* share the opinion of
the Party leader, where the primacy of the nuclear weapons is concerned.

Unless these weapons [strategic, missiles] are destroyed or neutralized, it is impossible to protect
the country's vital centers from destruction, and
one cannot count on successfully achieving the aim
of the war even if the enemy troop formations in the
military theaters, are destroyed.

V.D. Sokolovsky, *Military Strategy*, Translation of the
first edition, fully analyzed and annotated by H.S. Dinerstein, Leon Gouré and Th. Wolfe, New York 1963, pp.
399-400. But elsewhere they express their doubts regarding a reduction of the standing forces:

The advocates of such armies [of nuclear primacy]
fail to consider that the new equipment, far from
reducing the requirements of the armed forces for
personnel, increase them. For this reason, massive
armies of millions of men will be needed to wage a
future war. (*Ibid.*, p. 338)

In the second edition--fifteen months after the first--
the importance of the massive army is maintained and is
given extended attention. Also the third edition stresses
the need for both strategic weapons and "mass armed forces," (p. 210).

57. *Pr.*, October 25, 1961. (*CDSP*, Vol. XIV, No. 1, p. 19)

58. *Ibid.*

59. The decisive character of the initial period and surprise

330

was, and still is, generally recognized. Also, about the nature of a future war being a nuclear war, mutually destructive and of short duration, agreement existed to a large extent, but no unanimity is found. Although the duration will presumably be short and modern weaponry "will significantly shorten the duration of a war," the first edition of Military Strategy finds "it necessary to make serious preparations for a protracted war." In the second edition the same passage is put more strongly:

> It is necessary to develop and perfect the ways and means of armed combat, anticipating the attainment of victory over the aggressor first of all within the shortest possible time, in the course of a rapidly moving war. But the war may drag on and this will demand protracted and all-out exertion of army and people. Therefore we must also be ready for a protracted war and get the human and material resources into a state of preparedness for this eventuality. (2nd ed. passage underlined)

3rd ed., op.cit., p. 211.

60. Malinovsky, loc.cit., p. 20.

61. Ibid., pp. 19-20.

62. Jacobson, op.cit., p. 53.

63. 1st ed., Gouré et al., p. 130.

64. Harriet Fast Scott points at the tribute paid by Cherednichenko "who eulogized Sokolovsky as being the key figure in the revolution in military affairs." Editor's Introduction, op.cit., p. XXV.

65. Ibid., pp. 281-282.

66. Ibid., p. 282.

67. Ibid., p. 284.

68. Idem.

69. Ibid., p. 281.

70. Grechko, On Guard, J.P.R.S., p. 43.

71. For example, William Lee concludes:

> The nuclear targeting doctrine stated by Marshal
> Krylov in 1967 was worked out by (Long-Range Avia-
> tion) LRA not long after World War II, probably be-
> fore the USSR began to stockpile nuclear weapons.
> The early strategic missile units evidently shared
> LRA's nuclear-targeting strategy and carried it over
> to the SRF (Strategic Rocket Forces). (p. 121)

Even though Lee recognizes the differences between various
TVDs, the thrust of his article is a translation of Eura-
sion TVD targeting strategy into one for the transatlan-
tic theater, as is also suggested by the title. William
T. Lee, "Soviet Targeting Strategy and SALT," Air Force
Magazine, September 1978, pp. 120-129. Douglass corrects
his earlier--at least implicit--confusion between the
American and European theater in Soviet Military Strategy in Europe. (New York 1980) Unlike in his--and Hoeber's
--Soviet Strategy for Nuclear War, he distinguishes between the two theaters, although incorrectly as to the
Soviet meaning of "strategic" and "theater." Moreover,
his distinction between the 1960s and 1970s is difficult
to warrant.

> In comparing the available Soviet literature of the
> 1970s with that of the early and mid-1960s, one of
> the most noticable differences appears to be a cer-
> tain separation of strategic from theater war. Recent
> discussions on the conduct of theater operations
> (e.g., in The Offensive and The Basic Principles of
> Operational Art and Tactics) seems to be much more
> detached from strategic war than similar writings
> have been in the past. (p. 191)

One wonders whether "similar writings" on operations and
tactics in the American theater could ever have existed.
A "certain separation" between the theaters is an under-
statement at the least. Savkin's book The Basic Principles
of Operational Art and Tactics focusses, moreover, on the
period 1953-1959, a period preceeding Soviet intercontinental capabilities. Finally, although Soviet military do
not fully exclude the possibility that some day a "first-
strike" against ICBMs may become technically possible,
they time and again point to the remaining retaliatory
might and its inevitable use given the level of damage
already suffered. A "first-strike" is, however, not possible, since "there can be no counting on the complete
destruction of the enemy's strategic weapons, especially
if the growing number of mobile launchers of strategic
rockets and nuclear rocket-carrying submarines in their

inventory is taken into account." (part underlined is
added to the second edition, Sokolovsky, op.cit., 3rd
ed., p. 61).

The countervailing strategy is seen as "pointless without
the first-strike concept" (New Times, No. 43, 1980, p.
21). But, despite the increased kill-probability of 300
Minuteman and of the programmed MX and Trident-2, the
Soviet Union still relied on the land-based strategic
forces and continues to do so. Furthermore, the Soviet
Union had been willing to forego the option deploying
mobile ICBMs for the duration of the SALT-II Treaty until 1985. Apparently, the Soviet leaders do not believe
in intercontinental nuclear war not being a holocaust.
It is deterrence, not war-fighting, that lies at the basis of their approach to the superpower strategic relationship. (For a discussion about a counterforce capability of American SLBMs see Desmond Ball, "The Counterforce Potential of American SLBM Systems," Journal of
Peace Research, No. 1, 1977, pp. 23-40; Kosta Tsipis,
Anne H. Cahn, Bernard T. Feld (eds.), The Future of the
Sea-Based Deterrent, Cambridge, Mass. 1973; Aviation
Week and Space Technology, June 16, 1980.)

72. V. Andreev, "The Subdivision and Classification of Thea-
     ters of Military Operations," Voennaya Mysl, No. 9, 1964,
     quoted by Joseph D. Douglass, Jr., "Soviet Nuclear Stra-
     tegy in Europe: A Selective Targeting Doctrine?," Strate-
     gic Review, Fall 1977, p. 25.

73. Thomas Wolfe, Soviet Power and Europe, 1945-1970, Balti-
     more 1970, p. 197.

74. Col. M. Shirokov, "The Question of Influences on the Mi-
     litary and Economic Potential of Warring States," Voen-
     naya Mysl, quoted in Strategic Review, Winter 1980, p.
     82.

75. Military Strategy, 3rd ed., pp. 64-69; quoted by Wolfe,
     Soviet Power, p. 454.

76. G. Trofimenko, "On a Pivotal Course," MEMO, No. 2, 1975.
     (FBIS, February 24, p. AA 5)

77. Sokolovsky, op.cit., 3rd ed., p. 67.

78. Ibid., p. 64; cf. The conclusion of Army General Kuroch-
     kin in 1977 is not different; "Thus, each use of nuclear
     weapons conceals in itself a constant risk for a world
     war with unlimited use of the nuclear potential." Inter-

view in <u>Narodna Armiya</u>, February 6, 1977. (<u>FBIS</u>, February 10, p. A 1)

79. No single aspect of a "land-war" is overlooked. The "Officers Library" approaches war from a variety of fields including psychology and pedagogy. Soviet military theory, developed at hundreds of academies and institutes, calls for a total preparation for war of both the military and population. cf. Skirdo, <u>op.cit.</u>, Chapter II, "The General Populace: A Decisive Force in Modern Warfare."

80. G. Arbatov, "Strength-Policy Impasses," <u>Military Review</u>, No. 1, 1975, p. 46.

81. Col. L.S. Semeiko, "New Forms, but the same Content," <u>Kr.Zv.</u>, April 8, 1975. (<u>Strategic Review</u>, Fall 1975, p. 86) For a Western view, rejecting the feasibility of limited exchanges, see Sydney D. Drell and Frank Van Hippel, "Limited Nuclear War," <u>Scientific American</u>, November 1976, pp. 27-37.

82. <u>Ibid.</u>, p. 85.

83. Milshtein and Semeiko conclude that McNamara's counterforce "plans proposed at the very beginning of the 1960s ...disappeared quite soon, <u>and the gamble on 'assured destruction' became the main one.</u>" (Emphasis added) Under conditions of strategic parity, reality is "mutual assured destruction," however dreadful a situation that may be.

> Of course, the concept of "nuclear deterrence" which <u>presupposes</u> the existence of <u>giant nuclear forces</u> capable of <u>certain</u> destruction, is not an ideal solution of the problem of peace and of preventing nuclear conflict. But it is <u>a question of whether</u> to move from this concept, which reflected, according to the widespread opinion, the real state of affairs. (Emphasis added)

Limited nuclear war will not develop according to flexible "rules of the game" as suggested by Schlesinger. According to the authors, prevention of war and "the limitation of the arms race are the central problem of Soviet-American relations." M.A. Milshtein and L.S. Semeiko, "The Problem of the Inadmissibility of a Nuclear Conflict," SShA, No. 11, 1974, pp. 2-13. (<u>FBIS</u>, November 12, pp. AA 1-10)

84. <u>Pr.</u>, April 7, 1974.

85. Milshtein and Semeiko, <u>loc.cit.</u> (<u>FBIS</u>, pp. AA 7-8);
86. Milshtein quotes Brown (<u>Newsweek</u>, July 17, 1978) saying

> The Soviets will have to consider the possibility
> that our Minuteman missiles would no longer be in
> their silos when their ICBMs arrive. We have not
> adopted a doctrine of launching our missiles after
> receiving a signal that the other side's missiles
> have been launched..., but they would doubtless have
> to take such a possibility into consideration.

M.A. Milshstein, "At a Dangerous Crossroads," <u>SShA</u>, No.
10, 1978. (<u>FBIS</u>, October 26, p. 10) On the American side
fear for a Soviet "lauch-upon-warning" doctrine exists
as well. Raymond Garthoff reports from the SALT-I negotiations:

> During the exchange on strategic stability in the
> SALT plenary meetings in the Spring of 1970, the
> Soviet side referred to the possibility that ICBM
> silos might be empty by the time of an enemy strike,
> since the ICBMs in them could already be in flight
> owing to information gained from technical early-
> warning systems. The US delegation took the occasion
> of this remark to make clear that the US held any
> "launch on warning" doctrine abhorrent, and a state-
> ment to that effect by the Secretary of Defense was
> subsequently placed on the SALT plenary record.

"SALT and the Soviet Military," <u>Problems of Communism</u>,
January-February 1975, p. 34.

cf. R. Simonyan, "Suicide Syndrome," <u>New Times</u>, No. 33,
1980, pp. 5-6; Trofimenko raises two major objections
against nuclear war scenarios; a political and a technical one.

> In various speculative exercises of the Pentagon ex-
> perts (here, again, we are in the sphere of theology),
> it is contended that under certain circumstances the
> Soviet Union might limit itself to strike only against
> selected military targets in the United States (e.g.,
> only bomber bases). What for?, one feels bound to ask.
> How can one ascribe to the Soviet Union the belief
> that it is possible to deliver a nuclear strike
> against several bases in the United States and get
> off cheap with only a limited retaliatory strike?

Moreover, what would be proved by such a trial of strength, regardless of which side might resort to it? Such hypothetical speculations are sheer mental calisthenics. They are not strategy-given, of course, that military strategy and war are a continuation of policy and not vice versa....

...The Pentagon has estimated that such a disarming strike would require the launch of more than 2,000 warheads against the enemy targets. Tell me, who, with the exception of God himself, in the few minutes available could determine that this vast number of warheads already in mid-flight is a "limited" counterforce rather than an all-out countervalue attack and, accordingly, give the command for an appropriate limited retaliation? That this is humanly possible is beyond belief.

G. Trofimenko, "The 'Theology' of Strategy," _Orbis_, Fall 1977, p. 513.

87. Semeiko, _loc.cit._

88. Milshtein and Semeiko, _loc.cit._ (_FBIS_, p. AA 9); cf. M. A. Milshtein, "At a Dangerous Crossroads," _SShA_, No. 10, 1978.

89. _Pr._, January 19, 1977. (_CDSP_, Vol. XXIX, No. 3, p. 3)

90. Col. Gen. N.A. Lomov (ed.), _Scientific-Technical Progress and the Revolution in Military Affairs_, Moscow 1973. (_Series A Soviet View_, No. 3, p. 272)

91. McGwire, _op.cit._, p. 112. Warner (_op.cit._, p. 192) also doubts the counterforce intention by deploying the huge SS-9. Ross does not exclude the counterforce rationale of the SS-9, primarily as a means of catching up with the United States in a qualitative respect. (The large numbers of the SS-11 gave quantitative equality.) But Ross argues in his article that:

Soviet weapons systems are the product of a number of variable inputs....
...In the case of the SS-9, the supportive confluence of bureaucratic tradition-routine (e.g., the "big-missile" design team and the Strategic Rocket Forces) and a set of strategic-military needs and values (e.g., more secure ABM penetration, offsetting US qualitative advantages in guidance and targetting), probably directed and determined SS-9 deployment far

more than any long-range and inchoate "first-strike" design or intent.

Dennis Ross, "Rethinking Soviet Strategic Policy: Inputs and Implications," The Journal of Strategic Studies, No. 1, 1978, p. 20. The same pattern is highlighted by Warner, op.cit., and Spielmann, op.cit. His case study concerns the SS-6.

92. G. Trofimenko, Changing Attitudes Toward Deterrence, Center for International and Strategic Affairs, Los Angelos 1980, p. 24.

93. The past few years have seen some war-scenarios worked out by Western military experts. General Close assumes a Soviet conventional offensive being so successful that NATO is defeated within 48 hours without the chance or time to employ nuclear weapons. From the Soviet point of view, a conventional-only war would be the most attractive option. However, the Soviet leaders must have very high confidence in their conventional power and be convinced that NATO is lacking the political will and military capability to resort to nuclear weapons. If these conditions are not met, a conventional-only offensive is an unlikely choice.
General Hacket and Brigadier Bidwell, respectively, draw the picture of a war starting with conventional means and escalating into a nuclear war by a Soviet attack on Birmingham and by British employment on the battlefield. Hacket's Third World War stops after retaliation against Minsk, but Bidwell's war continues to escalate by the use of selective nuclear employment on military targets in Poland and East Germany, on the one hand, and in Britain, on the other. Then

> ...the President, forced to choose between the complete destruction of the NATO defenses and nuclear war, gave the fatal order. (p. 153)

The civilian analyst, Wettig, concludes that the Soviet Union is "gradually acquiring a first strike capability on the Euro-strategic level." (p. 39, see also p. 13) In a time of crisis, according to him, the Soviet leaders might decide to pre-empt a Western attack when this seems imminent to them. A most unlikely scenario, for-- even if it were technically possible to destroy "500 nuclear targets in Western Europe" (?) simultaneously-- in time of crisis few Western nuclear systems would not be dispersed and/or on Quick Reaction Alert. Moreover,

337

what sense would it make to destroy Western Europe so thoroughly? Finally, Soviet military theory and the improving accuracy of weapons systems point to the--most conceivable, albeit extremely difficult and risky--option of selective nuclear employment in the rear of Western forces, while mounting--as far as possible--a conventional attack. The decision of NATO to modernize LRTNF is precisely aimed at strengthening the deterrent against a Soviet SEO (Selective Employment Option). Whatever strategic operations are technically possible, Sokolovsky's judgment that "it is difficult to imagine now the results of their conduct" would be even more valid in 1980 than it was in 1962.

> May one consider that in a future war any one form
> of strategic operation will be used?
> Of course not. War always was an extremely complex
> and varied phenomenon. This is even more true of a
> future nuclear war. (p. 288)

R. Close, Europe without Defense?, New York 1979; J. Hackett, The Third World War, 1985, A Future History, London 1978; S. Bidwell, World War 3: A Military Projection Founded on Today's Facts," London 1978; Gerhard Wettig, East-West Security Relations on the Eurostrategic Level, Berichte des Bundesinstituts für Ostwissenschaftliche und Internationale Studien, Cologne, No. 27, August 1980; cf. G.D. Vernon, "Soviet Options for War in Europe: Nuclear or Conventional?," Strategic Review, Winter 1979; Douglass, "Soviet Nuclear Strategy in Europe: A Selective Targeting Doctrine?," loc.cit.; Douglass, Soviet Military Strategy, op.cit.

94. A.S. Zheltov, T.R. Kondratkov, and Ye.A. Khomenko, Methodological Problems of Military Theory and Practice, Moscow 1969, p. 336, quoted by Joseph D. Douglass, Jr., and Amoretta M. Hoeber, "The Nuclear War-fighting Dimension of the Soviet Treat to Europe," The Journal of Social and Political Studies, No. 2, 1979.

95. Compare, for example, the assurances of Secretary of State Kissinger with the alarming remarks of the academic and lecturer Kissinger highlighted by his speech in Brussels, September 1, 1979.

96. See, for example, François de Rose, "The Future of SALT and Western Security in Europe," Foreign Affairs, Summer 1979, pp. 1065-1074; cf. J.J. Martin, "Nuclear Weapons in NATO's Deterrent Strategy," Orbis, Winter 1979, pp.

875-895; Robert A. Gessert and Harvey B. Seim, <u>Improving NATO's Theater Nuclear Posture: A Reassessment and a Proposal</u>, Center for Strategic and International Studies, Washington D.C. 1977. And, as Hoffman estimates the importance of regional balances,

> ...the primary U.S. military effort ought to be aimed at shoring up regional balances because of the very autonomy of these balances, not because the United States can no longer count on offsetting a conventional imbalance with nuclear superiority. (In any event, the real deterrent is the risk of nuclear war, not American nuclear superiority.) None of the scenarios that entail the use of strategic nuclear weapons really make sense--not massive retaliation and not limited counterforce. The function of these weapons is likely to remain deterrence from their use. This means that the real danger lies in problems of regional instability, in a world strategically fragmented under a stable superpower nuclear umbrella.

Stanley Hoffman, "Muscle and Brains," <u>Foreign Policy</u>, Winter 1979-1980, pp. 6-7.

97.   Like the Soviet military,

> ...the American military also prepares to fight efficiently. It is certainly not getting ready to capitulate and surrender to the enemy. And if one leaves out differing war goals for different states, then technically the military in every country has one and the same mission: to do its utmost in case of war to ensure its country the favorable outcome of every battle and of the war. In this sense, trying to attribute some objectives other than efficient war-fighting to the American military is pure demagoguery. One can only express amazement at what is now written on the subject in the United States. (p. 23)

Trofimenko, "Changing Attitudes....," p. 24.

339

CHAPTER VII

1. K. Sheidin, "Program for Peace and International Coopera-
    tion," Kommunist, No. 9, June 1971, p. 89.

2. Ibid., pp. 89-99.

3. G.A. Arbatov, "American Imperialism and the New Realities
    of the World," Pr., May 4, 1971; cf. N. Inozemtsev, "Capi-
    talism of the 1970s: An Intensification of Contradictions,"
    Pr., August 20, 1974.

4. Idem.

5. B. Dmitriev, "A Policy of Relaxing Tension," Novoye Vremya,
    No. 43, 1971, p. 7.

6.   Nobody expects that the normalization of Soviet-Ameri-
        can relations and the conclusion of the present and
        even more all-embracing agreements on arms limitations
        between our country and the United States will lead
        to an end to competition between our two social sys-
        tems....
        ...It is a question of creating optimum conditions for
        the competition between the two systems by switching
        to the channel of peaceful coexistence and cooperation
        in the name of averting a global catastrophe.

    G. Trofimenko, "An Important Problem," Pr., June 5, 1973.

7. Arbatov, "American Imperialism," loc.cit.

8. Pr., June 12, 1971.

9. G. Trofimenko, "On a Pivotal Course," MEMO, No. 2, 1975.
    (FBIS, February 24, p. AA 3)

10. G.A. Arbatov, "Strategic Parity and the Policy of the Car-
    ter Administration," SShA, No. 11, 1980, p. 36.

11. Trofimenko, "Pivotal Course," loc.cit., p. AA 4.

12.   From early 1972 until mid-1975, a circumscribed en-
        thusiasm characterized one mode of Soviet writing,
        while a second mode expressed growing distrust of the
        U.S. In mid-1975, both groups of Soviet writers began

to assert that the United States was blatantly igno-
ring the Soviet conditions for cooperation. From mid-
1975 on, statements of distrust, based on the fear
that the U.S. would try to reassert its military pro-
wess, emerged more frequently. Soviet-American relations have continued to worsen; by mid-1978, Soviet
scholars of all persuasions maintained a silence on
the topic of cooperation as such and referred to it
only tangentially in their writings on other subjects.

William B. Husband, "Soviet Perceptions of U.S. 'Positions-of-Strength' Diplomacy in the 1970s," World Politics,
July 1979, p. 507.

13. Arbatov, Pr., May 4, 1971; cf. Brezhnev's remark at the
XXIV Party Congress that "adaptation to the new conditions
does not mean the stabilization of capitalism as a system."

14. G. Trofimenko, "Political Realism and the 'Realistic Deterrence' Strategy," SShA, No. 12, 1971. (FBIS, December
10, p. H 2)

15. Ibid., p. H 13.

16. V.V. Larionov, "The Transformation of the 'Strategic Sufficiency' Concept," SShA, No. 11, 1971. (FBIS, November
12, p. H 10)

17.   First use could conceivably, let me underscore con-
        ceivably, involve what we define as strategic forces
        and possibly, possibly, underscore possibly involve
        selective strike at the Soviet Union. We do not ne-
        cessarily exclude that, but it is indeed a very, very
        low probability.
        Any use of nuclear weapons would be a most agonizing
        decision for any political leader...The purpose and
        thrust of U.S. military strategy in recent years is
        to raise the nuclear threshold so that we have serious
        conventional options that will not drive us to early
        resource to nuclear weapons....
        We, however, will make use of nuclear weapons should
        we be faced with serious aggression likely to result
        in defeat in an area of very great importance to the
        United States. This has clearly been the case in
        Western Europe for many years....

Washington Post, July 2, 1975, quoted in Lawrence T.
Caldwell, Soviet American Relations: One Half Decade of
Detente, Problems and Issues. Atlantic Paper, Paris 1975,

p. 45. Caldwell continues:

> Although its charge that Schlesinger threatened a possible first strike was technically accurate, Pravda's distorted interpretation (July 12, 1975) illustrates the great complexity of interaction between the two powers on strategic affairs. However one views the substance of the Schlesinger doctrine, it surely is not an irresponsible threat to use "nuclear weapons in any crisis situation," as Pravda charged. (p. 45)

18. V.V. Larionov, Pr., April 7, 1974.

19. Arbatov, "Strategic Parity," loc.cit.

20. cf. David Holloway, "The Soviet Style of Military R&D," in Franklyn A. Long and Judith Reppy (eds.), The Genesis of New Weapons, Decision Making for Military R&D, New York 1980, p. 154.

21. Western policy on economic interdependence is important, but the major determinant in long-term Soviet economic and technological performance is its military policy. If the Soviets choose to stay on their current course of military superpower augmentation, they must defer or forgo the option of joining the Western industrial nations as an economic superpower.

   John P. Hardt, "Soviet Economic Capabilities and Defense Resources," in Grayson Kirk and Nils H. Wessel (eds.), The Soviet Threat, Myths and Realities, New York 1978, p. 133; cf. "The Soviet Economy in 1978-1979 and Prospects for 1980," U.S. Central Intelligence Agency, Washington D.C., June 1980.

22. Holloway, "Soviet Style," loc.cit.

23. These aspects are well illustrated by Gallagher and Spielmann, op.cit., Chapter IV, "The Scientists."

24. Col.Gen. N.A. Lomov (ed.), Scientific-Technical Progress and the Revolution in Military Affairs, Moscow 1973, (Series A Soviet View, No. 3, p. 32).

25. Gallagher and Spielmann, op.cit., p. 73.

26. Col. V. Bondarenko, "The Scientific Potential and the Defense of the Country," Kr.Zv., August 20, 1971. (FBIS,

August 24, p. M 7) See also his "Soviet Science and
Strengthening the Defense of the Country," <u>KVS</u>, September, No. 18, 1974.

27. <u>Ibid.</u>, p. M 8.

28. <u>Idem.</u>; cf. Holloway, Adelphi Paper No. 76.

29.   A study of Soviet technology from the early 1950s
        to the early 1970s has concluded that the Soviet
        Union did not close the technological gap with the
        West, and even fell further behind in some advanced
        areas; but there are traditional areas--such as the
        iron and steel industry or high-voltage electric po-
        wer transmission--where the Soviet Union has remained
        among the world leaders.

        Holloway, "Military R&D," <u>loc.cit.</u>, p. 138.

30. Myers and Simes conclude about the publication of <u>The</u>
    <u>First Strike</u> in 1971 that it had as the main purpose

        ...to influence Soviet strategic deployments in a
        particular direction--that is, away from quantita-
        tive growth in the direction of qualitative improve-
        ments. Moreover, it served as a powerful warning to
        those, particularly in the military, who believed
        that time always worked in the favor of Soviet stra-
        tegic programs.

    Kenneth A. Myers and Dimitri Simes, <u>Soviet Decision Ma-</u>
    <u>king, Strategic Policy, and SALT</u>, Report prepared for
    ACDA, Washington D.C. 1974, p. 54.

31. Cf. Grechko's book of 1974, <u>The Armed Forces of the So-</u>
    <u>viet State</u>.

32. Col. V. Rutkov, "The Military-Economic Might of the So-
    cialist Countries is a Factor in the Security of Peoples,"
    <u>KVS</u>, No. 23, 1974. (<u>J.P.R.S.</u>, Translations on USSR Mili-
    tary Affairs, No. 1110, January 17, 1975, p. 15.)

33. Bondarenko, "Soviet Science," <u>loc.cit.</u>, p. 25.

34. <u>Khrushchev Remembers</u>, Vol. II, pp. 27-28.

35. Bondarenko, "Soviet Science," <u>Idem.</u>

36. Col.Gen. M. Kozlov, "An Important Factor in the Might of

the Armed Forces," Kr.Zv., April 21, 1976.

37. Col.Gen. N.V. Ogarkov, "The Theoretical Arsenal of the Military Leader," Kr.Zv., September 3, 1971. (FBIS, September 10, p. M 3)

38.   It is not like producing tanks, where you put so much steel and labor into process and you get the tank out the other end. In R&D the relationship between inputs and outputs is very tenuous...It is not that the Soviets don't desire to have some of these advanced technologies. It is our feeling that they have not been able to acquire these technologies as rapidly as we have.

And in the sphere of hardware the CIA estimates also appeared to have been too high.

What we have come to is a realization that the Soviet military production complex is not as efficient as we thought it was, and much closer to the civilian efficiency.

Hearings before the Subcommittee on Priorities and Economy Allocation of Resources in the Soviet Union and China-1976, Washington D.C. 1976, pp. 55-56.

39. Pr., January 19, 1977. (CDSP, Vol. XXIX, No. 3, p. 3)

40. Pr., May 4, 1978.

41. Pr., June 15, 1974. (CDSP, Vol. XXVI, No. 24)

42. International Affairs, No. 4, 1975, p. 11.

43. G.A. Arbatov, "The Impasses of the Policy of Force," World Marxist Review, No. 2, 1974. (FBIS, February 20, p. B 6)

44. N.V. Ogarkov, "The Fatherland's Reliable Shield," Sovetskaya Litva, February 23, 1974. (FBIS, March 1, p. V 6)

45. V. Kulikov, "Mighty Guard of Peace and Socialism," Izv., February 23, 1974.

46. Col. S. Tyushkevich, "The Development of the Doctrine on War and the Army on the Basis of the Experience of the Great Patriotic War," KVS, No. 22, 1975. (FBIS, July 24, p. B 8)

47. NATO C-M (80) 59, October 17, 1980, p. 2 and 4; For a discussion and critique of the CIA's so-called "building block" approach, also used by NATO, see Franklyn D. Holzman, "Dollars or Rubles: The CIA's Military Estimates," Bulletin of the Atomic Scientists, June 1980, pp. 23-27. For example, with regard to the important area of technology, Holzman finds

> The fallacy of the CIA procedure is that the very dimension of the arms race in which the United States has the greatest advantage, namely, advanced technology--which dimension makes much of the difference between military superiority and inferiority--is enormously undervalued. In fact, significant technological superiority is given a zero price instead of the "almost uncountable" or often "infinite" price the CIA admits it should have. The CIA's ruble calculation implicitly asks: Which country's defense package would cost the Soviet Union more to produce, assuming U.S. equipment is not technologically superior? This question is a proxy for: Which country's defense package is stronger assuming the U.S. has no lead in weapons technology? This is like asking: Would Wilt Chamberlain have been a greater basketball player than most if he had been a foot shorter? (p. 26)

See also Paul Cockle, op.cit.; M. Boretsky and A. Nove, "The Growth of Soviet Arms Technology: A Debate," Survival, July-August 1972.

48. Radio Moscow, November 24, 1973. (FBIS, November 26, p. BB 2)

49. Radio Vilnius, November 23, 1973. (FBIS, December 6, pp. R 11 and R 8)

50. Trofimenko, "Strategic 'Theology'," loc.cit., p. 515.

51. Raymond L. Garthoff, "Mutual Deterrence and Strategic Arms Limitation in Soviet Policy," International Security, Summer 1978, p. 112.

52. For example, Senator Moynihan describes the SALT process and its result for U.S. security as follows:

> The United States entered into the negotiations for SALT I with a pronounced advantage in strategic weapons and those for SALT II with sufficient advantage.

The prospect is that the SALT III negotiations will
begin with the Soviets anticipating strategic suprem-
acy by the end of the process. In such circumstances,
to hold out hopes for any real reduction is self-
deception or worse.

International Herald Tribune, August 4-5, 1979.

53. Cf. Myers and Simes, op.cit.

54. The distinction is made by Garthoff, Soviet Strategy in
the Nuclear Age, New York 1962, p. 8.

55. Izv., February 6, 1971; Pr., February 3, 1971; cf. Raymond L. Garthoff, "Negotiating with the Russians: Some
Lessons from SALT," International Security, Summer 1978,
pp. 3-24; Newhouse, op.cit.; Mason Willrich and John B.
Rhinelander (eds.), SALT, The Moscow Agreements and Beyond, New York 1974; Gerald C. Smith, SALT: The First
Strategic Arms Negotiation, New York 1977.

56. Reprinted in Survival, 1970, pp. 268-269.

57. Y. Tomilin, "A Topical Problem," Izv., July 9, 1971.

58. Stanley Sienkiewicz, "SALT and Soviet Nuclear Doctrine,"
International Security, Spring 1978, p. 94.

59.   Perhaps the biggest problem for the American side in
          SALT has not been the Russians--tough negotiating
          partners that they are--but the absence of high-level
          consensus in Washington on American negotiating ob-
          jectives and the burden of continually negotiating
          (and maneuvering) among various factions within the
          U.S. government....
          ...Nowhere more clearly than in SALT have differen-
          ces within the American government so shaped and
          reshaped negotiating approaches and goals in ways
          that undercut and complicated a sound and effective
          negotiating strategy.

          Raymond L. Garthoff, "Negotiating SALT," The Wilson
          Quarterly, Autumn 1977, p. 85; cf. Thomas Wolfe, The
          SALT Experience, op.cit.

60. Strobe Talbott, Endgame, The Inside Story of SALT-II,
New York 1979, p. 73.

61. Craig R. Whitney, "Kremlin Admits SALT Debate," Interna-

tional Herald Tribune, November 8, 1978; David Linebaugh, "Hawks in Kremlin's Towers," International Herald Tribune, May 23, 1979; Special Report: "Who Conceded What to Whom," Time, May 21, 1979, pp. 9-19.
A report from the Congressional Budget Office concludes about the American concerns as to the survivability of the ICBM force and the costs of MX:

> It is clear, however, that the SALT II agreement-- and, especially, the extension of SALT II-type limits into the 1990s--could enhance the survivability of the planned U.S. ICBM force. The agreement also might add somewhat to the ability of the U.S. bomber force to escape safely from its bases in the event of an attack. For the ICBM force, the survivability gain can be measured in dollar terms--the cost avoided by not having to overcome the effects of additional Soviet warheads. At very high levels of Soviet build- up, of course, such cost estimates may be a poor measure of the nature of the U.S. problem. Were re- jection of SALT II to result in a very rapid Soviet build-up, the United States might be compelled to undertake a fundamental rethinking of its strategic force posture, resulting in a very different force mix from that now planned. As noted earlier, many of these gains form SALT II limits will come only if the limits are extended into the deployment period for MX, illustrating the potential importance of SALT III.

SALT II and the costs of Modernizing U.S. Strategic For- ces, Washington D.C., September 1979, p. 33.

62. Paul H. Nitze, "Assuring Strategic Stability in an Era of Detente," Foreign Affairs, January 1976, pp. 207-232; The response of Jan M. Lodal, "Assuring strategic stabi- lity: An Alternate View," Foreign Affairs, April 1976, pp. 462-481; Nitze, "Strategy in the Decade of the 1980s," Foreign Affairs, Fall 1980, pp. 82-101.

63. Marshal N. Ogarkov, "The Myth of the 'Soviet Military Threat' and Reality," Pr., August 2, 1979. General Kuli- kov tells the Supreme Soviet in 1972 that the agreements are the result of Soviet military might. "We are fully aware that they do not mean a change in the nature of imperialism or denial of its aggressive essence." Izv., August 23, 1972.

64. M.A. Milshtein and L.S. Semeiko, "Strategic Arms Limita-

tion: Problems and Prospects," SShA, No. 12, 1973. (FBIS, December 17, p. AA 6) Western scholars and activists in the field of disarmament can, however, hardly agree. As one advocate of unilateral steps concludes:

> Unilateral reciprocated disarmament initiatives would respond to the long felt need for making the disarmament process more transparent and understandable to public opinion. Disarmament talks and measures would acquire greater concreteness and drawing strength from the climate of detente.would themselves contribute to a better atmosphere of understanding. The process of disarmament could be accelerated and further armaments halted. Unilateral moves may not solve all the problems. But as an alternative supplement to current endeavours they are full of promise. They may be a step in the right direction.

Marek Thee, "Disarmament Through Unilateral Initiatives," Bulletin of Peace Proposals, No. 4, 1974, p. 383.

65. Paul Warnke quoted by Barry M. Blechman, "Do Negotiated Arms Limitations Have a Future?," Foreign Affairs, Fall 1980, p. 108.

66. Helmut Sonnenfeldt and William Hyland, Soviet Perspectives on Security, Adelphi Paper No. 150, London 1979, p. 21. Most Soviet actors are probably in agreement with Colin Gray who warns that:

> ...for overriding political reasons, military rationales might be disregarded in negotiating an arms control treaty, but that would not constitute a victory for any arms control perspective.

Colin Gray, "Who's Afraid of the Cruise Missile," Orbis, Fall 1977, p. 517. According to Garnett's thoughtful description, arms control

> ...merely implies co-operation between enemies to establish qualities of weapons likely to reduce the chances and ferocity of war, and to control the development, deployment and use of weapons along mutually acceptable lines.

John Garnett, "Disarmament and Arms Control since 1945," in Martin, p. 191.

67. M. Kostko, Survival, September–October 1972, p. 238, re-

printed from MEMO, June 1972.

68. "We have in no way ruled out," said the French Chief
     of Staff, "the possibility of participating in for-
     ward line combat...."

     Pr., June 9, 1979. (CDSP, Vol. XXVIII, No. 23) The speech-
     es of President Giscard d'Estaing and General Méry are
     in part reprinted in Survival, September-October 1976,
     pp. 226-230.

69. Kostko, loc.cit., p. 237.

70. V. Viktorov, "At the Vienna Talks," Mezhdunarodnaya Zhizn,
     No. 7, 1974, p. 32. (FBIS, July 17, p. BB 8)

71. Ibid., p. 30. (FBIS, p. BB 7)
     McNamara is quoted saying in 1968:

         I consider that NATO and the Warsaw Pact have approxi-
         mately equal capabilities in ground troops.

     and Schlesinger, in 1973:

         The situation in Europe is now quite stable. We would
         like to keep it that way.

     cf. D. Proektor, "Dangers, Real and Imaginary," Pr., Ja-
     nuary 8, 1977:

         Despite all the differences in the configuration of
         the armed forces of Warsaw Pact and NATO countries,
         their levels in Europe are roughly the same, and
         there is an essential balance. It engenders stability.

72. The parties may find agreement about the nuclear-capable
     systems that complement the conventional forces in "deter-
     rence by denial." This weapons category would consist of
     dual-capable artillery and Lance missiles on the
     Western side, and dual-capable artillery (?), Frog and
     Scud missiles on the Soviet side. It could be argued that
     MBFR, at least, would deal with a category of weapons
     systems whose missions are comparable. As outlined in
     Chapter VI, doctrinal asymmetries between NATO and Warsaw
     would require a trade-off of Soviet missiles against
     NATO's nuclear-capable artillery in order to offset of-
     fensive and defensive capabilities and to balance the li-
     mitations or reductions according to the military value
     attached by each side to the various systems. Obviously,

to reach agreement on values and weapons systems different in kind will be extremely difficult--not to mention
problems regarding verification, numbers, dual-capability,
etc. Geographic asymmetries and the longer strike reach
of Soviet weapons into Western Europe, moreover, nullify
the effectiveness of such agreements if no restraints can
be put on these systems. As Burt concludes about the prospect of MBFR in which military equipment is included:

> ...the geographical consequences of an MBFR accord
> would be much more significant if, as now seems like-
> ly, an agreement also limited military equipment,
> particularly nuclear delivery vehicles. The concept
> of a nuclear balance in Central Europe is meaningless
> because the countries there can be targeted by Soviet
> weapons lying outside the boundaries covered in the
> negotiations.

Richard Burt, "The Future of Arms Control, A Half Glass
Empty," Foreign Policy, Fall 1979, p. 39.

73. Pr., October 27, 1973. The Soviet military and in particular the ground forces are very likely to oppose MBFR.
A significant reduction, such as a tank army or its equivalent in divisions, would run counter to the desired
flexibility and the further development of the combined-
arms concept. Erickson's conclusion about the political
weight of the ground forces, then, may also have its
consequences for Soviet negotiating behavior in Vienna.

> The ground forces must be counted as not merely major
> component of Soviet military capability but also a
> persistent influence on Soviet military policy and
> organization....

John Erickson, "The Ground Forces in Soviet Military Policy," Strategic Review, Winter 1978, p. 78. It is noteworthy, that Proektor's only explicit explanation for Soviet objections against "a sharp cutback in the Warsaw
Treaty countries ground forces" is that this would upset
"their defence structure." (Emphasis added)
D. Proektor, "Military Detente: Primary Task," International Affairs, No. 6, 1976, p. 41.

74. Lawrence T. Caldwell, Soviet Security Interests in Europe
and MFR, California Seminar on Arms Control and Foreign
Policy Research Paper No. 72, 1976, p. 43.
Garthoff's experience in the SALT I negotiations is similar.

The United States and the Soviet Union took markedly different approaches to SALT. As is often the case, the Russians sought "agreement in principle" prior to agreement on specifics, or even before disclosing their proposals. By contrast the more pragmatic American approach was to offer a fairly complete, complex, and detailed package proposal. Arguments can be advanced for each technique, but the two are difficult to reconcile.... Where the Russians wanted a general, "politically" significant accord, American negotiators favored specific measures that would add up to a "militarily" significant agreement.

Garthoff, "Negotiating SALT," loc.cit., p. 82.

75. Leslie H. Gelb, "The Future of Arms Control, A Half Glass Full," Foreign Policy, Fall 1979, p. 24.

76. Warner, op.cit., p. 222.

77. Aspaturian, in Farrell, p. 268-269.

78. Thomas Wolfe, Soviet Strategy, p. 238.

79. Eran, op.cit., pp. 240-243.

80. Myers and Simes, op.cit., p. 30.

81. Ibid., pp. 88-89, 92-93.

82. Pr., June 12, 1971.

83. A.A. Grechko, "The Fleet of our Homeland," Morskoi Sbornik, No. 7, 1971. (FBIS, August 11, p. M 5)

84. Pr., July 21, 1974. (CDSP, Vol. XXXVI, No. 29)

85. Pr., July 28, 1974. Gorshkov notes that "this directly affects U.S. Naval seamen" and that "such an agreement would unquestionably facilitate the transformation of the Mediterranean into a stable zone of peace"; cf. B. Svetlov who calls his article incorrectly, perhaps not unintentionally, "An Important New Initiative," Izv., August 17, 1974; Podgorny was the first political leader who picked up this new formulation in a speech in Sofia. Pr., September 9, 1974; Brezhnev repeats his proposal in the GDR.

As I have said recently, the Soviet Union is prepared

at any time to come to an agreement regarding the nuclear fleet in the Mediterranean.

Pr., October 7, 1974.

86. See Morton Schwartz, Soviet Perceptions of the United States, Berkeley 1978.

87. M.A. Milshtein, "Progress Along the Main Salient," SShA, No. 2, 1975. (FBIS, February 12, p. AA 2)

88. H. Kissinger, White House Years, p. 1213.

89. Milshtein, loc.cit., p. AA 10.

90. G.A. Trofimenko, "On a Pivotal Course," MEMO, No. 2, 1975. (FBIS, February 24, p. AA 1)

91. G.A. Trofimenko, "Problems of Peace and Security in Soviet-American Relations," SShA, No. 9, 1974. (FBIS, September 24, pp. A 5-6)

92. G.A. Trofimenko, "The USSR and the United States: Peaceful Coexistence as the Norm of Mutual Relations," SShA, No. 2, 1974. (FBIS, February 12, p. B 13)

93. Pr., June 5, 1973.

94. Trofimenko, "Problems of Peace," loc.cit., pp. AA 6-7.

95. M.G. Vladimirov, "The Arms Control and Disarmament Agency Report," SShA, No. 7, 1974, p. 51.

96. Proektor, "Military Detente," loc.cit., p. 35.

97. D. Proektor, "European Security; Some Problems," MEMO, No. 9, 1973. (FBIS, October 31, p. BB 9)

98. Ibid.

99. Trofimenko, "Strategic 'Theology'," loc.cit., p. 515.

100. Burt, loc.cit., p. 42.

101. Radio Riga, December 26, 1973. (FBIS, January 3, p. R 11)

102. Ibid., p. R 12.

103. Ibid., p. R 13.

104. Trofimenko, "Peaceful Coexistence," p. B 7.

105. <u>Pr.</u>, April 23, 1976.

106. Erickson characterizes the political and military view-
points quite well, saying that military power is an
"indispensable element in maintaining political status
at large." There is a difference, however.

> In a narrower context, military weight is seen in
> Europe and elsewhere as the real arbiter of natio-
> nal security, which is to say, there is a substan-
> tial difference in the perception of the utility
> of military force. Simply having it is significant
> in its own right.

John Erickson, "European Security: Soviet Preferences
and Priorities," <u>Strategic Review</u>, Winter 1976, p. 41.

107. Stern, <u>op.cit.</u>, p. 84.

108.
> In general, the notion of a Soviet global thrust
> has less to do with the application of power (to-
> ward control) than it does with status and access
> (derived from power). That is, the key proposition
> is Gromyko's* namely, the Soviet Union as a parti-
> cipant in decisions of concern to it. This indis-
> putably depends, in the Soviet mind and, in part,
> in reality, on the growing mass of Soviet military
> power, strategic nuclear power in particular. But
> it also depends, in larger part, on the nature of
> local circumstances and, as events in the Middle
> East have proved since the 1973 war, these are of-
> ten more powerful.

Robert Legvold, "The Nature of Soviet Power," <u>Foreign
Affairs</u>, October 1977, p. 67.

*Gromyko has said that there may be "no question of any
significance which can be decided without the Soviet
Union or in opposition to it." (p. 66)

109. Sheidin, <u>op.cit.</u>, p. A 12.

110. Nikolai V. Sivachev and Nikolai N. Yakovlev, <u>Russia and
the United States</u>, Chicago 1979, p. 73.

Selected Bibliography

Adams, Jan S. Citizen Inspectors in the Soviet Union: The People's Control Committee. New York 1977.

Adomeit, Hannes, and Boardman, Robert. Foreign Policy Making in Communist Countries: A Comparative Approach. Saxon House 1979.

Alexander, Arthur J. Decision-Making in Soviet Weapons Procurement. Adelphi Paper No. 147-148. London 1978/1979.

Allison, Graham T. Essence of Decision: Explaining the Cuban Missile Crisis. Boston 1971.

Arbatov, Georgi. The War of Ideas in Contemporary International Relations. Moscow 1973.

Arms Control: Readings from 'Scientific American'. With Introductions by Herbert F. York. San Francisco 1973.

Aron, Raymond. Peace and War: A Theory of International Relations. New York 1966.

Aspaturian, Vernon V. Process and Power in Soviet Foreign Policy. Boston 1971.

_____. "The Soviet Military-Industrial Complex: Does it exist?" In Testing the Theory of the Military-Industrial Complex. Edited by Steven Rosen. London 1973.

Barghoorn, Frederic C. Politics in the USSR. Boston 1972.

Barton, John H., and Weiler, Lawrence D. eds. International Arms Control, Issues and Agreements. Stanford 1976.

Beaufre, André. An Introduction to Strategy. New York 1965.

Bertram, Christoph. The Future of Arms Control (Part I and II): Arms Control and Technological Change, Elements of a new Approach. Adelphi Paper 145 and 146. London 1978.

Bidwell, S. World War 3: A Military Projection Founded on Today's Facts. London 1978.

Bornstein, Morris., and Fusfeld, Daniel R. The Soviet Econo-
    my--A Book of Readings. 4th edition. Homewood 1974.

Boulding, Kenneth E. Conflict and Defense: A General Theory.
    New York 1963.

Brecht, Arnold. Political Theory: The Foundations of Twen-
    tieth-Century Political Thought. Princeton 1959.

Brezhnev, L.I. Ob Osnovykh Voprosakh Ekonomicheskoi Politiki
    KPSS na Sovremennom Etape. Moscow 1975.

——————. How it was: The War and Post-War Reconstruction
    in the Soviet Union. Oxford 1979.

Brown, A.H. Soviet Politics and Political Science. New York
    1974.

Brown, H. Department of Defense Annual Report, FY 1979.
    Washington D.C. 1978.

Brzezinski, Zbigniew, and Huntington, Samuel P. Political
    Power: USA/USSR. New York 1964.

Brzezinski, Zbigniew K. Ideology and Power in Soviet Politics.
    Revised edition. New York 1967.

Bull, Hedley. The Control of the Arms Race. 2nd edition. New
    York 1965.

Butterfield, H. History and Human Relations. London 1951.

Caldwell, Lawrence T. Soviet Attitudes to SALT. Adelphi Paper
    No. 75. London 1971.

——————. Soviet American Relations: One Half Decade of
    Detente, Problems and Issues. Paris 1975.

——————. Soviet Security Interests in Europe and MFR.
    California Seminar on Arms Control and Foreign Policy
    Research Paper No. 72. Santa Monica 1976.

Carr, E.H. The Twenty Years Crisis, 1919-1939; An Introduc-
    tion to the Study of International Relations. 2nd edi-
    tion. London 1946.

——————. What is History? Penguin edition, 1961.

355

Churchward, L.G. *Contemporary Soviet Government*. 2nd edition. London 1975.

Clemens, Walter. *The Superpowers and Arms Control*. Lexington 1973.

Close, R. *Europe without Defense?* New York 1979.

Cocks, Paul. "The Rationalization of Party Control." In *Change in Communist Systems*, pp. 153-190 . Edited by Chalmers Johnson. Stanford 1970.

_____. "Science Policy and Soviet Decision-Making: PPBS Soviet to the Kremlin." Paper presented at the APSA Annual Meeting. San Francisco, September 2-5, 1975.

_____. "The Policy Process and Bureaucratic Politics." In *The Dynamics of Soviet Politics*, pp. 156-178. Edited by Paul Cocks, Robert V. Daniels, and Nancy Whittier Heer. Harvard 1976.

_____. "Retooling the Directed Society: Administrative Modernization and Developed Socialism." In *Political Development in Eastern Europe*, pp. 53-92. Edited by Jan F. Triska and Paul Cocks. New York 1977.

_____. "Science Policy and Soviet Development Strategy." In *The XXV Congress of the CPSU: Assessment and Context*, pp. 39-52. Edited by Alexander Dallin. Stanford 1977.

_____. "Rethinking the Organizational Weapon: The Soviet System in a Systems Age." *World Politics*, January 1980: pp. 228-257.

Coffey, J.I. *New Approaches to Arms Reduction in Europe*. Adelphi Paper No. 105. London 1974.

Cohen, Lenard J., Shapiro, Jane P., eds. *Communist Systems in Comparative Perspective*. New York 1974.

Collins, John M. *Grand Strategy: Principles and Practices*. Annapolis 1973.

_____. *United States/Soviet Military Balance: A Frame of Reference for Congress*. Washington D.C. 1976.

_____, and Cordesman, Anthony H. *Imbalance of Power: An Analysis of Shifting US-Soviet Military Strengths* and Net Assessment Appraisal. San Rafael 1978.

_____. American and Soviet Military Trends since the Cuban Missile Crisis. Washington D.C. 1978.

Colton, Timothy J. "The Party-Military Connection: A Participatory Model." In Civil-Military Relations in Communist Systems, pp. 53-75.   Edited by Dale R. Herspring and Ivan Volgyes. Boulder 1978.

_____. Commissars, Commanders and Civilian Authority, The Structure of Soviet Military Politics. Harvard 1979.

Congress of the United States. Office of Technological Assessment. The Effects of Nuclear War. Washington D.C. 1979.

Conquest, Robert. Power and Policy in the U.S.S.R. London 1962.

Cox, Arthur Macy. The Dynamics of Detente; How to End the Arms Race. New York 1976.

Dallin, Alexander, and Larson, Thomas B. eds. Soviet Politics since Khrushchev. Englewood Cliffs 1968.

Dallin, Alexander. "Soviet Foreign Policy and Domestic Politics: A Framework for Analysis." In The Conduct of Soviet Foreign Policy, pp. 36-49. Edited by Erik P. Hoffman and Frederic J. Fleron. Chicago 1971.

_____. "Domestic Factors Influencing Soviet Foreign Policy." In The USSR and the Middle East, pp. 31-58. Edited by M. Confino and S. Shamir. Jerusalem 1973.

_____., ed. The XXV Congress of the CPSU: Assessment and Context. Stanford 1977.

_____. "The Domestic Sources of Soviet Foreign Policy." In The Domestic Context of Soviet Foreign Policy. Edited by Seweryn Bialer. Boulder 1981.

Deane, Michael J. Political Control of the Soviet Armed Forces. New York 1977.

Dismukes, Bradford, and McConnell, James M., eds. Soviet Naval Diplomacy. New York 1979.

Dodge, Norton T., ed. Analysis of the USSR's 24th Party Congress and 9th Five-Year Plan. Maryland 1971.

Dornberg, John. *Brezhnev, the Masks of Power*. London 1974.

Douglass, Joseph D. Jr., and Hoeber, Amoretta. *Soviet Strategy for Nuclear War*. Stanford 1979.

Douglass, Joseph D. Jr. *Soviet Military Strategy in Europe*. New York 1980.

Edmonds, Robin. *Soviet Foreign Policy 1962-1973: The Paradox of Super Power*. London 1975.

Eran, Oded. *The Mezhdunarodniki; An Assessment of Professional Expertise in the Making of Soviet Foreign Policy*. Tel Aviv 1979.

Erickson, John. "The Soviet Military, Soviet Policy and Soviet Politics." *Strategic Review*. Fall 1973, pp. 23-36.

_____. *The Road to Stalingrad, Stalin's War with Germany*. Volume I. London 1975.

_____. "European Security: Soviet Preferences and Priorities." *Strategic Review*. Winter 1976.

_____. "The Ground Forces in Soviet Military Policy." *Strategic Review*. Winter 1978. pp. 64-79.

Fleron, Frederic J., ed. *Communist Studies and the Social Sciences*. Chicago 1969.

Friedgut, Theodore H. *Political Participation in the USSR*. Princeton 1979.

Friedrich, Carl J., and Brzezinski, Zbigniew. *Totalitarian Dictatorship and Autocracy*. Cambridge 1956.

Friedrich, Carl J. *Man and his Government: An Empirical Theory of Politics*. New York 1963.

Gallagher, Matthew P., and Spielmann, Karl F. Jr. *Soviet Decision-Making for Defense: A Critique of U.S. Perspectives on the Arms Race*. New York 1972.

Garthoff, R.L. *Soviet Military Doctrine*. Glencoe 1953.

_____. *Soviet Strategy in the Nuclear Age*. New York 1962.

_____. *Soviet Military Policy*. New York 1966.

Gehlen, M.P. The Politics of Coexistence. Bloomington 1967.

Gessert, Robert A., and Hehir, J. Bryan. The New Nuclear Debate. New York 1976.

George, Alexander L., and Smoke, Richard. Deterrence in American Foreign Policy, Theory and Practice. New York 1974.

Ginsburgs, George, and Rubinstein, Alvin Z., eds. Soviet Foreign Policy towards Western Europe. New York 1978.

Goldhamer, Herbert. The Soviet Soldier, Soviet Military Management at the Troop Level. New York 1975.

Goodpaster, Andrew J., and Huntington, Samuel P. Civil-Military Relations. Washington D.C. 1977.

Gorshkov, S.G. The Sea Power of the State. (Moscow 1976) New York 1979.

Gouré, Léon., et al. The Role of Nuclear Force in Current Soviet Strategy. Coral Gables. 1975.

Gray, Colin S. The Geopolitics of the Nuclear Era: Heartland, Rimlands, and the Technological Revolution. New York 1977.

Grechko, A.A. "On Guard for Peace and the Building of Communism." Moscow 1971. Translation by JPRS No. 54602. December 2, 1971.

—————. The Armed Forces of the Soviet State. Moscow 1974.

Griffiths, Franklyn. "A Tendency Analysis of Soviet Policy-Making." In Interest Groups in Soviet Politics, pp. 335-377. Edited by H. Gordon Skilling and Franklyn Griffiths. Princeton 1971.

—————. Genoa plus 51: Changing Soviet Objectives in Europe. Toronto 1973.

Gessert, Robert A., and Seim, Harvey B. Improving NATO's Theater Nuclear Posture: A Reassessment and a Proposal. Washington D.C. 1977.

Hackett, J. The Third World War, 1985. A Future History. London 1978.

Hahn, Werner G. The Politics of Soviet Agriculture, 1960-1970. Baltimore 1972.

Halperin, Morton H. Bureaucratic Politics and Foreign Policy. Washington D.C. 1974.

_____. National Security Policy-Making. Toronto 1975.

Heilbrunn,Otto. Conventional Warfare in the Nuclear Age. New York 1965.

Herspring, Dale R., and Volgyes, Ivan., eds. Civil-Military Relations in Communist Systems. Boulder 1978.

Hoffman, Erik P., and Fleron, Frederic J., eds. The Conduct of Soviet Foreign Policy. Chicago 1971.

Hoffman, Stanley. "An American Social Science: International Relations." Daedalus, Summer 1977, pp. 41-60.

Holliday, George D. Technology Transfer to the USSR, 1928-1937 and 1966-1975: The Role of Western Technology in Soviet Economic Development. Boulder 1979.

Holloway, David. "Technology and Political Decision in Soviet Armaments Policy." Journal of Peace Research, No. 4. 1974, pp. 257-279.

Holzman, Franklyn D., and Legvold, Robert. "The Economics and Politics of East-West Relations." International Organization. Winter 1975, pp. 275-320.

Horelick, Arnold L., Johnson, Ross A., and Steinbruner, John D. The Study of Soviet Foreign Policy: A Review of Decision-Theory-Related Approaches. Santa Monica 1973.

Hough, Jerry F. The Soviet Prefects. Cambridge 1969.

_____. The Soviet Union and Social Science Theory. Cambridge 1977.

_____., and Fainsod, Merle. How the Soviet Union is Governed. Cambridge 1979.

Huntington, Samuel P. The Soldier and the State: The Theory and Politics of Civil-Military Relations. New York 1957.

_____. Political Order in Changing Societies. New Haven 1968.

Husband, William B. "Soviet Perceptions of U.S. 'Positions-of-Strength' Diplomacy in the 1970s." World Politics. July 1979, pp. 495-517.

Jacobson, Harold K., and William Zimmerman, eds. The Shaping of Foreign Policy. New York 1969.

Jacobson, C.G. Soviet Strategy, Soviet Foreign Policy. 2nd ed. Glasgow 1974.

Janowitz, Morris. The Professional Soldier. New York 1960.

——————. Military Conflict: Essays in the Institutional Analysis of War and Peace. Beverley Hills 1975.

Johnson, Chalmers, ed. Change in Communist Systems. Stanford 1970.

Jowitt, Ken. "Inclusion and Mobilization in European Leninist Regimes." World Politics. October 1975, pp. 69-96.

Jurrjens, Rudolf Th. The Free Flow: People, Ideas and Information in Soviet Ideology and Politics (forthcoming, Sijthoff, Leiden).

Kahan, Jerome H. Security in the Nuclear Age. Washington 1975.

Kaiser, Robert G. Russia: The People and the Power. New York 1976.

Kalb, Marvin., and Kalb, Bernard. Kissinger. New York 1975.

Kanet, Roger E., ed. The Behavioral Revolution and Communist Studies. New York 1971.

——————., and Batry, D. Soviet Economic and Political Relations with the Developing World. New York 1975.

Kéhayan, Nina and Jean. Rue du Prolétaire Rouge; Deux Communistes Francais en USSR. Paris 1978.

Kemp, Geoffrey, Pfaltzgraff, Robert L. Jr., and Ra'anan, Uri., eds. The Other Arms Race. Toronto 1975.

Kirk, Grayson, and Wessell, Nils H., eds. The Soviet Threat, Myths and Realities. New York 1978.

Kissinger, Henry. White House Years. Boston 1979.

Knorr, Klaus. On the Uses of Military Power in the Nuclear Age. Princeton 1966.

_____., ed. Historical Dimensions of National Security Problems. Lawrence 1976.

Kolkowicz, Roman. The Soviet Military and the Communist Party. Princeton 1967.

Korbel, Josef. Detente in Europe: Real or Imaginary? Princeton 1972.

Kulski, W.W. The Soviet Union in World Affairs: A Documented Analysis 1964-1972. Syracuse 1973.

Kuypers, G. Grondbegrippen van Politiek [Fundamental Concepts of Politics]. Utrecht-Antwerpen 1973.

Lee, William T. "The 'Politico-Military-Industrial Complex' of the USSR." Journal of International Affairs. No. 1. 1972, pp. 73-86.

Legault, Albert, and Lindsey, George. The Dynamics of the Nuclear Balance. Revised edition. Ithaca 1976.

Liddell Hart, B.H. Strategy. Second revised edition. New York 1975.

Lider, Julian. The Political and Military Laws of War. Westmead 1979.

Lodal, Jan M. "Assuring Strategic Stability: An Alternate View." Foreign Affairs. April 1976, pp. 462-481.

Lomov, N.A., ed. Scientific-Technical Progress and the Revolution in Military Affairs. Moscow 1973. Series A Soviet View, No. 3. Translated and Published under the Auspices of the United States Air Force.

Long, Franklyn A., and Reppy, Judith, eds. The Genesis of New Weapons, Decision Making for Military R&D. New York 1980.

Luttwak, Edward N. Strategic Power: Military Capabilities and Political Utility. Washington D.C. 1976.

Martin, Lawrence, ed. Strategic Thoughts in the Nuclear Age. London 1979.

McAuley, Mary. Politics and the Soviet Union. Middlesex 1977.

McLaurin, R.D. The Middle-East in Soviet Policy. Lexington 1975.

Medvedev, Zhores A. The Rise and Fall of T.D. Lysenko. New York 1969.

_____. Soviet Science. Oxford 1979.

Milovidov, A.S., and Kozlov, V.G., eds. The Philosophical Heritage of V.I. Lenin and Problems of Contemporary War. Moscow 1972. Series A Soviet View, No. 5. Translated and Published under the Auspices of the United States Air Force.

Myers, Kenneth A., and Simes, Dimitri. Soviet Decision Making, Strategic Policy, and SALT. Washington D.C. 1974.

Newhouse, John. Cold Dawn; The Story of SALT. New York 1973.

Nitze, Paul H. "Assuring Strategic Stability in an Era of Detente." Foreign Affairs. January 1976, pp. 207-232.

_____. "Strategy in the Decade of the 1980s." Foreign Affairs. Fall 1980, pp. 82-101.

Nove, Alec. East-West Trade, Problems, Prospects and Issues. Washington D.C. 1978.

Odom, W.E. The Soviet Volunteers. Princeton 1973.

_____. "The 'Militarization' of Soviet Society." Problems of Communism. September, October 1976, pp. 34-51.

Perlmutter, Amos. The Military and Politics in Modern Times. London 1977.

_____., and Bennett, Valerie Plave, eds. The Political Influence of the Military. New Haven 1980.

Pipes, Richard. "Why the Soviet Union Thinks it Could Fight and Win a Nuclear War." Commentary. July 1977, pp. 21-34.

Ponomarev, B.N., Izbrannoe, Rechi i Stati. Moscow 1977.

Ponomarev, B.N., Gromyko, A., Khostov, V., eds. History of Soviet Foreign Policy 1945-1970. Moscow 1974.

Pranger, Robert J. Detente and Defense: A Reader. Washington 1976.

Pye, Lucian W. Political Science and Area Studies: Rivals or Partners? Bloomington 1975.

Record, Jeffrey. U.S. Nuclear Weapons in Europe, Issues and Alternatives. Washington D.C. 1974.

Remnek, Richard B., ed. Social Scientists and Policy Making in the USSR. New York 1977.

Rigby, T.H. "The Soviet Leadership: Towards a Self-Stabilizing Oligarchy?." Soviet Studies. October 1970, pp. 167-191.

_____. "Crypto-Politics." In Communist Studies and the Social Sciences, pp. 116-129. Edited by Frederic J. Fleron, Jr. Chicago 1971.

Rosenau, James N. "Pre-Theories and Theories of Foreign Policy." In Approaches to Comparative and International Politics, pp. 27-92. Edited by R. Barry Farrell. Evanston 1966.

_____., ed. International Politics and Foreign Policy. New York 1969.

_____., ed. Linkage Politics. New York 1969.

_____. "Muddling, Meddling and Modelling: Alternative Approaches to the Study of World Politics in an Era of Rapid Change." Millennium: Journal of International Studies. Autumn 1979, pp. 130-144.

Savkin, V.Ye. The Basic Principles of Operational Art and Tactics. Moscow 1972. Series A Soviet View, No. 4. Translated and Published under the Auspices of the United States Air Force.

Schapiro, Leonard. The Communist Party of the Soviet Union. 2nd edition. New York 1971.

Schwartz, Morton. The Foreign Policy of the USSR: Domestic Factors. Encino 1975.

_____. Soviet Perceptions of the United States. Berkeley 1978.

Selected Soviet Military Writings 1970-1975. Series A Soviet View, No. 11. Translated and Published under the Auspices of the United States Air Force.

Seliger, Martin. _Ideology and Politics_. New York 1976.

Sidorenko, A.A. _The Offensive_. Moscow 1970. Series A Soviet View, No. 1. Translated and Published under the Auspices of the United States Air Force.

Silverman, David. _The Theory of Organizations: A Sociological Framework_. London 1970.

Simes, Dimitri K. _Detente and Conflict, Soviet Foreign Policy 1972-1977_, Washington D.C. 1977.

Sivachev, Nikolai V., and Yakovlev, Nikolai N. _Russia and the United States_. Chicago 1979.

Skilling, H. Gordon, and Griffiths, Franklyn, eds. _Interest Groups in Soviet Politics_. Princeton 1971.

Skirdo, M.P. _The People, the Army and the Commander_. Moscow 1970. Series A Soviet View, No. 14. Translated and Published under the Auspices of the United States Air Force.

Smith, Dan. _The Defence of the Realm in the 1980s_. London 1980.

Smith, Hedrick. _The Russians_. New York 1976.

Smith, Gerard C. _SALT: The First Strategic Arms Negotiation_. New York 1977.

Spielmann, Karl F. _Analyzing Soviet Strategic Arms Decisions_. Boulder 1978.

Stern, Paula. _Water's Edge, Domestic Politics and the Making of American Foreign Policy_. London 1979.

Stockholm International Peace Research Institute. _Tactical Nuclear Weapons: European Perspectives_. London 1978.

Sonnenfeldt, Helmut, and Hyland, William. _Soviet Perspectives on Security_. Adelphi Paper No. 150. London 1979.

Talbott, Strobe. _Endgame, The Inside Story of SALT-II_. New York 1979.

Tatu, Michel. _Power in the Kremlin from Khrushchev to Kosygin_. New York 1968.

Triska, Jan F., and Finley, David D. Soviet Foreign Policy 1917-1967. New York 1968.

_____., and Paul Cocks, eds. Political Development in Eastern Europe. New York 1977.

Trofimenko, G. Changing Attitudes Toward Deterrence. Los Angeles 1980.

Tsipis, Kosta., Cahn, Anne H., and Feld, Bernard T., eds. The Future of the Sea-Based Deterrent. Cambridge 1973.

Twitchett, Kenneth J., ed. Reflections on Survival and Stability. Oxford 1971.

Ulam, A. Expansion and Coexistence: Soviet Foreign Policy 1917-1973. 2nd edition. New York 1974.

United States Central Intelligence Agency. The Soviet Economy in 1978-1979 and Prospects for 1980. Washington D.C. 1980.

United States Congressional Budget Office. Planning U.S. General Purpose Forces, The Theater Nuclear Forces. Washington D.C. 1977.

United States Congressional Budget Office. SALT II and the Costs of Modernizing U.S. Strategic Forces. Washington D.C. 1979.

Vigor, Peter. The Soviet View of War, Peace and Neutrality. London 1975.

Voennaya Sila: Mezhdunarodnye Otnosheniya: Voennye Aspekty Vneshne-Politicheskykh Kontseptsy S.Sh.A. Moscow 1972.

Warner, Edward L. III. The Military in Contemporary Soviet Politics: An Institutional Analysis. New York 1977.

Welch, William. American Images of Soviet Foreign Policy. New Haven 1970.

Wettig, Gerhard. Frieden und Sicherheit in Europa: Probleme der KSZE und der MBFR. Stuttgart 1975.

_____. East-West Security Relations on the Eurostrategic Level. Berichte des Bundesinstituts für Ostwissenschaftliche und Internationale Studien. No. 27. Cologne 1980.

Whetten, Lawrence L. _Contemporary American Foreign Policy_. Lexington 1974.

_____., ed. _The Future of Soviet Military Power_. New York 1976.

White, Stephen. _Political Culture and Soviet Politics_. London 1979.

Willrich, Mason., and Rhinelander, John B., eds. _SALT: The Moscow Agreements and Beyond_. New York 1974.

Wolfe, Th. _Soviet Strategy at the Crossroads_. Harvard 1964.

_____. _Soviet Power and Europe, 1945-1970_. Baltimore 1970.

_____. _The SALT Experience: Its Impact on U.S. and Soviet Strategic Policy and Decision Making_. Santa Monica 1974.

_____. _Military Power and Soviet Policy_. RAND 1975.

Wrong, Dennis H. _Power; Its Forms, Bases and Uses_. Oxford 1979.

Yanov, Alexander. _Detente After Brezhnev: The Domestic Roots of Soviet Foreign Policy_. Berkeley 1977.

Young, Oran R. _Systems of Political Science_. Englewood Cliffs 1968.

Zheltov, A.S., Kondratkov, T.R., and Khomenko, Ye.A. _Methodological Problems of Military Theory and Practice_. Moscow 1969.

Zimmerman, William. _Soviet Perspectives on International Relations 1956-1967_. Princeton 1969.

_____. "Issue Area and Foreign Policy Process: A Research Note in Search of a General Theory." _American Political Science Review_. December 1973, pp. 1204-1211.

Zorin, V.A. _Osnovy Diplomaticheskoi Sluzhby_. Moscow 1977.

Abbreviations

ABM	Anti-ballistic missile
ALCM	Air-launched cruise missile
ASW	Anti-submarine warfare
CEP	Circular error probable
CPSU	Communist Party of the Soviet Union
FBS	Forward-based systems
GLCM	Ground-launched cruise missile
ICBM	Inter-continental ballistic missile
KT	Kiloton (1,000 tons TNT equivalent)
LNO	Limited nuclear option
LRTNF	Long-range theater nuclear forces
MBFR	Mutual and balanced force reductions
MIRV	Multiple independently-targetable re-entry vehicle
MT	Megaton (1 million tons TNT equivalent)
PLS	Pre-launch survivability
PTP	Probability to penetrate
SALT	Strategic arms limitation talks
SEO	Selective employment option
SLBM	Submarine-launched ballistic missile
SLCM	Sea-launched cruise missile
TNF	Theater nuclear forces
TVD	Teatr voennikh deistvy (theater of military operations)

Papers, Periodicals, Translations

CDSP	Current Digest of the Soviet Press
FBIS	Foreign Broadcast Information Service (Daily Report Soviet Union)
Izv.	Izvestia
Kr.Zv.	Krasnaya Zvezda
KVS	Kommunist Voorozhennykh Sil
MEMO	Mirovaya Ekonomika i Mezhdunarodnye Otnosheny
Pr.	Pravda
SShA	Soyediyonnye Shtaty Ameriki; Ekonomika, Politika, Ideologia